"Amazingly easy to use. Very portable, very complete."

*—Booklist*

♦

"The only mainstream guide to list specific prices. The Walter Cronkite of guidebooks—with all that implies."

*—Travel & Leisure*

♦

"Complete, concise, and filled with useful information."

*—New York Daily News*

♦

"Hotel information is close to encyclopedic."

*—Des Moines Sunday Register*

# Frommer's®

5th Edition

# Toronto

## by Marilyn Wood

Macmillan • USA

## ABOUT THE AUTHOR

Formerly the editorial director of Macmillan Travel, Marilyn Wood is an acclaimed travel writer and editor. Once a resident of Toronto, she has covered the city and all of central Canada for years and is a co-author of *Frommer's Canada*. She has also written *Frommer's London from $60 a Day*, *Frommer's Wonderful Weekends from New York*, and *Frommer's Wonderful Weekends from San Francisco*.

## MACMILLAN TRAVEL

A Simon & Schuster Macmillan Company
1633 Broadway
New York, NY 10019

Find us online at www.frommers.com

ISBN 0-02862106-9
ISSN 1047-7853

Editor: Dan Glover
Production Editor: Lori Cates
Map Editor: Douglas Stallings
Digital Cartography by John Decamillis and Ortelius Design
Design by Michele Laseau

## SPECIAL SALES

Bulk purchases (10+ copies) of Frommer's and selected Macmillan travel guides are available to corporations, organizations, mail-order catalogs, institutions, and charities at special discounts, and can be customized to suit individual needs. For more information write to: Special Sales, Macmillan General Reference, 1633 Broadway, New York, NY 10019.

Manufactured in the United States of America

# Contents

**1  Introducing Toronto, a Multicultural Mosaic  1**

   1  Frommer's Favorite Toronto Experiences  1

   2  Toronto Today  5

   3  History 101  6

   ★  *Dateline*  6

**2  Planning a Trip to Toronto  14**

   1  Visitor Information & Entry Requirements  14

   2  Money  15

   ★  *What Things Cost in Toronto*  16

   ★  *The Canadian Dollar & the U.S. Dollar*  16

   3  When to Go  17

   ★  *Toronto Calendar of Events*  17

   4  Travel Insurance  20

   5  Tips for Travelers with Special Needs  20

   6  Getting There  21

   ★  *CyberDeals for Net Surfers*  22

**3  Getting to Know Toronto  26**

   1  Orientation  26

   ★  *Neighborhoods in Brief*  27

   2  Getting Around  30

   ★  *Fast Facts: Toronto*  33

**4  Accommodations  37**

   1  Best Bets  38

   2  Downtown  39

   3  Midtown  49

   ★  *Family-Friendly Hotels*  53

   4  Uptown  55

   5  At the Airport  56

   6  Metro East  59

## 5    **Dining   61**

  1  Best Bets   62

  2  Restaurants by Cuisine   63

  3  Downtown West   65

  4  Downtown East   81

★  *A Passion for Patios*   82

  5  Midtown West   85

  6  Midtown East/The East End   93

★  *Family-Friendly Restaurants*   94

  7  Uptown   95

  8  Cafes & Java Joints   98

## 6    **What to See & Do in Toronto   100**

★  *Suggested Itineraries*   100

  1  The Top Attractions   101

  2  More Museums   112

  3  Exploring the Neighborhoods   114

  4  Architectural Highlights   116

  5  Historic Buildings   118

★  *Did You Know?*   119

  6  Markets   119

  7  Parks & Gardens   120

  8  Cemeteries   120

  9  Especially for Kids   121

10  Tours   122

11  Outdoor Activities   124

12  Spectator Sports   126

## 7    **City Strolls   128**

★  *Walking Tour 1—Harbourfront*   128

★  *Walking Tour 2—The Financial District*   130

★  *Walking Tour 3—St. Lawrence & Downtown East*   136

★  *Walking Tour 4—Chinatown & Kensington Market*   141

## 8    **Shopping   146**

  1  The Shopping Scene   146

  2  Shopping A to Z   146

★  *Shopping Tour—Browsing Queen Street West*   165

**9    Toronto After Dark    170**

   1  The Performing Arts    170

   ★  *Canada—The Funny Country*    176

   2  The Club & Music Scene    179

   3  The Bar Scene    184

   4  The Gay & Lesbian Scene    189

   5  Cinemas & Movie Houses    190

**10    Side Trips from Toronto    191**

   1  Niagara-on-the-Lake    191

   ★  *From Vinegar to Vintage—Ontario Wines Come of Age*    194

   2  Niagara Falls    201

   ★  *The Power & Pace of Niagara Falls*    204

   3  Stratford    211

**Index    219**

General Index    219

Accommodations Index    225

Restaurant Index    226

# List of Maps

Metropolitan Toronto   2

Underground Toronto   28

The TTC Subway System   32

Downtown Toronto
  Accommodations   40

Midtown Toronto
  Accommodations   50

Downtown Toronto Dining   66

Dining—Chinatown to
  Bloor Street   73

Midtown Toronto Dining   86

Downtown Toronto
  Attractions   102

Midtown Toronto
  Attractions   108

Walking Tour—
  Harbourfront   130

Walking Tour—Financial
  District   133

Walking Tour—St. Lawrence
  & Downtown East   137

Walking Tour—Chinatown
  & Kensington Market   143

Shopping Highlights—Bloor/
  Yorkville   147

Shopping Tour—Queen Street
  West   167

Downtown After Dark   172

After Dark—Chinatown to
  Bloor Street   185

Side Trips from Toronto   193

Niagara-on-the-Lake   195

Niagara Falls   203

Stratford   213

## AN INVITATION TO THE READER

In researching this book, we discovered many wonderful places—hotels, restaurants, shops, and more. We're sure you'll find others. Please tell us about them, so we can share the information with your fellow travelers in upcoming editions. If you were disappointed with a recommendation, we'd love to know that, too. Please write to:

*Frommer's Toronto,* 5th edition
Macmillan Travel
1633 Broadway
New York, NY 10019

## AN ADDITIONAL NOTE

Please be advised that travel information is subject to change at any time—and this is especially true of prices. We therefore suggest that you write or call ahead for confirmation when making your travel plans. The authors, editors, and publisher cannot be held responsible for the experiences of readers while traveling. Your safety is important to us, however, so we encourage you to stay alert and be aware of your surroundings. Keep a close eye on cameras, purses, and wallets, all favorite targets of thieves and pickpockets.

## WHAT THE SYMBOLS MEAN

### ✪ Frommer's Favorites

Our favorite places and experiences—outstanding for quality, value, or both.

The following abbreviations are used for credit cards:

| | | | |
|---|---|---|---|
| AE | American Express | EURO | Eurocard |
| CB | Carte Blanche | JCB | Japan Credit Bank |
| DC | Diners Club | MC | MasterCard |
| DISC | Discover | V | Visa |
| ER | enRoute | | |

## FIND FROMMER'S ONLINE

Arthur Frommer's Outspoken Encyclopedia of Travel (www.frommers.com) offers more than 6,000 pages of up-to-the-minute travel information—including the latest bargains and candid, personal articles updated daily by Arthur Frommer himself. No other website offers such comprehensive and timely coverage of the world of travel.

# Introducing Toronto, a Multicultural Mosaic

**O**nce lampooned as a dull and ugly city, Toronto, now with a population of more than four million, has burst forth from its stodgy past and grabbed attention as one of North America's most exciting cities. In 1996 it was voted the best city to live and work in by *Fortune Magazine.*

How did it happen? Toronto got a chance to change its image with a substantial blood transfusion from other cultures. A post–World War II influx of large numbers of Italians, Chinese, and Portuguese, plus Germans, Jews, Hungarians, Poles, Ukrainians, Greeks, East Indians, West Indians, and French Canadians infused this once quiet, conservative community with new energy. Now, there are neighborhoods where residents can eat an authentic Portuguese, Greek, or Italian meal; see a Hong Kong action film; or catch a late-night reggae set—all within a few blocks of their doorstep. And many Torontonians do these things, regarding their incredible diversity as nothing particularly out of the ordinary.

In recent years, this cultural growth has been accompanied by new developments—from theaters and concert halls to sports stadiums and major projects like the BCE building, the Canadian Broadcasting complex, and the National Trade Centre. Yet through it all, Toronto has managed to preserve the old while creating the new. Progress has not inevitably brought in the wrecker's ball; much has survived. When you see Holy Trinity Church and the Scadding House, one of the oldest residences in the city, standing proudly against the glass-galleried Eaton Centre, preserved because the people demanded it, you know that certain values and a great deal of thoughtful debate have gone into the making of this city.

In Toronto, people walk to work from their restored Victorian town houses (no developer can erect downtown commercial space without including living space), the subway positively gleams, and the streets are safe. Here, old buildings are saved and converted to other uses; architects design around the contours of nature instead of just bulldozing the trees. This is a city created with flair and imagination, but also a sense of traditional values.

## 1 Frommer's Favorite Toronto Experiences

- **Picnicking on the Toronto Islands.** A short ferry ride will transport you to another world of lagoons and rush-lined backwaters,

# Metropolitan Toronto

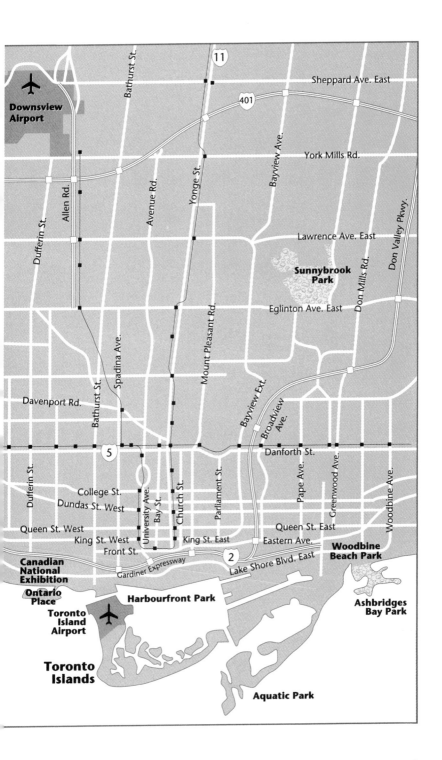

miles away from the urban tarmac—a world of houseboats and bicycles, a place to stroll beside the weeping willows.

- **Exploring Harbourfront.** Bring a model boat; watch artisans blowing glass; take a sailing lesson; tour the harbor; shop the quay and the antique mart—and this is just the beginning.
- **Relaxing in the Beaches.** Stroll or bike along the boardwalk, picnic in the adjacent parkland and gardens, and browse the stores 1 block from the beach.
- **Viewing the McMichael Collection at Kleinburg.** The McMichael—a log and stone gallery amid quiet stands of pine trees—is a peaceful oasis that's completely appropriate for the famous Group of Seven landscape paintings, inspired by the wilderness of Northern Ontario, displayed inside. It's well worth the 40-minute drive from downtown.
- **Playing and Learning at the Ontario Science Centre.** Here you can test your reaction time, play exotic musical instruments, experiment with the Internet, and play all kinds of interactive, enlightening, and fun games.
- **Strolling Through Chinatown or Queen Street West.** Chinatown is crowded, bustling, and lined with teashops, restaurants, bakeries, groceries, and herb stores; Queen Street West is a gathering place for artists and a street that is known for its assortment of eclectic stores selling everything from funky junk and antique clothing to fabrics and antiquarian books.
- **Hanging Out in the Evening in the Two Hottest Neighborhoods in Town, Little Italy and the Danforth.** In Little Italy, people crowd into the cafes and restaurants, as well as the bars that feature pool tables. Along the Danforth—the one area where you can dine after 11pm (to the strains of bouzouki music)—sidewalk cafes and restaurants are jammed long past last call.
- **Shopping St. Lawrence Market on Saturday Morning.** The St. Lawrence food hall is a veritable forest of edible delights. Here you can assemble all the ingredients for a picnic—cheeses and cold cuts of all kinds, breads, deli items, and desserts—or else enjoy a Canadian peameal bacon sandwich at one of the stands.
- **Sipping Cocktails atop the CN Tower.** On a clear day, you can see at least as far as Lake Simcoe or, if you're lucky, all the way to Georgian Bay. If it's foggy, forget it.
- **Watching a Game at Maple Leaf Gardens.** Join the crowds of loyal fans watching their beloved Maple Leafs battle it out on the ice. In the world of hockey, it's hard to find a more dedicated bunch, especially when you consider the years of lackluster performance the team's had. This is one place to see Canadians verging on the out of control.
- **Seeing a Baseball Game at the SkyDome.** If you're a baseball fan, you owe yourself a look at the SkyDome, the state-of-the-art home of the former world champion Blue Jays. If you want to go the luxury route, book one of the 70 rooms with field views at the complex's hotel. The retractable roof is nothing short of amazing.
- **Riding the Streetcar Along College and Carlton Streets or Along Queen Street West and East.** Enjoy the clang of the bell and the hiss of the air brakes as you glide along the rails. On the College route, you'll pass the University of Toronto, going through Little Italy and Little Portugal to the West End. The Queen Street car takes you through the funky area of Queen Street West or, if you're traveling in the opposite direction, to the Beaches, favorite residential neighborhood of young boomers and their families.
- **Viewing the Spectacular Collection of Henry Moore Sculptures at the Art Gallery of Ontario.** Henry Moore was so grateful to the citizens of Toronto for their

support, he donated many of his works to this museum, giving it the best collection of his sculpture in North America.

- **Shopping in the Chic Complex of Hazelton Lanes.** Hazelton Lanes shelters all the big names of world retail, conveniently located under one roof. There are also a couple of fine places for an energizing snack. Once you're refreshed, check out a few galleries in surrounding Yorkville.
- **Cruising the Harbor Aboard a Schooner.** Feel the wind in the ship's sails pushing you across the surface of the lake, as you weave in and out between the islands. The view of the Toronto skyline, dominated by the CN Tower, is superb.
- **Day Tripping to the Shaw Festival in Niagara-on-the-Lake or to the Stratford Festival.** Both are attractive historic towns. In Niagara-on-the-Lake, there's the added advantage of tasting the region's increasingly fine wines, while Stratford offers some of the finest dining opportunities in Ontario at its top-notch restaurants.

## 2  Toronto Today

The city's multiethnic mosaic continues to grow in richness with a steady flow of immigrants from around the world. The recent exodus from Hong Kong helped swell Toronto's Chinese population to more than 300,000 and has led to the development of several suburban Chinatowns. The original downtown Chinatown has been largely taken over by Vietnamese families, while the other, more recently minted Chinatowns with large shopping malls have developed around Kennedy and Lawrence. Asian immigrants from India, Pakistan, Korea, Thailand, and Vietnam have added new dimensions and flavor to the city's cultural life, as have newcomers from the Caribbean islands (most notably Trinidad and Tobago) and Central America.

It would be naive not to acknowledge the stresses and strains this rapid increase in population has created in the social fabric of Toronto, and the typical urban problems that have resulted. The situation has been aggravated by the actions of the most recently elected Tory provincial government, which has slashed budgets and cut back on social spending, closing services formerly taken for granted and amalgamating hospitals and other vital facilities. Overall, though, Toronto's quality of life is still far higher than a comparably sized American city, and much less violent.

The most visible problems are the homeless on the streets, the squeegee kids who line up with pails at intersections to clean car windshields, the steady deterioration of Yonge Street into the Times Square of Toronto, and the increased reports of violent, drug-related crime, especially in Regent Park, a public housing development bounded by Parliament, Shuter, River, and Gerrard streets, near Allan Gardens.

The new Progressive Conservative Provincial Government—known as the "Tories"—elected in June 1995 and headed by Mike Harris, has trimmed Ontario's social welfare budgets by 22%, which hasn't exactly ameliorated the situation.

Despite cuts in social services, money is being invested in the development of several major public facilities, most notably a new stadium for Toronto's basketball team, the Raptors, that will open in 1999. When they hit the courts as the first NBA team outside the United States, the Raptors created massive excitement. Basketball fever has swept the city, with fans packing the SkyDome for their games (the team's home until the new stadium is erected). Other major recent new developments include the doubling of the size of the Metro Toronto Convention Centre and the opening of the new National Trade Centre—Canada's largest.

When the sun goes down, the fashionable crowd continues to hang out along Queen Street, with new restaurants, boîtes, and jazz clubs pushing ever farther west;

but other neighborhoods are also bursting forth with new life—the Danforth and Little Italy, in particular. These last two are hot, hot, hot dining and late-night spots.

The biggest political issue at the moment is how the merging of the six municipalities into one megacity will work after the local elections in late 1997. Prior to this sea change, Metropolitan Toronto consisted of the cities of Toronto, North York, Etobicoke, Scarborough, and York, and the borough of East York. Each had its own city (or borough) hall. City government was a complex and often inefficient tangle of overlapping responsibilities. Metro was responsible for public transportation, police services, social services, traffic control, and the borrowing and issuing of debentures. Fire, health, and some other services were provided by the local municipalities; still other responsibilities, including sewage disposal, water supply, and libraries, were shared.

Reform was needed and a plan for enlarging Metro and amalgamating the municipalities was presented and a referendum held. Despite the results of the referendum, which showed that 60 to 70 percent of the population were against the amalgamation, and despite the protests that accompanied the passage of the bill, the Provincial Government pushed ahead, arousing some of the most contentious politicking the city has ever seen. The opposition Liberals and New Democrats attempted to stop the passage of the bill by attaching 13,000 amendments and leading a filibuster that lasted 10 long days. Nonetheless, the conservatives prevailed. It remains to be seen what will happen to the city during this period of change and reorganization.

## 3 History 101

### Dateline

- **1615** Etienne Brûleé travels the Toronto Trail.
- **1720** France establishes post at Toronto.
- **1751** Fort Rouille built.
- **1763** Treaty of Paris effectively ends French rule in Canada.
- **1787** Lord Dorchester, British governor of Québec, purchases land from Scarborough to Etobicoke from the Mississauga tribe.
- **1791** British colony of Upper Canada formed.
- **1793** Governor of Upper Canada, Col. John Simcoe, arrives and names settlement York.
- **1796** Yonge Street laid out, a 33-mile oxcart trail.
- **1797** Center of government transferred from Niagara to York.
- **1813** War of 1812: Americans invade, blow up Fort York, and burn Parliament buildings.

*continues*

**FROM FUR TRADING POST TO MUDDY YORK**  As with most cities, geography, trade, and communications are the influences that have shaped Toronto and its history. Although the city today possesses a downtown core, it also sprawls across a large area—a gift of geography, for there are no physical barriers to stop it. Initially, the flat broad plain rising from Lake Ontario to an inland ridge of hills (around St. Clair Avenue today) and stretching between the Don River in the east and the Humber in the west made an ideal location for a settlement.

Native Canadians had long stopped here at the entrance to the Toronto Trail—a short route between the Lower and Upper lakes. French fur trader Etienne Brûleé was the first European to travel this trail in 1615, but it wasn't until 1720 that the first trading post, known as Fort Toronto, was established by the French to intercept the furs that were being taken across Lake Ontario to New York State by English rivals. This trading post was replaced in 1751 by Fort Rouille, which was built on the site of today's CNE grounds. When the 1763 Treaty of Paris ended the Anglo-French War after the fall of Québec, French rule in North America was effectively ended and the city's French antecedents were all but forgotten.

Only 20 miles across the lake from the United States, Toronto has always been affected by what happens south of the border. When the American Revolution established a powerful and potentially hostile new nation, Toronto's location became strategically more important, or it certainly seemed so to John Graves Simcoe, lieutenant-governor of the newly formed province of Upper Canada, which had been established in 1791 to administer the frontiers—from Kingston and Quinte's Isle to Windsor and beyond—settled largely by Loyalists fleeing the Revolution. To Simcoe, Toronto was more defensible than Fort Niagara and a natural arsenal for Lake Ontario, which also afforded easy access to Lake Huron and the interior.

The governor had already purchased a vast tract of land from the Mississauga tribe for the paltry sum of £1,700 plus such baubles as blankets, guns, rum, and tobacco. In 1793 Lieutenant-Governor Simcoe, his wife, Elizabeth, and the Queen's Rangers arrived to build a settlement. Simcoe ordered a garrison built, renamed the settlement York, and laid it out in a 10-block rectangle around King, Front, George, Duke, and Berkeley streets. Beyond stretched a series of 100-acre lots from Queen to Bloor, which were granted to government officials to mollify their resentment about having to move to this mosquito-plagued, marshy, muddy outpost. Its muddiness was indeed prodigious, and in fact there is a story told of a fellow who saw a hat lying in the middle of a street, went to pick it up, and found the head of a live man submerged below it! In 3 short years a small hamlet had grown, and Simcoe had laid out Yonge Street—then a 33-mile oxcart trail—and 4 years later the first Parliament meeting confirmed York as the capital of Upper Canada.

## FROM MUDDY YORK TO THE FAMILY COMPACT

The officials were a more demanding and finicky lot than the sturdy frontier farmers, and businesses sprang up to serve them. By 1812 the population had grown to 703 and included a brewer-baker, a blacksmith, a watchmaker, a chairmaker, an apothecary, a hatter, and a tailor.

During the War of 1812, despite initial victories at Queenston and Detroit, Canada was under siege, and in April 1813, 14 ships carrying 1,700 American troops invaded York, blew up the uncompleted fort, burned the Parliament Buildings, and carried off the mace (which was not returned until 1934). The British general burned a 30-gun warship, the *Sir Isaac Brock,* which was being built, and retreated, leaving young John Strachan to negotiate the capitulation. This event did much to reinforce the town's

- **1820s** Immigration of Nonconformists and Irish Catholics fosters reform politics.
- **1828** Erie Canal extended to Oswego on Lake Ontario.
- **1830s** Orange Order becomes prominent influence in politics.
- **1832–34** Cholera epidemics.
- **1834** City named Toronto: City Council replaces magistrates; William Lyon Mackenzie becomes first mayor.
- **1837** Rebellion led by former mayor William Lyon Mackenzie, sparked by bad economic times.
- **1840s–50s** Mass Irish immigration.
- **1841** Act of Union establishes the United Province of Canada, with Kingston as ruling seat; Toronto loses status as a capital.
- **1842** Streets are gaslit.
- **1843** The university, King's College, opens.
- **1844** City hall built; George Brown founds the Globe.
- **1849** Great fire destroys much of city; Anglican King's College converts to secular University of Toronto.
- **1851** Population 30,000 (33% Irish); Anglican Trinity College founded; St. Lawrence Hall built.
- **1852** Toronto Stock Exchange opens; Grand Trunk Railroad charted, linking Québec–Montréal–Toronto–Guelph–Sarnia.
- **1853** St. James Cathedral completed at King and Church.
- **1858** Storm creates the Toronto Islands.
- **1861** Population 44,000; horse-powered street railway runs along Yonge to Yorkville.
- **1867** Canadian Confederation; Toronto becomes

*continues*

capital of new province of Ontario.

- 1868 Canada First movement begins.
- 1869 Eaton's opens.
- 1871 Population 56,000.
- 1872 Simpson's department store opens.
- 1876 John Ross Robertson starts Evening Telegram, which wields influence for next 90 years.
- 1884 Streets electrically lit.
- 1886 Provincial parliament buildings erected in Queen's Park.
- 1891 Population 181,000.
- 1893 First Stanley Cup played.
- 1896 *Maclean's* magazine started.
- 1901 Population 208,000.
- 1904 Great Fire burns much of downtown.
- 1906 First autos produced by Canada Cycle and Motor Company; Toronto Symphony founded.
- 1907 Bell strike broken; Royal Alexandra opens.
- 1911 Population 376,538.
- 1912 Garment workers' strike broken; Royal Ontario Museum founded.
- 1914 New Union Station built.
- 1914–18 World War 1; 70,000 Torontonians enlist. 13,000 die.
- 1920 Group of Seven exhibit for the first time.
- 1921 Population 521,893.
- 1923 Chinese Exclusion Act.
- 1940–45 Toronto functions as war supplier.
- 1947 Cocktail lounges approved.
- 1950 Sunday sports allowed.
- 1951 Population 31% foreign-born.
- 1953 Metro created.
- 1960 O'Keefe Centre opens.
- 1961 Population 42% foreign-born.

*continues*

pro-British, anti-American attitude—an attitude that persists to some extent to this day. In retaliation for the burning of Fort York, some Canadians went down and torched the American president's residence. (The Americans later whitewashed it to hide the charred wood—hence, the White House.)

A conservative pro-British outlook permeated the official political oligarchy that dominated York, and this group was dubbed the Family Compact. Many of the names that visitors will see on street signs, subway stops, and maps are derived from this august group of early government officers and their families. Among them were William Jarvis, a New England Loyalist who became provincial secretary; John Beverley Robinson, son of a Virginia Loyalist, who at age 22 became attorney general and later chief justice of Upper Canada; Scottish-educated Dr. John Strachan, who rose from being a schoolmaster to an Anglican rector and the most powerful figure in York; Anglo-Irish Dr. William Warren Baldwin, doctor, lawyer, architect, judge, and parliamentarian, who laid out Spadina Avenue as a thoroughfare leading to his house of that name in the country; and the Boultons, prominent lawyers, judges, and politicians—Judge D'Arcy Boulton built a mansion, The Grange, which later became the core of the art museum and still stands today.

These men, extremely conscious of rank, were conformist, conservative, pro-British, Tory, and Anglican. Their power would be broken only later in the 19th century as a larger and more diverse population gave reformers a chance to challenge their control. But even today their influence still lingers in the corporate world where a handful of companies and individuals control 80% of the companies on the Toronto Stock Exchange.

**THE EARLY 19TH CENTURY—CANAL, RAILROAD & IMMIGRATION** The changes that would eventually dilute their control began in the early 19th century, especially during the 1820s, 1830s, and 1840s, when immigrants—Irish Protestants and Catholics, Scots, Presbyterians, Methodists, and other Nonconformists—poured in to settle the frontier farmlands. By 1832 York had become the largest urban community in the province, with a population of 1,600. Already well established commercially as a supply center, York was given another boost when the Erie Canal was extended to Oswego on Lake Ontario, giving it direct access to New York, and the Welland Canal was built across the Niagara Peninsula, giving it access to Lake Erie and points beyond. In 1834 the city was incorporated and York became Toronto, a city bounded by Parliament Street to the east, Bathurst to the west, the lakefront to the south, and 400 yards north of the current Queen Street (then called Lot) to the north. Outside this area—stretching west to Dufferin Street, east to the Don River, and north to Bloor Street—lay the "liberties," out of which new wards would later be carved. North of Bloor, local brewer Joseph Bloor and Sheriff Jarvis were already drawing up plans for the village of Yorkville.

As more immigrants arrived, the population grew more diverse and demands for democracy and reform were voiced. Among the reformers were such leaders as Francis Collins, who launched the radical paper *Canadian Freeman* in 1825; lawyer William Draper; and, perhaps most famous of all, fiery William Lyon Mackenzie, who was elected Toronto's first mayor in 1834.

Mackenzie had started his *Colonial Advocate* to crusade against the narrow-minded Family Compact, calling for reform and challenging their power to such an extent that some of them dumped his presses into the lake. Mackenzie was undaunted and by 1837 was calling for open rebellion.

A severe depression, financial turmoil, and the failure of some banks all contributed to the 1837 Rebellion, one of the most dramatic events in the city's history. On December 5 the rebels, a scruffy bunch of about 700, gathered at Montgomery's Tavern outside the city (near modern-day Eglinton Avenue). From here, led by Mackenzie on a white mare, they marched on the city. Two days later the city's militia, called out by Sheriff Jarvis, scattered the rebels at Carlton Street. Both sides then turned and ran. Reinforcements arrived and pursued the rebels and bombarded the tavern with cannonballs. Mackenzie fled to the United States and two other leaders—Lount and Matthews—were hanged. Their graves can be visited in the Necropolis cemetery.

Between 1834 and 1884 the foundations of an industrial city were laid: Water works, gas, and later, electrical lighting were installed, and public transportation was organized. Many municipal facilities were built, including a city hall, the Royal Lyceum Theatre (1848) on King near Bay, the Toronto Stock Exchange (1852), St. Lawrence Hall (1851), an asylum, and a jail.

During the 1850s the building of the railroads accelerated the economic pace. By 1860 Toronto was at the center of a railroad web that linked the city north, south, east, and west. Toronto became the trading hub for lumber and grain imports and exports. Merchant empires were founded; railroad magnates emerged; and institutions like the Bank of Toronto were established.

Despite its growth and wealth Toronto still lagged behind Montréal—its population being only half of Montréal's in 1861—but increasingly Toronto took advantage of its superior links to the south, an advantage that would eventually help it overtake its rival. Under the Confederation of 1867 the city was guaranteed another

- 1965 New city hall built.
- 1971 Ontario Place built.
- 1972 Harbourfront under development.
- 1974 Metro Zoo and Ontario Science Centre open.
- 1975 CN Tower opens for business.
- 1984 City's 150th anniversary.
- 1989 SkyDome opens.
- 1992 Residents of Toronto Islands win 40-year struggle to retain their homes.
- 1993 Princess of Wales Theatre and CBC Building
- 1930s Depression; thousands go on relief or ride the boxcars.
- 1931 Maple Leaf Gardens built.
- 1939 Canada enters World War II; thousands of troops leave from Union Station.
- 1995 Progressive Conservative Government elected; focuses on budget cuts.
- 1996 Toronto voted best city in the world to live and work in by *Fortune Magazine*.
- 1997 People protest in Queen's Park against social-service cuts and the passage of Bill 103 creating a megacity.

advantage when it was made the capital of the newly created Ontario, which, in effect, gave it control over the minerals and timber of the north.

During this same mid-Victorian period the growth of a more diverse population continued. In 1847 Irish famine victims flooded into Toronto, and by 1851 and 1852 the Irish-born were the largest single ethnic group in Toronto. While many of them were Ulster Irish Protestants who did not threaten the Anglo-Protestant ascendancy, these newcomers were not always welcomed—a pattern that was to be repeated whenever a new immigrant group threatened to change the shape and order of society. As the gap between the number of Anglicans and Catholics closed, sectarian tensions increased and the old-country Orange and Green conflicts flared into mob violence.

**LATE & HIGH VICTORIAN TORONTO**   Between 1871 and 1891 the city's population more than tripled, shooting from 56,000 to 181,000. This increasingly large urban market helped spawn two great Toronto retailers—Timothy Eaton and Robert Simpson—who both moved to Toronto from Ontario towns to open stores at Queen and Yonge streets in 1869 and 1872, respectively. Eaton developed his reputation on fixed prices, cash sales only, and promises of refunds if the customer wasn't satisfied—all unique gambits at the time. Simpson copied Eaton and also competed by providing better service, such as two telephones to take orders instead of one. Both developed into full-fledged department stores, and both entered the mail-order business, conquering the country with their catalogs.

The business of the city was business, and amassing wealth was the pastime of such figures as Henry Pellatt, stockbroker and president of the Electrical Development Company and builder of Casa Loma; E.B. Osler; George Albertus Cox; and A.R. Ames. Although these men were self-made entrepreneurs, not Family Compact officials, they still formed a traditional socially conservative elite linked by money, taste, investments, and religious affiliation. And they were still British to a tee. They and the rest of the citizens celebrated the Queen's Jubilee in 1897 with gusto and gave Toronto boys a rousing send-off to fight in the Boer War in 1899. They also, like the British, had a fondness for clubs—the Albany Club for the Conservatives and the National Club for the Liberals. As in England, their sports clubs carried a certain cachet—notably the Royal Yacht Club, the Toronto Cricket Club, the Toronto Golf Club, and the Lawn Tennis Club.

The boom spurred new commercial and residential construction, such as the first steel-frame building—the Board of Trade Building (1889) at Yonge and Front; George Gooderham's Romanesque-style mansion (1890) at St. George and Bloor (now the York Club); the provincial parliament buildings in Queen's Park (1886–92); and the city hall (1899) at Queen and Bay. Public transit was improved, and by 1891 people were traveling the 68 miles of horse-drawn tracks. Electric lights, telephones, and electrical streetcars also appeared in the 1890s.

**FROM 1900 TO 1933**   Between 1901 and 1921 the population more than doubled, climbing from 208,000 to 521,893, and the economy continued to expand, fueled by the lumber, mining, wholesale, and agricultural machinery industries, and after 1911 by hydroelectric power. Toronto began to seriously challenge Montréal. Much of the new wealth went into construction, and three marvelous buildings from this era can still be seen today: the Horticultural Building at the Exhibition Grounds (1907), the King Edward Hotel (1903), and Union Station (1914–19). Most of the earlier wooden structures had been destroyed in the Great Fire of 1904, which wiped out 14 acres of downtown.

The booming economy and its factories attracted a wave of new immigrants—mostly Italians and Jews from Russia and Eastern Europe. They were very different from the British and Irish who had come earlier. They settled in the city's emerging ethnic enclaves. By 1912 Kensington Market was well established, and the garment center and Jewish community were firmly ensconced around King and Spadina. Little Italy clustered around College and Grace. By 1911 more than 30,000 Torontonians were foreign-born, and the slow march to change the English character of the city had begun.

It was still a city of churches worthy of the name "Toronto the Good," with a population of staunch religious conservatives, who barely voted for Sunday streetcar service in 1897 and in 1912 banned tobogganing on Sundays. As late as 1936, 30 men were arrested at the lakeshore resort of Sunnyside because they exposed their chests—even though the temperature was 105°F! In 1947 cocktail lounges were approved, but it wasn't until 1950 that commercialized sports could be played on Sundays.

Increased industrialization brought social problems, largely concentrated in Cabbagetown and the Ward, a large area that stretched west of Yonge and north of Queen. Here, poor people lived in crowded, wretched conditions: Housing was inadequate, health conditions were poor, and rag-picking or sweatshop labor was the only employment.

As industry grew unionism also increased, but the movement, as in the United States, failed to organize politically. Two major strikes—at Bell in 1907 and in the garment industry in 1912—were easily broken.

As the city became larger and wealthier it also became an intellectual and cultural magnet. Artists like Charles Jefferys, J.H. MacDonald, Arthur Lismer, Tom Thomson, Lawren Harris, Frederick Varley, and A.Y. Jackson, most associated with the Group of Seven, set up studios in Toronto, their first and now-famous group show opening in 1920. Toronto also became the English-language publishing center of the nation, and national magazines like *Maclean's* (started in 1896) and *Saturday Night* were launched. The Art Gallery of Ontario, the Royal Ontario Museum, the Toronto Symphony Orchestra, and the Royal Alexandra Theatre all opened before 1914.

Women advanced, too, at the turn of the century. In 1880 Emily Jennings Stowe became the first Canadian woman authorized to practice medicine. In 1886 women were admitted to the university. Clara Brett Martin was the first woman admitted to the law courts, and the women's suffragist movement gained strength, led by Dr. Stowe, Flora McDonald Denison, and the Women's Christian Temperance Union.

During World War I, Toronto sent 70,000 men to the trenches; about 13,000 were killed. At home, the war had a great impact economically and socially: Toronto became Canada's chief aviation center; factories, shipyards, and power facilities expanded to meet the needs of war; and women entered the workforce in great numbers.

After the war the city took on much more of the aspect and tone that is still recognizable today. Automobiles appeared on the streets—the Canadian Cycle and Motor Company had begun manufacturing them in 1906 (the first parking ticket was given in 1908); one or two skyscrapers appeared; and although 80% of the population still boasted British origin, ethnic enclaves were clearly defined.

The 1920s roared along, fueled by a mining boom, which saw Bay Street turned into a veritable gold-rush alley where everyone was pushing something hot. The Great Depression followed, racking up 30% unemployment in 1933. The only distraction from its bleakness was the opening of Maple Leaf Gardens in 1931, which besides being an ice-hockey center also hosted large protest rallies during the depression and later such diverse groups and personalities as the Jehovah's Witnesses, Billy Graham, the Ringling Bros. Circus, and the Metropolitan Opera.

As in the United States, hostility toward new immigrants was rife during the 20s, and it reached one of its peaks in 1923, when the Chinese Exclusion Act was passed, banning Chinese immigration. In the 1930s antagonism toward the Jews intensified. Signs such as NO JEWS, NIGGERS, OR DOGS were posted occasionally at Balmy and Kew beaches; and in August 1933, the display of a swastika at Christie Pits caused a battle between Nazis and Jews.

**AFTER WORLD WAR II**   In 1939 Torontonians again rallied to the British cause, sending thousands to fight in Europe. At home, plants turned out fighter bombers and Bren guns, and people endured rationing—one bottle of liquor a month and ration books for sugar and other staples—while they listened to the war-front news delivered by Lorne Greene.

Already prosperous by World War II, Toronto continued to expand during the 1940s. The suburbs alone added more than 200,000 to the population between 1940 and 1953. By the 1950s the urban area had grown so large, disputes between city and suburbs were so frequent, and the need for social and other services was so great that an effective administrative solution was needed. In 1953 the Metro Council was established, composed of equal numbers of representatives from the city and the suburbs.

Toronto became a major city in the 1950s, with Metro providing a structure for planning and growth. The Yonge subway opened, and a network of highways was constructed, linking the city to the affluent suburbs, which were populated by families who were buying cars, TVs, barbecues, refrigerators, and washing machines—all the modern conveniences associated with house-and-backyard suburbia. Don Mills, the first new town, was built between 1952 and 1962; Yorkdale Center, a mammoth shopping center, followed in 1964. Much of this growth was also fueled by the location of branch plants by American companies that were attracted to the area.

The city also began to loosen up, and while the old social elite (still traditionally educated at Upper Canada College, Ridley, and Trinity College) continued to dominate the boardrooms, politics, at least, had become more accessible and fluid. In 1954 Nathan Phillips became the first Jewish mayor, signifying how greatly the population had changed from earlier days when immigrants were primarily British, American, or French. In 1947 the Chinese Exclusion Act of 1923 was repealed, opening the door to the relatives of Toronto's then-small Chinese community. After 1950 the door swung open further. Germans and Italians were allowed to enter, adding to the communities that were already established; and then, under United Nations pressure, Poles, Ukrainians, Central European and Russian Jews, Yugoslavs, Estonians, Latvians, and other East Europeans poured in. Most arrived at Union Station, having journeyed from the ports of Halifax, Québec City, and Montréal. At the beginning of the 1950s the foreign-born were 31% of the population; by 1961 they were 42%, and the number of people claiming British descent had fallen from 73% to 59%. The 1960s were to bring an even richer mix of people—Portuguese, Greeks, West Indians, South Asians, and Chinese, Vietnamese, and Chilean refugees—changing the city's character forever.

In the 1960s the focus shifted back from the suburbs to the city. People moved back downtown, renovating the handsome brick Victorians so characteristic of today's downtown. Yorkville emerged briefly as the hippie capital—the Haight-Ashbury of Canada. Gordon Lightfoot and Joni Mitchell sang in the coffeehouses, and

## Impressions

*Los Angeles is one very obvious example of an edge, but Toronto is also a city at the edge of American history. With its draft dodgers, deserters, and émigré academics, it is almost Tolkien's Rivendell, safe from the ragings of the archaic darkness of Sauron and the Ring wraiths. Whether one can live permanently in Rivendell is a question I ask myself daily but at the moment Toronto seems the perfect retreat in which to look from one end of history to the other.*

—William Irwin Thompson, *At the Edge of History* (1971)

*Returning to Toronto was like finding a Jaguar parked in front of the vicarage and the padre inside with a pitcher of vodka martinis reading* Lolita.

—Article in *Maclean's,* January 1959

anti-Vietnam protests took over the streets. Perhaps the failure of the experimental, alternative Rochdale College in 1968 marked the demise of that era. By the mid-1970s Yorkville had been transformed into a village of elegant boutiques and galleries and high-rent restaurants, and the funky village had moved to Queen Street West.

In the 1970s Toronto became the fastest-growing city in North America. For years the city had competed with Montréal for first-city status, and now the separatist issue and the election of the Parti Québecois in 1976 hastened Toronto's dash to the tape. It overtook Montréal as a financial center, boasting the greatest number of corporate headquarters. Its stock market was more important, and it was also the country's prime publishing center. A dramatically different new city hall opened in 1965, symbol of the city's equally new dynamism. Toronto also began reclaiming its waterfront with the development of Harbourfront. New skyscrapers and civic buildings reflected the city's new power and wealth—the Toronto Dominion, the 72-story First Canadian Place, Royal Bank Plaza, Roy Thomson Hall, the Eaton Centre, the CN Tower—all of which transformed the old 1930s skyline into an urban landscape worthy of world attention.

Unlike the rapid building of highways and other developments completed in the 1950s, these developments were achieved with some balance and attention to the city's heritage. From the late '60s to the early '80s the citizens fought to ensure that the city's heritage was saved and that development was not allowed to continue as wildly as it had in the '50s. The best examples of the success of this reform movement were the stopping of the proposed Spadina Expressway in 1971 and the fight against several urban renewal plans.

During the 1970s the provincial government also helped develop attractions that would polish Toronto's patina and lure visitors: Ontario Place in 1971, Harbourfront in 1972, and the Metro Zoo and the Ontario Science Centre in 1974. Government financing also supported the arts and helped turn Toronto from a city with four theaters in 1965 to one boasting 22 in 1976 and more than 40 today.

The city's growth has continued with the 1989 downtown opening of the SkyDome, the first stadium in the world with a fully retractable roof, and the planned opening of the brand-new Air Canada Centre stadium in February 1999.

# 2 Planning a Trip to Toronto

This chapter is devoted to the where, when, and how of your trip—the advance-planning issues required to get it together and take it on the road.

After deciding where to go, most people have two fundamental questions: What will it cost? and How do I get there? This chapter will answer both of these questions and also resolve other important issues, such as when to go and where to obtain more information about Toronto.

## 1 Visitor Information & Entry Requirements

### VISITOR INFORMATION

**FROM NORTH AMERICA**    The best source for specific Toronto information is **Tourism Toronto, Metro Toronto Convention & Visitors Association,** Queen's Quay Terminal at Harbourfront, 207 Queen's Quay W., Toronto, ON, M5J 1A7 (☎ **800/363-1990** from the continental U.S., or 416/203-2600). Call them before you leave and request the kind of information you want.

For information about Ontario, contact **Tourism Ontario,** 1 Concorde Gate, Don Mills, ON, M3C 3M6 (☎ **800/ONTARIO** or 416/314-0944), or go to their travel center in the Eaton Centre on Level 1 at Yonge and Dundas. It's open Monday to Friday 10am to 9pm and Saturday 9:30am to 6pm and Sunday noon to 5pm.

The Canadian consulates in the U.S. do not provide tourist information. They will only refer you to the offices above.

Consular offices in Buffalo, Detroit, Los Angeles, New York, Seattle, and Washington, D.C. will deal with visas and other similar political/immigration issues.

**FROM ABROAD**    The following consulates can provide information or refer you to the appropriate offices that can: In the **UK and Ireland,** try the **Canadian High Commission,** MacDonald House, 1 Grosvenor Square, London W1X 0AB, ☎ **0171/258-6600,** fax 0171/258-6384; in **Australia,** contact the **Canadian High Commission,** Commonwealth Avenue, Canberra, ACT 2600, ☎ **02/6273-3844,** or the **Consulate-General of Canada,** Level 5, Quay West Building, 111 Harrington St., Sydney, NSW 2000 ☎ **02/9364-3000,** plus offices in Melbourne and Perth; in **New Zealand,** the **Canadian High Commission,** 3rd floor, 61 Molesworth St.,

Thomdon, Wellington ☎ **04/473-9577** or the **Consulate of Canada,** Level 9 Jetset Centre, 44–48 Emily Place, Auckland, New Zealand ☎ **09/309-3690;** in **South Africa,** the **Canadian High Commission,** 1103 Arcadia St., Hatfield 0083, Pretoria ☎ **012/342-6923** and offices in Capetown and Johannesburg.

## ENTRY REQUIREMENTS

**DOCUMENTS**    U.S. citizens and legal residents do not need passports or visas, but must show proof of citizenship (birth or voter's certificate, naturalization certificates or green card). Every person under 19 years of age is required to produce a letter from a parent or guardian granting him or her permission to travel to Canada. The letter must state the traveler's name and the duration of the trip. It is therefore essential that teenagers also carry proof of citizenship; otherwise their letter is useless at the border.

Citizens of Australia, New Zealand, the United Kingdom, and Ireland must have valid passports. Citizens of many other countries will need visas, which must be applied for in advance at the local Canadian embassy or consulate. For detailed information, call your local Canadian consulate or embassy.

**CUSTOMS**    Customs regulations are generous in most respects, but they get pretty complicated when it comes to firearms, plants, meats, and pets. Fishing tackle poses no problem (provided the lures are not made of restricted materials—specific feathers, for example), but the bearer must possess a nonresident license for the province or territory where he or she plans to use it. You can bring in free of duty up to 50 cigars, 200 cigarettes, and 2 pounds of tobacco, provided you're at least 18 years of age. You are also allowed 40 ounces (1.14l) of liquor or wine as long as you're over the minimum drinking age of the province you're visiting (19 in Ontario).

For more detailed information about customs regulations, write to **Revenue Canada,** 875 Heron Rd., Ottawa, ON, K1A 0L8.

## 2 Money

Canadians use dollars and cents, but with a distinct advantage for U.S. visitors—the Canadian dollar is worth 71¢ in U.S. money (give or take a couple of points' daily variation). So, in effect, your American money gets you 29% more the moment you exchange it into local currency. That makes quite a difference in your budget, and since the prices of many goods are roughly on a par with those in the United States, the difference is real, not imaginary. (Before you get too excited, though, keep in mind that sales taxes are higher.) You can bring in or take out any amount of money, but if you are importing or exporting sums of $5,000 or more, you must file a report of the transaction with U.S. Customs. Most tourist establishments in Canada will take U.S. cash, but for the best rate, withdraw cash from a Canadian ATM (most accept Cirrus or Plus) or exchange your funds into Canadian currency upon arrival.

If you do spend American money at Canadian establishments, you should understand how the conversion is calculated. Often there will be a sign at the cash register that reads "U.S. Currency 25%." This 25% is the "premium," which means that for every U.S. greenback you hand over, the cashier will consider it $1.25 in Canadian dollars. For example, for an $8 tab you need pay only $6.40 in U.S. bills.

It used to be that before leaving home, you were well advised to purchase traveler's checks and arrange to carry some ready cash (usually about $200), but now that **ATMs** are virtually everywhere in the world, and often deliver a better exchange rate, I recommend obtaining money from them. You can find them at most banks. For the location of the nearest ATM that services the **Cirrus** network, dial ☎ **800/424-7787** (a global access number); for **Plus,** call ☎ **800/843-7587** (U.S. only). On

## What Things Cost in Toronto | U.S. $

| | U.S. $ |
| --- | --- |
| Taxi from the airport to downtown | 30.00 |
| Subway/bus from the airport to downtown | 6.80 |
| Local telephone call | .18 |
| Double at the Four Seasons (very expensive) | 207.15 |
| Double at Bond Place (moderate) | 92.85 |
| Double at Victoria University (inexpensive) | 64.00 |
| Two-course prix-fixe lunch for one at La Bodega (moderate)* | 12.40 |
| Two-course lunch for one at Kensington Kitchen (inexpensive)* | 7.70 |
| Three-course dinner for one at Scaramouche (very expensive)* | 47.65 |
| Three-course dinner for one at Grano (moderate)* | 26.95 |
| Three-course dinner for one at Jerusalem (inexpensive)* | 15.80 |
| Pint of beer | 3.50 |
| Coca-Cola | .90 |
| Cup of coffee | .75 |
| Roll of ASA 100 Kodacolor film, 36 exposures | 5.00 |
| Admission to the Royal Ontario Museum | 7.15 |
| Movie ticket | 6.05 |
| Theater ticket at the Royal Alex | 28.55–67.85 |

*Includes tax and tip but not wine.

*Note: Prices are listed here in U.S. dollars.*

## The Canadian Dollar & the U.S. Dollar

The prices quoted in this guide are given in Canadian dollars with the equivalent in U.S. currency in parentheses. The rate we've used is $1.40 Canadian to $1 American.

Here's a quick table of equivalents:

| Canada $ | U.S. $ | Canada $ | U.S. $ |
| --- | --- | --- | --- |
| 1 | 0.72 | 50 | 36.00 |
| 5 | 3.60 | 80 | 57.60 |
| 10 | 7.20 | 100 | 72.00 |
| 20 | 14.40 | | |

the Web, try **www.visa.com** or **www.mastercard.com** for the location of the nearest Plus ATM. Most ATMs will make cash advances against MasterCard and Visa, but make sure you have your personal identification number with you.

For those who prefer the extra security of **traveler's checks,** U.S. dollar traveler's checks and credit cards are accepted in almost all hotels, restaurants, shops, and attractions, and they can be exchanged for cash at banks. You're best off cashing them at banks. As in the United States, most small businesses will not cash traveler's checks in a denomination greater than $50, or perhaps even $20.

**American Express** (☎ **800/221-7282** in the U.S. and Canada) is the most widely recognized traveler's check; depending on where you purchase them, expect to pay between 1% and 4% commission. Checks are free to members of the American Automobile Association (AAA).

**Citicorp** (☎ **800/645-6556** in the U.S., or **813/623-1709** collect in Canada) issues checks in U.S. dollars or British pounds.

**MasterCard International** (☎ **800/223-9920** in the U.S.) issues checks in about a dozen currencies.

**Thomas Cook** (☎ **800/223-7373** in the U.S.) issues checks in a variety of currencies.

# 3  When to Go

## THE CLIMATE

As a general rule, you can say that spring runs from late March to mid-May (though occasionally there'll be snow in mid-April); summer, from mid-May to mid-September; fall, from mid-September to mid-November; and winter, from mid-November to late March. The highest recorded temperature was 105°F; the lowest, –27°F. The average date of first frost is October 29; the average date of last frost is April 20. The blasts from Lake Ontario can sometimes be fierce, even in June. Bring a windbreaker or something similar.

### Toronto's Average Temperatures (°F)

|      | Jan | Feb | Mar | Apr | May | June | July | Aug | Sept | Oct | Nov | Dec |
|------|-----|-----|-----|-----|-----|------|------|-----|------|-----|-----|-----|
| High | 30  | 31  | 39  | 53  | 64  | 75   | 80   | 79  | 71   | 59  | 46  | 34  |
| Low  | 18  | 19  | 27  | 38  | 48  | 57   | 62   | 61  | 54   | 45  | 35  | 23  |

## HOLIDAYS

Toronto celebrates the following holidays: New Year's Day (January 1), Good Friday and/or Easter Monday (variable; in March or April), Victoria Day (last Monday in May), Canada Day (July 1), Civic Holiday (first Monday in August), Labour Day (first Monday in September), Thanksgiving (second Monday in October), Remembrance Day (November 11), Christmas Day (December 25), and Boxing Day (December 26).

On Good Friday and Easter Monday, both schools and government offices are closed; most corporations are closed on one or the other, and some are closed on both. Only banks and government offices close on Remembrance Day (November 11).

### TORONTO CALENDAR OF EVENTS

January, February, March, and April are dominated by trade shows, such as the International Boat and Automobile shows, Metro Home Show, Outdoor Adventure Sport Show and more. For information, call **Tourism Toronto** at ☎ **800/363-1990** or 416/203-2600.

February
- **North York Winter Fair,** Mel Lastman Square. This 3-day celebration features ice-skating shows, snow play, midway rides, performances, ice sculpting, arts-and-crafts shows, and more. For information, call ☎ **416/395-7350.** Usually around Valentine's Day.

## March

- **St. Patrick's Day Parade,** downtown. Toronto's own version of this classic Irish celebration. March 17. For information, call ☎ **416/487-1566.**

## May

- **Milk International Children's Festival,** Harbourfront. This is a 9-day celebration of the arts for kids—from theater and music to dance, comedy, and storytelling. For information, call ☎ **416/973-3000.** Usually starts on Mother's Day.

## June

- ✪ **Metro International Caravan,** citywide. This popular 9-day event (North America's largest international festival) features craft demonstrations, opportunities to sample authentic dishes, and traditional dance performances by 100 different cultural groups with a tie to Toronto. Usually third and fourth weekends. For information, call ☎ **416/977-0466.**
- **Du Maurier Ltd. Downtown Jazz Festival,** citywide. Begun in 1987, this 10-day festival showcases more than 1,600 artists playing in every jazz style conceivable— blues, gospel, Latin, African, traditional, and more—at more than 50 venues throughout town. For information, call ☎ **416/363-8717.** For **tickets,** call ☎ **416/973-3000.** Usually the last 11 days in June.
- **Benson & Hedges, Inc. Symphony of Fire,** Ontario Place. Boats fill the harbor and people flock to the waterfront to view this spectacular display of gunpowder art. Six shows are given on several Saturdays and Wednesdays. For information, call ☎ **416/442-3667.** Ongoing all month.
- **Gay & Lesbian Pride Celebration,** citywide. A week of events, performances, symposiums, parties, and more culminates in the great annual Sunday parade. For information call ☎ **416/92PRIDE** or 416/927-7433. Usually the last week in June.
- **Fringe of Toronto Festival,** citywide. This 10-day celebration presents new and challenging theater performed by as many as 80 different artists/groups. Each performance lasts no more than an hour. Shows are given on several different stages and ticket prices are low, with only 50% sold in advance (the most expensive ticket at the time of this writing is C$8/U.S.$6 at the door, C$10/U.S.$7 in advance). Every evening at the Fringe Club (292 Brunswick Ave.), a free cabaret that combines comedy, clowning, music, dance, and literary presentations is held. For information, call ☎ **416/534-5919** or e-mail the festival at fringeto@interlog.com. Usually the last week in June and the first week in July.

## July

- **Molson Indy,** the Exhibition Place Street circuit. This is one of Canada's major races on the IndyCar circuit. Call ☎ **416/872-4639.** Usually third weekend in July.
- ✪ **Caribana,** citywide. Toronto's version of Carnival transforms the city in midsummer, complete with traditional foods from the Caribbean and Latin America, ferry cruises, island picnics, concerts, and arts-and-crafts exhibits. Call ☎ **416/ 465-4884** for more information. Last week in July and first week in August.

## August

- ✪ **Canadian National Exhibition,** Exhibition Place. One of the world's largest exhibitions, this 18-day extravaganza features midway rides, display buildings, free shows, and grandstand performers. The 3-day Canadian International Air Show (first staged in 1878) is an added bonus. Call ☎ **416/393-6000** for information. Mid-August to Labour Day.

- **Du Maurier Ltd. Open,** National Tennis Centre at York University. Canada's international tennis championship is an important stop on the pro-tennis tour that attracts players such as Sampras, Agassi, Seles, and Sanchez Vicario. The Open is run in conjunction with a tournament in Montréal during the middle of August. In 1998, the men play in Toronto and the women in Montréal. In 1999, they alternate, and so on in subsequent years. For information, call ☎ **416/665-9777.** Usually third to fourth weekend in July or August.

September

- **Toronto International Film Festival,** citywide. The second-largest film festival in the world, showing more than 270 films in 10 days. For information, call ☎ **416/967-7371.** Early September.
- **Bell Canadian Open,** the Glen Abbey Golf Club in Oakville. Canada's national golf tournament has featured the likes of Greg Norman and Tiger Woods in recent years (☎ **905/844-1800**). It's almost always held at Glen Abbey, though Montréal hosted the event in 1997. Usually held over Labour Day weekend.

October

- **Oktoberfest,** in Kitchener-Waterloo, about 1 hour (60 miles) from Toronto. This famed drinkfest features cultural events plus a pageant and parade. For information, call ☎ **519/570-4267.** October 9 to 17 (1998).
- **International Festival of Authors,** at the Harbourfront. This prestigious 11-day literary festival draws more than 50 participants from around the world to readings and on-stage interviews. Among the literary luminaries who have appeared are Margaret Drabble, Thomas Kenneally, Joyce Carol Oates, A.S. Byatt, and Margaret Atwood. For information, call Harbourfront at ☎ **416/973-3000;** for tickets, call ☎ **416/973-4000.** Usually starts the third weekend of October.

November

- ☉ **Royal Agricultural Winter Fair and Royal Horse Show,** Exhibition Place. At this 12-day show, the largest indoor agricultural and equestrian competition in the world, vegetables and fruits are on display, along with crafts, farm machinery, livestock, and more. The horse show is traditionally attended by a member of the British royal family. Call ☎ **416/393-6400** for information. Usually second and third weekends of November.
- **Toronto International Pow Wow,** SkyDome. More than 1,500 Native American dancers, drummers, and singers attend this weekend celebration. There's also an arts-and-crafts marketplace and traditional foods to savor. Call ☎ **519/751-0040.** Usually last weekend in November.
- **The Cavalcade of Lights.** During this holiday celebration, the trees in and around Nathan Phillips Square are lit up, the skating rink hosts parties and performances, and ice sculptures decorate the square. Late November through December 31.

December

- **First Night Toronto and New Year's Eve at City Hall,** December 31. First Night is a nonalcoholic family New Year's Eve celebration. The purchase of a $7 button entitles you to attend a variety of musical, theatrical, and dance performances at downtown venues. To celebrate New Year's Eve, Torontonians gather in Nathan Phillips Square and also Mel Lastman Square in North York, where concerts begin around 10pm to usher in the countdown to the New Year.

## 4 Travel Insurance

Before you decide to purchase travel insurance, check your existing policies to see whether they'll cover you while you're traveling. Check with your health-insurance company to make sure that your coverage extends to Canada. Some credit cards offer automatic flight insurance when you purchase an airline ticket with that credit card. These policies insure against death or dismemberment in the event of a plane crash.

Also, check your credit cards to see if any of them pick up the collision damage waiver in Canada (CDW) if you plan to rent a car. The CDW can run as much as $14 a day and add as much as 50% to the cost of renting a car. Check your automobile insurance policy, too; it might cover the CDW as well. If you own a home or have renter's insurance, see if that policy covers off-premises theft and loss wherever it occurs. Find out what procedures you need to follow to make a claim. If you're traveling on a tour or package deal and have prepaid a large chunk of your travel expenses, you might want to ask a travel agent about trip-cancellation insurance.

If, after checking all your existing insurance policies, you decide that you need additional insurance, a good travel agent can give you information on a variety of different options. Or you can contact **Wallach & Company,** 107 W. Federal St., P.O. Box 480, Middleburg, VA 20118 ( ☎ **800/237-6615** or 540/687-3166). They provide a comprehensive travel policy that covers all contingencies—cancellation, health, emergency assistance, and loss.

## 5 Tips for Travelers with Special Needs

### FOR TRAVELERS WITH DISABILITIES

Toronto is a very accessible city. Curb cuts are well made and common throughout the downtown area; special parking privileges are extended to people with disabilities who have disabled plates or a special pass that allows parking in "No Parking" zones. The subway and trolleys are, unfortunately, not accessible, but the city operates a special service for those with disabilities, called **Wheel-Trans.** Visitors can register for this service. For information, call ☎ **416/393-4111.**

The **Community Information Centre of Metropolitan Toronto,** 425 Adelaide St. W., at Spadina, Toronto, ON, M5V 3C1 ( ☎ **416/392-0505,** weekdays 8am–10pm; weekends 10am–10pm) may be able to provide limited information and assistance about social-service organizations in the city, but does not have any accessibility information per se on tourism or hotels.

### FOR SENIORS

Bring some form of photo ID, as many city attractions grant special senior discounts. Some hotels, too, will offer special discounted rates.

If you haven't already done so, think about joining the **American Association of Retired Persons (AARP),** 601 E St. NW, Washington, DC 20049 ( ☎ **202/434-2277**).

Also look into the fun courses that are offered at incredibly low prices by **Elderhostel,** 75 Federal St., Boston, MA 02110 ( ☎ **617/426-7788**) in the Toronto region. For a catalog, write Elderhostel, P.O. Box 1959, Wakefield, MA 01880-5959.

### FOR STUDENTS

The key to securing discounts and other special benefits is the **International Student Identity Card (ISIC),** available to any bona fide high school or university student.

Contact the **Council on International Educational Exchange (CIEE),** 205 E. 42nd St., New York, NY 10017 (☎ **212/822-2600** or 212/822-2700). The card is available at all Council Travel offices and at many U.S. college campuses. To find the office nearest you, call ☎ **888/COUNCIL** (888/268-6245) or ☎ **800/GETANID** (800/438-2643).

If you'd like to meet other students, you've come to the right place: Toronto has several major colleges in addition to the large and sprawling **University of Toronto.** The largest university in Canada, with more than 50,000 students (41,000 full-time), the University of Toronto offers many year-round activities and events that any visitor can attend—lectures, seminars, concerts, and more. U of T Day is usually celebrated in the middle of October, when the university holds an open house to the community and also celebrates with a children's fair and the annual homecoming football game and parade. Call ☎ **416/978-8342** for more information or 416/978-5000 for campus tours.

## FOR GAY & LESBIAN TRAVELERS

Toronto has a large gay population estimated at about 250,000. Community life is centered north and south of the intersection of Church and Wellesley streets. Any gay man or lesbian will find the following resources useful. First, pick up a copy of the biweekly *Xtra!,* available free at many bookstores, including the **Glad Day Bookshop,** 598A Yonge St., 2nd floor (☎ **416/961-4161**), open Monday to Wednesday 10am to 6:30pm, Thursday to Friday 10am to 9pm, Saturday 10am to 6pm, and Sunday from noon until 6pm. If you want to secure a copy of *Xtra!* ahead of time, contact *Xtra!* at 491 Church St., Suite 200, Toronto, ON, M4Y 2C6 (☎ **416/925-6665**).

For information on upcoming events, call **Tel-Xtra** (☎ **416/925-9872**).

## FOR WOMEN TRAVELERS

For books and information on the feminist scene, stop by the **Toronto Women's Bookstore,** 73 Harbord St., at Spadina (☎ **416/922-8744**). It's open Monday to Wednesday and Saturday from 10:30am to 6pm, Thursday and Friday until 8pm, and Sunday from noon to 5pm.

# 6  Getting There

## BY PLANE

Wherever you're traveling from, always shop the different airlines and ask for the lowest fare, if price is a factor. You may be able to fly for less than the standard APEX fare by contacting a ticket broker or consolidator. These companies, which buy tickets in bulk and then sell them at a discount, advertise in the Sunday travel sections of major city newspapers. You may not be able to get the lowest price they advertise, but you're likely to pay less than the price quoted by the major airlines. Bear in mind that tickets purchased through a consolidator are often nonrefundable tickets. If you change your itinerary after purchase, chances are you'll pay a stiff penalty.

**FROM THE U.S.  Air Canada** (☎ **800/776-3000**) operates direct flights to Toronto from most major American cities, including Allentown, Atlanta, Baltimore/Washington, Boston, Charlotte, Chicago, Cincinnati, Cleveland, Columbus, Denver, Harrisburg, Hartford, Houston, Kansas City, Los Angeles, Miami, Milwaukee, Minneapolis, Nashville, New York, Newark, Orlando, Philadelphia, Phoenix, Pittsburgh, Raleigh-Durham, St. Louis, San Francisco, Seattle, and Tampa. It also flies from major cities around the world and operates indirectly from other U.S. cities.

# CyberDeals for Net Surfers

It's possible to get some great deals on airfare, hotels, and car rentals via the Internet. So grab your mouse and start surfing before you head to Toronto—you could save a bundle on your trip. The Web sites I've highlighted below are worth checking out, especially since all services are free (but don't forget that time is money when you're on-line).

- **Air Canada (www.aircanada.ca)** and **Canadian Airlines (www.cdnair.ca)**    On Wednesdays, the Web sites of these two airlines offer highly discounted flights to Canada for the following weekend. You need to reserve the flight on Wednesday or Thursday to fly on Friday (after 7pm only) or Saturday (all day) and return on Monday or Tuesday (all day). Once you register with Air Canada's Web Specials page, they'll e-mail you every Wednesday about available discounts. For Canadian Airlines, just check out their site every Wednesday morning.

- **Travelocity (www.travelocity.com)**    This is one of the best travel sites out there. In addition to its **Personal Fare Watcher,** which notifies you via e-mail of the lowest airfares for up to five destinations, Travelocity will track in minutes the three lowest fares for any routes on any dates. You can book a flight then and there, and if you need a rental car or hotel, they'll find you the best deal via the SABRE computer reservations system (a huge database used by travel agents worldwide). Click on Last Minute Deals for the latest travel bargains.

- **Microsoft Expedia (www.expedia.com)**    The best part of this multipurpose travel site is the **Fare Tracker:** You fill out a form on the screen indicating that you're interested in cheap flights to Canada from your hometown, and, once a week, they e-mail you the best airfare deals. The site's Travel Agent will steer you to bargains on hotels and car rentals, and you can book everything, including flights, right on-line. This site is even useful once you're booked: Before you go, log on to Expedia for oodles of up-to-date travel info, including weather reports and foreign exchange rates.

- **Preview Travel (www.reservations.com** and **www.vacations.com)**    Another useful site, Reservations.com has a **Best Fare Finder** that'll search the Apollo computer reservations system for the three lowest fares for any route on any days of the year. Say you want to go from New York to Toronto and back between December 6 and 13: Just fill out the form on the screen with times, dates, and destinations, and within minutes, Preview will show you the best deals. If you find an airfare you like, you can book your ticket on-line—you can even reserve hotels and car rentals on this site. If you're in the preplanning stage, head to Preview's Vacations.com site, where you can check out the latest package deals by clicking on Hot Deals.

- **Trip.Com (www.thetrip.com)**    This site is really geared toward the business traveler, but vacationers-to-be can also use Trip.Com's valuable fare-finding engine, which will e-mail you every week with the best city-to-city airfare deals on your selected route or routes.

*—Jeanette Foster*

Jeanette Foster is co-author of *Frommer's Hawaii from $60 a Day* and *Frommer's Honolulu, Waikiki & Oahu*

The other Canadian airline, **Canadian Airlines International** (☎ **800/ 426-7000**), operates direct flights into Toronto from Chicago, Dallas, Miami, Los Angeles, and New York City.

Among U.S. airlines, **US Airways** (☎ **800/428-4322**) operates directly into Toronto from a number of U.S. cities, notably Baltimore, Indianapolis, Philadelphia, and Pittsburgh. **American** (☎ **800/433-7300**) has daily direct flights from Chicago, Dallas, Miami, and New York. **United** (☎ **800/241-6522**) has direct flights from Chicago, San Francisco, and Washington (Dulles). **Northwest** (☎ **800/225-2525**) flies directly from Detroit and Minneapolis only. **Delta** (☎ **800/221-1212**) flies direct from Atlanta and Cincinnati.

**FROM ABROAD**    There's frequent service either directly or indirectly to Toronto from around the world.

Several airlines operate from the **United Kingdom. British Airways** (☎ **0345/ 222-111**), **Air Canada** (☎ **0990/247-226**), and **Air India** fly direct from London's Heathrow. Air Canada also flies direct from Glasgow and Manchester. **Canadian Airlines** (☎ **0181/577-7722** in London, 0345/616-767 outside London) flies from Gatwick.

In **Australia, Canadian International** (☎ **1300/655-767**) has an agreement with Qantas and flies from Sydney to Toronto, stopping in Honolulu en route. From **New Zealand, Canadian International** (☎ **0800/802-245**) cooperates with Air New Zealand, scheduling on average three flights a week from Auckland to Toronto with one or two stops in Honolulu and/or Fiji.

From Cape Town in **South Africa, Delta** (☎ **800/221-1212**) operates via New York, **Air Canada** (call Cardinal Associates in Johannesburg at ☎ **011/880-8931**) via Frankfurt, **Swissair** (☎ **021/214-938**) via Zurich, and **South African Airways** (☎ **021/254-610**) via Miami or New York. An assortment of airlines flies from Johannesburg, including **British Airways** (☎ **011/441-8600**) via Heathrow, **South African Airways** (☎ **011/333-6504**) via Miami or New York, and **Swissair** (☎ **011/484-1980**) via Zurich.

## ARRIVING IN TORONTO

Most flights arrive at **Pearson International Airport,** located in the northwest corner of Metro Toronto approximately 30 minutes from downtown, although a few (mostly commuter flights) land at the **Toronto Island Airport,** a short ferry ride from downtown.

Three terminals, serviced by more than 50 airlines, cater to the traveler at Pearson. The most spectacular is the **Trillium Terminal 3** (☎ **905/612-5100**) used by American, Canadian Airlines International, British Airways, Air France, KLM, Lufthansa, and United, among others. This is a supermodern facility with moving walkways, a huge food court, and many retail stores.

To get from the airport to downtown, take Highway 427 south to the Gardiner Expressway East. A taxi along this route will cost about C$40 (U.S.$29). A slightly sleeker way to go is by flat-rate limousine, which will cost C$36.50 to C$38 (U.S.$26 to U.S.$27). Two limo services are **Aaroport** (☎ **416/745-1555**) and **AirLine** (☎ **905/676-3210**). Also very convenient is the **Airport Express** bus (☎ **905/ 564-6333**), which travels between the airport, the bus terminal, and all major downtown hotels—Harbour Castle Westin, the Royal York, Crowne Plaza Toronto Centre, the Sheraton Centre, and the Delta Chelsea Inn—every 20 minutes all day. The adult fare costs C$12.50 (U.S.$9) one way, the round trip C$21.50 (U.S.$15); the service is free for children under 11 accompanied by an adult. In addition, most first-class hotels run their own hotel limousine services, so check when you make your reservation.

The cheapest way to go is by subway and bus, which will take about an hour. The **TTC** has an airport bus (#58A) that travels between the Lawrence West subway station and Terminal Two at Pearson Airport for a total fare of C$4 (U.S.$2.85), C$2 of which is a supplement due at the airport. For more information, call ☎ **416/393-4636.**

## BY TRAIN

Amtrak's *Maple Leaf* links New York City and Toronto via Albany, Buffalo, and Niagara Falls, departing daily from Penn Station. The journey takes 11 3/4 hours. From Chicago, the *International* carries passengers to Toronto via Port Huron, Michigan (a 12 1/2-hour trip). Note that these lengthy schedules allow for extended stops at customs and immigration checkpoints at the border. With either routing, you'll arrive in Toronto at Union Station on Front Street, 1 block west of Yonge Street, opposite the Royal York Hotel. The station has direct access to the subway, so you can easily reach any Toronto destination from here.

To secure the lowest round-trip fares, book as far in advance as possible and try to travel midweek. Seat availability determines price levels; the earlier you book the more likely you are to secure a lower fare. Here though are a few sample one-way fares for use as guidelines only: New York to Toronto, US$65–$99 one way, depending on seat availability (for round trip, double the fare); from Chicago, US$98 one way, US$108–$196 round trip, depending on seat availability. Meals are not included in these prices. Always ask about the availability of discounted fares, companion fares, and any other special tickets. Call **Amtrak** at **800/USA-RAIL** or 800/872-7245.

From Buffalo's Exchange Street Station, you can also make the trip to Toronto's Union Station on the **Toronto/Hamilton/Buffalo Railway (THB).** Connecting services are also available from other major cities along the border.

## BY BUS

**Greyhound/Trailways** (☎ **800/231-2222**) is the only bus company that crosses the border into Canada from the United States. You can travel from almost anywhere in the United States, changing buses along the way until you reach Toronto. You'll arrive at the Metro Coach Terminal downtown at 610 Bay St., near the corner of Dundas Street.

The bus may be faster and cheaper than the train, and its routes may be more flexible if you want to stop along the way, but it's also more cramped, toilet facilities are meager, and meals are taken at somewhat depressing rest stops along the way.

Depending on where you are coming from, you should check into Greyhound/Trailways' special unlimited-travel passes as well as into any discount fares that might be offered. It's hard to provide sample fares because bus companies, like the airlines, are adopting yield-management strategies, causing prices to change from one day to the next depending on demand.

## BY CAR

Hopping across the border by car is no problem, as the U.S. highway system leads directly into Canada at 13 points. If you're driving from Michigan, you'll either enter at Detroit–Windsor (via I-75 and the Ambassador Bridge) or Port Huron–Sarnia (via I-94 and the Bluewater Bridge). If you're coming from New York, you have more options. Via I-190, you can enter at one of three places: Buffalo–Fort Erie; Niagara Falls, N.Y.–Niagara Falls, Ont.; or Niagara Falls, N.Y.–Lewiston. Via I-81, you'll cross the Canadian border at Hill Island; and via Rte. 37, you'll enter at either Ogdensburg–Johnstown or Rooseveltown–Cornwall.

From the United States you are most likely to enter Toronto via either Hwy. 401 or Hwy. 2 and the Queen Elizabeth Way if you come from the west. If you come from the east via Montréal, you'll also use hwys. 401 and 2.

Here are a few approximate driving distances in miles to Toronto: from Boston, 566; from Buffalo, 96; from Chicago, 534; from Cincinnati, 501; from Detroit, 236; from Minneapolis, 972; and from New York, 495.

Obviously, be sure you are carrying your driver's license and car registration if you plan to drive your own vehicle into Canada. It isn't a bad idea to carry proof of your automobile liability insurance, either.

If you are a member of the American Automobile Association (AAA) and your car breaks down once you've crossed the border, the **Canadian Automobile Association (CAA),** 60 Commerce Valley Dr. E., Thornhill (☎ **905/771-3111**), provides emergency road service.

# 3

# Getting to Know Toronto

This chapter helps you get your bearings in Toronto by describing the city's layout, offering options for getting around, and listing useful resources to assist you in handling any contingency that might crop up during your trip—from hiring a baby-sitter to removing a stain from your favorite shirt.

## 1 Orientation

### VISITOR INFORMATION

For tourist information about Toronto, go to (or write) **Tourism Toronto,** 207 Queens Quay W., Suite 590, in the Queens Quay Terminal at Harbourfront (P.O. Box 126), Toronto, ON, M5J 1A7 (☎ **800/363-1990** or 416/203-2500), open Monday to Friday from 9am to 5pm. Take the LRT from Union Station to the York Street stop.

More conveniently located is the drop-in **Ontario Visitor Information Centre** in the Eaton Centre, on Yonge Street at Dundas Street. It's located on "Level 1" and is open year-round Monday to Friday, 10am to 9pm, Saturday from 9:30am to 6pm, and Sunday from noon to 5pm.

If you happen to be in the neighborhood, the **Community Information Centre,** 425 Adelaide St. W. (☎ **416/392-0505**), specializes in social, government, and health-service information for residents or potential residents, but will try to answer any question. And if they can't, they will direct you to someone who can.

If you want to pick up a few brochures and a map before you leave **Pearson International Airport,** stop by the **Transport Canada Information Centre** in your terminal (there's one in each), where a staff fluent in 10 languages can also answer questions about tourist attractions, ground transportation, and more (☎ **905/676-3506** or 416/247-7678).

### CITY LAYOUT

Toronto is laid out in a grid system. **Yonge** (pronounced *Young*) **Street** is the main north-south street, stretching from Lake Ontario in the south well beyond Highway 401 in the north; the main east-west artery is **Bloor Street,** which cuts right through the heart of downtown. Yonge Street divides western cross streets from eastern cross streets.

"Downtown" usually refers to the area stretching south from Eglinton Avenue to the lake between Spadina Avenue in the west and Jarvis Street in the east. Because this is such a large area, I have divided it into **downtown** (from the lake north to College/Carlton Street), **midtown** (College/Carlton Street north to Davenport Road), and **uptown** (north from Davenport Road). In the first area you'll find all the lakeshore attractions—Harbourfront, Ontario Place, Fort York, Exhibition Place, the Toronto Islands, plus the CN Tower, City Hall, SkyDome, Chinatown, the Art Gallery, and the Eaton Centre. Midtown includes the Royal Ontario Museum, the Gardiner Museum, the University of Toronto, Markham Village, and chic Yorkville, a prime area for browsing and dining alfresco. Uptown is a fast-growing residential and entertainment area for the young, hip, and well heeled.

**Metropolitan Toronto** sprawls so widely that quite a few of its primary attractions exist outside the downtown core, such as the Ontario Science Centre, the Metropolitan Zoo, Canada's Wonderland, and the McMichael collection. Be prepared to journey somewhat.

**UNDERGROUND TORONTO**    It is not enough to know the streets of Toronto; you also need to know the warren of subterranean walkways underneath the city streets. Consult our map, "Underground Toronto," or look for the large clear underground PATH maps throughout the concourse.

Currently, you can walk from the Queen Street subway station west to the Sheraton Centre, then south through the Richmond-Adelaide Centre, First Canadian Place, and Toronto Dominion Centre all the way (through the dramatic Royal Bank Plaza) to Union Station. En route, branches lead off to the stock exchange, Sun Life Centre, and Metro Hall. Additional walkways also link Simcoe Plaza to 200 Wellington West and to the CBC Broadcast Centre.

Other walkways exist around Bloor Street and Yonge Street and elsewhere in the city. So if the weather's bad, you can eat, sleep, dance, shop, and go to the theater without even donning a coat.

## NEIGHBORHOODS IN BRIEF

Most of the following neighborhoods are in the downtown city center:

**The Toronto Islands**    These three islands in Lake Ontario—Ward's, Algonquin, and Centre—are home to a handful of residents and also a welcome summer haven to Torontonians where they can go to in-line skate, bicycle, boat, and picnic. Centre Island is the most visited. Catch the ferry at the foot of Bay Street by the Westin Hotel.

**Harbourfront/Lakefront**    The landfill on which the railroad yards and dock facilities were built is now a glorious playground opening onto the lake.

**Financial District**    Toronto's major banks and insurance companies have their headquarters here, from Front Street north to Queen Street, between Yonge and York streets. It's where Toronto's first skyscrapers were built.

**Old Town/St. Lawrence Market**    During the 19th century, this area, east of Yonge Street between the Esplanade and Adelaide Street, was the focal point of the community. Today the market's still going strong, and a stroll around the surrounding area will recapture an earlier era.

**New Town/King Street West Theater District**    An area of dense cultural development, this area stretches from Front Street north to Queen Street, and from Bay

# Underground Toronto

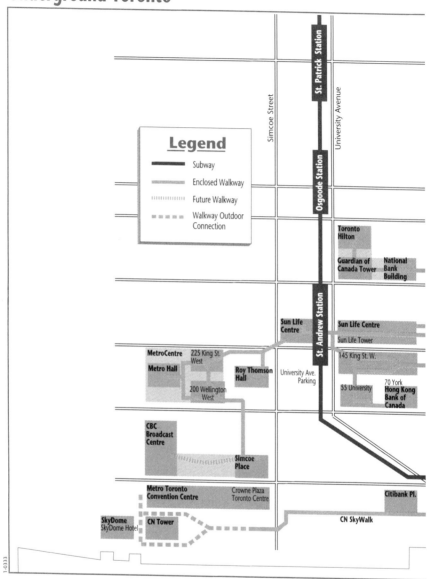

Street west to Bathurst Street. It contains the Royal Alex, Princess of Wales Theatre, Roy Thomson Hall, the CBC building, Metro Hall, the Convention Centre, and the CN Tower.

**Chinatown** Dundas Street West from University Avenue to Spadina Avenue, and north to College Street are the boundaries of Chinatown. As the Chinese community has grown, it has extended along Dundas Street and north along Spadina Avenue. Here, you'll see a fascinating mixture of the old and the new, as tiny hole-in-the-wall restaurants that have been in business for years share the sidewalks with glitzy shopping centers built with Hong Kong money.

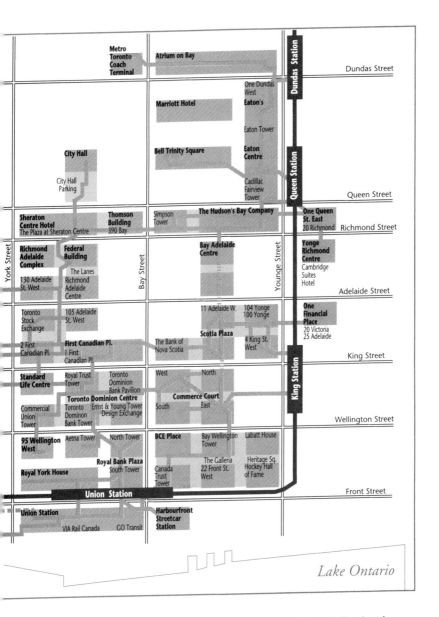

**Yonge Street**  Toronto's main commercial drag, Yonge Street is lined with stores and restaurants of all sorts. It's seedy in many places, especially around College and Dundas streets, where there's a section of strip and porno joints.

**Queen Street West**  This stretch of Queen Street from University Avenue to Bathurst Street is youthful, hip, and home to many of the city's young fashion designers. It offers an eclectic mix—antiques stores, secondhand bookshops, hip fashion boutiques and antique clothing emporiums, reasonably priced dining, and more. Despite the intrusion of such mega-retailers as the Gap, many independently owned boutiques flourish here, lending a decidedly local funk to the scene.

**Queen's Park and the University**   Home to the Ontario Legislature and many of the colleges and buildings that make up the University of Toronto, this neighborhood extends from College Street to Bloor Street between Spadina Avenue and Queen's Park Crescent.

**Cabbagetown**   Once described by writer Hugh Garner as the largest Anglo-Saxon slum in North America, this area stretching east of Parliament Street to the Don Valley between Gerrard Street and Bloor Street has been gentrified and is now a sought-after residential district. It's so named because the front lawns of the homes occupied by the Irish immigrants who settled here in the late 1800s were, it is said, covered with row upon row of cabbages.

**Yorkville**   Originally a village outside the city, this area north and west of Bloor Street and Yonge Street became Toronto's Haight-Ashbury in the 1960s. Now, it's a fashionable enclave of designer boutiques, galleries, cafes, and restaurants.

**The Annex**   An architecturally unique residential community, in which the streets are lined with handsome turn-of-the-century homes. It stretches from Bedford Road to Bathurst Street, and from Bloor Street to Bernard Street. Its residents are reputed to have a more liberal, independent spirit than some other neighborhoods; they led the fight against the Spadina Expressway project, which would have bisected downtown Toronto with a highway.

**Rosedale**   Curving tree-lined streets and elegant homes are the hallmarks of this leafy suburb, northeast of Yonge Street and Bloor Street to Castle Frank and the Moore Park Ravine. Named after Sheriff Jarvis's residence, its name alone is synonymous with Toronto's wealthy elite.

**Forest Hill**   After Rosedale, the second prime residential area in Toronto. Forest Hill is home to Upper Canada College and Bishop Strachan School for girls, and stretches west of Avenue Road between St. Clair Avenue and Eglinton Avenue.

**Little Italy**   A thriving, lively neighborhood filled with authentic Italian coffee bars, trattorias, and other stores serving the Italian community along College Street between Euclid and Shaw. It positively hums at night.

**The Beaches**   Communal, youthful, safe, and comfortable. These adjectives best describe the Beaches, just 15 minutes from downtown at the end of the Queen Street East streetcar line. A summer resort in the mid-1800s, its boardwalk and beach continue to make it a relaxing, casual family-oriented neighborhood.

**The East End—the Danforth**   This continuation of Bloor Street across the Don Valley Viaduct is largely a Greek neighborhood, lined with old-style Greek tavernas and new, happening contemporary Greek bars and restaurants crowded from early evening until early morning. The most concentrated Greek area starts in the 400 block.

**North York**   The redevelopment of this largely white suburban community about 13km (8 miles) north of Toronto's Queen Street has made it one of the hottest real-estate markets in the country. There's very little here for the visitor, other than the Ford Centre for the Performing Arts. In November 1997, its perpetually flamboyant mayor, Mel Lastman, became the mayor of the new, larger Toronto.

## 2 Getting Around

### BY PUBLIC TRANSPORTATION

Public transit is operated by the **Toronto Transit Commission (TTC)** (☎ **416/ 393-4636** daily from 7am to 10pm for information), which provides an overall interconnecting subway, bus, and streetcar system.

**Fares** (including transfers to buses or streetcars) are C$2/U.S.$1.45 (or 10 tickets for C$16/U.S.$11) for adults, C$1.35/U.S.96¢ (10 tickets for C$10.70/U.S.$7.65) for students 19 and under and seniors, and C50¢/U.S.35¢ (10 tickets for C$4/U.S.$2.85) for children under 12. You can purchase a special C$6.50 (U.S.$4.65) day pass good for unlimited travel for one person after 9:30am on weekdays, and good for up to six persons (a maximum of two adults) anytime Saturday, Sunday, and holidays.

For surface transportation, you need a ticket, a token, or exact change. Tickets and tokens may be obtained at subway entrances or authorized stores that display the sign TTC TICKETS MAY BE PURCHASED HERE. Always obtain a transfer *where you board the train or bus,* just in case you need it. They are obtainable free of charge in the subways from a push-button machine just inside the entrance or directly from drivers on streetcars and buses.

**THE SUBWAY**   It's a joy to ride—fast, quiet, and clean. It's a very simple system to use, too, consisting of two lines—Bloor-Danforth and Yonge-University-Spadina—designed basically in the form of a cross: The Bloor Street east-west line runs from Kipling Avenue in the west to Kennedy Road in the east, where it connects with Scarborough Rapid Transit traveling to Scarborough Centre and McCowan Road. The Yonge Street north-south line runs from Finch Avenue in the north to Union Station (Front Street) in the south. From here, it loops north along University Avenue and connects with the Bloor line at the St. George station. A Spadina extension runs north from St. George to Wilson Avenue.

A light rapid transit system connects downtown to Harbourfront, running from Union Station along Queen's Quay to Spadina with stops at Queen's Quay ferry docks, York Street, Simcoe Street, and Rees Street, and then continuing up Spadina to the Spadina/Bloor subway station. No transfer is needed from subway to LRT and vice versa.

The subway operates Monday to Saturday from around 6am to around 1:30am and Sunday from 9am to 1:30am. From 1am to 5:30am a Blue Night Network operates on basic surface routes running about every 30 minutes. For route information, pick up a Ride Guide at subway entrances or call ☎ **416/393-4636.** Multilingual information is available. You can also use the automated information service at ☎ **416/393-8663.**

Smart commuters park their cars at subway terminal stations at Kipling, Islington, Finch, Wilson, Warden, Kennedy, York Mills, Victoria Park, and Keele. Certain conditions apply. Call ☎ **416/393-8663** for details. You'll have to get there very early.

**BUSES & STREETCARS**   Where the subway leaves off, buses and streetcars take over to carry you east-west or north-south along the city's arteries. When you pay your fare (on bus, streetcar, or subway), always pick up a transfer, so that if you want to transfer to another mode of transportation, you won't have to pay another fare. For complete TTC information, call ☎ **416/393-4636.**

# BY TAXI

As usual, this is an expensive mode of transportation: It's C$2.50 (U.S.$1.80) the minute you step in, and C25¢ for each additional 0.275 kilometers. There's also a C10¢ charge for each bag. Cab fares can quickly mount up, especially during rush hours. Nevertheless, if you need a cab you can hail one on the street (they also line up in front of the big hotels), or call one of the major companies: **Diamond** (☎ **416/366-6868**), **Yellow** (☎ **416/504-4141**), or **Metro** (☎ **416/504-8294**). If you experience any problems with cab service, call the Metro Licensing Commission at ☎ **416/392-3082.**

# The TTC Subway System

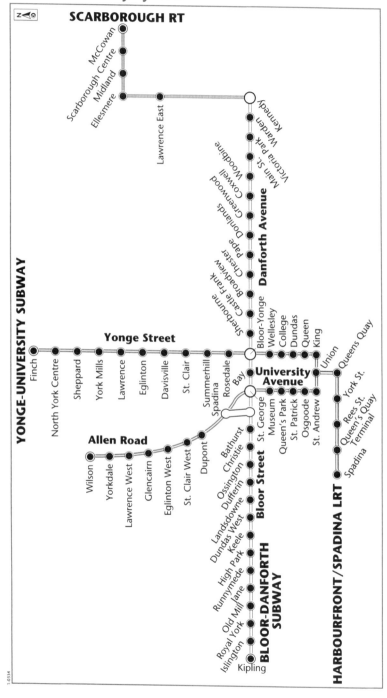

## BY CAR

Toronto may be spread out, but that doesn't necessarily mean that a car is the best way to get around. Driving in the city can be very frustrating because there's lots of traffic and parking is expensive. This is particularly true downtown, where traffic moves slowly and parking lots are scarce.

**RENTAL CARS**   Prices on car rentals change so frequently and vary so widely that your best bet is to shop around before you make your reservations. At the time of this writing, **Budget,** 141 Bay St. (☎ **416/364-7104**), charges C$38/U.S.$27 (including 200km/124 miles free) per day plus C12¢ per kilometer, or C$204 (U.S.$146) per week (including 1,400km/868 miles free), for a compact car. **National Tilden,** 930 Yonge St. (☎ **416/925-4551**), charges C$39/U.S.$28 per day (including 225km/140 miles free) plus C15¢ per kilometer, or C$245 (U.S.$175) per week, (including 1600km/992 miles free). Always ask about special weekend rates and other discounts.

*Note:* If you're under 25, check with the company—many will rent on a cash-only basis, some only if you have a credit card, and others will not rent to you at all.

**Parking**   Parking lots downtown run about C$4 (U.S.$2.85) per half hour, with a C$15 to C$18 (U.S.$11 to U.S.$13) maximum between 7am and 6pm. After 6pm and on Sunday, rates go down to around C$6 (U.S.$4.30). Generally the city-owned lots, marked with a big green "P," are slightly cheaper. Observe the parking restrictions—otherwise the city will tow your car away.

**Driving Rules**   A right turn at a red light is permitted after coming to a full stop, unless posted otherwise. The driver and front-seat passenger must wear seat belts (if you're caught not wearing one, you'll pay a substantial fine). The speed limit within the city is 30 miles per hour (50kmph). You must stop at pedestrian crosswalks. If you are following a streetcar and it stops, you must stop well back from the rear doors so that passengers can exit easily and safely. (Where there are concrete safety islands in the middle of the street for streetcar stops, this rule does not apply, but exercise care nonetheless.) Radar detectors are illegal.

## BY FERRY

Metro Parks operates ferries that travel to the Toronto Islands. Call ☎ **416/ 392-8193** for schedules and information. Round-trip fares are C$4 (U.S.$2.85) adults, C$2 (U.S.$1.40) seniors and students 15–19, and C$1 (U.S.70¢) children under 15.

## BY BICYCLE

You can secure a pamphlet outlining biking routes from Tourism Toronto. The Toronto Islands, the Beaches, Harbourfront/Lakefront/Sunnyside, and High Park are all great biking areas.

You can **rent bicycles** at Harbourfront right across from Queen's Quay; on Centre Island from **Toronto Island Bicycle Rental** (☎ **416/203-0009**) May to September; and year-round at **High Park Cycle and Sports,** 24 Ronson Dr. (☎ **416/ 614-6689**). Prices range from C$12 to C$22 (U.S.$9 to U.S.$16) per day.

### FAST FACTS: Toronto

**Airport**   See "Getting There," in chapter 2.

**Area Code**   Toronto's area code is **416;** outside the city, the code is **905.**

**Business Hours**   Banks are generally open Monday to Thursday from 10am to 3pm and Friday from 10am to 6pm. Stores are generally open Monday to Wednesday from 9:30 or 10am to 6pm and Saturday and Sunday from 10am to 5pm, with extended hours (until 8 to 9:30pm) on Thursday and usually Friday.

**Car Rentals**   See "Getting Around," earlier in this chapter.

**Climate**   See "When to Go," in chapter 2.

**Currency Exchange**   Generally, the best place to exchange your currency is at an ATM or bank. Currency can also be exchanged at the airport, but at a less favorable rate.

**Dentist**   For emergency dental services call ☎ **416/485-7121** or call **The Royal College of Dental Surgeons** (☎ **416/961-6555**) for a referral. Otherwise, ask at the front desk or the concierge at your hotel.

**Doctor**   If you need the services of a doctor while in Toronto, **The College of Physicians and Surgeons,** 80 College St. (☎ **416/967-2600** ext. 626 ), operates a referral service from 9am to 5pm. See also "Emergencies," below.

**Documents**   See "Visitor Information & Entry Requirements," in chapter 2.

**Driving Rules**   See "Getting Around," earlier in this chapter.

**Electricity**   It's the same as in the United States—110 volts, 50 cycles, AC.

**Embassies/Consulates**   All embassies are in Ottawa, the national capital. They include: the **Australian High Commission,** 50 O'Connor St., Suite 710, Ottawa, ON, K1P 6L2 (☎ **613/236-0841**); the **British High Commission,** 80 Elgin St., Ottawa, ON, K1P 5K7 (☎ **613/237-1530**); the **Irish Embassy,** 130 Albert St., Ottawa, ON, K1P 5G4 (☎ **613/233-6281**); the **New Zealand High Commission,** 727–99 Bank St., Ottawa, ON, K1P 6G3 (☎ **613/238-5991**); the **South African High Commission,** 15 Sussex Dr., Ottawa, ON, K1M 1M8 (☎ **613/ 744-0330**); and the **U.S. Embassy,** 100 Wellington St., Ottawa, ON, K1P 5T1 (☎ **613/238-4470**). Many nations maintain consulates in Toronto, including the following: **Australian Consulate-General,** 175 Bloor St. E., Suite 314, at Church St. (☎ **416/323-1155**); **British Consulate-General,** 777 Bay St. Suite 2800 at College (☎ **416/593-1290**); and the **U.S. Consulate,** 360 University Ave. (☎ **416/595-1700**).

**Emergencies**   Call ☎ **911** for fire, police, and ambulance. The **Toronto General Hospital** provides 24-hour emergency service (☎ **416/340-4611** or 416/ 340-4800). There are two entrances: the main entrance at **200 Elizabeth St.** and a second entrance at **150 Gerrard St. W.**

**Hospitals**   Try **Toronto General Hospital,** 200 Elizabeth St. (emergency ☎ **416/ 340-4611**). There's another entrance at 150 Gerrard St. W..

**Hot Lines**   To reach the rape crisis hot line, call ☎ **416/597-8808;** the victim assault line is ☎ **416/863-0511;** and the suicide prevention line is ☎ **416/ 598-1121.**

**Laundry/Dry Cleaning**   **Bloor Laundromat,** 598 Bloor St. W., at Bathurst Street (☎ **416/588-6600**) is conveniently located. At the **Laundry Lounge,** 531 Yonge St., at Wellesley Street (☎ **416/975-4747**), you can do your wash while sipping a cappuccino and watching TV in their lounge (open 7am to 11pm daily).

**Liquor Laws**   The minimum drinking age is 19 and drinking hours are daily 11am to 2am. Liquor, wine, and some beers are sold at **Liquor Control Board of Ontario**

(LCBO) stores, open Monday to Saturday. Most are open from 10am to 6pm (some stay open evenings).

True wine lovers will want to check out **Vintages** stores (also operated by the LCBO), which carry a more extensive and more specialized selection of wines. The most convenient downtown locations are in the lower-level concourse of **Hazelton Lanes** (☎ 416/924-9463) and at Queen's Quay ☎ 416/864-6777. Look also for the **Wine Rack** at 560 Queen St. W. (☎ 416/504-3647) and at 77 Wellesley St. E. at Church (☎ 416/923-9393). This last chain sells only Ontario wines.

Beer is sold at **The Beer Store,** most of which are open Monday to Friday from 10am to 10pm and Saturday from 10am to 8pm. There's a downtown location at 614 Queen St. W. (☎ 416/504-4665).

**Lost Property**   If you left something on a bus, streetcar, or the subway, call the **TTC Lost Articles Office** (☎ 416/393-4100) at the Bay Street subway station. They're open Monday to Friday from 8am to 5pm.

**Luggage Storage/Lockers**   Lockers are available at Union Station.

**Mail**   Postage for letters and postcards to the United States costs C52¢ (U.S.37¢); overseas, C90¢ (U.S.64¢). Mailing letters and postcards within Canada costs C45¢ (U.S.32¢).

**Maps**   Free maps of Toronto are available in every terminal at **Pearson International Airport** (look for signs directing you to the nearest Transport Canada Information Centre), the Metropolitan Toronto Convention & Visitors Association at **Harbourfront,** and the Visitor Information Centre in the **Eaton Centre,** on Yonge Street at Dundas Street. You can purchase a greater variety of maps at all convenience stores and bookstores, or try **Canada Map Company,** 63 Adelaide E. between Yonge and Church (☎ 416/362-9297) or **Open-Air Books and Maps,** 25 Toronto St., near Yonge and Adelaide streets (☎ 416/363-0719).

**Newspapers/Magazines**   The three daily newspapers are the *Globe & Mail,* the *Toronto Star,* and the *Toronto Sun. Eye* and *Now* are free arts-and-entertainment weeklies. In addition, there are many English-language ethnic Toronto newspapers serving the Portuguese, Hungarian, Italian, East Indian, Korean, Chinese, and Caribbean communities. *Toronto Life* is the major monthly city magazine. *Where Toronto* is usually provided free in your hotel room.

**Pharmacies**   One big chain is **Pharma Plus,** with a store at 68 Wellesley St., at Church Street (☎ 416/924-7760), which is open daily from 8am to midnight. Other Pharma Plus branches are in College Park, Manulife Centre, Commerce Court, and First Canadian Place.

**Police**   In a life-threatening emergency, call ☎ 911. For all other matters, you can reach the Metro police (40 College St.) at ☎ 416/808-2222.

**Post Office**   Postal services are available at convenience and drug stores. Look for the sign in the window indicating such services. There are also post-office windows open throughout the city in **Atrium on Bay** (☎ 416/506-0911), **Commerce Court** (☎ 416/956-7452), and at the **TD Centre** (☎ 416/360-7105).

**Radio**   The programming of the Canadian Broadcasting Corporation is one of the joys, as far as I'm concerned, of traveling in Canada. It offers a great mix of intelligent discussion and commentary as well as drama and music. In Toronto, the CBC broadcasts on 740 AM and 94.1 FM.

CHIN, at 1540 AM and 100.7 FM, will get you in touch with the ethnic/multicultural scene in the city, broadcasting in more than 30 different languages.

**Safety**   As large cities go, Toronto is generally safe, but be alert and use common sense, particularly at night. In the downtown area, Moss Park is considered one of the toughest areas to police. Avoid Allan Gardens and other parks at night.

**Taxes**   The provincial retail sales tax is 8% (on accommodations it's only 5%); there is an additional national goods-and-services tax (GST) of 7%.

In general, nonresidents may apply for a refund of these taxes for nondisposable merchandise that will be exported for use provided it was removed from Canada within 60 days of purchase. Note, though, that the following do not qualify for rebate: meals and restaurant charges, alcohol, tobacco, gas, car rentals, and such services as dry cleaning and shoe repair. The quickest and easiest way to secure the refund is to stop in at a duty-free shop at the border. You must have proper receipts with GST registration numbers. Or you can apply through the mail, but it will take about 4 weeks to receive your refund. For an application form and information, write or call **Visitor Rebate Program, Revenue Canada,** Summerside Tax Center, Summerside, PEI C1N 6C6 ☎ **902/432-5608,** *well in advance* of your trip. You can also contact **Ontario Travel,** Queen's Park, Toronto, ON, M7A 2R9 (☎ **800/668-2746** or 416/314-0944).

**Taxis**   See "Getting Around," earlier in this chapter.

**Telephone**   A local call from a telephone booth costs C25¢ (U.S.18¢). Watch out for hotel surcharges on local and long-distance calls; often a local call will cost *at least* C$1 (U.S.70¢) from a hotel room. The United States and Canada are on the same long-distance system. To make a long-distance call between the United States and Canada, use the area codes as you would at home. Canada's international prefix is 1.

**Time**   Toronto is on eastern standard time. Daylight saving time is in effect from April to October.

**Tipping**   Basically it's the same as in the United States: 15% in restaurants, 15% to 20% for taxis, and C$1 (U.S.70¢) per bag for porters.

**Transit Information**   For information on the subway, bus, and streetcar system, call ☎ **416/393-4636.**

**Weather**   Call the **talking yellow pages** at ☎ **416/292-1010** for a current weather report and lots of other information.

# Accommodations

Although Toronto has many fine hotels, it's not easy to find good-value accommodations downtown. The city is expensive. Most of the top hotels are pricey and cater to a business clientele; and even at the more moderate establishments, you can expect to pay C$100 (U.S.$71) a night. A few budget hotels charge under C$90 (U.S.$64) a night, while nonhotel accommodations, such as university dorms, start at C$45 to C$50 (U.S.$32 to U.S.$35) per night. Bed-and-breakfasts are a good bet for frugal travelers, but even they are creeping upward in price. The situation is not helped by a 5% accommodations tax and the national 7% GST.

There are some things you can do to combat the situation. I cannot stress enough how important it is to ask for a discount. Just like the airlines, hotels practice yield-management strategies and adjust the cost of a room depending on occupancy. This means that the official rack rate has virtually disappeared. For example, a single room with a rack rate of C$199 (U.S.$141) could rent for as little as C$130 (U.S.$93) or even lower. In fact, it's pretty standard today to sell rooms at 30% to 40% off the rack rate. If a room goes unsold, that revenue is lost forever, thus creating a nice incentive for a hotel's management to move to flexible room rates. If you're lucky and the market is slow, asking for a discount or stating simply what you're prepared to pay will certainly secure you a rate much lower than the published rack rate.

No matter what, always ask about discounts for special groups of people—corporate personnel, government employees, the military, seniors, students—whatever group to which you legitimately belong. These will be substantially lower than rack rates. Also ask about seasonal discounts, especially summer rates and weekend packages, which can help you secure some great bargains at even the most luxurious establishments. In addition, always ask in advance about parking charges and surcharges on local and long-distance phone calls. Both can make a big difference in your bill.

In the pages that follow I have categorized my favorites according to price and location. **Downtown** runs from the lakeshore to College/Carlton Street between Spadina Avenue and Jarvis Street; **midtown** refers to the area north of College/Carlton Street to where Dupont crosses Yonge Street, also between Spadina and Jarvis; **uptown** is north of the city core. I have also included a few hotels close to **Pearson International Airport** and a few to the east of the city.

AN IMPORTANT NOTE ON PRICES    The prices quoted in this chapter are rack rates. The accommodations tax is 5%, and the goods and services tax is 7%, but both are refunded to nonresidents upon application (see "Taxes" under "Fast Facts: Toronto," in chapter 3).

BED-&-BREAKFASTS    For interesting, truly personal accommodations, contact **Toronto Bed & Breakfast,** 253 College St. (P.O. Box 269), Toronto, ON, M5T 1R5 (☎ **416/588-8800;** Mon–Fri 9am–noon and 2–7pm), for their list of homes offering bed-and-breakfast accommodations within the city for an average of C$65 to C$90 (U.S.$46 to U.S.$64) per night per double. The association will reserve for you, or you can choose an establishment and make all the arrangements yourself.

Other organizations to try include the **Downtown Toronto Association of Bed-and-Breakfast Guesthouses,** P.O. Box 190, Station B, Toronto, ON, M5T 2W1 (☎ **416/368-1420;** fax 416/368-1653). This association represents about 30 non-smoking bed-and-breakfasts and is operated by Linda Lippa, an enthusiastic bed-and-breakfast host herself, who has a spacious Victorian home where she welcomes guests. The best time to call is between 8:30am and 7pm. All homes are nonsmoking. Room prices range from C$60 to C$90 (U.S.$43 to U.S.$64) double. **Metropolitan Bed and Breakfast,** Suite 269, 615 Mount Pleasant Rd., Toronto ON, M4S 3C5 (☎ **416/964-2566;** fax 416/960-9529), lists about 25 good bed-and-breakfasts ranging from C$50 to C$90 (U.S.$36 to U.S.$64). **Bed and Breakfast Homes of Toronto,** Box 46093, College Park Post Office, 44 Yonge St., Toronto, ON, M5B 2L8 (☎ **416/363-6362**) is a cooperative of about 18 independent B&B operators who offer rooms from C$60 to C$135 (U.S.$43 to U.S.$96).

# 1  Best Bets

- **Best Historic Hotel:** The **King Edward Hotel,** 37 King St. E. (☎ **416/863-9700**), is an oasis of Edwardian extravagance that has the grand style and service of that era yet offers up-to-the-minute amenities. Built in 1903 during the reign of King Edward VIII, it was the pet project of George Gooderham, the wealthiest man in Toronto and the owner of what was said to be the largest distillery in the British Empire. Daughters of Toronto society made their debuts in the Crystal Ballroom, and the Victoria Room was a favorite dining room for the elite. Anyone who was anyone stayed at the King Eddie: Past guests included Rudyard Kipling, Teddy Roosevelt, Rudolph Valentino, the Duke of Windsor, and the Beatles, who had to be barricaded in their rooms against the 3,000 fans who stormed the lobby. Though it has had its ups and downs, today it positively radiates grand style, and everything—the marble, the etched glass, the brass, and the baroque plasterwork—glows with the patina of age.
- **Best for Business Travelers:** The premier hotel for business travelers and one that is acclaimed regularly as such by *Fortune* and *Institutional Investor* is **The Four Seasons Hotel,** 21 Avenue Rd. (☎ **800/268-6282**). The Executive suites are 50% larger than standard rooms and spacious enough for informal meetings. In-room facilities include a multiline speaker phone and fax/modem computer hookup. The business center is available 24 hours and so too is the concierge and room service. Also, the Studio Cafe, Truffles, and La Serre are tops for business meals or cocktails. To top it off, limousine service is provided to the financial district.
  - **Best for a Romantic Getaway:** In town, the waterfront **Radisson Plaza Hotel Admiral,** 249 Queen's Quay W. (☎ **800/333-3333**), is small enough to make you feel like you're in a romantic hostelry, while the outdoor rooftop pool provides a resortlike atmosphere. Out of town, luxury abounds at **Langdon Hall,**

RR 3, Cambridge, ON, N3H 4R8 (☎ 519/740-2100), an accommodation that transports visitors as close as they can come to a romantic English country experience near Toronto (see chapter 10, page 216).

- **Best for Families:** The **Delta Chelsea Inn,** 33 Gerrard St. W. (☎ 800/ 243-5732), has been catering to families for years. The special children's programs, the day-care center, and the separate health club for adults only all help smooth the way for family vacationers.
- **Best Moderately Priced Hotel:** The **Holiday Inn on King,** 370 King St. W. (☎ 800/263-6364), has a great location near the SkyDome and the theater and entertainment district. It's only 5 years old and has a fine jazz bar below ground level.
- **Best Budget Hotel:** The **Venture Inn,** 89 Avenue Rd. (☎ 800/387-3933), can't be beaten for its location in expensive Yorkville. It has no-frills rooms and lacks a restaurant and other services, but that's precisely why it can charge the prices it does.
- **Best Alternative Accommodation: Victoria University,** 140 Charles St. W. (☎ 416/585-4524), wins this category hands down because of its excellent downtown location, right across from the Royal Ontario Museum (ROM), and the facilities it offers—a pool, tennis courts, and a fitness center. It's simply furnished, but a clean room with fresh linens costs only C$64 (U.S.$46) a night.
- **Best Service:** No matter what you ask for at **The Four Seasons** (see above), it will be delivered to you graciously. Such personal attention can be lavished on guests because the hotel is relatively small and has a very high staff-to-guest ratio.
- **Best Location:** If you're in Toronto on vacation, the **Westin Harbour Castle,** 1 Harbour Sq. (☎ 800/228-3000), on the lake, is a very alluring summer location, even if it is a convention hotel. For the business traveler, the **Crowne Plaza Toronto Centre,** 225 Front St. W. (☎ 800/422-7969), is actually connected to the convention center, a factor not to be minimized at the end of a long day standing behind or strolling past convention booths.
- **Best Outdoor Pool:** The **Radisson Plaza Hotel Admiral** (see above), with its outdoor rooftop pool overlooking the lake, gives your afternoon swim a Caribbean resort air.
- **Best Indoor Pool:** The **Royal York,** 100 Front St. W. (☎ 416/368-2511), has an exquisitely decorated pool complete with classical murals and potted palms.
- **Best Views:** Every room that faces south at the **Westin Harbor Castle** (see above) has a view of the lake.
- **Best for Sports Fans:** It's hard to be closer to the action than at the **SkyDome Hotel,** 1 Blue Jays Way (☎ 800/441-1414), where more than half of the rooms have views of the diamond where the Toronto Blue Jays play their home games.

## 2 Downtown

The downtown area runs from the lakefront to College/Carlton Street between Spadina Avenue and Jarvis Street.

### VERY EXPENSIVE

**Cambridge Suites Hotel.** 15 Richmond St. E. (close to the corner of Yonge St.), Toronto, ON, M5C 1N2. ☎ 800/463-1990 or 416/368-1990. Fax 416/601-3751. 231 suites. A/C MINIBAR TV TEL. C$310–$330 (U.S.$229–$236) single, C$330–$350 (U.S.$236–$250) double. Rates include continental breakfast. AE, DC, DISC, ER, MC, V. Parking C$16 (U.S.$11). Subway: Queen.

Ideally situated for the business traveler in the financial district, this all-suites hotel features comfortable accommodations and the extra-special conveniences that make

# Downtown Toronto Accommodations

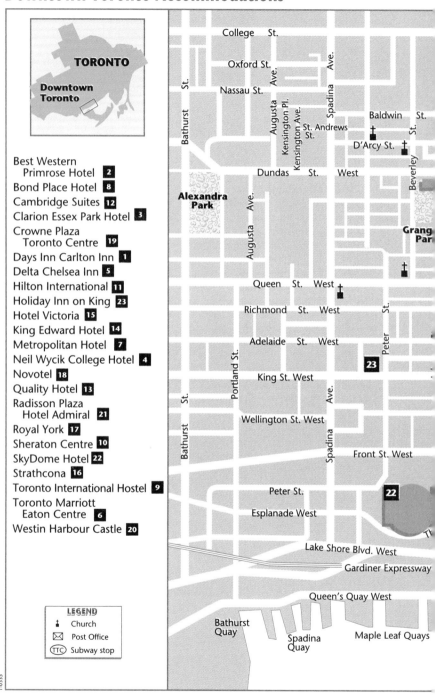

Best Western
  Primrose Hotel **2**
Bond Place Hotel **8**
Cambridge Suites **12**
Clarion Essex Park Hotel **3**
Crowne Plaza
  Toronto Centre **19**
Days Inn Carlton Inn **1**
Delta Chelsea Inn **5**
Hilton International **11**
Holiday Inn on King **23**
Hotel Victoria **15**
King Edward Hotel **14**
Metropolitan Hotel **7**
Neil Wycik College Hotel **4**
Novotel **18**
Quality Hotel **13**
Radisson Plaza
  Hotel Admiral **21**
Royal York **17**
Sheraton Centre **10**
SkyDome Hotel **22**
Strathcona **16**
Toronto International Hostel **9**
Toronto Marriott
  Eaton Centre **6**
Westin Harbour Castle **20**

**LEGEND**
✝ Church
✉ Post Office
(TTC) Subway stop

1-0335

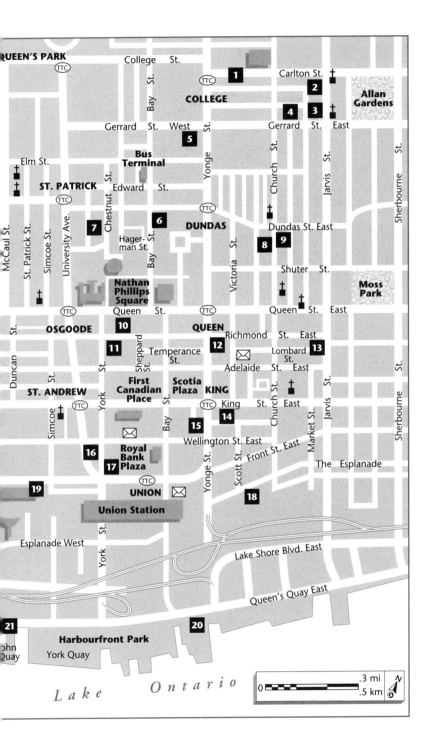

QUEEN'S PARK

(TTC)

College St.

1

COLLEGE

Carlton St.

2

Allan Gardens

Bay St.

4

3

Gerrard St. West

Gerrard St. East

5

Yonge St.

Church St.

Jarvis St.

Sherbourne St.

Elm St.

ST. PATRICK

(TTC)

Bus Terminal

Edward St.

Chestnut St.

Bay St.

7

6

DUNDAS

Dundas St. East

Hager-man St.

Victoria St.

8

9

McCaul St.

St. Patrick St.

Simcoe St.

University Ave.

Shuter St.

Nathan Phillips Square

Moss Park

(TTC)

Queen St.

(TTC)

Queen St. East

OSGOODE

10

QUEEN

Richmond St. East

St.

11

Sheppard St.

Temperance St.

12

Lombard St.

13

Duncan St.

Adelaide St. East

ST. ANDREW

First Canadian Place

Scotia Plaza

KING

Church St.

Market St.

Jarvis St.

Sherbourne St.

Simcoe St.

(TTC)

(TTC) King St. East

14

15

York St.

Bay St.

Wellington St. East

16

Yonge St.

Scott St.

Front St. East

The Esplanade

17

Royal Bank Plaza

(TTC)

UNION

19

18

Union Station

Esplanade West

York St.

Lake Shore Blvd. East

Queen's Quay East

21

20

John Quay

Harbourfront Park

York Quay

Lake Ontario

0 .3 mi .5 km

N

all the difference. Each large 550-square-foot suite has a refrigerator, a microwave, and dishes, along with a supply of coffee, tea, and cookies, plus a sizable working area with a desk, two two-line telephones, and a fax. If you like, you can leave a list and your grocery shopping will be done for you. The furnishings are extremely comfortable and include a couch, armchairs, and a coffee table. There's also a dressing area with a full-length mirror, and a marble bathroom equipped with a full complement of amenities. The penthouse luxury suites are duplexes that have Jacuzzis. Gold Club suites have everything the standard suites have, plus free local calls, complimentary shoe shine, and complimentary breakfast and snacks.

**Dining/Entertainment:** Facilities include a small, comfortable bar and a fine dining room that serves reasonably priced entrees at dinner, such as salmon teriyaki or breast of chicken with cilantro and lime beurre blanc.

**Services:** Room service 11am to 11pm; daily maid service, valet, concierge.

**Facilities:** Business center; laundry; convenience store; fitness center, boasting a fine view of the city and equipped with whirlpool; exercise room and sauna.

**King Edward Hotel.** 37 King St. E., Toronto, ON, M5C 2E9. ☎ **416/863-9700.** Fax 416/ 367-5515. 315 rms and suites. A/C MINIBAR TV TEL. C$195–$330 (U.S.$139–$236) double; from C$385 (U.S.$275) suite. AE, DC, MC, V. Parking C$24 (U.S.$17). Subway: King.

Affectionately known as The King Eddy, this is the city's oldest hotel. In its heyday, it welcomed such guests as Edward, Prince of Wales, Rudolph Valentino, Charles de Gaulle, Richard Burton and Liz Taylor, and the Beatles. Built in 1903 by distiller George Gooderham, the richest man in Toronto, it underwent a C$40 million renovation in the 1980s that restored all of its architectural features—marble Corinthian columns, sculpted stucco, and a glass-domed rotunda above the lobby. The lobby today is a serene and lovely place for tea or cocktails.

The 299 rooms are extremely spacious and beautifully decorated. Each room has a telephone in the bathroom, a clock radio, and such niceties as complimentary newspaper delivery, bathrobes, super-fluffy towels, makeup mirrors, hair dryers, and marble bathtubs.

**Dining/Entertainment:** Traditional English afternoon tea—complete with clotted cream, strawberry preserves, and cucumber finger sandwiches—is served in the Lobby lounge. The famous old Victoria Room has been turned into the **Café Victoria,** where baroque plasterwork and etched glass is matched with extravagant potted shrubs. Eight-foot-high windows in the main-floor **Consort Bar** look out onto King Street. For formal dining, **Chiaro's** specializes in fine continental cuisine with main dishes priced from C$25 to C$30 (U.S.$18 to U.S.$21).

**Services:** 24-hour room service, concierge, laundry/valet, complimentary shoe shine and newspaper, nightly turndown.

**Facilities:** Health club.

# EXPENSIVE

**Crowne Plaza Toronto Centre.** 225 Front St. W., Toronto, ON, M5V 2X3. ☎ **800/ 422-7969** or 416/597-1400. Fax 416/597-8128. 587 rms and suites. A/C MINIBAR TV TEL. C$219–$309 (U.S.$156–$221) double. Extra person C$20 (U.S.$14). Weekend packages available. AE, DC, DISC, MC, V. Parking C$20.50 (U.S.$15). Subway: Union.

The Crowne Plaza Toronto Centre is ideally located for the CN Tower, SkyDome, Roy Thomson Hall, the theater district, and the Convention Centre (to which is it is attached). The rooms are finely appointed with marble bathroom counters, writing desks, elegant table lamps, and two telephone lines. All contain such additional amenities as a coffeemaker and iron/ironing board.

**Dining:** Located in the garden court, the **Trellis Bistro and Lounge** is well known for its Sunday brunch and after-theater menu; there's fine dining in the elegant **Chanterelles,** which also offers a special pre-theater fixed-price menu.

**Services:** Room service 6am to 2am, concierge, and laundry/valet.

**Facilities:** Indoor pool, whirlpool, saunas, a well-equipped exercise room, squash courts, and sundeck.

**Hilton International.** 145 Richmond St. W., Toronto, ON, M5H 3M6. ☎ **800/445-8667** or 416/869-3456. Fax 416/869-1478. 601 rms and suites. A/C MINIBAR TV TEL. C$200–$300 (U.S.$143–$214) double. Extra person C$20 (U.S.$14). One child under 18 stays free in parents' rm. Weekend packages available. AE, MC, V. Parking C$18 (U.S.$13) overnight. Subway: Osgoode.

Conveniently located near the Convention Centre and financial district, this 32-story hotel has all the facilities one expects from the Hilton chain. The refurbished rooms are large, well decorated, and have many amenities. Executive rooms have a trouser press, a terry-cloth bathrobe, and access to a private lounge where complimentary breakfast and hors d'oeuvres are served.

**Dining/Entertainment:** The **Garden Court** offers breakfast, lunch, afternoon tea, and dinner in a Singapore-style atmosphere created by lush greenery and cushioned rattan chairs. **Barristers** has a clubby atmosphere, with wonderful leather armchairs and couches.

**Services:** 24-hour room service, concierge, laundry/valet, twice-daily housekeeping, baby-sitting.

**Facilities:** Heated indoor/outdoor pool with attractive sundeck, sauna, whirlpool, exercise room, massage specialist, executive business center.

**The Metropolitan Hotel.** 108 Chestnut St., Toronto, ON, M5G 1R3. ☎ **416/977-5000.** Fax 416/977-9513. 441 rms, 39 suites. A/C MINIBAR TV TEL. C$205–$250 (U.S.$146–$179) double. Children under 16 stay free in parents' rm. AE, DC, DISC, ER, EURO, JCB, MC, V. Parking C$18.25 (U.S.$13). Subway: St. Patrick.

A few years ago, the Metropolitan was purchased by a Hong Kong hotel company, which completed a C$28 million renovation of the hotel. Everything has been revamped and redecorated, including the dining facilities with the help of one of Toronto's star chefs—Susur Lee. The ambiance is sleek and modern, with some Oriental accents throughout. At the time of writing, though, service was not as swift or smooth as it should be.

The rooms are spiffily furnished and well equipped for the business traveler—with large desks, telephones with computer- and fax-compatible jacks, and in-closet safes. Bathroom amenities include lighted swing mirrors, massage showerheads, bathrobes, and hair dryers. The luxury and executive suites have Jacuzzis, Dolby Surround Sound TVs, stereos, and CD players.

The Metropolitan is conveniently located 2 blocks from the Eaton Centre on Chestnut Street, just off Dundas Street between Bay Street and University Avenue.

**Dining: Hemispheres,** with its Kandinsky-inspired painting and curvaceous glass walls, has to be one of the most attractive all-day dining rooms in the city, and one of the few with a special chef's table. Overlooking the lobby, the **Alibi bar and restaurant** serves casual fare. **Lai Wah Heen** is an elegant contemporary Chinese restaurant that serves really fine Cantonese cuisine (see page 71 for a review).

**Services:** 24-hour room service, concierge, and laundry/valet.

**Facilities:** Indoor swimming pool; fitness center with sauna, whirlpool, and massage therapy services; business center.

**Novotel.** 45 The Esplanade, Toronto, ON, M5E 1W2. ☎ **800/668-6835** or 416/367-8900. Fax 416/360-8285. 262 rms, 8 suites. A/C MINIBAR TV TEL. From C$195 (U.S.$139) double. AE, DC, ER, MC, V. Parking C$11.75 (U.S.$8). Subway: Union.

Located just off Yonge Street near the St. Lawrence Centre and Hummingbird Centre, the Novotel is an ultramodern hotel, built in French Renaissance style with a Palladian entrance leading to a marble lobby with oak and Oriental decorative accents. The rooms are nicely appointed with all the expected conveniences, including two telephones, hair dryers, radio and TV speakers in the bathrooms, and skirt hangers.

**Dining:** The unremarkable **Café Nicole** serves breakfast, lunch, and dinner.

**Services:** Room service is available from 6am to midnight; there's also a concierge, laundry and valet service, and airport shuttle service.

**Facilities:** An indoor pool, sauna, whirlpool, and exercise room.

**✪ Radisson Plaza Hotel Admiral.** 249 Queen's Quay W., Toronto, ON, M5J 2N5. ☎ **800/333-3333** or 416/203-3333. Fax 416/203-3100. 157 rms and suites. A/C MINIBAR TV TEL. C$175–$220 (U.S.$125–$157) double. Extra person C$20 (U.S.$14). Weekend packages available. AE, DC, ER, MC, V. Parking C$15 (U.S.$11). Subway: Union, then take the LRT.

As the name and the harborfront location suggest, the Radisson Plaza Hotel Admiral has a strong nautical flavor. The lobby combines polished woods and downtown Toronto brass with nautical paintings. The horseshoe-shaped roofdeck comes complete with a pool and cabana-style bar and terrace.

The rooms are elegantly furnished with campaign-style chests of drawers with brass trimmings, marble-top side tables, and desks, all set on jade carpets. Extra amenities include two phones, real wood hangers, and in the bathroom, a hair dryer and clothesline.

**Dining/Entertainment:** Looking out onto the harbor and Lake Ontario, **The Commodore's Dining Room** serves classic continental cuisine, with main courses ranging from C$20 to C$28 (U.S.$14 to U.S.$20). **The Galley** serves a more modest menu, while the adjacent **Bosun's Bar** offers light snacks.

**Services:** 24-hour room service, concierge, and complimentary newspaper delivery.

**Facilities:** Resort style outdoor swimming pool on extra-large roofdeck complete with cabana-style bar, whirlpool, and squash court.

**Royal York.** 100 Front St. W., Toronto, ON, M5J 1E3. ☎ **800/441-1414** or 416/863-6333. 1,365 rms and suites. A/C MINIBAR TV TEL. C$175–$230 (U.S.$125–$164) double; from C$300 (U.S.$214) suites and Entree Gold service. Many special packages available. AE, DC, DISC, MC, V. Parking C$18 (U.S.$13). Subway: Union.

To many citizens and regular visitors, the Royal York *is* Toronto because in its 35 banquet and meeting rooms, many of the city's landmark historical and social events have taken place. Today, conveniently located for the business and theater districts, it's a huge enterprise and, as such, not to everyone's taste. Still, there is a magnificence to this hotel, which opened in 1929 and has hosted a raft of royalty, heads of state, and celebrities. The lobby is vast, impressive, and crowned by an incredible inlay coffered ceiling that is lit by large cast-bronze chandeliers. If you stay here, do go down and look at some of the banquet rooms, several of which have splendid ceiling murals, and the series of provincial meeting rooms, each with a unique decor.

The statistics relating to it are mind boggling. It can sleep 2,800 guests; it contains an eighth of a mile of carpeting; and it can accommodate 10,000 people at one meal sitting. The kitchen bakes 10,000 rolls daily, uses 18,000 eggs per week, and washes 25,000 pieces of china and 45,000 pieces of silverware daily.

The hotel has undergone major renovations in the last few years. Rooms vary in size, but a standard room will have a king-size bed and antique reproduction furnishings including an armchair and a well-lit desk. Nice features are solid-wood doors, windows that open, and wall moldings. Rooms for travelers with disabilities are exceptionally well equipped for wheelchair guests and for those guests who have hearing or visual impairments. Entree Gold provides a superior room on a private floor with separate check-in, a private lounge, complimentary breakfast and newspaper, and nightly turndown.

**Dining/Entertainment:** The Royal York boasts 10 restaurants and lounges. Among them, **The Acadian Room** offers Canadian cuisine in an elegant atmosphere. The wine list features one of the most extensive selections of Ontario wines anywhere. **The Benihana** offers a show of Japanese finesse. **The Gazebo** affords a gardenlike setting for lunch, and **York's Deli and Bakery** offers an array of salads, soups, hot dishes, and super-sized sandwiches. **Piper's Bar & Eatz** has a full range of drinks, a tavern menu, and singing waiters. The **Lobby Bar** features a sports screen; the more intimate **Library Bar** is highly rated for its martinis.

**Services:** 24-hour room service, laundry/valet, concierge.

**Facilities:** Skylit indoor lap pool with hand-painted trompe l'oeil murals and potted palms, exercise room, saunas, steam rooms and whirlpool, barbershop and beauty salon, shopping arcade with an American Express Travel Centre, business center.

**The Sheraton Centre.** 123 Queen St. W., Toronto, ON, M5H 2M9. ☎ **800/325-3535** or 416/361-1000. Fax 416/947-4854. 1,382 rms and suites. A/C MINIBAR TV TEL. C$265 (U.S.$189) double. Extra person C$20 (U.S.$14). 2 children under 18 stay free in parents' rm. Special packages available. AE, CB, DC, ER, EURO, JCB, MC, V. Parking C$22 (U.S.$16) a day, more for valet parking. Subway: Osgoode.

A very large convention hotel that nevertheless provides exceptional service, the Sheraton Centre is located right across from City Hall and near the Convention Centre. It occupies a 43-story shopping complex with six restaurants and bars and two movie theaters. At the back of the lobby, there are 2 acres of landscaped gardens with a waterfall and terrace restaurant enclosed behind glass walls.

All of the spacious rooms are attractively furnished and well equipped. The Club level in the Queen Tower provides such extra amenities as a private lounge with complimentary continental breakfast and evening hors d'oeuvres; Club-level rooms are equipped with combo fax/printer/copier, ergonomic chair, and a two-line speaker phone.

**Dining/Entertainment:** In the shopping concourse, **Good Queen Bess** is an authentic-looking English pub (shipped from England in sections) where you can enjoy a glass of Newcastle brown. Off the lobby, **the Reunion** is a lively bar with 14 television monitors, pool tables, and weekend djs, while the **Long Bar and Lounge** provides a spectacular view of City Hall and live entertainment on weekends. **Postcards Cafe and Grill** features cuisines from the Americas and also hosts the "Fast Break Breakfast," which is free if it's not served in 5 minutes.

**Services:** 24-hour room service, laundry/valet, concierge, supervised play center and baby-sitting available.

**Facilities:** Large indoor/outdoor pool with sundeck, sauna, game room, hot tub, exercise room, business center.

**SkyDome Hotel.** 1 Blue Jays Way, Toronto, ON, M5V 1J4. ☎ **800/441-1414** or 416/341-7100. Fax 416/341-5090. 346 rms. A/C MINIBAR TV TEL. City view, from C$165 (U.S.$118) double; field side, from C$289 (U.S.$206). AE, DC, DISC, JCB, MC, V. Parking C$17 (U.S.$12); C$11 (U.S.$8) self parking (higher rates in spring and summer). Subway: Union.

For sports fans (baseball fans in particular), this is hotel heaven. Imagine having a room that overlooks the bull pen and the splendid green of the field, as 70 rooms of this hotel located right inside the SkyDome stadium do.

Standard rooms come with a view window, more expensive field-side rooms have raised living areas, and then there are the suites. The city-view rooms are the least expensive. Each unit has modern furnishings and is equipped with full amenities, including a hair dryer, coffeemaker, and clock radio.

**Dining/Entertainment: Cafe on the Green** overlooks the field, and, adjacent to the hotel, so do **Sightlines** and the **Hard Rock Cafe.**

**Services:** 24-hour room service, laundry/valet, concierge.

**Facilities:** Fitness center with pool, squash courts, sauna, and exercise room.

**Toronto Marriott Eaton Centre.** 525 Bay St., at Dundas, Toronto, ON, M5G 2L2. ☎ **800/ 228-9290** or 416/597-9200. Fax 416/597-9211. 459 rms and suites. A/C MINIBAR TV TEL. C$179–$219 (U.S.$128–$156) double. AE, DC, MC, V. Subway: Dundas.

Conveniently located alongside Eaton Centre, this is a modern hotel with all the hallmarks of the Marriott chain. In addition to the amenities listed above, rooms contain clock radios and attractive furnishings. Nonsmoking rooms and rooms for travelers with disabilities are available, too.

**Dining/Entertainment: The Parkside** restaurant offers all-day dining while **JW's** offers fine dining. **Characters,** a bar, features billiards and table games as well as music and sporting events.

**Services:** 24-hour room service, laundry and valet, a concierge, and baby-sitting. It's refreshing that the staff (porters, car valets, and others) do not expect or accept tips.

**Facilities:** Indoor rooftop swimming pool, whirlpool, sauna, health club.

✪ **Westin Harbour Castle.** 1 Harbour Sq., Toronto, ON, M5J 1A6. ☎ **800/228-3000** or 416/869-1600. Fax 416/361-7448. 980 rms and suites. A/C MINIBAR TV TEL. C$160–$300 (U.S.$114-$214) double. Extra person C$20 (U.S.$14). Children stay free in parents' rm. Weekend packages (double occupancy) and special long-term rates available. AE, DC, ER, MC, V. Parking C$21 (U.S.$15). Subway: Union; then LRT to the hotel.

A popular convention hotel, the Harbour Castle is located right on the lakefront, ideally situated for those who want to explore the Harbourfront. The rooms are located in two towers joined at the base by a five-story podium. Marble, oak, and crystal adorn the spacious lobby, which commands a great harbor view.

Each room has a view of the lake and is well furnished with a marble-top desk and night tables, table and floor lamps, and an extra phone in the bathroom. There are 442 nonsmoking rooms.

**Dining/Entertainment:** On the 38th floor of the south tower, **the Lighthouse** is a revolving restaurant with fabulous views that is open for all three meals. Entrees range from C$17 to C$38 (U.S.$12 to U.S.$27). Chinese cuisine is offered in the ground-floor **Grand Yatt.** Tea and cocktails are served in the **Lobby Lounge.** Off the main lobby, **the Chartroom** offers a comfortable haven for a drink with piano entertainment in the evenings.

**Services:** 24-hour room service, concierge, laundry/valet, guest-room voice mail, beauty shop.

**Facilities:** Fitness center with indoor pool, whirlpool, sauna, steam room, two squash courts, two outdoor tennis courts, massage clinic, shopping arcade.

# MODERATE

**Best Western Primrose Hotel.** 111 Carlton St. (between Church and Jarvis sts.), Toronto, ON, M5B 2G3. ☎ **800/268-8082** or 416/977-8000. Fax 416/977-6323. 338 rms, 4 suites.

A/C TV TEL. C$119–$169 (U.S.$85–$121) double. Extra person C$10. Weekend packages available (except July–Sept). AE, DC, MC, V. Parking C$12.50 (U.S.$9). Subway: College.

The Primrose offers spacious rooms, all with wall-to-wall carpeting and color-coordinated furnishings, color TVs, and individual climate control. About 25% contain king-size beds and sofas; the rest have two double beds. The downstairs coffee shop charmingly evokes the atmosphere of a Viennese cafe with its painted-wood decor. Room service is available from 7am to 10pm, and there's also laundry and valet service, as well as a complimentary newspaper every morning. An outdoor pool and sauna are available for guests' use.

**Bond Place Hotel.** 65 Dundas St. E., Toronto, ON, M5B 2G8. ☎ **416/362-6061.** Fax 416/360-6406. 286 rms and suites. A/C TV TEL. C$130 (U.S.$93) single or double. Extra person C$15 (U.S.$11). Weekend packages available. AE, DC, DISC, ER, MC, V. Parking C$12 (U.S.$9). Subway: Dundas.

Ideally located just a block from Yonge Street and the Eaton Centre and near the Pantages and Elgin theatres, the Bond Place Hotel has decent, if somewhat old fashioned rooms at reasonable prices.

Off the lobby, the casual Garden Café serves breakfast, lunch, and dinner, while downstairs, Freddy's serves lunch and dinner and complimentary hors d'oeuvres from 5 to 7pm.

There's laundry and valet service, and room service from 7am to 10pm.

**Clarion Essex Park Hotel.** 300 Jarvis St. (just south of Carlton), Toronto, ON, M5B 2C5. ☎ **800/567-2233** or 416/977-4823. Fax 416/977-4830. 58 rms, 44 suites. A/C TV TEL. C$145–$155 (U.S.$104–$111) double. AE, DISC, ER, JCB. Parking C$12 (U.S.$9).

Conveniently located within walking distance of the Eaton Centre, Pantages Theatre, and City Hall, the Clarion Essex Park is a comfortable, moderately priced hotel that's used by a lot of tour groups but is located in a slightly dubious neighborhood. All rooms have queen- or king-size beds, and each is nicely furnished with a sofa, a desk, and a coffee table. Amenities include phones, cable color TVs, refrigerators, and a fully tiled bathroom with a hair dryer. Closets are large.

There's a bistro with a bar that's open for all meals, and room service is available from 7am to 9pm. Facilities include an indoor pool, sauna, whirlpool, fitness center, squash courts, and a room containing billiards and Ping-Pong tables.

**Days Inn Carlton Inn.** 30 Carlton St., Toronto, ON, M5B 2E9. ☎ **800/329-7466** or 416/977-6655. Fax 416/977-0502. 536 rms and suites. A/C TV TEL. C$119–$169 (U.S.$85–$121) double. Extra person C$15 (U.S.$11). Children under 18 stay free in parents' rm. Summer discounts available. AE, DC, DISC, MC, V. Parking C$12 (U.S.$9). Subway: College.

Nicely furnished rooms with modern conveniences at fair prices are the hallmark of the Carlton Inn, a modern, centrally air-conditioned high-rise. Besides offering reasonably priced (for Toronto) accommodations, the inn is well located, only a few steps from Yonge Street, right next door to Maple Leaf Gardens.

Besides the regular amenities, refrigerators are available on request. There is a lounge, a sports bar, and a restaurant. Laundry and valet services are available. Facilities include an indoor pool, saunas, and a hair salon.

**Delta Chelsea Inn.** 33 Gerrard St. W., Toronto, ON, M5G 1Z4. ☎ **800/243-5732** or 416/595-1975. Fax 416/585-4362. 1,547 rms, 47 suites. A/C TV TEL. C$129–$235 (U.S.$92–$168) double with standard service; C$139–$245 (U.S.$99–$175) double with signature service; C$15 (U.S.$11) additional on business floor; from C$275 (U.S.$196) suite. Extra person C$20 (U.S.$14). Children under 18 stay free in parents' rm. Weekend packages available. AE, DC, DISC, MC, V. Parking C$18 (U.S.$13)—but only 575 spaces. Subway: College.

The Delta Chelsea, located between Yonge and Bay streets, is still one of Toronto's best buys—particularly for families and on weekends—although prices have risen considerably in recent years. The crowded scene in the lobby, though, testifies to its continued popularity.

All rooms have color TVs with in-room movies, phones, and bright, modern furnishings. Some rooms have kitchenettes. The south tower has 600 rooms featuring dual phones with data jacks, call waiting, and conference-call features. This tower also contains a penthouse lounge, a business center, and more dining facilities.

All rooms have 24-hour room service, baby-sitting, and laundry and valet service. For a little more, you can have a signature service room, with complimentary tea and coffee service, a minibar, a terry-cloth bathrobe, and an iron and ironing board.

The hotel also offers a special business floor, where rooms contain ergonomic chairs; cordless speaker phones, with a speaker in the bathroom; desks with supplies; in-room faxes with confidential numbers; terry-cloth bathrobes, minibars, and irons and ironing boards. Guests staying here also receive such amenities as free local calls, complimentary copies of the *Globe & Mail*, and access to a business center located on the same floor—all for an additional C$15 (U.S.$11).

**Wittles** offers casual but elegant dining, while the **Market Garden** is an attractive self-service cafeteria with an outdoor courtyard that sells salads, sandwiches, and grilled items at reasonable prices. The restaurants offer a good-value children's menu, and children under 6 eat free. The **Chelsea Bun** offers live entertainment daily and Dixieland jazz on Saturday afternoon. For a relaxing drink, there's the **Elm Street Lounge** or **Deck 27,** which offers a great view of the skyline.

Facilities include an adult-only pool and fitness center with an adjacent bar as well as an additional pool, whirlpool, sauna, exercise room, lounge, game room with three pool tables, beauty salon, business center, and—a blessing for parents—a children's creative center where 3 to 12 year-olds can play under expert supervision (it's open until 10pm on Friday and Saturday, and there's a nominal charge).

**Holiday Inn on King.** 370 King St. W. (at Peter), Toronto, ON, M5V 1J9. ☎ **800/263-6364** or 416/599-4000. Fax 416/599-7394. 425 rms, 10 suites. A/C TV TEL. C$169–$179 (U.S.$121–$128) double. Extra person C$15 (U.S.$11). AE, DISC, ER, MC, V. Parking C$16 (U.S.$11.50). Subway: St. Andrew.

Housed in an odd-looking Miami-style building, the Holiday Inn is close to the theater district, the CN Tower, and SkyDome. The rooms are pleasantly furnished in pastels, with sage-green carpeting and floral bedspreads; each is fully equipped with a phone, clock radio, wet bar, and a decently lit desk. Many have balconies. The bathrooms have a number of amenities, including hair dryers. There's a restaurant, a lounge that's famous for its live jazz, and a deli. An outdoor pool, sauna, and fitness center round out the facilities.

## INEXPENSIVE

**Hotel Victoria.** 56 Yonge St. (at Wellington), Toronto, ON, M5E 1G5. ☎ **416/363-1666.** Fax 416/363-7327. 48 rms. A/C TV TEL. C$90–$107 (U.S.$64–$76) double. Extra person C$15 (U.S.$11). Special weekend rates available. AE, DC, DISC, MC, V. Parking C$16 (U.S.$11.50). Subway: King.

In search of a small, personal hotel? Try the Hotel Victoria, with only 48 rooms spread over six floors. It's located in a landmark building in the heart of the financial district, only 2 blocks from the Hummingbird Centre. The lobby is small and elegant, and retains the marble columns, staircase, and decorative moldings of an earlier era.

The rooms are either standard or select (the latter are larger). They have modern furnishings, a gray and burgundy decor, and private baths. Some have coffeemakers and minirefrigerators. Complimentary *Globe & Mail* is available on request.

There's a restaurant, lounge, and lobby bar; room service is available from 7am to 2pm; laundry and valet service is also available.

**Quality Hotel.** 111 Lombard St. (between Adelaide and Richmond sts.), Toronto, ON, M5C 2T9. ☎ **416/367-5555.** Fax 416/367-3470. 196 rms and suites. A/C TV TEL. C$99–$139 (U.S.$71–$99) double. AE, DC, DISC, MC, V. Parking C$11.75 (U.S.$8). Subway: King or Queen.

Formerly a Journey's End, the Quality Hotel has modern rooms fully appointed with color TVs, coffeemakers, hair dryers, and irons/ironing boards. Continental breakfast is included in the rate. Facilities include a small exercise room.

**Neil Wycik College Hotel.** 96 Gerrard St. E. (between Church and Jarvis), Toronto, ON, M5B 1G7. ☎ **800/268-4358** or 416/977-2320. Fax 416/977-2809. 304 rms (none with bath). C$46–$55 (U.S.$33–$39) double, C$50–$62 (U.S.$36–$44) family rm (2 adults plus children). MC, V. Mid-May to late Aug. Parking C$9 (U.S.$6) nearby. Subway: College.

Right downtown, the Neil Wycik College Hotel offers basic modern, clean accommodations at very reasonable rates from early May to late August. Since these are primarily student accommodations, rooms contain only the most essential furniture—beds, chairs, and desks—and lack air-conditioning and TVs. Family rooms have two single beds and room for three rollaways. Four to five bedrooms share two bathrooms and one kitchen with a refrigerator and stove. If you wish to cook, you have to furnish your own utensils. Other facilities include a TV lounge, a rooftop sundeck, a sauna, a laundry room, and a breakfast cafeteria.

**The Strathcona.** 60 York St., Toronto, ON, M5J 1S8. ☎ **416/363-3321.** Fax 416/363-4679. 193 rms. A/C TV TEL. May 1–Oct 30 C$90–$100 (U.S.$64–$71) double, Nov 1–Apr 30 C$70 (U.S.$50). AE, DC, MC, V. Parking C$12 (U.S.$9) nearby. Subway: Union.

Currently one of Toronto's best buys, the Strathcona is located right across from the Royal York Hotel, within easy reach of all downtown attractions. Although the rooms are small, they are decently furnished with modern blond-wood furniture, gray carpeting, and brass floor lamps.

The coffee shop/restaurant is open daily; there's also a luncheon snack bar and a lounge with a large-screen TV for sports watching. Room service is offered from 6am to 7pm. It's a great location for a great price.

**Toronto International Hostel.** 160 Mutual St. at Gerrard, Toronto, ON, M5B 2M2. ☎ **416/971-4440.** Fax 416/971-4088. 225 beds. A/C. C$26 (U.S.$19) per person in a double, C$22.50 (U.S.$16) per person in a 4-person rm; C$30.28 (U.S.$22) and C$26.78 (U.S.$19) respectively for nonmembers. MC, V. Parking C$7 (U.S.$5) in a nearby lot. Subway: Dundas.

Hostel accommodations are arranged in suites of four rooms sharing two bathrooms. Furnishings are simple: bed, closet, and sink with a kitchen in each suite. Each floor has a common room with TV, and there are laundry facilities and an exercise room on the premises. Guests have access to a complete health facility in an adjacent building with squash courts, running track, and pool for only C$1 (U.S.70¢).

## 3 Midtown

The midtown area runs north from College/Carlton Street between Spadina Avenue and Jarvis Street to where Dupont crosses Yonge Street.

### VERY EXPENSIVE

✪ **The Four Seasons Hotel.** 21 Avenue Rd., Toronto, ON, M5R 2G1. ☎ **800/268-6282** or 416/964-0411. Fax 416/964-2301. 210 rms, 170 suites. A/C MINIBAR TV TEL. C$290–$365

# Midtown Toronto Accommodations

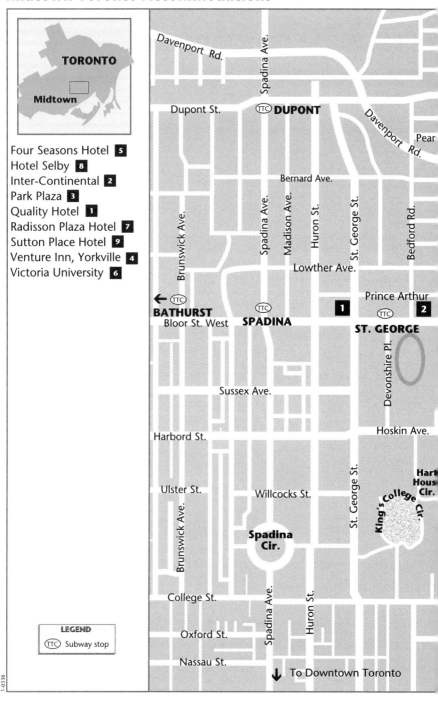

Four Seasons Hotel **5**
Hotel Selby **8**
Inter-Continental **2**
Park Plaza **3**
Quality Hotel **1**
Radisson Plaza Hotel **7**
Sutton Place Hotel **9**
Venture Inn, Yorkville **4**
Victoria University **6**

TORONTO

Midtown

Davenport Rd.

Spadina Ave.

Dupont St.

(TTC) **DUPONT**

Davenport Rd.

Pear

Bernard Ave.

Brunswick Ave.

Spadina Ave.

Madison Ave.

Huron St.

St. George St.

Bedford Rd.

Lowther Ave.

Prince Arthur

← (TTC)
**BATHURST**
Bloor St. West

(TTC)
**SPADINA**

**1**

(TTC)

**2**

**ST. GEORGE**

Devonshire Pl.

Sussex Ave.

Harbord St.

Hoskin Ave.

Ulster St.

Willcocks St.

St. George St.

Hart
Hous
Cir.

King's College Cir.

Brunswick Ave.

Spadina
Cir.

College St.

Spadina Ave.

Huron St.

**LEGEND**
(TTC) Subway stop

Oxford St.

Nassau St.

↓ To Downtown Toronto

1-0336

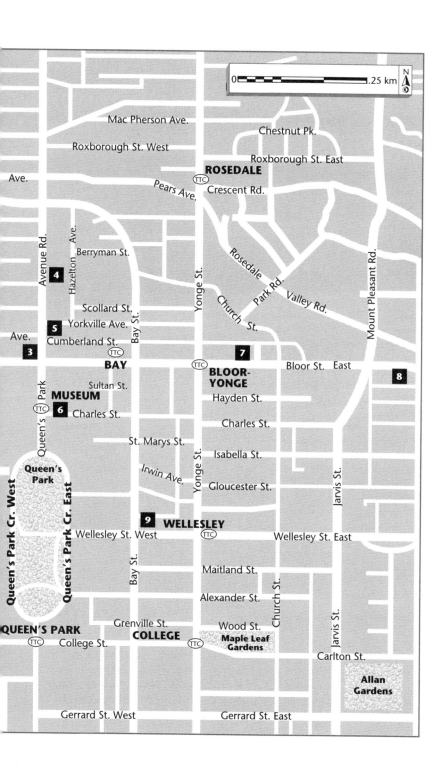

0                 .25 km

N

Mac Pherson Ave.

Roxborough St. West

Chestnut Pk.

Roxborough St. East

**ROSEDALE**

Ave.

Pears Ave.

Crescent Rd.

Avenue Rd.

Hazelton Ave.

Berryman St.

**4**

Rosedale Valley Rd.

Park Rd.

Yonge St.

Church   St.

Mount Pleasant Rd.

Scollard St.

**5** Yorkville Ave.

Ave.

Cumberland St.

Bay St.

**3**

TTC

**BAY**

TTC

**7**

Bloor St.   East

**8**

**BLOOR-
YONGE**

Queen's Park

TTC

Sultan St.

**MUSEUM**

Hayden St.

**6** Charles St.

Charles St.

St. Marys St.

Isabella St.

**Queen's
Park**

Irwin Ave.

Gloucester St.

Yonge St.

Queen's Park Cr. West

Queen's Park Cr. East

**9** **WELLESLEY**

Wellesley St. West

TTC

Wellesley St. East

Jarvis St.

Bay St.

Maitland St.

Alexander St.

Church St.

Grenville St.

Wood St.

**QUEEN'S PARK**

**COLLEGE**

TTC     College St.

TTC

**Maple Leaf
Gardens**

Carlton St.

Jarvis St.

**Allan
Gardens**

Gerrard St. West

Gerrard St. East

(U.S.$207–261) double; from C$415 (U.S.$296) suite. Weekend rates available. AE, CB. DC, ER, JCB, MC, V. Parking C$20 (U.S.$14). Subway: Bay.

Located in the heart of the Bloor-Yorkville area, the Four Seasons has a well-deserved reputation for consistently fine and highly personal service, attention to detail, quiet but unimpeachable style, and total comfort. The lobby, with its marble and granite floors, Savonnerie carpets, and stunning fresh-flower arrangements, epitomizes the style.

The spacious rooms are furnished with king-size, queen-size, or twin beds and boast dressing rooms and marble bathrooms. The table lamps are porcelain, the furnishings elegant, and the fabrics plush. Extra amenities include bathrobes, hair dryers, makeup and full-length mirrors, tie bars, closet safes, and windows that open. Corner rooms have balconies. Four Seasons Executive Suites each have an additional seating area separated from the bedroom by French doors, two TVs, and a deluxe telephone with two lines and conference-call capacity. Nonsmoking rooms and special rooms for those with disabilities are available.

**Dining/Entertainment:** ✪ **Truffles,** on the second floor, has been named one of the world's 10 great hotel restaurants (see chapter 5, page 85, for a review). Two sculptures of Uffizi wild boars adorn the entrance to the lavish dining area, which features murals, ceramics, and furniture designed by Canadian artists. Only the finest materials have been used in the design elements: curly maple for the paneling and 11,000 pieces of walnut, oak, jojoba, and purple-heart wood in the magnificent marquetry floor. The tables are amply spaced and the cuisine is extraordinary. Main courses are priced from C$28 to C$37 (U.S.$20 to $26).

**The Studio Cafe** has become the city's place to see and be seen. It serves meals all day, features an open kitchen, and is filled with light. The modern Italian decor and furnishings include gorgeous Gianni Versace fabrics on the tables and display cases filled with original glass artworks, all of which are for sale. The menu is inspired by the Mediterranean and offers several gourmet pizzas (delicious!), pastas, salads, and light entrees, all priced from C$12 to C$24 (U.S.$9 to U.S.$17). Evening hors d'oeuvres and a Sunday brunch are served in **La Serre,** which also features entertainment in the evenings. **The Lobby Bar** serves a traditional afternoon tea. There are special kids' menus, too, with meals served either in Animal World wicker baskets or on Sesame Street plates.

**Services:** 24-hour concierge, 24-hour room service and valet pickup, 1-hour pressing, complimentary shoe shine, twice-daily maid service, baby-sitting, doctor on call, children's activities, weekday courtesy limo to downtown, complimentary coffee and newspaper.

**Facilities:** Business center; health club with indoor/outdoor pool, whirlpool, Universal equipment, and massage; free bicycles and video-game units for children.

**Inter-Continental.** 220 Bloor St. W., Toronto, ON, M5S 1T8. ☎ **416/960-5200.** Fax 416/960-8269. 209 rms. A/C MINIBAR TV TEL. C$265–$345 (U.S.$189–$246) double. AE, DC, JCB, MC, V. Parking C$22 (U.S.$16) valet. Subway: St. George.

The Inter-Continental, conveniently located on Bloor Street at St. George, is small enough to provide excellent, very personal service. The spacious rooms are well furnished with comfortable French-style armchairs and love seats. The marble bathrooms, with separate showers, are large and equipped with every imaginable amenity—each has a two-line telephone with a personal computer/fax hookup, a clothesline, large fluffy towels, a bathrobe, and a scale. Extra special room features include closet lights, a large desk-table, a clock radio, a full-length mirror, and windows that open.

## 👪 Family-Friendly Hotels

**Delta Chelsea Inn** *(see p. 47)* This hotel has always been on the cutting edge of the hospitality industry, and their Family Fun rooms attest to this. They're jam-packed with lots to do: in-room family movies, Super Nintendo, bubble bath, and such extras as a nighttime gift, night-light, and a cookie jar with a supply of cookies that's refreshed daily. The Delta Kids Have Fun program for kids aged 3 to 12 sponsors special activities in the Children's Creative Centre and throughout the hotel. When kids check in at the life-size gingerbread house, they get a registration card and passport. Children 6 and under eat free; kids 7 to 12 eat for half-price. All this goes a long way toward creating a smooth and more economical family stay.

The **Four Seasons** *(see p. 49)* Free bicycles, video games, and the pool should keep most kids occupied. The meals served in Animal World wicker baskets or on Sesame Street plates, and the complimentary room-service cookies and milk on arrival make them feel special. To top it all off, housekeeping provides all the amenities parents need.

The **Sheraton Centre** *(see p. 45)* This hotel operates a Very Important Kids program, which includes a free welcome gift for each child upon check-in, free dining from the kid's menu for children under 12 accompanied by an adult in Postcards Cafe, plus 2 complimentary hours of supervised play at Kids & Quackers, which is a supervised play area for kids aged 18 months to 12 years, and of course in-room Super Nintendo. Don't forget that the hotel has two movie theaters on the premises.

**Dining/Entertainment: Signatures** offers fine dining with dinner entrees priced from C$16 to C$28 (U.S.$11 to U.S.$20). The attractive, comfortable **Harmony Lounge,** with a marble bar, fireplace, and cherry paneling, is a pleasant retreat for afternoon tea or cocktails accompanied by piano entertainment. From here, French doors lead out to an inviting patio.

**Services:** 24-hour room service, laundry/valet, twice-daily maid service, nightly turndown, concierge, complimentary shoe shine and newspaper.

**Facilities:** Lap pool with adjacent patio; fitness room with treadmill, bikes, Stairmaster, and Paramount equipment; sauna and massage room; business center.

**The Park Plaza.** 4 Avenue Rd., Toronto, ON, M5R 2E8. ☎ **416/924-5471** or 800/268-4927. Fax 416/924-4933. 348 rms and suites. A/C MINIBAR TV TEL. C$260–$395 (U.S.$186–$282) double. Children under 18 stay free in parents' rm. AE, DC, DISC, MC, V. Parking C$18 (U.S.$12). Subway: Museum or Bay.

The Park Plaza is located in fashionable Yorkville and close to the ROM and the Bata Shoe Museum. Purchased in 1997 by Grand Bay Hotels and Resorts, it is currently undergoing extensive renovations. During the makeover, all 64 rooms and 20 suites in the original South Tower, which were recently renovated and redecorated to exceptionally high standards, will remain open. The amenities in these rooms include two telephones with voice mail, louvered closets, and a full-length mirror. Suites have additional features: scales, umbrellas, and two-line telephones with fax-computer hookups. Rooms in the North Tower are currently being enlarged and totally renovated.

**Dining/Entertainment: The Roof Restaurant,** on the 18th floor, is open all day. The adjacent lounge has inviting couches, a wood-burning fireplace, and a spectacular view, ensuring that its fame as a gathering place for Toronto literati will be retained. Additional restaurants are also planned for July 1998.

**Services:** 24-hour room service, twice-daily maid service, laundry/valet, complimentary newspaper and shoe shine, concierge.

**Facilities:** Business center; off-site fitness privileges. A spa is also planned for July 1998.

## EXPENSIVE

**Radisson Plaza Hotel.** 90 Bloor St. E., Toronto, ON, M4W 1A7. ☎ **800/333-3333** or 416/961-8000. Fax 416/961-4635. 238 rms, 18 suites. A/C MINIBAR TV TEL. From C$185 (U.S.$132) double; from C$290 (U.S.$207) suite. Extra person C$15 (U.S.$11). Children under 18 stay free in parents' rm. Weekend packages available. AE, DC, DISC, JCB, MC, V. Parking C$18.50 (U.S.$13) Subway: Bloor.

Occupying the 7th to 12th floors of a multiuse complex, the Radisson Plaza is designed around an inner cobblestone courtyard with flowers, shrubbery, and trees. The lobby is on the street level.

All the rooms have double beds and are tastefully decorated. Appointments include the standard ones listed above as well as clock radios, makeup mirrors, and hair dryers. Plaza Club rooms have a concierge and private lounge.

**Dining/Entertainment: Matisse** pays homage to the artist with floor-to-ceiling replicas of his paintings. It serves all day, featuring California-style cuisine with international accents. Main courses are priced from C$15 to C$28 (U.S.$11 to U.S.$20). There's also a bar.

**Services:** Room service from 6:30am to 11pm; laundry/valet, concierge.

**Facilities:** Squash, sauna, and whirlpool facilities are in the Bloor Park Club in the building.

**The Sutton Place Hotel.** 955 Bay St., Toronto, ON, M5S 2A2. ☎ **800/268-3790** or 416/924-9221. Fax 416/924-1778. 230 rms, 62 suites. A/C MINIBAR TV TEL. C$235–$300 (U.S.$168–$214) double; from C$400 (U.S.$286) suite. Extra person C$20 (U.S.$14). Children under 18 stay free in parents' rm. Weekend rates available. AE, DC, JCB, MC, V. Parking C$21 (U.S.$15). Subway: Museum or Wellesley.

A small luxury hotel, the Sutton Place caters to a business and leisure clientele, including a healthy sprinkling of celebrities, who are drawn by its European flair, elegant decor, and fine service. Throughout the public areas are antiques, tapestries, Oriental carpets, and crystal chandeliers. The very spacious rooms are luxuriously furnished in a French style. Each contains a couch, desk, and two telephones with fax/computer hookup.

**Dining: Accents Restaurant and Bar** offers a relaxed bistro-style setting for all meals.

**Services:** 24-hour room service, laundry/valet, complimentary newspaper and shoe shine, twice-daily maid service, concierge, limousine to the financial district.

**Facilities:** Indoor pool with spacious sundeck, sauna, massage, fully equipped fitness center, business center.

## MODERATE

**Quality Hotel.** 280 Bloor St. W. (at St. George), Toronto, ON, M5S 1V8. ☎ **416/968-0010.** 210 rms. A/C TV TEL. C$137 (U.S.$98) double. Weekend and other packages available. AE, DC, DISC, MC, V. Parking C$11.50 (U.S.$8).

Part of the well-known chain, this hotel is only a few blocks west of the Inter-Continental and represents a great value for the location. Rooms are modern and well equipped, with remote-control cable TVs and modern light furnishings, including useful, well-lit work tables. The Executive rooms have dataport phones for computer hookup. There's a restaurant and coffee shop, and room service from 7am to noon and from 5 to 11pm. Guests may use the facilities at a nearby fitness center.

**Venture Inn, Yorkville.** 89 Avenue Rd., Toronto, ON, M5R 2G3. ☎ **800/387-3933** or 416/964-1220. Fax 416/964-8692. 71 rms. A/C TV TEL. C$100–$150 (U.S.$71–$107) double. Rate includes continental breakfast. AE, DC, DISC, ER, MC, V. Parking C$6.50 (U.S.$4.65). Subway: Bay

A clean, no-frills hotel in exclusive Yorkville, the Venture Inn is a good value. The modern rooms are attractively furnished in pine. Laundry and dry-cleaning services are available.

## INEXPENSIVE

**Hotel Selby.** 592 Sherbourne St., Toronto, ON, M4X 1L4. ☎ **800/387-4788** or 416/921-3142. Fax 416/923-3177. 67 rms (59 with bath). A/C TV TEL. C$80–$90 (U.S.$57–$64) double; C$100–$125 (U.S.$71–$89) suite. All rates include continental breakfast. AE, MC, V. Limited free parking on first-come first-serve basis; otherwise C$8 (U.S.$6).

This hotel, located in a large turn-of-the-century Victorian, represents a great downtown bargain. The clientele, a mixture of gay and straight couples, seems to enjoy the comfortable lobby/sitting area with a chandelier and a fireplace near the front desk downstairs. The rooms are individually decorated with an eclectic mix of furniture. Ceilings are high, making the rooms airy and dramatic; many have stucco decoration and moldings. In several rooms, the old bathroom fixtures have been retained. Furnishings include a couch, a TV, and a phone. There's a large walk-in closet, and the bathroom has a claw-foot tub and pedestal sink. Notable rooms include the very large Hadley Hemingway Suite, which boasts a fireplace; the Gooderham Suite, with a brass-hooded fireplace, an oak dresser, a couple of wingbacks, and a small tub with a shower in the bathroom; and room 401, with an old-fashioned burled-wood bed, angled ceilings, track lighting, and a pair of leatherette wingbacks. There's also a coin laundry on premises. Guests have access to a nearby health club for a small fee.

**Victoria University.** 140 Charles St. W., Toronto, ON, M5S 1K9. ☎ **416/585-4524.** Fax 416/585-4530. 700 rms (none with bath). C$64 (U.S.$45.70) double. Rate includes breakfast. Discounts available for seniors and students. MC, V. Early May to late Aug. Nearby parking C$12 (U.S.$9). Subway: Museum.

For a great summer bargain downtown, stay at Victoria University, right across from the Royal Ontario Museum. Rooms in the 425-room student residence are available from mid-May to late August. Each is furnished as a study/bedroom and supplied with fresh linen, towels, and soap. Bathrooms are down the hall. Guests enjoy free local calls and use of laundry facilities, as well as access to the dining and athletic facilities (including tennis courts).

## 4 Uptown

## MODERATE

**Best Western Roehampton Hotel.** 808 Mount Pleasant Rd., Toronto, ON, M4P 2L2. ☎ **800/387-8899** or 416/487-5101. Fax 416/487-5390. 110 rms and suites. A/C TV TEL. C$145–$160 (U.S.$104–$114) double. Special discount packages available. AE, DC, DISC, ER, MC, V. Parking C$7 (U.S.$5). Subway: Eglinton.

Situated at the center of the Eglinton Avenue business district, the Roehampton has spacious, recently renovated rooms. The corner rooms are especially large and attractive, with pleasant views. All units are well equipped; some have refrigerators. The **Champs sports lounge/restaurant** serves an all-day menu; room service is available from 10am to 11pm. Laundry and valet service and an outdoor rooftop pool and sundeck on the third floor round out the hotel's features.

## 5 At the Airport

### EXPENSIVE

**Sheraton Gateway at Terminal Three.** Toronto AMF, Box 3000, Toronto, ON, L5P 1C4. ☎ **800/325-3535** or 905/672-7000. Fax 905/672-7100. 474 rms, 6 suites. A/C MINIBAR TV TEL. C$170–$220 (U.S.$121–$157) double. AE, DC, DISC, ER, MC, V. Parking C$8 (U.S.$6).

Connected by skywalk to Terminal 3, this is the most convenient place to stay at the airport. All rooms are soundproofed and luxuriously decorated, containing all the expected amenities, plus hair dryers, irons/ironing boards, and coffeemaker. For travelers it's also convenient to be able to view flight departure and arrival times on your own personal TV. Club rooms offer upgraded features like ergonomic chairs, halogen lighting, bathrobe, fax/printer/copier, plus private lounge serving complimentary breakfast and hors d'oeuvres.

**Dining/Entertainment:** Three buffets are served daily in the **Café Suisse,** while the **Mahogany Grill** is reserved for fine dining (main dishes C$16–$30/U.S.$11–$21). There's also a lobby bar.

**Services:** 24-hour room service.

**Facilities:** Business center, hair salon, indoor pool, whirlpool, 24-hour fitness center. Massage therapists are also available.

**Toronto Airport Hilton International.** 5875 Airport Rd., Mississauga, ON, L4V 1N1. ☎ **800/567-9999** or 905/677-9900. Fax 905/677-7782. 413 rms, 152 minisuites. A/C MINIBAR TV TEL. C$195 (U.S.$139) double; minisuites from C$225 (U.S.$161) double. Extra person C$20 (U.S.$14). Children stay free in parents' rm. Weekend packages available. AE, CB, DC, DISC, ER, MC, V. Free parking. Take the Gardiner Expwy. west to Hwy. 427 north, to Airport Expwy. (Dixon Rd. exit).

The Airport Hilton has all the comfort and conveniences associated with the Hilton name. A 12-story tower added to the hotel contains minisuites, each featuring separate bedroom, bathroom, and parlor areas. Each minisuite comes fully equipped with a king-size bed, a sofa bed, two color TVs, three telephones, and a table for working or dining. The hotel's other 259 rooms are not suites, and they contain only a TV and telephone.

**Dining/Entertainment:** The **Harvest Restaurant/Café** features international cuisine; **the Lobby Coffee Bar** offers flavored coffees and snacks. **Misty's Club** is well known for its musically themed evenings—from country to reggae (Wednesday to Sunday).

**Services:** 24-hour room service, laundry/valet, concierge, baby-sitting.

**Facilities:** Business center, outdoor heated pool with poolside deck, squash and racquetball courts, exercise room.

**Wyndham Bristol Place.** 950 Dixon Rd., Rexdale, ON, M9W 5N4. ☎ **416/675-9444.** Fax 416/675-4426. 287 rms and suites. A/C TV TEL. C$165 (U.S.$118) double; from C$400 (U.S.$286) suite. Extra person C$15 (U.S.$11). Children under 18 stay free in parents' rm. Special packages available. AE, DC, DISC, JCB, MC, V. Parking C$5 (U.S.$3.55).

For really personal service—the kind that caters to the idiosyncrasies of each guest— and chic surroundings, try the Wyndham Bristol Place, a select hotel where contemporary architecture and facilities blend with old-fashioned attention to detail and service. Outside, the redbrick building is striking enough, but inside the lobby is luxuriously comfortable with its cherry-wood pillars, marble walls, and rich carpeting. The standard rooms are beautifully designed, decorated, and appointed. Each has custom-made contemporary furniture, double or king-size beds, geometric design throws, two telephones, a color TV, a bedside console, an alarm clock, iron/ironing board, dataport line, and large parlor lights in the bathroom.

**Dining: Le Café,** raised slightly to overlook the lobby, is a plush coffee shop with comfortable banquettes. **Zachary's** dining room is delightfully contemporary and graced with a kaleidoscopic tapestry hung over white tile. The dinner specialties range from C$23 to C$32 (U.S.$16 to U.S.$23), and may include oven-braised red snapper in a lobster sauce or a filet of beef tenderloin baked with a caramelized shallot crust on Pinot Noir and chive reduction.

**Services:** 24-hour room service, laundry/valet, concierge.

**Facilities:** Indoor/outdoor pool with skylight dome and sundeck; flower gardens; reflecting pools; health club with exercise room, sunroom, sauna.

## MODERATE

**Best Western Toronto Airport.** 33 Carlson Court, Toronto, ON, M9W 6H5. ☎ **800/ 528-1234** or 416/675-1234. Fax 416/675-3436. 524 rms. A/C MINIBAR TV TEL. C$119–$180 (U.S.$85–$129) double. Extra person C$15 (U.S.$11). AE, DC, DISC, ER, MC, V. Parking C$4 ($2.85).

Best Western's Carlton Place Hotel has been thoroughly renovated in the last few years. The lobby and public areas have been spruced up with marble or tile flooring and new decor. The modern functional rooms are equipped with two telephones (one with fax/computer hookup), coffeemakers, and a hair dryer, in addition to the standard amenities. Premier Service provides a pullout sofa bed, a skylight, nightly turndown, a cotton bathrobe, and a pass to nearby Health Club with squash courts; Business Plus rooms contain an oversized lounge chair and ottoman plus desk with halogen lighting and upgraded amenities including iron/ironing board. The Willow Tree restaurant offers all-day dining. There's also 24-hour room service, an indoor swimming pool, a sauna and whirlpool, exercise room, and laundry room.

**Regal Constellation Hotel.** 900 Dixon Rd., Etobicoke, ON, M9W 1J7. ☎ **416/675-1500.** Fax 905/675-4611. 710 rms and suites. A/C TV TEL. C$105–$175 (U.S.$75–$125) double. Extra person C$15 (U.S.$11). Children under 16 stay free in parents' rm. Weekend and honeymoon packages available. AE, DC, DISC, MC, V. Parking C$5 (U.S.$3.55).

Even though it was built 37 years ago and has been turned into a large hotel since, it still has a certain elegance. Because the hotel has expanded so often, rooms come in myriad styles, with color schemes running from beige to green. Every room is a minisuite featuring L-shaped sofas, large desks, king-size or twin/double-bed arrangements, and a color TV with in-house movies.

The hotel is a veritable entertainment and dining complex, including the **Atrium** off the main lobby for all-day buffet dining, the **Grill** specializing in steaks and other grilled items, the **Mitaka** offering Japanese fare, and even a Chinese restaurant. At night, you can sit under a spreading banyan tree overlooking a tropical garden and enjoy a cocktail or dance to live entertainment in the Banyan Tree bar.

There's 24-hour room service; other services include concierge, laundry/valet, and baby-sitting. An unusual indoor/outdoor pool (it's shaped like a river around a tropical island and reached by small wooden footbridges), a bank, a hair salon, and a full recreation complex with exercise room and saunas round out the hotel's facilities.

## INEXPENSIVE

**Comfort Inn—Airport.** 240 Belfield Rd., Rexdale, ON, M9W 1H3. ☎ **416/241-8513.** Fax 416/249-4203. 122 rms. A/C TV TEL. C$86 (U.S.$61) double. Extra person C$10 (U.S.$7). AE, DC, MC, V. Free parking. Take Hwy. 27 north to Belfield Rd.

Off the airport strip, but close enough to be convenient, the Comfort Inn—Airport has modern rooms with up-to-date, color-coordinated decor and pine furnishings, plus individual climate control, color TVs, and phones. Irons/ ironing boards and hair dryers are available on request. Complimentary continental breakfast is included in the rate.

**Days Inn—Toronto Airport.** 6257 Airport Rd., Mississauga, ON, L4V 1N1. ☎ **800/387-6891** or 905/678-1400. Fax 905/678-9130. 201 rms. A/C TV TEL. C$90–$169 (U.S.$64–$121) double. Extra person C$10 (U.S.$7). Children under 18 stay free in parents' rm. Weekend packages available. AE, DC, DISC, ER, JCB, MC, V. Free parking.

The Days Inn offers facilities similar to those of the larger hotels on the airport strip, but at lower prices. It's a small, friendly place set in a streamlined seven-story block. The lobby has a comfy air with its natural-stone fireplace. The rooms are bright and airy and feature natural-pine furniture, color TVs, phones, irons/ironing board, a coffeemaker, and a vanity outside each bathroom.

The hotel has a restaurant-bar, and room service is available from 5 to 11pm. There's also an indoor pool and exercise room.

**Delta Meadowvale Resort & Conference Centre.** 6750 Mississauga Rd. (at Hwy. 401), Mississauga, ON, L5N 2L3. ☎ **800/422-8238** or 905/821-1981. Fax 905/542-4036. 374 rms, 13 suites. A/C TV TEL. C$89–$190 (U.S.$64–$136) double. Weekend packages available. AE, DC, DISC, MC, V. Free parking.

About 30 minutes from downtown, 15 minutes from the airport, and accessible from the 401, 403, and QEW, the Meadowvale is set on 23 acres of landscaped grounds and is distinguishable because of its resortlike features—bicycles and trails, tennis (four) and squash courts as well as indoor/outdoor pools, fitness center, and children's creative program. The ambiance is cozy and rustic; wood and brass are used in the decor, and there's a fireplace in the lobby. The rooms are functional and modern and have the added attraction of a balcony. Facilities include two restaurants, a bar, and in summer an outdoor dining patio. Signature service rooms include terry-cloth bathrobes, complimentary newspaper, and upgraded amenities. Services include 24-hour room service and laundry/valet.

**Four Points Hotel.** 5444 Dixie Rd. (at Hwy. 401), Mississauga, ON, L4W 2L2. ☎ **800/737-3211** or 905/624-1144. Fax 416/624-9477. 289 rms, 8 suites. A/C TV TEL. C$109–$199 (U.S.$78–$142) double. Extra person C$15 (U.S.$11). Weekend rates are lower. AE, DC, DISC, ER, MC, V. Free parking.

The Four Points Hotel is located on a 6-acre woodland site 10 minutes from the airport. The rooms are modern and functional, and are equipped with coffeemakers and hair dryers. There's a restaurant on the premises, as well as 24-hour room service and laundry/valet service; baby-sitting can also be arranged. An indoor pool, sauna, and exercise room round out the facilities.

**Venture Inn at the Airport.** 925 Dixon Rd., Etobicoke, ON, M9W 1J8. ☎ **888/483-6887** or 416/674-2222. Fax 416/674-5757. 283 rms. A/C TV TEL. C$110 (U.S.$79) double. Extra person C$10 (U.S.$7). Rate includes breakfast. AE, DC, ER, MC, V. Free parking. Take the Gardiner Expwy. west to Hwy. 427 north, exit Dixon Rd., and turn right.

This hotel is part of the moderately priced Venture Inn chain, which features modern rooms furnished in a country style. Some upgraded rooms have coffeemakers, hair dryers, and more than one phone. **Pat and Mario's** is connected to the hotel, and there are plenty of other dining choices nearby. Coffee/tea is provided 24 hours. Room service is available 11am to 1am plus laundry/valet. Facilities include an indoor pool, sauna, and whirlpool.

# 7  Metro East

Accommodations here are conveniently located to the Metro Zoo, the science center, and Scarborough Town Centre, a vast shopping mall.

There are a number of moderately priced chain hotels in this area, including: **Embassy Suites,** 8500 Warden Ave., Markham, ON, L6G 1A5 (☎ 905/470-8500); **Radisson,** 1250 Eglinton Ave. E., Don Mills, ON, M3C 1J3 (☎ 416/449-4111); and **Sheraton,** 2035 Kennedy Rd., Scarborough, ON, M1T 3G2 (☎ 416/299-1500).

## EXPENSIVE

**Westin Prince Hotel.** 900 York Mills Rd., Don Mills, ON, M3B 3H2. ☎ **800/WESTIN** or 416/444-2511. Fax 416/444-9597. 381 rms and suites. A/C TV TEL. C$210–$245 (U.S.$150–$175) double. Extra person C$20 (U.S.$14). Children under 18 stay free in parents' rm. Weekend packages available. AE, DC, MC, V. Free parking. Subway: York Mills.

Located 20 minutes from downtown, this luxury hotel offers a quiet ambiance. It is set on 15 acres of private parkland where you can wander marked nature trails.

A warm, soft decor is found in the rooms, many of which have handsome bay windows or appealing balconies. Each of the oversized rooms has a marble bathroom with a hair dryer, two telephones, unstocked refrigerator, and an in-room safe.

**Dining/Entertainment: Le Continental** features a walk-in cellar and fine cuisine with main courses priced from C$20 to C$40 (U.S.$14 to U.S.$29). **Katsura,** the specialty restaurant, has four separate dining areas, a tempura counter and sushi bar, tatami-style dining, teppanyaki-style cuisine, and a robata bar. Complete dinners range from C$37 to C$47 (U.S.$26 to U.S.$34). **The Coffee Garden** restaurant overlooks a grove of 30-foot-tall trees, as does **The Brandy Tree,** a sophisticated piano bar, restfully decorated in gray and plum.

**Services:** 24-hour room service, laundry/valet, concierge, baby-sitting.

**Facilities:** Business center, outdoor heated pool, sauna, three tennis courts, fitness center, game room, putting green, nature trails, jogging track.

## INEXPENSIVE

**University of Toronto at Scarborough, Student Village.** Scarborough Campus, University of Toronto, 1265 Military Trail, Scarborough, ON, M1C 1A4. ☎ **416/287-7369.** Fax 416/287-7323. C$160 (U.S.$114) for 2-night minimum; each additional night C$80 (U.S.$57) to a maximum of C$470 (U.S.336) per week. Family rates available. MC. V. Open mid-May to the end of Aug. Free parking. Take the subway to Kennedy, then the Scarborough Rapid Transit to Ellesmere, then bus no. 95 or 95B to the college entrance. Or take exit 387 north from Hwy. 401.

From mid-May to the end of August, the University of Toronto in Scarborough has accommodations available in town houses that sleep four to six people and contain equipped kitchens. None has air-conditioning, a TV, or a telephone. There is a cafeteria, pub, and recreation center (with squash and tennis courts, a gym, and an exercise room). The parklike setting is appealing.

## A RURAL RETREAT

**The Guild Inn.** 201 Guildwood Pkwy., Scarborough, ON, M1E 1P6. ☎ **416/261-3331.** Fax 416/261-5675. 90 rms, 6 suites. TV TEL. C$88 (U.S.$63) double. Extra person C$10 (U.S.$7); children under 12 stay free in parents' rm. Special packages available. AE, ER, MC, V. Free parking. Subway: Kennedy.

Beautifully situated 30 minutes from downtown on the Scarborough Bluffs, the Guild Inn offers tranquillity and gracious surroundings. Enter the tall wrought-iron gates at the head of the drive into the 90-acre grounds, which are dotted with historic architectural fragments, such as limestone Ionic columns rescued from Toronto's Banker Bond building, torn down to make way for Canadian Place.

Inside, the lobby has the air of an English manor, with its broad staircase, oak beams, and wrought-iron chandeliers. You'll also find wonderful art and china collections, a legacy from the 1930s when the property was occupied by the Guild of All Arts, which operated art-and-craft workshops that attracted so many visitors here that rooms and dining facilities were added. During these halcyon years many notables visited including Queen Juliana of the Netherlands, Dorothy and Lillian Gish, Moira Shearer, Rex Harrison, Sir John Gielgud, and Lilli Palmer.

Some of the rooms have a view of the rear gardens, which sweep down to the Scarborough Bluffs, rising 200 feet above Lake Ontario. The inn's original central section was built in 1914, and the rooms here have been renovated. All 86 rooms have air-conditioning, AM/FM radios, color TVs, and private balconies.

**Dining:** The dining room is still a popular gathering place for Sunday brunch; at dinner it serves primarily grills, roasts, and seafood, priced from C$17 to C$28 (U.S.$12 to U.S.$20). In summer, cocktails are served outside on a lovely veranda.

**Facilities:** Outdoor swimming pool, tennis court, fitness room, nature trails.

# Dining 5

The city's palate is wide-ranging and adventurous, making dining in Toronto a delightful round-the-world experience that can be enjoyed for a moderate price. Current trends seem to lean toward Latin and Mediterranean cuisine, with ever more concentrated doses of Southeast Asian and Pacific Rim flavors. You can eat at the fashionable hot spots, and by all means do so; but it's more fun, in my opinion, to explore the city's neighborhoods and visit the prime ethnic dining spots found along College Street in Little Italy, in Chinatown near Dundas and Spadina, and at Greek tavernas along the Danforth. Queen Street West is a terrific stomping ground featuring bistro and other reasonably priced cuisines and so too is Baldwin Street, just north of and parallel to Dundas and conveniently located near the Art Gallery.

Another charming and welcome aspect of the city's dining scene is the incredible number of outdoor dining spots and the tolerance extended to those of us who just want to linger for a few hours over an iced coffee or a lemonade. It's refreshing and very European in flavor. Supposedly there are 5,000-plus restaurants in the city. Below is a quick-reference list of 120 or so of my favorites organized by cuisine (with the neighborhood and an abbreviation of the price category in parentheses), followed by write-ups of each establishment, categorized by location and price.

**SOME DINING NOTES**   Although dining in Toronto can be expensive, it usually seems that way not so much because of the food, but because of the extras—like the 8% provincial sales tax on meals and the 7% GST. In addition, wine prices are higher than those in the United States, largely because of the tax on all imported wines. You will pay as much as C$6 (U.S.$4.30) for a glass of house wine in the better restaurants, and as much as C$25 (U.S.$18) for a 1-liter (1.1 qt.) carafe. Most wine lists start at around C$25 (U.S.$18). There's also a 10% tax on all alcohol—keep in mind that the prices quoted often do not reflect that tax.

Locations are as follows: **Downtown** refers roughly to streets from the waterfront to and including College/Carlton Street between Ossington Avenue and Jarvis Street; **Midtown** refers to the area north of College/Carlton Street to Davenport and Yonge streets and also between Ossington and Jarvis; I have also further subdivided both of these sections into west and east. **Uptown** covers the area north of Davenport Street.

# 1 Best Bets

- **Best for a Romantic Dinner:** The dining room at **Scaramouche,** 1 Benvenuto Place (☎ **416/961-8011**), affords sparkling views of the downtown skyline, but it's the combination of ambiance, cuisine, and service that makes this a romantic dining experience.
- **Best for a Business Lunch: Jump Cafe and Bar,** 1 Wellington St. W. (☎ **416/363-3400**), is right in the heart of the financial district. Its patrons appreciate the well-spaced tables, the handsome surroundings, the up-to-the-minute service and food, and the extensive selection of single malts and grappas at the bar.
- **Best for a Celebration:** At **N 44,** 2537 Yonge St. (☎ **416/487-4897**), the room positively glows at night. Whatever you choose on the menu will be beautifully presented and taste exquisite. Accompany it with a selection from the extensive wine list (more than 300 choices), and then, when you've finished, take the party upstairs to the piano bar.
- **Best Decor: Palavrion,** 270 Front St. W. (☎ **416/979-0060**), has to be one of the most dramatic restaurants in the city for the way its decor combines colors and textures. Wall colors are brilliant—orange, yellow, and turquoise—and further il-luminated with trompe l'oeil art—while the floors are studded with individually crafted art tiles.
- **Best View:** The 360° view from the **revolving restaurant** atop the **CN Tower,** 301 Front St. W. (☎ **416/362-5411**), is nothing short of amazing, and the food is somewhat better than most similarly located restaurants.
- **Best Wine Lists: Centro,** 2472 Yonge St. (☎ **416/483-2211**), has the most well-rounded list anywhere, and what's even better, many of its great wines can be sampled in the downstairs wine bar. There are 540 labels on the list including 67 California Chardonnays and 30 different champagnes. The list is also strong in Italian reds, featuring the superb Tuscans (Sassicaia, Ornellaia, Tignanello, and Solais) and also lists several lustrous back vintage Bordeaux. Prices range from C$26 to C$2,000 (U.S.$19 to U.S.$1,429).
- **Best Bistro:** For really tried-and-true favorites like pan-roasted salmon or calf's liver in mustard sauce, seek out **Herbs,** 3187 Yonge St. (☎ **416/322-0487**), a color-filled bistro in uptown. You'll always find a warming cream soup, a steak if you want one, and a buttery caramel tarte tatin plus some more innovative spe-cialties here.
- **Best Greek: Pan on the Danforth,** 516 Danforth Ave. (☎ **416/466-8158**), offers contemporary Greek cuisine that goes far beyond the typical kebab house basics.
- **Best Italian:** If you want to be transported to Italy and to experience the heady scents and flavors of updated Northern Italian cuisine, **Centro** (see above) is the place to go. Here in a splendid room with soaring ceilings, classical pillars, slabs of marble, and portraits of Asolo, you can bask at tables set with the finest china and crystal, relishing a simple but wonderful appetizer of local Woolwich goat cheese with yellow pepper, herb oil, and balsamic vinegar, and finishing with a lemon mascarpone tart laced with blackberries. What comes in between will sur-prise and delight.
- **Best Latin:** At **Xango,** 106 John St. (☎ **416/593-4407**), diners can taste a full range of South American cuisines—from Ecuador, Chile, Peru, and Argentina. The flavors are tongue-tingling and fiery, though not distastefully so. There are beautifully served tropical drinks, too.

- **Best Portuguese:** At **Chiado,** 864 College St. at Concord Avenue (☎ **416/ 538-1910**), diners will discover authentic Portuguese cuisine—fish dishes such as grilled fillet of salted cod or *parrilhada* of seafood, and desserts like *natas do ceu*, a very rich cream dessert served over ladyfingers and soaked with bitter almond liqueur.
- **Best Seafood:** Toronto is not a great city for fresh seafood, but at **Joso's,** 202 Davenport, just east of Avenue Road (☎ **416/925-1903**), you'll always be presented with a good selection of fresh fish on a board, so you can select the freshest for cooking.
- **Best Desserts: Dufflet Pastries,** 787 Queen St. W. (☎ **416/504-2870**), is great for tarts and cakes, and in fact supplies many of the city's restaurants; **Sicilian Ice Cream Company,** 710–712 College St. (☎ **416/531-7716**), scoops the best ice cream and gelati. As far as restaurants go, there are many great places for dessert, but **Scaramouche** (see above) stands out for its wonderful crème brûlée, chocolate cake, and bread pudding. Innovative desserts, like coconut custard served with chocolate-dipped plantain chips, can be found at **Xango,** 106 John St. (☎ **416/ 593-4407**).
- **Best Late-Night Dining:** The Danforth is the only place in Toronto where you can dine after midnight, until 3am or so, and there are several places along the strip that serve a full range of delicious, small dishes—**Ouzeri,** 500A Danforth Ave. (☎ **416/778-0500**), is the liveliest.
- **Best People-Watching:** There's a very good chance you'll see some visiting celebrities in the **Studio Cafe** at The Four Seasons Hotel, 21 Avenue Rd. (☎ **416/ 964-0411**), or at **Prego della Piazza,** around the corner from The Four Seasons in Renaissance Plaza (☎ **416/920-9900**).
- **Best Brunch:** Among Toronto's hotels, the most outstanding brunch can be enjoyed at **The Four Seasons,** 21 Avenue Rd. (☎ **416/964-0411**). At the buffet, you can sample fresh smoked fish and shellfish and choose from a fantastic selection of breads, pâtés, antipasti, roasts, and salads, plus omelets and egg dishes made to order. The king of the restaurant Sunday brunch scene is **Mildred Pierce,** 99 Sudbury St. (☎ **416/588-5695**). Their version of eggs Benedict—poached eggs with smoked salmon on a croissant, served with a Gorgonzola cream sauce— and their banana pecan pancakes with honey-bourbon butter sauce are especially good.

# 2  Restaurants by Cuisine

## ASIAN
Tiger Lily's (Downtown West, *I*)

## BURGERS
Toby's Goodeats (Downtown West, *I*)

## CAJUN
N'Awlins (Downtown West, *M*)
Southern Accent (Midtown West, *M*)

## CANADIAN
Canoe (Downtown West, *E*)

Fred's Not Here Smokehouse and Grill (Downtown West, *M*)
Red Tomato (Downtown West, *I*)

## CHINESE
The Eating Counter (Downtown West, *I*)
Lai Wah Heen (Downtown West, *E*)
Lee Garden (Downtown West, *I*)
Pink Pearl (Downtown West, *M*)
Wah Sing (Downtown West, *I*)

**Key to abbreviations:** *I* = Inexpensive, *M* = Moderate, *E* = Expensive, *VE* = Very Expensive

## CALIFORNIAN

Far Niente (Downtown West, *VE*)

## CONTINENTAL

Arlequin (Midtown West, *M*)
Chiaro's (Downtown West, *VE*)
Herbs (Uptown, *E*)
Jacques Bistro du Parc (Midtown West, *M*)
La Maquette (Downtown East, *E*)
Mildred Pierce (Downtown West, *M*)
Movenpick Bistretto (Midtown West, *M*)
Movenpick Marché (Downtown West, *I*)
Palavrion (Downtown West, *M*)
Rivoli (Downtown West, *I*)
Scaramouche (Uptown, *VE*)
360 Revolving Restaurant (Downtown West, *VE*)
Trapper's (Uptown, *E*)
Truffles (Midtown West, *VE*)

## CREPES

Le Papillon (Downtown East, *I*)

## DELI

The Bagel (Downtown West, *I*)
Shopsy's (Downtown East, *I*)

## ECLECTIC

Avalon (Downtown West, *E*)
Cities (Downtown West, *M*)
Jump Cafe and Bar (Downtown West, *E*)
Mildred Pierce (Downtown West, *M*)

## FRENCH/BISTRO

Bistro 990 (Midtown West, *E*)
Brownes Bistro (Uptown, *M*)
La Bodega (Downtown West, *M*)
Le Paradis (Uptown, *M*)
Le Select (Downtown West, *M*)
Mildred Pierce (Downtown West, *M*)
Opus (Midtown West, *E*)
St. Tropez (Downtown West, *M*)
Taro Grill (Downtown West, *M*)

## FUSION

Boba (Midtown West, *E*)
Left Bank (Downtown West, *M*)
Mercer Street Grill (Downtown West, *E*)
Pangaea (Midtown West, *E*)
Peter Pan (Downtown West, *M*)
Queen Mother Cafe (Downtown West, *I*)

## GREEK

Astoria (Midtown East/The East End, *I*)
Byzas (Midtown East/The East End, *I*)
Lolita's Lust (Midtown East/The East End, *I*)
Myth (Midtown East/The East End, *M*)
Omonia (Midtown East/The East End, *I*)
Ouzeri (Midtown East/The East End, *I*)
Pan on the Danforth (Midtown East/The East End, *M*)

## INDIAN

Babur (Downtown West, *M*)
Indian Rice Factory (Midtown West, *I*)

## INTERNATIONAL

N 44 (Uptown, *VE*)

## ITALIAN

Acqua (Downtown West, *E*)
Biagio (Downtown East, *E*)
Borgo Antico (Midtown West, *M*)
Centro (Uptown, *VE*)
Coppi (Uptown, *E*)
Galileo (Downtown East, *E*)
Grano (Uptown, *M*)
Grappa (Downtown West, *M*)
Il Fornello (Downtown West, *I*)
Il Posto (Midtown West, *E*)
KitKat Bar & Grill (Downtown West, *M*)
La Fenice (Downtown West, *E*)
Myth (Midtown East/The East End, *I*)

N'Awlins (Downtown West, *M*)

Prego della Piazza (Midtown West, *E*)

Pronto (Uptown, *E*)

Spiaggia (Downtown East, *M*)

Splendido Bar and Grill (Midtown West, *E*)

Trattoria Giancarlo (Downtown West, *M*)

ZooM Caffe & Bar (Downtown East *E*)

## JAPANESE

Masa (Downtown West, *M*)

Mori (Midtown West, *I*)

Nami Japanese Seafood (Downtown East, *E*)

## LAOTIAN

Vanipha (Downtown West, *I*)

## LIGHT FARE

Bloor Street Diner (Midtown West, *I*)

Free Times Café (Downtown West, *I*)

Kalendar (Downtown West, *I*)

Langolino (Downtown West, *M*)

## LATIN AMERICAN

The Boulevard Café (Midtown West, *I*)

Xango (Downtown West, *E*)

## MEDITERRANEAN

Lolita's Lust (Midtown East/ The East End, *I*)

Messis (Midtown West, *M*)

Opus (Midtown West, *E*)

Taro Grill (Downtown West, *M*)

## MIDDLE EASTERN

Aïda's Falafel (Midtown West, *I*)

Jerusalem (Uptown, *I*)

Kensington Kitchen (Midtown West, *I*)

## PORTUGUESE

Chiado (Downtown West, *E*)

## QUÉBECOIS

Montréal Bistro and Jazz Club (Downtown East, *M*)

## SEAFOOD

Filet of Sole (Downtown West, *M*)

Joso's (Midtown West, *M*)

Rodney's Oyster House (Downtown East, *M*)

Whistling Oyster Seafood Cafe (Downtown West, *M*)

## STEAK

Barberian's (Downtown West, *E*)

Black & Blue Smoke Bar (Midtown West, *E*)

The Senator (Downtown East, *E*)

## SWISS

Movenpick Bistretto (Midtown West, *M*)

## THAI

Thai Magic (Uptown, *M*)

Vanipha (Downtown West, *I*)

Young Thailand (Downtown East, *I*)

## VEGETARIAN

Annapurna Vegetarian Restaurant (Midtown West, *I*)

Free Times Café (Downtown West, *I*)

# 3  Downtown West

There's plenty of pleasurable dining to choose from in this area. One of the best streets on which to look for a selection of reasonably priced bistros frequented by artists and young professionals is **Queen Street West.** Dining in the theater district is, as in most other cities, fraught with pitfalls—high prices and poor quality—but I describe some exceptions below. **Chinatown** and the streets north of it—like Baldwin Street—are also good places to look for restaurants, as is **College Street** in Little Italy.

# Downtown Toronto Dining

Acqua **45**
Avalon **12**
Babur **21**
Barberian's **29**
Biagio **45**
Canoe **33**
Chiaro's **41**
Cities **1**
The Eating Counter **20**
Far Niente **34**
Filet of Sole/Whistling Oyster **25**
Fred's Not Here/Red Tomato **14**
Free Time's Café **5**
Galileo **46**
Il Fornello **32**
Jump Cafe and Bar **38**
Kitkat Bar & Grill **18**
Lai Wah Heen **28**
La Bodega **7**
La Fenice **15**
La Maquette **44**
Lee Garden **6**
Left Bank **3**
Le Papillon **48**
Le Select **10**
Masa **24**
Mercer Street Grill **19**
Montréal Bistro and Jazz Club **47**
Movenpick Marché **36**
Nami Japanese Seafood **42**
N'Awlins **17**
Palavrion **26**
Peter Pan **11**
Pink Pearl **49**
Queen Mother Café **22**
Red Tomato/Fred's Not Here **14**
Rivoli **9**
Rodney's **39**
St. Tropez **16**
The Senator **31**
Shopsy's **37**
Taro Grill **2**
360°Revolving Restaurant **27**
Tiger Lily's **23**
Toby's Goodeats **30**
Vanipha **4**
Wah Sing **8**
Whistling Oyster/Filet of Sole **25**
Young Thailand **43**
Xango **13**
Zoom **40**

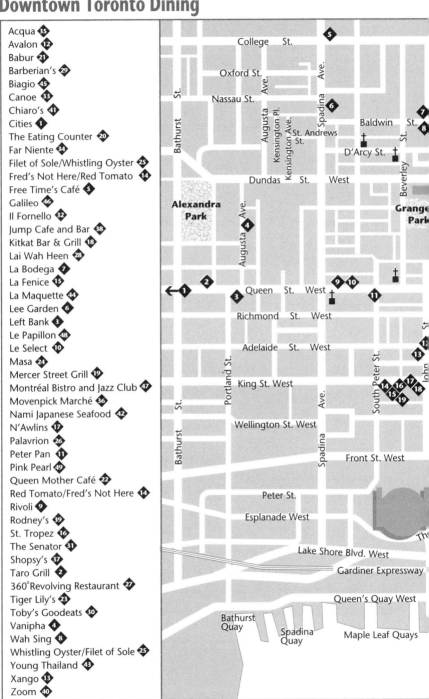

1-0337

# VERY EXPENSIVE

**Chiaro's.** In the King Edward Hotel, 37 King St. E. ☎ **416/863-9700.** Reservations recommended. Main courses C$28–$38 (U.S.$20–$27). AE, CB, DC, MC, V. Mon–Sat 5:30–10:30pm. Subway: King. CONTINENTAL.

For formal dining, Chiaro's, decorated in stunning gray lacquer with etched-glass panels and French-style chairs, specializes in fine French and continental cuisine. The cuisine has won many awards, and if you really want an experience, request the Chef's Table in the kitchen. At dinner you might start with delicious Scottish and Irish smoked salmon carved from the trolley, or escargots and woodland mushrooms on a garlic essence. You might follow with a poached Dover sole tartare with shrimp, tomato, parsley, capers, and cornichons; or a roast lamb with a lemon-thyme reduction; or a shelled lobster with lemon, orange, and honey sauce. Finish with a luscious rendering of tiramisu on cafe au lait zabaglione. The wine list is excellent and extensive.

**Far Niente Napa Grill.** 30 Wellington St. W. at Bay ☎ **416/368-1444.** Main courses C$15–$40 (U.S.$11–$29). AE, DC, MC, V. Mon–Fri 11:30am–11:30pm, Mon–Sat 5:30–11pm. Subway: St. Andrew. CALIFORNIA.

It's meant to remind you of sunny California and it does with its vineyard landscapes, walls of wine-filled wine racks, barrel stave chairs, and terra-cotta colors. The food is California-inspired too, featuring simply grilled dishes that retain the flavor of the ingredients. In addition to steaks, there are five options for grilled salmon, plus other grilled dishes like lamb chops in a mango and mint barbecue sauce or swordfish in a balsamic vinaigrette. Pastas and vegetarian dishes also abound. You can choose to "graze" by opting for the small portion, or order a whole dish. There are plenty of appetizers to enjoy—from bruschetta to grilled calamari in a white-wine, tomato garlic, and scallion-butter sauce. Downstairs, **Soul of the Vine** is a more casual stop for pasta and antipasti and offers a wide range of wine by the glass from a 10,000 bottle stock. Stone walls and brick vaulted ceilings make for a cellarlike ambiance. There's late-night dancing to retro sounds.

**360 Revolving Restaurant.** CN Tower, 301 Front St. W. ☎ **416/362-5411.** Main courses C$25–$36 (U.S.$18–$26). AE, DC, MC, V. Mon–Sun 10:30am–2:30pm and 4:30pm–10:30pm. Subway: Union. CONTINENTAL.

Dining at such dizzy heights usually means that the view is terrific but the food is far from it. In this case, the food is almost equal to the view, even if some of the ingredients are a trifle rarefied, like the herb-seared steak of Canadian-raised ostrich served with oyster mushroom and okra ratatouille. The menu certainly emphasizes Canadian ingredients—there's Angus beef, Aurora chicken, and New Brunswick salmon, the last served with a redolent smoked-tomato vinaigrette.

The decor uses a lot of natural elements—stone, slate, wood, stainless steel, and glass, but it's not so inspiring that it distracts from the view. The art showcased on the interior walls is worth viewing, though. There's an excellent wine list with more than 400 selections.

# EXPENSIVE

**Acqua.** 10 Front St. W. ☎ **416/368-7171.** Reservations recommended. Main courses C$20–$29 (U.S.$14–$21). AE, DC, ER, MC, V. Mon–Fri 11:30am–11:30pm, Sat 5–11:30pm. Subway: Union. ITALIAN.

One of the trendiest and most dramatic restaurants in Toronto, Acqua attracts the Bay Street crowd—investment bankers, traders, and brokers—especially during happy hour, when the bar is filled with suits. Evoking the drama and color of Venice at

Carnival, the bar area (where you can dine) features curvaceous tables standing under sail-like flags. There's also a courtyard dining area that spills out into the BCE galleria; it's defined by striped poles, reminiscent of those that line Venetian canals. Starfish patterns decorate the floors and water cascades down a wall fashioned out of metal fish.

The cuisine is contemporary Italian. Pan-seared Lake Huron whitefish with mashed lobster potatoes, asparagus, and caviar; and a grilled veal chop with buttered green beans, chanterelle potato puree morels, and sweet garlic reduction are just two of the menu's main attractions. In addition, there are a few pastas, plus a grand selection of appetizers, such as salmon tartare with sticky rice salad, tempura shrimp, and pencil asparagus, or peppered beef carpaccio on mesclun lettuce with aged Parmesan. For dessert, chocoholics won't be able to pass up the Belgian chocolate and raspberry crème brûlée with blackberry preserve. There's a great selection of dessert wines, ports, and grappa as well as a top-of-the-line wine list.

✪ **Avalon.** 270 Adelaide St. W. at John St. ☎ **416/979-9918.** Main courses C$19–$32 (U.S.$14–$23). AE, DC, MC, V. Wed–Fri noon–2:30pm; Mon–Thurs 5:30–10pm, Fri–Sat 5:30–11pm. Subway: Osgoode or St. Andrew. ECLECTIC.

The room is small, comfortable, and elegant, and the cuisine is fresh and expertly prepared by one of the city's premier young chefs. Climb the short marble staircase past the dramatic floral centerpiece and you'll find yourself in an elegant room with handsome demi-lune stained-glass windows. You'll sit on floral fabric-covered banquettes at tables with beautiful place settings. The menu changes daily, but will likely feature eight or so dishes prepared from the day's freshest seasonal ingredients. There might be a simple but tasty wood-grilled Cornish hen with mashed potatoes, pearl onions, and Swiss chard, or perhaps yellowfin tuna with roasted Jerusalem artichokes, braised greens, and Bordelaise sauce. Much of the produce is locally or organically raised. Appetizers are similarly inspired—on a recent visit, there were simple flavor-concentrated soups and a particularly lovely warm salad made with white asparagus, fresh cèpes, and arugula with hazelnut vinaigrette. Among the desserts, the most spectacular is the Valrhona molten chocolate cappuccino cake. There's also a good international wine list.

✪ **Barberian's.** 7 Elm St. ☎ **416/597-0335.** Reservations required. Main courses C$20–$34 (U.S.$14–$24). AE, DC, MC, V. Mon–Fri noon–2:30pm; daily 5pm–midnight. Subway: Dundas. STEAK.

Barberian's isn't all red velvet and brass like most steak houses. Instead, it's located in a pre-Confederation building and is decorated with Canadiana including some Group of Seven paintings; a bust of Canada's first prime minister, Sir John A. Macdonald; an early Canadian grandfather clock; plus pre-Confederation money, coal-oil lamps, and firearms. It's a casual, friendly place and the occasional host to a number of sports, theater, and film celebrities. The menu features 10 or so steaks from a 9-ounce sirloin to chateaubriand for two along with veal chop, surf and turf, and grilled salmon. After 10pm, a fondue-and-dessert menu offers such additional delights as Grand Marnier soufflé. The 500-plus selections on the wine list and a decent martini selection suit the traditional crowd that dines here.

✪ **Canoe.** 54th floor, Toronto Dominion Bank Tower, 66 Wellington St. W. ☎ **416/364-0054.** Main courses C$21–$32 (U.S.$15–$23). AE, DC, ER, MC, V. Mon–Fri 11:30am–2:30pm, 5–10:30pm. Subway: King. CANADIAN.

The foyer, with its framed autumn leaves, sets a natural tone for this restaurant, where the floors are fashioned from mushroom-stained walnut and the tables from cherry. On a clear day, the view is magnificent; when the clouds are low and mist envelops the tower, the setting is dramatic. The cuisine spotlights the very best Canadian ingredients (Digby scallops, Alberta beef, Yukon caribou, Ontario pheasant), and includes some spa-inspired dishes, such as skin-roasted Arctic char on a warm salad of crooked spinach, goat's cheese, and tomato vinaigrette. There's a full and extensive wine list and great desserts, too.

✪ **Chiado.** 864 College St. (at Concord Ave.). ☎ **416/538-1910.** Reservations recommended. Main courses C$17–$28 (U.S.$12–$20). AE, DC, MC, V. Mon–Sat noon–3pm and Mon–Thurs 5–10pm, Fri–Sat 5pm–11pm. Subway: Queen's Park, then streetcar west. PORTUGUESE.

Chiado refers to the district in Lisbon that's filled with small bistrettos like this one. It draws a professional, sophisticated crowd. Beyond the appetizing display at the front of the room, you'll discover a long, narrow, elegant dining room with marble floors, walls adorned with art, and tables set with specially painted fresh orchids. In summer, the storefront opens entirely onto the street, adding to the atmosphere. Among the appetizers, the *pinheta* of salted cod and the marinated sardines with lemon and parsley will appeal to the true Portuguese; others might prefer the grilled tiger shrimp served with piri piri sauce (made with Portuguese chili oil). On the main menu, the poached fillet of salted cod is pure Portuguese. Of the less traditionally Portuguese dishes, there are a few meat offerings, but I recommend the unusual fish dishes (fresh fish is flown in daily). For a traditional Portuguese dessert, try the *natas do ceu*, a very rich cream dessert served over ladyfingers and soaked with bitter almond liqueur. There's a good, reasonably priced wine list.

✪ **Jump Cafe and Bar.** 1 Wellington St. W. ☎ **416/363-3400.** Reservations recommended for lunch and dinner. Main courses C$17–$22 (U.S.$12–$16). AE, DC, ER, MC, V. Mon–Fri 11:30am–4:30pm; Mon–Thurs 5–10pm, Fri–Sat 5–11pm. Subway: King. ECLECTIC.

A little hard to find, tucked away in Commerce Court, Jump is a lively New York–style cafe that has become a popular power-dining and drinking spot. It vibrates with energy. The streamlined atrium dining room has polished granite floors and warm maple tables; the grand space is broken up by palms and other strategically placed trees and shrubs. The bar area to the right of the entrance is presided over by a bust of Bacchus and features a good selection of single malts and grappas. In summer, it's pleasant to sit out in Commerce Court.

In addition to the fresh daily specials, the menu features about nine dishes, such as five-herb marinated halibut with charred corn, pineapple, mango, and spinach salad in a wild-ginger yellow-tomato vinaigrette or New York steak in a smoky bourbon peppercorn sauce served with truffle-whipped potatoes and grilled portobello mushrooms. At least six pasta dishes are also available. To start, try the richly flavored wild and tame mushroom soup made with six different kinds of fungi, or the terrific black tiger shrimp with a Cajun Creole–spiced sweet-pepper sauce and wild-mushroom ragout. Among the desserts, I long for the banana coconut cream pie with freshly grated coconut and Jamaican rum butterscotch, but you may be seduced by the dense chocolate cake spiked with rum-soaked raisins and layered with sweet mascarpone filling. The bar is so lively, it's sometimes hard to compete with the noise level of your fellow patrons.

✪ **La Fenice.** 319 King St. W. ☎ **416/585-2377.** Reservations recommended. Main courses C$16–$26 (U.S.$11–$27). AE, DC, MC, V. Mon–Fri noon–2:30pm; Mon–Sat 5:30–11pm. Subway: King. ITALIAN.

La Fenice's traditional northern Italian cuisine and understated decor draw a conservative business crowd. Really fresh ingredients and fine, authentic olive oil are the hallmarks of its cuisine. There are 18 or so pasta dishes—*agnolotti al Gorgonzola e salvia* made with Gorgonzola, sage, and tomato, and also fettuccine salmonate with fresh salmon, dill, leeks, and cream are just a couple examples—plus a fine selection of Provimi veal, chicken, and fresh fish dishes. Desserts include a refreshing raspberry sherbet, zabaglione, tiramisu, and fresh fruits in season. It can be noisy at La Fenice, and the service sometimes seems too precise and detached.

**Lai Wah Heen.** 110 Chestnut St. in the Metropolitan Hotel. ☎ **416/977-9899.** Main courses C$12–$24 (U.S.$9–$17), with some dishes priced C$40–$80 (U.S.$29–$57). AE, DC, MC, V. Daily 11:30am–3pm; Sun–Thurs 5:30–10:30pm, Fri–Sat 5:30–11pm. Subway: St. Patrick. CHINESE.

In Chinese, Lai Wah Heen means "beautiful meeting place"; and indeed, this restaurant is that, with two levels joined by broad black granite steps, and handsome, dramatically large pictograms decorating the walls. A specially equipped Cantonese kitchen delivers top-quality Chinese food that has attracted many patrons from the local Chinese community. This is the place to try shark's-fin soup or abalone. There are nine soups to choose from, ranging from Alaskan king crab bisque to shrimp wonton suspended in clear consommé and shark's fin, which begins at C$25 (U.S.$18) per person. Similarly extravagant dishes can be found among the main courses—braised sliced abalone in oyster sauce runs C$80 (U.S.$57)—along with more modest items, like the barbecued duckling in a coconut curry cream, or the oysters in a spiced Malaysian chili sauce. There's also a good selection of casseroles and rice and noodle dishes. At lunch, in addition to a short luncheon menu, there's a list of 30 or so dim sum offerings. They're priced from C$2 to C$6.50 (U.S.$1.45 to U.S.$4.65).

✪ **Mercer Street Grill.** 36 Mercer St. ☎ **416/599-3399.** Main courses C$18–$27 (U.S.$13–$20). AE, ER, MC, V. Winter Mon–Fri noon–2:15pm, Summer Thurs–Fri only; Sun–Wed 5:15–10pm, Thurs 5:15–10:30pm, Fri–Sat 5:15–11pm. Subway: St. Andrew. FUSION.

Great for pre- or posttheater dining, Mercer Street Grill has drawn rave reviews from local foodies for its inspired Asian fusion cuisine. Each finely prepared dish that emerges from the open kitchen in back is dramatically presented. Start with the wonderful lotus roll of teriyaki beef with crimini mushrooms and a chili basil essence, or the Malaysian black tiger shrimp with crispy noodles and Szechuan spices. Each of the main dishes has a complex and enticing combination of flavors—from the roasted breast of chicken with yellow curry flavors, roasted beet crispy lentil wonton and natural jus to the steamed swordfish and lobster roll with tomato curry and Napa greens.

The dining room is sleek and modern with wood floors and polished wooden tables, set against olive-drab walls with geometric mirrors as accents. The lighting is Milan modern, and the minimal decor is in keeping with the modern ambiance. Both lemon lovers and chocoholics are catered to with two spectacular desserts—the lemon treasure box, containing lemon brûlée, lemon ice, and raspberry lemon roulade and the chocolate sushi, which are hand-rolled sheets of Belgian chocolate filled with raspberry, hazelnut, and white chocolate served with a raspberry nectar. In summer, the serene Japanese-style patio is a must.

✪ **Xango.** 106 John St. ☎ **416/593-4407.** Main courses C$18–$24 ($U.S.13–$17). AE, DC, MC, V. Mon–Sat 5–11pm. Subway: St. Andrew. LATIN AMERICAN.

This is a major player in the latest trend toward authentic Latin cuisine. It's housed in an intimate, low-lit room furnished with wrought-iron chairs set on a tile floor. There's a small outdoor balcony. Each dish is beautifully presented and so are the drinks—order a margarita and it will come in an extravagant art-glass goblet. The cuisine is derived from several different Latin American countries. Among the specialty starters are the four or so ceviches. For me, the most flavorful is the

Honduran version made with fresh tuna, chilies, ginger, and fresh coconut. For a tasty vegetarian appetizer, select the *empanada cebolla*—an empanada filled with braised onions and served with sliced pears, crumbled Spanish blue cheese, and walnut vinaigrette. Entrees range from the Chilean salmon, which is wrapped in a banana leaf and baked with celery, carrots, mushrooms, capers, and corn, and served with saffron rice and orange-scented sofrito, to the spicy adobo-rubbed beef tenderloin served over garlic mash with roasted onions and sweet-corn salsa. These dishes are complemented by a wide selection of reasonably priced Spanish, South American, and Portuguese wines. Besides the daily selection of ice creams and sorbets, there are such additional desserts as the delicious pudin Cubano, a warm bread pudding with guava and dark rum sauce, or the chocolate flan with peanut brittle and whiskey cream.

## MODERATE

**Babur.** 273 Queen St. W. ☎ **416/599-7720.** Main courses C$7–$19 (U.S.$5–$14). AE, MC, V. Daily 11:45am–2:30pm and 5–10:30pm. Subway: Osgoode. INDIAN.

This is an appealing restaurant that serves some fine, non-greasy Indian cuisine. It's a comfortable place with white cloth-covered tables and minimal decor, except for a few shrubs. A portrait of Babur, the first Mughal Emperor, adorns one wall. A full range of Indian dishes is offered, from biryanis and vegetarian specialties to tandoori and other classic dishes like rogan josh and Goan prawn curry.

**Cities.** 859 Queen St. W. ☎ **416/504-3762.** Main courses C$12–$19 (U.S.$9–$14). MC, V. Tues–Fri noon–2pm, Sun–Wed 5:30–10pm, Thurs–Sat 5:30–11pm. Subway: Osgoode, then streetcar west. ECLECTIC.

A small outpost, attracting a hip, young and not-so-young crowd, Cities offers great value. Tables are covered with butcher paper, chairs are basic black, and the art on the coral-colored walls is original. The cuisine is eclectic. Although the menu changes daily, you might find a tongue-tingling black tiger shrimp accompanied by a charred pineapple salsa or a three-mushroom salad with warm walnut vinaigrette to start. Among the eight or so main dishes, there will always be a good balance between meat and seafood, such as a rack of lamb with rosemary-infused glaze, breast of duck with blueberries and mint glaze, or grilled swordfish on a mango-papaya salsa. Their *tarte tatin* is as good as you'll find anywhere.

**Filet of Sole.** 11 Duncan St. ☎ **416/598-3256.** Reservations required 2 days in advance. Main courses C$14–$44 (U.S.$10–$31). AE, DC, MC, V. Mon–Fri noon–2:30pm; daily 5–11pm. Subway: Osgoode. SEAFOOD.

Conveniently located near the CN Tower and the theater district, this high-volume restaurant attracts theatergoers and conventioneers. Here, you'll find an oyster bar and an exhaustive seafood menu that also features daily specials. The restaurant serves everything from fish-and-chips to a 2$^{1}/_{2}$-pound lobster. Most of the dishes—bluefish, monkfish, red snapper, salmon, swordfish, tuna, mahimahi, and many other varieties—are in the range of C$14 to $18 (U.S.$10 to U.S.$13). Daily specials have more zing, like the salmon with a horseradish pepper caper crust or the Cajun-spiced bluefish. For non–fish eaters, there's roasted chicken and several steak dishes. This is a bustling, busy, down-to-earth place.

**Fred's Not Here Smokehouse and Grill.** 321 King St. W. ☎ **416/971-9155.** Reservations recommended. Main courses C$14–$40 (U.S.$10–$29). AE, DC, MC, V. Mon–Fri noon–2pm; Mon–Sat 6–10pm. Subway: St. Andrew. CANADIAN.

An extensive menu and lively bar scene attract tourists and theatergoers to this down-stairs locale. The menu ranges from back ribs with maple-chili barbecue sauce, to roasted rack of lamb in a Creole-mustard crust with rosemary garlic jus, served with

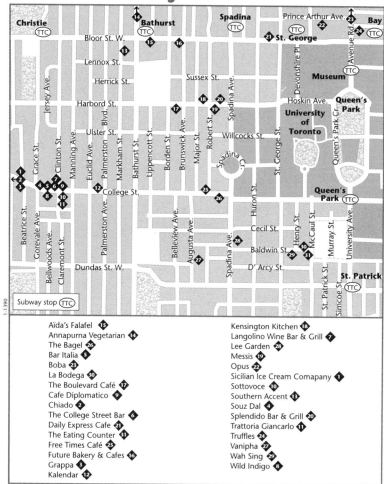

Aïda's Falafel 15
Annapurna Vegetarian 14
The Bagel 26
Bar Italia 5
Boba 23
La Bodega 30
The Boulevard Café 17
Cafe Diplomatico 9
Chiado 2
The College Street Bar 6
Daily Express Cafe 21
The Eating Counter 31
Free Times Café 25
Future Bakery & Cafes 16
Grappa 3
Kalendar 12

Kensington Kitchen 18
Langolino Wine Bar & Grill 7
Lee Garden 28
Messis 19
Opus 22
Sicilian Ice Cream Comapany 1
Sottovoce 10
Southern Accent 13
Souz Dal 4
Splendido Bar & Grill 20
Trattoria Giancarlo 11
Truffles 24
Vanipha 27
Wah Sing 29
Wild Indigo 8

apple-mint relish, to grilled salmon with green lentils pancetta and caramelized shallots. The equally eclectic appetizers might include mixed dim sum along with a fiery Portuguese piri piri lamb satay with crumbled feta cheese and peanut sauce. My favorites among the desserts are the pâté of white and dark chocolate with pistachio sauce and the banana fritters with caramel ice cream and chocolate sauce.

**Grappa.** 797 College St. (1½ blocks west of Beatrice). ☎ **416/535-3337.** Reservations recommended at dinner. Main courses C$12–$18 (U.S.$9–$13). AE, ER, MC, V. Tues–Sun 5–11pm. Subway: Queen's Park, then streetcar west. ITALIAN.

Pass the small bar up front and enter the low-lit romantically old-fashioned dining room, where the only decor is the oak curio cabinets filled with Barolos and other fine wines, and the mural on the back wall depicting the *vendange.* The meal will start with a dish of black olives, crusty fresh bread, and olive oil. The food is fresh and good, with such daily specials as a *zuppa di pesce* with shrimp, scallops, and mussels in a tomato-lemon broth. Other dishes you might find are mixed grill of seasonal fish and shrimp served with risotto verde and a roast-pepper chutney; or grilled calf's liver with braised red onions, and portobello mushrooms in a balsamic jus. The pastas—penne flavored with Italian sausage, smoked bacon, and onions or the gnocchi made with smoked salmon, sundried tomatoes, dill, vodka, and cream, for example—are all outstanding. Raspberry *clafoutis*, dark chocolate mousse cake, and tiramisu are just a few of the dessert musts.

**KitKat Bar & Grill.** 297 King St. W. ☎ **416/977-4461.** Main courses C$14–$19 (U.S.$10–$14). AE, DC, MC, V. Daily 11:30am–12:30am. Subway: St. Andrew. ITALIAN.

Al Carbone presides over this restaurant at the heart of the theater district, making everyone who passes through the front door feel welcome and special. It's a favorite spot among American and Canadian on-camera personalities, journalists, TV and film producers and directors, and the occasional rock star or Hollywood actor. The room is long and narrow, the decor eclectic (old movie posters and cats), and there's even a live tree rising up in the kitchen preparation area. You'll dine at tables spread with blue gingham tablecloths; the simple, comfort food includes such dishes as lemon chicken, honey garlic back ribs, steak, and several pasta choices. It's eminently friendly and down-home. Singles are also made to feel very welcome. The Italian wine list is fairly priced.

**La Bodega.** 30 Baldwin St. ☎ **416/977-1287.** Reservations recommended for dinner. Main courses C$10–$24 (U.S.$7–$17); prix-fixe special lunch C$13 (U.S.$9), dinner C$18.50 (U.S.$13). AE, DC, ER, MC, V. Mon–Fri noon–2:30pm; Mon–Sat 5–10:30pm. Subway: St. Patrick. FRENCH.

Ensconced in an elegant town house, La Bodega, 2 blocks south of College and 2 blocks west of University Avenue, has been in business for more than 25 years. It's still a neighborhood favorite for its fine fresh food, moderate prices, and very comfortable atmosphere. The main menu features traditional French dishes—veal medallions with a morel mushroom sauce and filet mignon seasoned with a foie gras red-wine sauce are two examples—as well as a pasta of the day and usually a game dish. Every day, the specials, usually inspired by the freshest produce at the market, are written on the blackboard menu. There are usually three or four interesting choices, including several fresh fish dishes, such as horseradish-encrusted monkfish. The best bet of all, though, is the prix-fixe dinner for C$18.50 (U.S.$13), offering a choice of two set menus—one meat, the other fish—with soup or salad and tea or coffee. At lunchtime, when the restaurant is especially popular, lighter fare is served, and a prix-fixe lunch is available for C$13 (U.S.$9).

The dining rooms are quite fetching—the walls are graced with French tapestries, and the windows have swag curtains. French music adds a certain Gallic air. There's a definite glow about the place. In summer, the shaded floral-decorated patio, with umbrella-sheltered faux-marble tables, is a popular dining spot.

**Langolino Wine Bar & Grill.** 50C Clinton St. at College St. ☎ **416/530-4710.** Main courses C$9–$15 (U.S.$6–$11). AE, ER, MC, V. Sun–Thurs 11am–11pm, Fri–Sat 11am–midnight. Subway: Queen's Park, then streetcar west. LIGHT FARE.

This restaurant/wine bar has a warm Provençal glow about it with its burnt-orange walls and tile floors. The antiqued mural adds a lot to the atmosphere too. It's a casual place where you sense you can linger over coffee or a drink. The cuisine is plain: fettuccine alfredo or linguine with grilled vegetables in a tomato sauce and other pasta dishes, or veal or chicken in a lemon sauce or a simple grilled salmon. Their Sunday brunch features Eggs Benedict and Eggs Florentine beginning at C$5 (U.S.$3.55).

**✪ Le Select.** 328 Queen St. W. ☎ **416/596-6405.** Reservations recommended. Main courses average C$9 (U.S.$6) at lunch, C$13–$18 (U.S.$9–$13) at dinner; fixed-price meal C$20

(U.S.$14). AE, DC, MC, V. Mon–Thurs 11:30am–11:30pm, Fri–Sat 11:30am–midnight, Sun noon–10:30pm. Subway: Osgoode. FRENCH.

One of Queen Street's longest-lasting bistros, Le Select still attracts a mixed crowd of well-heeled artists and professionals. They come for the Left-Bank atmosphere, created by the authentic zinc bar, numerous French posters, French-style breakfronts, fringed fabric lampshades over the tables, and jazz music in the background.

Another draw is the moderately priced, French bistro food—from mussels steamed in white wine and shallots to *bavette aux echalottes,* or confit de canard served with an orange sauce. Most dishes, such as the fillet of salmon with basil, lemon, and ginger sauce, are under C$16 (U.S.$11). The wine list is well rounded.

**Left Bank.** 567 Queen St. W., just east of Portland St. on the south side of the street. ☎ **416/504-1626.** Reservations recommended for dinner. Main courses C$16–$26 (U.S.$11–$19). AE, DC, ER, MC, V. Tues–Thurs 6–10pm, Fri–Sat 6–11pm. Subway: Osgoode, then streetcar west. FUSION.

The heavy tapestries and ornate carved French doors and bar give this restaurant a rich, renaissance feel that's more akin to the Loire Valley than to the Left Bank. The cuisine mixes classical French with nouvelle and other flavors from the Caribbean and Asia. The 10 or so main courses range from fettuccine with black tiger shrimp, roasted red peppers, oyster mushrooms, and saffron marjoram butter; lamb sirloin with minted rhubarb jus; or salmon trout with a tomato and porcini mushroom fumé. To start, try the beer-glazed wild mushroom and pancetta mille feuille with Parmesan cheese and a spiced smoked-corn salad. The wine list offers a selection mainly of California and French wines. The crowd is less Queen Street and composed more of conservative 20- or 30-somethings, with the occasional celebrity visitor in the brocade and satin VIP room. There's a bar/billiards room downstairs.

**Masa.** 205 Richmond St. W. ☎ **416/977-9519.** Reservations recommended. Sushi from C$2.60 (U.S.$1.85) per piece; dinners C$14–$39 (U.S.$10–$28). AE, DC, MC, V. Mon–Fri noon–2:30pm; Mon–Sat 5–11pm, Sun 5–10pm. Subway: Osgoode. JAPANESE.

Well known to Toronto aficionados of Japanese cuisine, Masa offers some of the most authentic Japanese food in the city. Seat yourself at the sushi bar and choose from a huge assortment, or dine Western- or tatami-style. Sake containers, Japanese prints, fans, and screens are scattered around the large room. There's a full range of appetizers—broiled squid, oysters in rice vinegar, and fiddleheads with sesame sauce, to name just a few—or you can preface your dinner with one of the many fascinating soups—Tororo seaweed soup, for instance. The best deals, though, are the fixed-price dinners, which include clear soup, a small appetizer, rice, and such main courses as salmon teriyaki, raw tuna sashimi, or garlic beef yakiniku. Don't miss the *mitsu mame* dessert—seaweed jelly with black peas.

**✪ Mildred Pierce.** 99 Sudbury St. ☎ **416/588-5695.** Reservations not accepted. Main courses C$14–$19 (U.S.$10–$14). ER, MC, V. Mon–Fri noon–3pm, Sun 11am–3pm; Sun–Thurs 6–10pm, Fri–Sat 6–11pm. Subway: Osgoode, then take streetcar west to Dovercourt. Walk south on Dovercourt, then take a right on Sudbury. The restaurant is located on the left at the back of a parking lot attached to Studio 99. FRENCH/CONTINENTAL/ECLECTIC.

This atmospheric, offbeat spot, which resembles a movie set, is frequented by in-the-know locals and is well worth seeking out. From the handful of tables outside, there's a great view of the CN Tower and the downtown skyline. The outdoor terrace is awaft in billowing cloth screens and climbing shrubs. Inside, the room has a theatrical flair with scrim curtains and vast murals of a large Roman feast featuring the apparent likenesses of the owner, the electrician, and other local foodies, including a critic or two. The glowing faux-copper tables are set on a mosaic floor.

Out of the open kitchen comes a variety of fine daily specials, such as a loin of pork with a cabernet-cassis sauce and chutney. The menu features 10 or so main courses that range from linguine tossed in garlic, chilies, white wine, and olive oil, with cherry tomatoes, oregano, and grated Parmesan, to beef filet with a red-wine thyme jus. Start with the grilled calamari with roasted tomato confit and black- and green-olive tapenades, or the delicious warm chevre in vine leaves with roasted red peppers, herbed olive oil, and parchment flat bread.

Depending on your passions, you'll want to save some room for dessert. I can recommend the rhubarb-meringue tartlet with strawberry-rhubarb sauce, but you might prefer the chocolate-pistachio pâté served with white and dark chocolate sauce, or the profiteroles filled with vanilla ice cream and drizzled with chocolate sauce. The reasonably priced wine list is good, and an excellent brunch menu is also served Sundays.

**N'Awlins.** 299 King St. W. ☎ **416/595-1958.** Reservations recommended for dinner. Main courses C$16–$22 (U.S.$11–$16). AE, DC, MC, V. Mon–Fri noon–11pm, Sat 5pm–1am, Sun 5pm–midnight. Subway: St. Andrew. CAJUN/ITALIAN.

Jazz is played here every night, and the walls are studded, top to bottom, with photographs of historic and contemporary jazz greats. There's a long, narrow bar in back and outdoor dining, too. The cuisine complements the ambiance—just take the blackened chicken breast with a sweet honey glaze and grilled Cajun chicken in a Creole sauce, for example. Other dishes are more eclectic, such as tiger shrimp sautéed with garlic, leeks, and white wine on a bed of rice, or veal in a spinach and mushroom pesto sauce. There are pasta dishes, too. The Cajun/Italian combined influence on the cuisine is most apparent on the appetizer menu: Cajun calamari, anyone? This is a pre- and posttheatergoer's favorite.

**Palavrion.** 270 Front St. W. ☎ **416/979-0060.** Reservations accepted. Most items C$12–$16 (U.S.$9–$11). AE, DC, ER, MC, V. Sun–Thurs 11:30am–11pm, Fri–Sat 11:30am–1am. Subway: Union. CONTINENTAL.

This huge (380-seat) concept restaurant has to be one of the most expensive restaurant stage sets ever constructed, certainly the most expensive in Toronto. It cost C$6.5 million to create, and the results are dramatic, to say the least. The original concept, which mimicked Movenpick Marché, has been modified so that it now functions as a full-service restaurant offering light dishes, noodles, and such fish dishes as poached or grilled salmon. The prime attractions come from the Swiss grill—steak-frites and bratwurst, for example. People still flock here, attracted by the exciting, inspired decor featuring brilliant wall colors—orange, yellow, and turquoise—which are further illuminated with trompe l'oeil art. Huge light fixtures that look like old-style microphones loom over the bar area. In the area serving dessert and gelato, the floors are studded with individually crafted tiles. Even the bathrooms feature tiles in spectacularly different and inspiring his. Upstairs, there's an Homage to Dalí table designed by French tile artist Alain Vagh, which is reserved for special guests.

**Peter Pan.** 373 Queen St. W. ☎ **416/593-0917.** Reservations recommended for parties of 6 or more. Main courses C$8–$17 (U.S.$6–$12). AE, MC, V. Mon–Sat noon–4:30pm; Sun–Wed 5pm–midnight, Thurs–Sat 6pm–1am; brunch Sun noon–4pm. Subway: Osgoode. FUSION.

Another venerable survivor on Queen Street, Peter Pan still delivers exciting, moderately priced cuisine in a stylish 1930s ambiance, complete with a tin ceiling and high-back booths lit by art deco sconces. The patrons are mostly bourgeois boomers. On the menu, you'll find pastas and entrees often flavored with Asian, Caribbean, and Mexican herbs and spices. You might start with mussels in a lime, cilantro, and bourbon broth with fennel and gingered black beans, followed by a breast of chicken with apple chipotle marmalade, or New York strip loin with wild mushrooms, charred tomato, and rosemary. Desserts are always enticing, such as a pear tart with almond cream, or a Brazilian fig tart with kirsch sabayon.

**Pink Pearl.** 207 Queen's Quay W. ☎ **416/203-1233.** Reservations recommended. Main courses C$10–$26 (U.S.$7–$19). AE, DC, MC, V. Daily 11am–3pm and 5–11pm. Subway: Union, then LRT. CHINESE.

An attractive Chinese restaurant with views of Lake Ontario, Pink Pearl has been a local favorite for many years because of the quality of its Cantonese-Szechuan food and the comfort of its decor. It caters more to Western palates than do the restaurants of Chinatown. To start, there are several hors d'oeuvres and a dozen soups to select from, including shark's-fin soup with chicken. The specialties of the house range from braised lobster with ginger and green onion, and sliced chicken sautéed with pineapple and green peppers, to shrimp Szechuan style. There's an intriguing dish called Rainbow Chopped in Crystal Fold, consisting of finely chopped pork, Chinese sausage, mushroom, bamboo shoots, water chestnuts, celery, and carrot sautéed and served in crisp lettuce. The wine list is French and Italian.

Another Pink Pearl can be found at 110 Bloor St. W. (☎ **416/975-1155**).

**St. Tropez.** 315 King St. W. ☎ **416/591-3600.** Reservations recommended for dinner. Main courses C$15–$20 (U.S.$11–$14). AE, DC, ER, MC, V. Mon–Wed 11:30am–11pm, Thurs–Sat 11:30am–midnight. Subway: St. Andrew. FRENCH.

Stucco, mock shutters, and pale washes of color effect a country-French atmosphere at St. Tropez. In summer, the back courtyard, with its awning, vine-encrusted walls, and statuary, is appealing to the mixture of tourists and local theatergoers who dine here. The bistro fare consists of such dishes as grilled salmon with mango salsa, chicken with honey rosemary glaze, and, of course, steak-frites and bouillabaisse. For dessert, try the classic crème brûlée or the *clafoutis*.

**Taro Grill.** 492 Queen St. W. (just west of Denison Ave. on the north side). ☎ **416/504-1320.** Reservations not accepted. Main courses C$13–$18 (U.S.$9–$13). AE, MC, V. Daily noon–4pm; Sun–Thurs 6–11pm, Fri–Sat 6pm–midnight. Subway: Osgoode, then streetcar west. FRENCH/MEDITERRANEAN.

This is a small, distinctly hip spot with a mosaic floor, red walls, and a short menu. Head past the small bar and kitchen up front to the small dining area behind. Expect pastas, pizzas, and a daily fish special, in addition to six or so entrees like stuffed chicken dijonnaise, or braised rack of lamb with a rosemary glaze. Appetizers are similarly straightforward—a warm goat cheese and walnut salad and steamed mussels are two examples.

**✪ Trattoria Giancarlo.** 41–43 Clinton St. (at College). ☎ **416/533-9619.** Reservations strongly recommended. Pasta and rice C$12–$14 (U.S.$9–$10); main courses C$17–$24 (U.S.$12–$17). AE, MC, V. Mon–Sat 6–10:30pm. Subway: Queen's Park, then streetcar west. ITALIAN.

This restaurant is one of my all-time favorite spots in Little Italy, if not in the city, and I find myself returning here time after time. It's small and cozy, and thoroughly Italian, with an outside dining area in summer. The tablecloths are covered with butcher paper, the floor is black-and-white tile, and the background music is opera or jazz.

For a real treat, start with the fresh wild mushrooms broiled with herbs, garlic, Parmesan, and oil; or *crostini chiantigiana* (mattone toasts topped with fresh ricotta, prosciutto, and Chianti-caramelized figs). Follow with any one of six pasta dishes—

one is linguini with oven-roasted tomatoes, sweet onions, and shrimp in a white-wine broth—or the risotto of the day. The grilled fish and meats are superb, like the tender lamb marinated in grappa, lemon, and olive oil; or the swordfish grilled with fresh mint, garlic, and olive oil. For dessert, try the tiramisu, the crème caramel, or the delicious chocolate-raspberry tartufo. The experience is always memorable, and the welcome is real.

**Whistling Oyster Seafood Cafe.** 11 Duncan St. ☎ **416/598-7707.** Reservations recommended for lunch only. Main courses C$14–$20 (U.S.$10–$14). AE, DC, ER, MC, V. Mon–Sat 11am–midnight, Sun 4–11pm. Subway: Osgoode. SEAFOOD.

Families and middle-class Torontonians head to the Whistling Oyster for its happy oyster hour and a happy dim sum hour on Sundays from 4:30 to 10pm. They enjoy 20 or so appetizers, including a variety of fresh clams and oysters, and such dishes as steamed clams in wine, tomato, and garlic; and blackened tiger shrimp with mangoes and Thai coleslaw. Most items are under C$4; everything is under C$7. Be sure to check out the glittering mermaid suspended over the central bar; she's a conversation piece.

## INEXPENSIVE

**The Bagel.** 285 College St. ☎ **416/966-7555.** Everything less than C$10 (U.S.$7). V. Mon–Fri 7am–9pm, Sat 8am–6pm, Sun 8am–5pm. Subway: Queen's Park. DELI.

You have to be a member of the "clean plate club" if you want to eat at The Bagel—otherwise the waitresses will scold you with "C'mon, eat already." Blintzes, bagels, lox, and cream cheese are the tops at this characterful spot. Sandwiches and dinner plates—Southern fried chicken, sweet-and-sour meatballs, fried fillet of sole—are also available.

**The Eating Counter.** 21–23 Baldwin St. ☎ **416/977-7028.** Reservations accepted for parties of 4–10 only. Main courses C$7–$13 (U.S.$5–$9). AE, DC, MC, V. Daily 11am–11pm. Subway: St. Patrick. CHINESE.

Lines extend into the street from The Eating Counter, near McCaul and Dundas streets. Many of the eager patrons here are Chinese who relish the perfectly cooked Cantonese fare—crisp, fresh vegetables; noodles; barbecue specialties; and, a particular favorite, fresh lobster with ginger and green onions. Ask the waiter to recommend the freshest items of the day. The decor is nonexistent, but the food is good.

**Free Times Café.** 320 College St. between Major and Robert. ☎ **416/967-1078.** Daily specials C$7–$8 (U.S.$5–$6). AE, MC, V. Mon–Sat 11:30am–12:45am, Sun 11:30am–10:45pm. Subway: Queen's Park, then streetcar west. VEGETARIAN/LIGHT FARE.

The Free Times Café has a casual, avant-garde ambiance. Original art is on display, and folk and original acoustic music is featured nightly. It attracts a college-age and older crowd that appreciates the vegetarian fare. Everything is reasonably priced, and the menu includes such daily specials as chicken Dijonnaise, scallop and veggie stir-fry, and various pasta dishes. On Sundays, the place is filled with Jewish families drawn by the brunch spread called "Bella, did you eat?," a buffet spread of blintzes, potato latkes, salmon patties, lox and onions, beet salad, gefilte fish, and more—all for C$11 (U.S.$8).

**Il Fornello.** 214 King St. W. ☎ **416/977-2855.** Reservations recommended. Main courses C$10–$14 (U.S.$7–$10). MC, V. Mon–Fri noon–10pm, Sat 5–11pm. Subway: St. Andrew. ITALIAN.

Il Fornello is famous for its 20 varieties of pizza, cooked in a wood-fired clay oven, and for a variety of popular Italian dishes—pasta, veal, and chicken. Also featured is an alternative menu with nondairy, nonyeast, and low-cholesterol items. There are several other locations, too.

**Lee Garden.** 331 Spadina Ave. between St. Andrews and Nassau sts. ☎ **416/593-9524.** Reservations not accepted. Main courses C$9–$16 (U.S.$6–$11). MC, V. Daily 4pm–midnight. Subway: Spadina, then LRT south. CHINESE.

Lee Garden is known for its seafood specialties—Dungeness crab or lobster with ginger and green onions; tiger shrimp with fresh pineapple; fresh oysters, clams, squid, and abalone; and steamed cod with black-bean sauce. The menu also features such pork, beef, and chicken dishes as honey-orange back ribs, chicken in black-bean sauce, and beef with chili peppers. But it's the fish dishes that win acclaim from most Torontonians, and rightly so—they're sublime.

**Kalendar.** 546 College St., west of Bathurst ☎ **416/923-4138.** Main courses C$8–$11 (U.S.$6–$8). MC, V. Mon–Fri 11am–midnight, Sat 10:30am–midnight, Sun 10:30am–11pm (the bar stays open later). Subway: Queen's Park, then streetcar west. LIGHT FARE.

Kalendar conjures a Paris-in-the-'20s air with smoke-colored walls, jazz moaning in the background, and a large brass coffeemaker. People linger over great bowls of coffee or else enjoy tasty flat pastry scrolls filled with everything from Havarti cheese, roasted red peppers, and fresh basil to chicken breast, snow peas, and julienne carrots with a sweet curry sauce. The nan topped with a variety of ingredients from plum tomatoes to smoked salmon with cream cheese dill capters and red onion is also good. There's pizza and pasta, too.

**Movenpick Marché.** On the galleria of BCE Place, Front St. W. ☎ **416/366-8986.** Reservations not accepted. Most items C$7–$9 (U.S.$5–$6). AE, DC, MC, V. Daily 7:30am–2am. Subway: Union. CONTINENTAL.

This large restaurant, with a variety of seating areas, is a relatively recent innovation in food merchandising that attracts an eclectic crowd of office workers and professionals as well as tourists and other curiosity seekers. Pick up a tab at the entrance and stroll through the bustling market, where various stands, carts, and trolleys display fresh foods and ingredients. Stop at the rosticceria and select a meat for the chef to cook. Pause at the seafood and raw bar and pick out a fish for the grill, or peruse the pasta bar. Then wander over to the *bistro de vin* and check out the cases of wine, or enjoy a *boccalino* of one of the open wines. This is a dependable place for breakfast, lunch, or dinner. If you hate standing and waiting in line for a meal, don't go at peak dining hours, when the place is mobbed, noisy, and frenetic.

**Queen Mother Cafe.** 208 Queen St. W. ☎ **416/598-4719.** Reservations not accepted. Main courses C$10–$14 (U.S.$7–$10). AE, MC, V. Daily 11:30am–1am. Subway: Osgoode. FUSION.

A simple restaurant with a granite bar, polished wood tables, and bentwood chairs, this is another longtime favorite on Queen Street. Desserts are displayed in a glass case in the back. The menu offers such Laotian-Thai items as crispy chicken with garlic, coriander, and black peppercorn served with lime coriander sauce, or crispy salmon with a coating of curry, turmeric, and coriander, finished in a curried white-wine and coconut-milk sauce, plus Asian-inspired appetizers and salads. The cafe has outdoor dining in summer.

**Red Tomato.** 321 King St. W. ☎ **416/971-6626.** Main courses C$8–$13 (U.S.$6–$9). AE, DC, MC, V. Mon–Fri 11:30am–12:30am, Sat noon–1am, Sun 4:30–10pm. Subway: St. Andrew. CANADIAN.

At night, this popular downstairs bar/restaurant with a large central bar, video screens, wild murals, and exposed plumbing is virtually filled to capacity. The youngish crowd feasts on an array of pasta dishes, including fettuccine with smoked salmon, tomato cream, and vodka; jalapeño linguine with rotisserie chicken, mushrooms, sundried tomato, wine, and jerk cream; and gnocchi with four cheeses. About eight or nine pizzas are also offered, along with the specialty of the house, hot rocks cuisine, which is cooked on a granite hot-rock grill. Six or so dishes are prepared this way, including green peppercorn salmon cooked tandoori style and honey-garlic-glazed lamb.

**Rivoli.** 332 Queen St. W. ☎ **416/597-0794.** Reservations not accepted. Main courses C$10–$15 (U.S.$7–$11). AE, MC, V. Daily 11:30–2am. Subway: Osgoode. CONTINENTAL.

Rivoli attracts a mixed, avant-garde artsy and boomer crowd. Its dinner menu features nine or so eclectic specialties such as *yuhukai,* which is a chicken breast stuffed with a pesto made from macadamia nuts and thai basil and served with red plum-wine ginger sauce, or liberation lamb—lamb chops marinated in garlic, balsamic vinegar, oil, and herbs and finished with a teriyaki cabernet glaze, or the signature burger with caramelized onions served on challah. Three or so daily specials supplement the menu—usually one pasta, one meat, and one fish dish. The lunch menu features sandwiches such as grilled cheese made with challah or pita stuffed with falafel. In summer, the sidewalk patio is jammed. There's pool upstairs, and good nightly entertainment in the back room, plus a video bar. The dining-room decor is appropriately surreal and basic black. Seating is not designed for comfort, and noise can make easy conversation problematic.

**Tiger Lily's.** 257 Queen St. W. ☎ **416/977-5499.** Reservations not accepted. Main courses C$7–$11 (U.S.$5–$8). AE, MC, V. Sun–Tues 11:30am–9pm, Wed 11:30am–10pm, Thurs 11:30am–11pm. Subway: Osgoode. ASIAN.

This casual noodle house attracts a youthful, health-conscious crowd that enjoys putting together its own Asian-style soup combinations and noodle dishes. At lunch, diners select cafeteria-style from the different-colored cardboard menus on the wall behind the counter. At dinner, there's table service and a menu featuring about a dozen noodle plates. Try the delicious mixed seafood in coconut or black-bean sauce, or the Vietnamese-style noodle dish made with wide rice noodles in a citrus-tomato sauce fragrant with lemongrass and chilies and garnished with fish. Beer and wine only.

**Toby's Goodeats.** Eaton Centre (Yonge St. between Dundas and Queen sts.). ☎ **416/591-6994.** Main courses C$5–$10 (U.S.$3.55–$7). AE, MC, V. Tues–Sat 11:30am–1am, Sun–Mon 11:30am–midnight. Subway: Dundas. BURGERS.

Capture those childhood dreams of milkshakes, Coke floats, and a good burger along with the rest of the crowd at Toby's Goodeats, a 1950s-style hamburger joint. The decor suits: a schizophrenic combination of Formica tables, cookie jars, funky posters, and the traditional brick-and-plants look. It's very crowded at lunchtime. Besides the burgers, there are salads, sandwiches, pizzas, and pastas.

Toby's Goodeats can also be found at 725 Yonge St. (☎ **416/925-9908**), 542 Church St. (☎ **416/929-0411**), and First Canadian Place (☎ **416/366-3953**).

**Vanipha.** 193 Augusta Ave. ☎ **416/340-0491.** Most items C$8–$13 (U.S.$6–$9). V. Mon–Sat noon–11pm. Subway: Queen's Park, then streetcar west. LAOTIAN/THAI.

A Laotian/Thai restaurant in a plain but comfortable step-down storefront, Vanipha serves authentic Southeast Asian cuisine. After indulging in one of the tempting appetizers, like the steamed mussels with Thai basil in a spicy garlic sauce, try one of the different curries—red, green, or yellow—or one of the more exotic dishes like the Gai Haw Bai Toey, marinated chicken with garlic, coriander, sesame oil, soy sauce, and whiskey wrapped in pandan leaves. Now that's a parcel of real flavor. Noodle and stir-fry dishes complete the menu. And there's also a special seasonal treat—Thai sticky rice.

**Wah Sing.** 47 Baldwin St. ☎ **416/599-8822.** Reservations accepted for large parties only. Most items C$8–$16 (U.S.$6–$11). AE, MC, V. Sun–Thurs 11:30am–10pm, Fri–Sat 11:30am–11:30pm. Subway: St. Patrick. CHINESE.

People come here to enjoy terrific seafood at reasonable prices—especially the lobster special, which is two lobsters for C$16 (with a minimum additional purchase of C$10)! There's plenty of other shellfish on the menu, like the mussels with garlic and black-bean sauce or the oysters with ginger and green onions, along with traditional Chinese fare, too. The decor is minimal, but the food makes for crowds. Expect to wait.

# 4 Downtown East

## EXPENSIVE

**Biagio.** 157 King St. E. ☎ **416/366-4040.** Reservations recommended. Pasta and risotto C$12–$16 (U.S.$9–$11); main courses C$16–$32 (U.S.$11–$23). AE, DC, MC, V. Mon–Fri noon–2:30pm; Mon–Sat 6–10:30pm. Subway: King. ITALIAN.

This restaurant has one of the most beautiful, inviting courtyards in the whole city, as well as attractive high-ceilinged dining rooms with large, well-spaced tables that are perfect for carrying on deal-making conversations comfortably—a feature that endears it to the power crowd that frequents Biagio. The kitchen serves some of the best Italian food in the city, with a menu that features an array of extra-special pasta and risotto dishes. The lasagna arrives in a light-pink sauce studded with salmon, scallops, and shrimp, and the tagliolini comes with choice morsels of lobster. Risotto can be prepared with porcini, saffron, Gorgonzola, and parsley, or shrimp and arugula. For the more robust appetite, there's *bistecca al barolo e funghi*, or a veal chop with wine, butter, and sage. To start, try the delicious carpaccio served with lemon, celery, arugula, and Parmesan cheese with a balsamic vinegar glaze; or the salmon with fennel, pink peppers, and orange.

**Galileo.** 193 King St. E. ☎ **416/363-6888.** Main courses C$15–$24 (U.S.$11–$17). AE, DC, MC, V. Mon–Fri noon–3pm; Mon–Sat 5:30–11pm. Subway: King. ITALIAN.

This handsome, modern Italian restaurant makes a statement with its curved-back chairs, impressive wine displays all set against lilac-colored walls, and dark-blue ceiling. The cuisine is innovative and inspirational, often using Asian spices and flavors combined with traditional Italian ingredients, such as rack of lamb with smoked garlic crisp, tamarind paste, and rosemary. Fish is also treated in exciting ways. Try the applewood-grilled salmon with coriander mashed potato. There's an expansive list of appetizers—from smoked venison carpaccio with salsa verde, pecorino cheese, capers, red onion, and olive oil to poached pear stuffed with sundried tomatoes, plum slivers, pancetta, roasted cashews, and field mushrooms in a veal jus with a hint of cream. For dessert, don't miss the tiramisu or the white-chocolate tart. The wine list is very extensive.

**La Maquette.** 111 King St. E. ☎ **416/366-8191.** Reservations recommended. Main courses C$16–$26 (U.S.$11–$19). AE, MC, V. Mon–Fri noon–2:30pm; Mon–Sat 5:30–10:30pm. Subway: King. CONTINENTAL.

At La Maquette, the dining rooms have a romantic ambiance. The main room has a fireplace; there's also a light and airy solarium overlooking the sculpture garden. The cuisine is a modern twist of Northern Italian, Californian, and French traditions. Start your meal with portobello mushroom and grilled eggplant, layered with goat cheese

# A Passion for Patios

By the time spring rolls around, the citizens of Toronto are desperate to lounge outside in the sunshine for as much of the day as possible. This may account for the city's profusion of patios, from tiny nooks tucked away in backyards to the vast expanse of patios that fill whole sidewalks, like those on John Street between Adelaide and Richmond, including **Al Frisco's,** 133 John St., and **Montana,** 145 John St. Perhaps the Torontonian passion for patios has something to do with the length and bitterness of Canadian winters.

To get you started on your own quest for the perfect patio, here are a few more of my favorites:

At the **St. Tropez,** 315 King St. W., you step through an archway into a brick-floored courtyard covered with a striped tent-style awning. The vine-covered walls and sculpted figure serving as a planter make this a lovely romantic spot. In a similar vein, across town there's also **Biagio,** 157 King St. E., which has to possess one of the most fetching courtyards in the city, complete with a gurgling classical fountain.

For a flavor of South Beach or the tropics, there are several downtown patios worth seeking out. My favorite is at **Alice Fazooli's,** 294 Adelaide St. W. (see page 184). From Adelaide Street, walk down the passageway lined with hibiscus and you'll find a large bar and terrace sheltered by what looks like camouflage cloth. Here in the evenings you can be serenaded by a mariachi band while the fountain plays and, if need be, the flames of a fire flicker, lighting up the jungle mural.

Cabana-style bars, a fountain and tropical plants, and a wonderful view are the lures at **the Oasis** atop Wayne Gretzky's, 99 Blue Jays Way. The rooftop and ground-floor patios at **Bamboo,** 312 Queen St. W., are other downtown hot spots that are easy on the eye with their tropical murals, glass brick styling, and fountains.

In Yorkville, rooftop patios can be found at **Hemingways,** 142 Cumberland St.; while the patio at the front and back of **Sassafraz,** 100 Cumberland St., is another crowd pleaser.

The Danforth and Little Italy are the neighborhoods where patios really take over. Along the Danforth, they are large and lively and right out front, except at **Lolita's Lust.** In Little Italy, along College Street, they are equally large and lively and placed square out front, like the one at **Cafe Diplomatico,** 594 College St., but they can also be tucked away romantically in the back, as at **Souz Dal,** 636 College St., and **Wild Indigo,** 607 College St.

Wherever you find yourself in Toronto in summer, you'll find a patio. Even if you don't see one at first, always ask, because it's axiomatic that there will be one somewhere, even if it's only a few square feet. Patios come in all shapes, sizes, and styles; somehow or other, you can bet your life that the management of any dining or drinking establishment will have figured out how to carve out a patio somewhere on the premises. So go ahead, suss out your own secret patios throughout the city.

and served on smoked tomato sauce; or pan-fried foie gras served with a port wine reduction. Follow with one of the 10 or so entrees that might include grilled tuna loin on a red-wine beurre blanc; or a grilled roast beef tenderloin served with a foie gras sauce and roast garlic mash. The menu also features pastas and risottos—including a delicious smoked pheasant-filled ravioli in roasted garlic Alfredo; and a

Cajun risotto made with chicken, sausage, and shrimp with bell peppers, tomato, and spice. The three-course pretheater menu is an excellent value at C$20 (U.S.$14). In summer, the outdoor dining area overlooks a small sculpture park with a particularly pleasant waterfall.

**Nami Japanese Seafood.** 55 Adelaide St. E. ☎ **416/362-7373.** Reservations recommended Thurs–Sat. Sushi C$4–$6; main courses C$12–$29 (U.S.$9–$21). AE, DC, MC, V. Mon–Fri noon–2:30pm; Mon–Sat 6–10:30pm. Subway: King. JAPANESE.

An upscale, expensive, and ultrastylish restaurant, Nami attracts wealthy Japanese Torontonians and businesspeople. The prime attraction is the fresh sushi and sashimi. Up front, there's a sushi bar, and behind it, attractive booth seating or traditional tatami-style dining.

Start with *kaki*, *ebi fry* (oysters or shrimp), or beef sashimi—thinly sliced beef lightly coated and served with *ponzu* sauce. For a real treat, order the *tenshin* bento, which provides an assortment of sushi and sashimi; or the Love Boat, which includes salad, miso, tempura, sushi, sashimi, salmon teriyaki, deep-fried chicken, and fruits.

**The Senator.** 249 and 253 Victoria St. ☎ **416/364-7517.** Reservations recommended for dinner in the dining room. Main courses C$8–$15 (U.S.$6–$11) at lunch, C$18–$24 (U.S.$13–$17) at dinner. AE, DC, MC, V. Diner: Mon–Fri 7:30am–8:30pm, Sat 8am–8:30pm, Sun 8am–3pm. Steak house: Tues–Fri 11:30am–2:30pm; Tues–Thurs 5–11:30pm, Fri 5pm–midnight, Sat 5pm–12:30am, Sun 5–10pm. Subway: Dundas. STEAK.

In the diner, green leatherette booths, tiled floors, and down-home cuisine take you back to the 1940s. Here, you can still order a full breakfast of bacon and eggs, beans, home fries, and toast for C$5 (U.S.$3.55). The luncheon menu features such comfort dishes as meat loaf, macaroni and cheese, fish-and-chips, liver and onions, burgers with fried onions and corn relish, and creamy rice pudding. And best of all, you can perch on a stool and order up a rich old-fashioned milkshake.

The adjacent dining room is decked out in mahogany, mirrors, and stained glass, with enclosed velvet booths. Theatergoers mingle with an artsy crowd waiting to attend the jazz-cabaret on the top floor. Some of the dishes served in the diner make an appearance here, but the prime attractions are steaks and chops, even though a few chicken and fish dishes, such as a chicken breast with rosemary lemon sauce and a grilled swordfish with a roasted red-pepper coulis, have also found their way onto the menu. Find room for the desserts, which are good. The fine wine list is primarily Canadian-American.

**ZooM Caffe & Bar.** 18 King St. E. ☎ **416/861-9872.** Main courses C$15–$27 (U.S.$11–$19). AE, DC, ER, MC, V. Mon–Fri noon–3pm, Mon–Tues 5–11pm, Wed–Sat 5pm–midnight. Subway: King. ITALIAN.

A soaring space, this is the latest darling of the Bay Street crowd. Ultramodern, with wrought-iron chairs with snail-like backs and spiked globes for lighting, it's very a la mode. The bar is stocked with wine from floor to ceiling and has inviting upholstered modern Italian seating. A large mirror hangs on the back wall of the restaurant to allow people to see the tables below. Specialties include a succulent banana-leaf-wrapped sea bass in black-bean moho sauce with whipped malanga, or spice-rubbed pork loin with a chipotle plum sauce accompanied by grilled pineapple, sauerkraut, and chili potato hash. To start, try the multi-mushroom tart with a zinfandel glaze, or the soup or salads.

# MODERATE

**Montréal Bistro and Jazz Club.** 65 Sherbourne St. (at Adelaide). ☎ **416/363-0179.** Reservations recommended, especially on weekends. Main courses C$10–$19 (U.S.$7–$14).

AE, MC, V. Mon–Fri 11:30am–3pm; Mon–Thurs 6–11pm, Fri–Sat 6pm–midnight. Subway: King, then streetcar east. QUÉBECOIS.

Montréal, at Adelaide and Sherbourne, is the place to try Québecois specialties, such as the famous pea soup and the *tourtière*, a tasty meat pie. The food is good and reasonably priced. Lunch specials include soup or salad and such main courses as chicken curry with mango chutney or fusili with oyster mushrooms, snow peas, tomato, and fresh herbs. At night, the specialties include roast duck with maple-syrup glaze or a stir-fry of tiger shrimp. Most items are around C$15 (U.S.$11). For dessert, try the crème caramel with orange zest or the Tia Maria chocolate mousse. To the left of the entrance, you'll find one of Toronto's best jazz clubs.

**Rodney's Oyster House.** 9 Adelaide St. E. ☎ **416/363-8105.** Oysters C$1.35–$3 (U.S.95¢–$2.15), main courses C$13–17 (U.S.$9–$12). AE, DC, MC, V. Mon–Sat 11:30am–midnight. Subway: King. SEAFOOD.

A fun place. Nudge into this basement and select some fresh oysters—the best in the city, according to most—or sample some of the piping-hot chowder from the cauldrons behind the bar. There's a serious drinking scene here, too.

**Spiaggia.** 2318 Queen St. E. ☎ **416/699-4656.** Reservations recommended. Main courses C$14–$16 (U.S.$10–$11). AE, DC, MC, V. Sun–Thurs 5–10pm, Fri–Sat 5–11pm. Subway: Queen, then streetcar east. ITALIAN.

A small, casual Beaches bistro, Spiaggia is filled with tables covered in blue gingham and glass. It caters to a mostly local crowd, with a short blackboard menu that changes daily. The menu usually features about seven pastas, such as gnocchi stuffed with ricotta; or linguine with clams, mussels, shrimp, and scallops in a tomato-basil sauce. In addition, there are usually three main courses featuring veal, chicken, or fish in such dishes as chicken con pesto. Desserts include tiramisu, chocolate-sambucca mousse, and a variety of gelati.

## INEXPENSIVE

**Le Papillon.** 16 Church St. (between Front St. E. and Esplanade). ☎ **416/363-0838.** Reservations recommended on weekends. Crepes C$8–$10 (U.S.$6–$7). AE, DC, MC, V. Tues–Fri noon–2:30pm; Tues–Wed 5–10pm, Thurs 5–11pm, Fri 5pm–midnight; Sat 11:30am–midnight; Sun noon–10pm. Subway: Union. CREPES.

When you arrive, there'll probably be a line of eager folks outside Le Papillon, since this continues to be a popular Toronto fixture, even after 25 years of business. Stucco walls, trees, skylights, and a wood-burning fireplace give it a Mediterranean air, which is completed by blue gingham tablecloths. Although it's primarily a creperie, it also offers such French-Canadian dishes as *cretons* (pork pâté) and *tourtière* (a meat pie of veal, pork, and beef), along with an excellent onion soup (*Bon Appetit* has supposedly requested the recipe three times). Among the 16 savory crepes, there's crêpe Marie Claude (with sausages, apples, and Cheddar cheese), crêpe Continental (chicken, mushrooms, and peppers in béchamel), and one filled with beef bourguignonne. In addition, there are six or so dessert crepes, made with ingredients such as sliced peaches and bananas, or cooked apples and cinnamon.

**Shopsy's.** 33 Yonge St. ☎ **416/365-3333.** Sandwiches and main courses C$7–$13 (U.S.$5–$9). AE, DC, MC, V. Mon–Wed 7am–11pm, Thurs–Fri 7am–midnight, Sat 8am–midnight, Sun 8am–11pm. Subway: Union. DELI.

Toronto's most famous deli was started in the garment district 72 years ago. Today, it's right across from the O'Keefe Centre, sporting a spiffy outdoor patio, arrayed with brilliant yellow umbrellas. They serve huge stuffed deli sandwiches, the most traditional being the corned beef and pastrami. It's a good breakfast spot, too.

**Young Thailand.** 81 Church St. (south of Lombard St.). ☎ **416/368-1368.** Reservations recommended. Main courses C$9–$16 (U.S.$6–$11). AE, DC, MC, V. Mon–Fri 11:30am–2pm; daily 4:30–11pm. Subway: Queen or King. THAI.

This large restaurant with minimal decor serves good Thai cuisine. Beef, pork, chicken, and seafood dishes make up the menu—sliced beef in hot, spicy, thick sauce; slices of chicken with shredded ginger, mushrooms, and onions; and pork with garlic, onions, chili pepper, and sweet basil leaves. Sweet-and-sour fish and spicy shrimp are among the close to 20 seafood dishes. Start with a stimulating *tom kha kai* soup made with coconut milk, lemongrass, chili, and chicken; or with one of the traditional salad or noodle dishes.

There are other branches at **111 Gerrard St. E.** between Jarvis and Church (☎ **416/599-9099**) and **165 John St.** (☎ **416/593-9291**), which is my favorite.

## 5  Midtown West

There's plenty of fine dining in this neighborhood, which includes Yorkville, but because of its many chic and expensive shopping areas, it's not always a pleasant experience. Rents are high, so consequently, prices are high, but the quality doesn't always match. That said, I have included in this section one or two selections that can be relied upon to deliver quality at a decent price.

### VERY EXPENSIVE

✪ **Truffles.** In The Four Seasons Hotel, 21 Avenue Rd. ☎ **416/964-0411.** Reservations recommended. Main courses C$28–$36 (U.S.$20–$26). AE, DC, MC, V. Mon–Sat 6–11pm. Subway: Bay. CONTINENTAL.

Named one of the 10 best hotel restaurants in the world by *Hotel* magazine, and carrying a 5-diamond AAA rating, Truffles is certainly the premier hotel dining room in the city. The room provides a lavish setting for some exquisite Provençal-style cuisine. Fine materials have been used in the design of all the elements—from the marquetry floor that's fashioned from 11,000 pieces of oak, jojoba, and purpleheart wood to the curly maple paneling and the custom-designed cabinets, mirrors, ceramics, and other art pieces. The cuisine is imaginative, fresh, and flavorful. For those who have to watch their diets, the alternative cuisine is a welcome feature on the menu, and not a hardship when you can enjoy steamed salmon with roasted five-roots fricassee and carrot-cumin sauce. Otherwise, you can start with the ravioli of Hudson Valley foie gras confit with wild mushrooms, potato, and garlic sauce; or the malpeque oysters with warm caviar-chive sauce. Follow with the pan-seared five-spice duck breast, shiitake mushroom, and potato cannelloni with lemongrass jus; or the seared veal tenderloin with garlic vintage balsamic sauce; or the oven-baked halibut with tomato caper sauce. At the conclusion, treat yourself to the spectacular flourless butter chocolate dome with passion-fruit coulis.

### EXPENSIVE

**Bistro 990.** 990 Bay St. (at St. Joseph). ☎ **416/921-9990.** Reservations required. Main courses C$17–$30 (U.S.$12–$21). AE, ER, MC, V. Mon–Fri noon–3pm; Mon–Sat 5–11pm. Subway: Museum or Wellesley. FRENCH.

Bistro 990 could have been air-lifted from the French provinces with its French doors, lace curtains, and outdoor cafe tables. The cuisine ranges from such traditional bistro dishes as roasted chicken with mashed potatoes, or steak and frites with Roquefort or bordelaise sauce, to stuffed duck with sage and apricot in a red-currant glaze. Among the appetizers, the steamed Prince Edward Island mussels in a red-tomato curry broth with ginger and fresh cilantro are extra-special, as are the escargots sautéed

# Midtown Toronto Dining

Annapurna ❶
Arlequin ⑫
Bistro 990 ㉒
Bloor St. Diner ⑳
Boba ⑬
Borgo Antico ⑰
Boulevard Café ❺
Il Posto ⑭
Indian Rice Factory ❷
Jacques' Bistro du Parc ⑯
Joso's ⑪
Kensington Kitchen ❻
Lakes ⑩
Le Paradis ❸
Messis ❽
Mori ⑱
Movenpick Bistretto ⑮
Opus ❹
Pangaea ⑲
Prego della Piazza ㉒
Splendido ❼
Thai Magic ❾
Truffles ㉑

1-0338

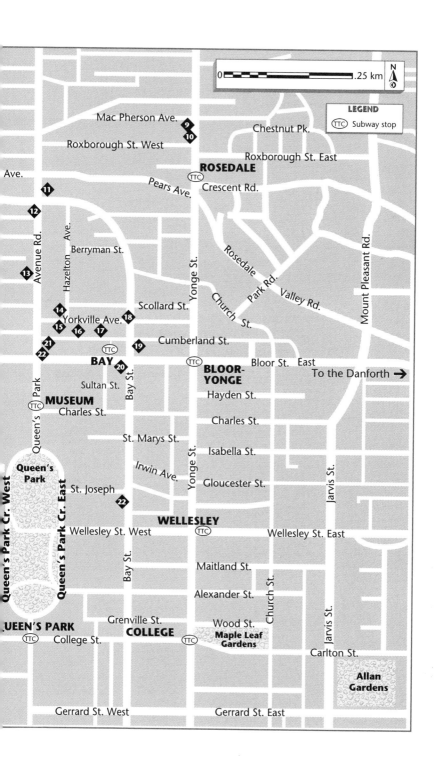

0      .25 km

N

LEGEND

(TTC) Subway stop

Mac Pherson Ave.

9
10

Chestnut Pk.

Roxborough St. West

Roxborough St. East

Ave.

**ROSEDALE**

Pears Ave.

(TTC)

Crescent Rd.

11

12

Hazelton Ave.

Avenue Rd.

Berryman St.

Yonge St.

Rosedale Valley Rd.

Park Rd.

13

Scollard St.

Church St.

Mount Pleasant Rd.

14

18

Yorkville Ave.

15   16   17

Cumberland St.

21

19

22

Park

Bay St.

**BAY**

20

(TTC)

(TTC)

**BLOOR-YONGE**

Bloor St.   East

**To the Danforth →**

Sultan St.

(TTC)

Queen's

**MUSEUM**

Charles St.

Hayden St.

Charles St.

St. Marys St.

Isabella St.

Yonge St.

Irwin Ave.

Gloucester St.

Jarvis St.

**Queen's Park**

St. Joseph

22

Queen's Park Cr. West

Queen's Park Cr. East

**WELLESLEY**

Wellesley St. West

(TTC)

Wellesley St. East

Maitland St.

Bay St.

Alexander St.

Church St.

Jarvis St.

Grenville St.

**QUEEN'S PARK**

(TTC)

College St.

**COLLEGE**

(TTC)

Wood St.

**Maple Leaf Gardens**

Carlton St.

**Allan Gardens**

Gerrard St. West

Gerrard St. East

with garlic, bacon, onion, and spinach in a white-wine cream sauce. Desserts change daily, but always include tarts and a selection of ice creams and sorbets.

✪ **Boba.** 90 Avenue Rd. ☎ **416/961-2622.** Main courses C$19–$27 (U.S.$14–$19). AE, DC, ER, MC, V. Mon–Thurs 5:30–10pm, Fri–Sat 5:30–10:30pm. Subway: Bay. FUSION.

Barbara Gordon and Bob Bermann were among the early Toronto restaurateurs to experiment with spicy, ethnic flavors at restaurants like Avocado Club. They continue to provide food lovers with a sophisticated, ethnic-inspired, modern American cuisine that uses fresh local products. Start, for example, with the grilled eggplant and smoked pepper salad with Woolwich chevre, or the Thai-flavored steak tartare served with shiitake mushroom salad and wonton crisps. Asian spices imbue the main dishes with delectable character—two good examples are the rice-paper–wrapped chicken breast on Thai black rice, with a spiced rice-wine vinegar sauce; and the rare grilled tuna with coconut noodles, mango and avocado salsa, and black-bean sauce. Desserts are also extraordinary, especially the Valrhona chocolate triangle with crème fraîche ice cream, fresh raspberries, and raspberry sauce, or the citrus trio, a divine blood-orange tart in a cookie crust, with lime-buttermilk pudding and lemon ice cream.

This finely prepared cuisine is served in a sunny garden ambiance, with large, spectacular floral arrangements. Mustard and lilac walls are adorned with paintings of flowers in profusion. It attracts a moneyed crowd—some in fine designer wear, others in jeans.

**Il Posto.** 148 Yorkville Ave. ☎ **416/968-0469.** Reservations recommended. Main courses C$19–$26 (U.S.$14–$19). AE, DC, MC, V. Mon–Sat noon–2:30pm and 6–10:30pm. Subway: Bay. ITALIAN.

Right in the heart of high-rent Yorkville, where restaurants are constantly opening and closing, Il Posto, tucked away in York Square, has thrived for many years and still offers a very attractive setting. You can dine inside or out on a brick terrace under a spreading maple tree. The menu features such Italian classics as *saltimbocca alla romana* (veal, prosciutto, and sage); as well as fresh fish dishes and flavorsome pastas, like the *penne alla puttanesca,* made with tomatoes, olives, garlic, and anchovies. For dessert, besides some very special tartes, you might relish the oranges marinated in Grand Marnier or the smooth, creamy zabaglione. The restaurant's beige walls, Italian prints, fresh flowers, and classical music create a serene dining atmosphere. The high-priced wine list doesn't intimidate the professional and moneyed clientele.

**Opus.** 37 Prince Arthur Ave. ☎ **416/921-3105.** Reservations recommended. Main courses C$19–$30 (U.S.$14–$21). AE, MC, V. Daily 5:30–11:30pm. Subway: St. George. FRENCH/MEDITERRANEAN.

A splashy place for the expense-account brigade. Beyond the small bar, you'll find a series of small, intimate rooms in a town house. The current menu features healthful contemporary Mediterranean cuisine using many organically grown ingredients. Among the eight main courses, you might find grilled medallions of tuna with a lime, coriander, and mango salsa, or a roast breast of "La Ferme" chicken with a roasted-pepper and goat-cheese glaze, or a roast leg of caribou with morel mushroom glaze. Whet your appetite with a startling hot-and-sour miso soup, flavored with braised leeks, shrimp wontons, coriander, enoki mushrooms, and poached quail egg, or the sauté of wild mushrooms, fresh herbs, and balsamic jus. Opus has one of the most extensive and best wine lists in the city, featuring French, Californian, and Italian selections.

**Pangaea.** 1221 Bay St. ☎ **416/920-2323.** Main courses C$19–$32 (U.S.$13–$23). Mon–Sat 11:30am–11:30pm. AE, DC, ER, MC, V. Subway: Bay. FUSION.

This dramatic space has been made into a perfect foil for elegant dining. The decor is muted and understated, using fine woods of distinction for the furnishings and the walls. One prominent organic-style wall sculpture is all that can be described as "decor," along with a bough that hangs above the bar, supporting another bronze sculpture. The cuisine is modern, in the best meaning of the word. Try sunflower-encrusted lamb rack in a port sauce or the succulent red snapper en papillote with lemon butter. Each dish is richly flavored. One of my favorites is the liver in a zinfandel reduction. Appetizers are tempting, too, from the simple salad made special by the addition of pickled Jerusalem artichoke to the tuna carpaccio served with a black pepper–horseradish vinaigrette and some arugula and truffled pecorino cheese. Desserts are worth indulging in, like the bread-and-butter brioche pudding scented with orange and vanilla and served warm with berries, mint coulis, and a scoop of Tahitian vanilla ice cream.

**Prego della Piazza/Black & Blue Smoke Bar.** 150 Bloor St. W., in Renaissance Plaza. ☎ **416/920-9900.** Main courses C$17–$30 (U.S.$12–$21). AE, DC, ER, MC, V. Mon–Sat noon–3pm and 5:30pm–midnight. Subway: Bay. ITALIAN/STEAK.

A darling of the celebrity crowd. Both of the rooms are luxuriously understated. The table settings are extravagant and the cuisine predominantly Italian. Although the crowd that comes here relishes the roasted veal chop with currant, grapes, capers, spinach, and potato or the beef tenderloin with a barbaresco reduction, the house specialty is the fish and the pastas. Try the fish of the day or flavorsome but pristinely simple taglierini with parmigiano, veal reduction, and fresh herbs. Pizzas are available too. Start with the calamari fritti or the beef carpaccio with a balsamic and basil vinaigrette.

The adjacent Black & Blue Smoke Bar is extraordinarily elegant. Dry-aged beef and lobster are the specialties priced from C$32 to C$45 (U.S.$23 to U.S.$32). They serve only the best, of course, and precede main courses with escargots, pâté, or caviar. Dinner only Monday through Saturday 6pm to midnight.

✪ **Splendido Bar and Grill.** 88 Harbord St. ☎ **416/929-7788.** Reservations recommended well in advance. Main courses C$20–$29 (U.S.$14–$21). AE, DC, ER, MC, V. Daily 5–11pm. Subway: Spadina, then LRT south. ITALIAN.

Splendido is one of the city's scene-stealers—for its absolutely stunning dining room. It stretches on behind the black-gray granite bar up front, a riot of brilliant yellow lit by a host of tiny, fairylike track lights. The walls are hung with huge flower canvases by Helen Lucas.

The food is Italian with international inspirations, and the menu changes monthly. Start with the signature antipasto of grilled chili-marinated prawns, smoked bocconcini, pickled octopus, cranberry bean salad, sweet pepper, and sweet garlic. Follow with either pasta or a main course. For example, you might choose the saffron tagliatelle with smoked salmon, mushroom duxelles, beets, and dill cream. Among the main courses, roast rack of veal with garlic mashed potatoes, asparagus, and sundried tomato aïoli jus is a special treat; but so, too, is the roasted chicken with herbs, warm Tuscan bread salad, currants, pine nuts and aged balsamic vinegar olive oil dressing. For a special finish, try a glass of one of the several ice wines, accompanied by a fragrant Tahitian vanilla bean crème brûlée, or the lemon meringue tart with vodka blueberry compote. It's a loud, lively place, so give it a pass if it's a romantic dinner you're seeking.

# MODERATE

**Arlequin.** 134 Avenue Rd. (between Davenport and Bernard sts.). ☎ **416/928-9521.** Reservations recommended. Main courses C$13–$19 (U.S.$9–$14) at dinner. AE, DC, MC, V.

Daily 11:30am–3pm; Mon–Sat 5:30–11pm. The front counter opens at 8am. Subway: Bay. CONTINENTAL.

Frequented by a well-heeled Rosedale and young professional crowd, Arlequin is a handsome, small restaurant with a counter display of fabulous pâtés, cheeses, salads, and baked goods up front. The menu is keyed to market-fresh ingredients and might include grilled loin of lamb on a gratin of plums, red wine, and aged chevre, served with crisp polenta; or fettuccine with oyster, chanterelle, and black trumpet mushrooms, leeks, garlic, and fresh herbs.

**Borgo Antico.** 29 Yorkville Ave. ☎ **416/969-9982.** C$10–$22 (U.S.$7–$16). AE, DC, ER, MC, V. Mon–Fri 11:30am–3pm, Mon–Sat 5–11pm. Subway: Bay. ITALIAN.

This is a romantic room with a cavelike atmosphere. The ceiling is barrel-vaulted and has been painted red with a gold fleur-de-lis pattern. Wine-filled racks are used decoratively. The polished wood tables seem to fit. Try one of the 10 pizzas—the spicy gorgonzola onion confit, for example, or one with roasted artichoke, red onion, capers, herbed tomato, and mozzarella. Or if you prefer, there are several fine pastas and risottos and a handful of such main dishes as steak with horseradish and red wine reduction or grilled swordfish with tomato coulis, capers, and olives. Finish with a vanilla crème brulée or the port-drunk berries served with double-cream ice cream.

**Jacques Bistro du Parc.** 126A Cumberland St. ☎ **416/961-1893.** Main courses C$11–$25 (U.S.$8–$18); prix fixe C$21 (U.S.$15). AE, MC, V. Mon–Sat 11:30am–3pm; daily 5–10:30pm. Subway: Bay. CONTINENTAL.

Ladies who lunch and French-speakers drop into this upstairs dining room in the heart of Yorkville for omelets and casual California-inspired fare. Everything about the small room is tasteful, from the fresh flowers on the bar and the French prints to the pictures of Paris. But the patrons come for the omelets—10 selections—and the half-dozen meat and fish dishes, such as coquilles St. Jacques in a California style with roasted green and red peppers, jalapeño, and tomato salsa; or rack of lamb with Dijon mustard. And, of course, there are salads, soups, and quiches, too.

**Joso's.** 202 Davenport (just east of Avenue Rd.). ☎ **416/925-1903.** Reservations recommended. Pasta C$9–$14; main courses C$14–$42 (U.S.$10–$30). AE, MC, V. Mon–Fri 11:30am–2:30pm and Mon–Sat 5:30–11pm. Subway: Bay. SEAFOOD.

Yugoslav Joseph Spralja—of Malka and Joso—has appeared on *The Tonight Show* and performed at Carnegie Hall, but since he gave up folk singing and guitar playing, he has taken to combing the fishmarkets for his restaurant, Joso's. Besides having a fascinating owner, this place has some interesting seafood, but also a rather idiosyncratic decor—erotic, ceramic sculptures of golf-ball-bosomed females—that might offend some.

If you don't care a fig about such indelicate matters, but you do care about fresh seafood prepared to retain its flavor, then stop by Joso's. At dinner, a selection of fresh fish will be presented to you; choose the one you like best, and it will be grilled and served with a salad (such dishes are priced by the pound). Or, you can have octopus steamed with a dressing of oil, garlic, parsley, capers, and olives; deep-fried squid with salad; or spaghetti with an octopus, clam, and squid tomato sauce. A selection of exotic coffees is available, along with a special baklava, and Italian ice creams and sorbets. Bentwood cane chairs and pale-lemon tablecloths complete the decor of the tiny downstairs room. A larger room upstairs is similarly appointed.

**Messis.** 97 Harbord St. ☎ **416/920-2186.** Main courses C$11–$18 (U.S.$8–$13). AE, DC, MC, V. Tues–Fri noon–2pm; Sun–Thurs 5:30–10pm, Fri–Sat 5:30–11pm. Subway: Spadina, then LRT south. MEDITERRANEAN.

A favorite among local foodies, Messis offers good, reasonably priced Northern Italian cuisine in warm and comfortable surroundings. The menu features a variety of pizzas, including one with oven-dried tomato tapenade, roasted onions, zucchini, mixed mushrooms, and mozzarella and asiago cheeses; plus such pasta dishes as fettuccine with shrimp, oven-dried tomatoes, black olives, and spinach in a garlic-tomato sauce. In addition, there are about six fish and meat dishes, including a honey-lemon-glazed salmon with a papaya ginger coulis and plum-wine drizzle; and a rack of lamb with herb-mustard crust and balsamic glaze, served with soft polenta, sautéed mushrooms, oven-dried tomatoes, and grilled white eggplant. The room is small, with a minimal decor. The walls are sponge-painted and stenciled in yellow, and the coral ceiling gives the dining area a warm glow. There's also an appealing awning-covered patio.

**Movenpick Bistretto.** 133 Yorkville Ave. ☎ **416/926-9545.** Reservations recommended at dinner, especially for small groups. Main courses C$9–$17 (U.S.$6–$12). AE, DC, ER, MC, V. Tues–Sat 7:30am–2am, Sun–Mon 7:30am–1am. Subway: Bay. CONTINENTAL/SWISS.

At this popular place, where people line up for dinner, you won't find fine dining, but you will find excellent value and gigantic desserts. Just ask for the Design Dessert menu, and you'll see what I mean. Although the menu features typical bistro fare like steak-frites, veal with mushroom cream sauce, and a croque-monsieur, my favorites are the Rösti dishes, like the one topped with fresh slices of Parmesan and prosciutto, mushrooms, peppers, and basil tomato sauce—all for C$9.80 (U.S.$7), an amazing value. The fresh shellfish—on display at the entrance—is another very popular draw. This is one place in Yorkville where you'll receive value for your money, in a bright, lively atmosphere.

**Southern Accent.** 595 Markham St. ☎ **416/536-3211.** Reservations recommended. Main courses C$12–$20 (U.S.$9–$14). AE, ER, MC, V. Daily 5:30–10:30pm. In summer, lunch is served 11:30am–2:30pm on the patio. Subway: Bathurst. CAJUN.

Southern Accent has a real down-home feel that draws Annex locals. The background music is cool, the art interesting, and the floral tablecloths somehow funky. There are three areas to dine in—upstairs in the dining room, downstairs on the bar level, or out on the tent-covered brick patio. The menu features picante black tiger shrimp, jambalaya, shrimp étouffée, and blackened lamb with horseradish-blackened tomato coulis. Don't miss the bread pudding with bourbon sauce.

## INEXPENSIVE

**Aïda's Falafel.** 553 Bloor St. W. ☎ **416/588-6900.** Main courses C$3.50–$7 (U.S.$2.50–$5). No credit cards. Sun–Thurs 11am–1:30am, Fri–Sat 11am–3am. Subway: Bathurst. MIDDLE EASTERN.

Aïda's Falafel, on Bloor Street at Bathurst, is a small, unassuming restaurant with a couple of tables out front. Tabbouleh, falafel, and shish kebab are the order of the day. There are also several branches on Yonge Street, plus a branch in the Beaches on Queen Street E. at Woodbine.

**Annapurna Vegetarian Restaurant.** 1085 Bathurst St. (just south of Dupont). ☎ **416/537-8513.** Everything less than C$6.50 (U.S.$4.65). No credit cards. Mon–Tues and Thurs–Sat noon–9pm, Wed noon–6:30pm. Subway: Bathurst. VEGETARIAN.

About 2 decades ago, Shivaram Trichur opened the Annapurna Vegetarian Restaurant, just south of Dupont. Beyond the counter, where you can purchase various goodies, including lemon poppy-seed cake, books on yoga, and copies of *Meditation at the U.N.,* you'll find a plant-filled room where you can enjoy some fine, low-priced food. Relax in the peaceful, entirely smoke-free atmosphere, listening to the meditative background music, along with the young, intellectual, and interesting crowd that gathers here.

Nothing on the menu is over C$6.50 (U.S.$4.65). My favorite choice is a *masala dosai*, a crepe filled with a spicy potato mixture and served with coconut chutney. Salads and vegetarian sandwiches supplement the south Indian dishes.

**Bloor Street Diner.** 55 Bloor St. W., Manulife Centre. ☎ **416/928-3105.** Most items C$5–$18 (U.S.$3.55–$13). Daily 7am–1am. Subway: Bloor/Yonge. LIGHT FARE.

The Bloor Street Diner is a convenient place for shoppers and late-nighters to stop for a wide selection of reasonably priced food. The handmade floor, wall tiles, and pottery evoke a Provençal atmosphere. The restaurant offers several dining experiences. The espresso bar serves a variety of coffees, plus salads, panini sandwiches, and crepes. La Rotisserie features roasted meats, poultry, and fish prepared in the style of Provence. Le Café/Terrasse serves light bistro-style meals and stays open until 1am daily. It's a great place to relax in summer on the stylish wicker-and-metal chairs. Les Billiards is the latest pool hot spot.

**The Boulevard Café.** 161 Harbord St. ☎ **416/961-7676.** Reservations recommended for upstairs dining. Main courses C$12–$16 (U.S.$9–$11). AE, MC, V. Tues–Sun 11:30am–3:30pm and 5:30–11pm; daily in summer. Subway: Spadina, then LRT south. LATIN AMERICAN.

A favorite gathering spot of young creative types as well as academics, The Boulevard Café is somehow reminiscent of Kathmandu in the 1960s, although the inspiration is Peruvian. Peruvian cushions and South American wall hangings soften the upstairs dining room. The outside summer cafe, strung with colored lights, attracts an evening and late-night crowd. To start, the menu features *empañadas* (spicy chicken or beef pastry); tangy shrimp in a spiced garlic, pimiento, and wine sauce; and *tamal verde* (spicy corn, coriander, and chicken pâté). For the main course, the major choice is *anticuchos*, marinated and charbroiled brochettes of your own choosing: sea bass, shrimp, pork tenderloin, beef, or chicken.

**Indian Rice Factory.** 414 Dupont St. ☎ **416/961-3472.** Reservations recommended. Main courses C$9–$15 (U.S.$6–$11). AE, DC, MC, V. Mon–Sat noon–11pm, Sun 5–10pm. Subway: Dupont. INDIAN.

A friend of mine raised in India swears by the Indian Rice Factory, operated by Mrs. Patel, who was born in the Punjab. It is an elegant place, with comfortable plush booths, a light-oak bar, and Indian artifacts. The food is decent and the prices are right. All the curries—chicken, beef, and shrimp—are under C$11 (U.S.$8). The restaurant also serves a wide selection of Indian vegetarian dishes, including *aloo gobi* (a curried mixture of potato and cauliflower), *matar paneer* (peas and cheese cooked with spices), and *aloo palak* (spinach with potatoes). The wine list is better than expected.

**☼ Kensington Kitchen.** 124 Harbord St. ☎ **416/961-3404.** Reservations recommended. Main courses C$8–$13 (U.S.$6–$9). AE, CB, DC, ER, MC, V. Mon–Sat 11:30am–11pm, Sun 11:30am–10pm. Subway: Spadina, then LRT south. MIDDLE EASTERN.

A mixed hip and academic crowd that appreciates the food and the prices frequents this comfortable, casual Mediterranean bistro. The menu changes weekly, although it will usually feature such basics as couscous, eggplant provençale, and meshwi (brochettes of marinated chicken, lamb, or kofta). The fresh fish changes daily and varies from salmon to Arctic char, featuring twists such as monkfish spiced with a fresh mango salsa. The appetizers are always appealing, like the steamed Prince Edward Island mussels with diced celery, carrots, and onions in a spicy tomato-coriander sauce. There are two dining rooms—one upstairs, the other downstairs—but my favorite spot is on the back deck under the spreading trees. There is a very well-selected wine list.

**Mori.** 1280 Bay St. ☎ 416/961-1094. Reservations recommended at dinner. Main courses C$9–$14 (U.S.$6–$10). AE, MC, V. Mon–Sat 11:30am–10pm. Subway: Bay. JAPANESE.

Mori, a tiny Japanese cafe with wrought-iron tables and deep-blue tablecloths, is great for budget dining. The sushi and the salmon or chicken teriyaki, served with soup, oshitashi, and green tea, are the highlights. The variety of vegetarian sushi (spinach, carrot, and the like) is notable. So, too, is the vegetarian sukiyaki.

## 6  Midtown East/The East End

In the East End along Danforth Avenue, you'll find yourself in a veritable Little Greece. Streets are lined with tavernas, bouzouki music spills out onto the sidewalk, and restaurant after restaurant bears a Greek name. Most of these places are inexpensively priced.

### MODERATE

**Myth.** 417 Danforth Ave. (between Logan and Chester). ☎ 416/461-8383. Reservations not accepted. Main courses C$10–$21 (U.S.$7–$15). AE, DC, MC, V. Summer Mon–Thurs 11:30am–2am, Fri 11:30am–4am, Sat 2pm–4am, Sun 2pm–2am; winter same except Mon–Wed 5pm–1am, and Sun 2pm–1am. Subway: Chester. GREEK/ITALIAN.

This large restaurant evokes the atmosphere of classical Greece, when huge sailing vessels plied the Mediterranean. Giant shields adorn the walls, while banks of TVs play movies of Greek myths. Choose from among the long list of hot and cold appetizers—lemongrass mussels or Mediterranean bean soup—or else select pasta, pizza, or a more substantial dish like barbecued salmon. The dramatic decor and five pool tables attract a huge, young crowd at night.

**Pan on the Danforth.** 516 Danforth Ave. ☎ 416/466-8158. Reservations accepted for parties of 6 or more only. Main courses C$13–$19 (U.S.$9–$14). AE, MC, V. Sun–Thurs 5pm–midnight, Fri–Sat 5pm–1am. Subway: Chester or Pape. GREEK.

Pan is different from the other kebab houses on the street, thanks to its owner-chef, who produces imaginatively updated Greek cuisine. It's served in a room painted in the brilliant palette of the Mediterranean—gold and azure. You can make a meal from the assortment of 20-odd dips, salads, and appetizers that are offered at this exciting, energetically charged hot spot. Among the more substantial dishes, try the grilled loin of lamb with a fig-and-orange glaze, and served with black-olive mash and marinated artichokes, or the grilled sea bass with tomato, onion, capers, and roasted garlic salsa served with delicious, authentically Greek lemon potatoes.

### INEXPENSIVE

**Astoria.** 390 Danforth Ave. ☎ 416/463-2838. Main courses C$9–$15 (U.S.$6–$11). AE, MC, V. Mon–Wed and Fri–Sat 11am–1am, Sun and Thurs 11am–midnight. Subway: Chester. GREEK.

Astoria is a little fancier than most of the Greek restaurants in the neighborhood, with an outdoor patio complete with playing fountain. The offerings include beef, lamb, and chicken souvlaki, quail over charcoal, a 12-ounce New York steak, and broiled seafood, plus nine or so appetizers.

**Byzas.** 535 Danforth Ave. ☎ 416/778-1100. Main courses C$9–$18 (U.S.$6–$13). AE, MC, V. Sun–Thurs 11am–3am, Fri–Sat 11am–5am. Subway: Chester or Pape. GREEK.

---

### 👪 Family-Friendly Restaurants

**Toby's Goodeats** *(see p. 80)*  Enough kid-appealing items to satisfy even the fussiest child. Lots of locations.

**Movenpick Bistretto** *(see p. 91)*  Caters to kids with a special menu, colored pencils, and drawing paper.

**Jerusalem** *(see p. 98)*  Features lots of finger-licking Middle Eastern foods that kids find very palatable and fun to boot.

**Kensington Kitchen** *(see p. 92)*  There are pita sandwiches, brownies, and other kid-friendly fare. The airplanes and other toys that decorate the walls only add to its attraction.

---

This large restaurant is meant to be cool, and it succeeds. Crowds come for the festive atmosphere and the large selection of traditional appetizers—dolmades, marinated octopus, jalapeños stuffed with cream cheese, or chickpeas sautéed with onions, tomatoes, and spices. There are also plenty of traditional lamb dishes to choose from, along with moussaka and a variety of souvlaki. The bar area up front has stone floors and comfortable banquettes, while behind, the raised dining room has tables set on polished wood floors. The walls are decorated with large, fine-quality photographs of Greece. The sidewalk patio is usually jammed with all manner of people—families, young couples, and the occasional suit. On weekend evenings (Thursday to Sunday), belly dancers entertain from 8:30 to 9:30pm, and the music goes on until 1:30 in the morning.

**Lolita's Lust.** 513 Danforth Ave. ☎ **416/465-1751.** Most items C$10–$16 (U.S.$7–$11). AE, MC, V. Sun–Thurs 6–11pm, Fri–Sat 6pm–midnight. Subway: Chester or Pape. GREEK/MEDITERRANEAN.

Lolita's is different from most of the other restaurants along Danforth, which is why it's currently so hip. It's small and low-lit, with only a handful of booths and tables; and its menu is more varied, with a broader range of Mediterranean, not just Greek, specialties. The traditional small plates, for example, go from roasted quail stuffed with onion, raisins, pine nuts, and dried cherry couscous to grilled calamari with anchovy, oven-dried tomato, and black olives. Among the seven or so main dishes, try the stuffed pork tenderloin with feta, pine nuts, and honey-roasted onion au jus; or the roasted chicken with lemon and fried green onion. There's a small, convivial bar and tiny patio in the back.

**Omonia.** 426 Danforth Ave. (at Chester). ☎ **416/465-2129.** Main courses C$8–$16 (U.S.$6–$11). AE, DC, ER, MC. Daily 11am–1am. Subway: Chester. GREEK.

Once one of the most popular local Greek tavernas, Omonia continues to offer a fun experience, complete with bouzouki sounds and jugs of wine to wash down the garlic-drenched food. Barbecued specialties, souvlaki, chicken, and pork selections are the main features. The Greek pictures, the patio, and the blue tablecloths provide an authentic ambiance.

**✪ Ouzeri.** 500A Danforth Ave. ☎ **416/778-0500.** Reservations not accepted. Main courses C$7–$13 (U.S.$5–$9). AE, DISC, ER, MC, V. Daily 11:30am–2am; lunch served until 3pm, dips and appetizers only served 4–5pm. Subway: Chester. GREEK.

Ouzeri is one of the hottest places on Danforth—it's spirited, casual, and mobbed. People either jam into the few small, circular tables outside or occupy the tables inside, drinking one of the numerous international beers or wines by the glass. It's all très Athens, with tile floors, sun-drenched pastel hues, and eclectic art objects and art. The food is good and cheap, ranging from seafood (prawns with feta and wine, sardines with mustard, calamari, broiled octopus) and meat (pork, lamb, and beef kebabs; moussaka) to rice, pasta, and phyllo pie dishes. Various snacks, like hummus, *tara-mosalata*, mushrooms *à la grecque*, and *dolmades*, complete the menu.

At lunch, Ouzeri dishes out its version of dim sum, *meze sum*—hot and cold appetizers that are wheeled by on carts. Sunday brunch is a filling repast that begins with a buffet spread of appetizers and proceeds through cooked-to-order main courses. It's a frenetic, noisy scene, especially at night.

# 7 Uptown

## VERY EXPENSIVE

✪ **Centro.** 2472 Yonge St. ☎ **416/483-2211.** Reservations recommended. Main courses C$23–$34 (U.S.$16–$24). AE, DC, MC, V. Mon–Sat 5–11:30pm. Subway: Eglinton. ITALIAN.

Occupying a huge space with a mezzanine and a downstairs wine and pasta bar, Centro has grand Italian style—dramatic fluted tulip lamps and classical columns, striking huge photographs of Italian scenes, and a brilliant blue-green ceiling.

A chic, animated crowd gathers here for Northern Italian cuisine with a California accent. The menu changes monthly, but among the dishes might be grilled Delft blue veal chop with chanterelles and chive cream, rack of Ontario lamb with honey-mustard crust and rosemary essence, or sautéed red snapper in a corn and jalapeño sauce. There are also three or more pasta dishes, all with flavorsome sauces. To start, try the terrine of Québec foie gras with Inniskillin ice-wine gelée, oven-dried pineapple, and warm brioche; or the local Woolwich goat cheese with yellow peppers, herb oil, and balsamic glaze. Desserts are worth anticipating—lemon mascarpone tart with blackberry sauce and chocolate pecan Napoléon with a Southern Comfort sauce are only two examples. The international wine list is extraordinary.

✪ **N 44.** 2537 Yonge St. ☎ **416/487-4897.** Reservations recommended. Main courses C$28–$37 (U.S.$20–$26). AE, DC, MC, V. Mon–Sat 5–11pm. Subway: Eglinton. INTERNATIONAL.

Those who really appreciate fine dining and have the money to indulge their habit, come north to this restaurant just south of Sherwood Avenue. A sleek art deco beauty, it occupies a dramatic space with soaring ceilings. In the back, chefs work in the glassed-in kitchen, which is etched with the compass logo (North 44° is Toronto's latitude). The atmosphere is enhanced by mirrors, burnished stainless steel, and soft lighting that makes the room positively glow at night. The food is inspired by several international cuisines, although the emphasis is on Italian. On the dinner menu, you might find roasted rack of lamb with a pecan-mustard crust, served with a peppercorn sauce; grilled salmon with crisp leeks and a citrus sauce; or grilled veal tenderloin with a herb-peppercorn crust and an aged balsamic sauce. Pizzas and pastas are also featured. It's worth saving some room for the warm chocolate tower—a dramatic creation with a liquid center, accompanied by banana rum ice cream and several different sauces. Besides an extensive (300-plus bottles) wine list, there are also 20 or so wines available by the glass. There's a very appealing mezzanine wine bar with piano entertainment Wednesday to Saturday.

✪ **Scaramouche.** 1 Benvenuto Place. ☎ **416/961-8011.** Reservations required. Main courses C$25–$30 (U.S.$35–$42); pasta dishes C$16–$22 (U.S.$11–$16). AE, DC, MC, V. Main room: Mon–Sat 6–10:30pm. Pasta bar: Mon–Fri 6–10:30pm, Sat 6–11pm. Subway: St. Clair. CONTINENTAL.

Scaramouche sustains its reputation as one of Toronto's top-class restaurants by drawing an "old money" crowd. A little difficult to find (it's located on the first floor of an apartment building, 4 blocks south of St. Clair Avenue and Avenue Road), it's certainly worth seeking out. Try to secure a window seat, which grants a view of the downtown city skyline. The decor, the flower arrangements, and the careful presentation of the food make the experience special.

Although the menu changes frequently, it will feature a selection of hot and cold appetizers such as the terrine of duck foie gras with grilled apple and mango in a port wine reduction, or lobster and scallop sausage enhanced by lobster nage and pepper aïoli. Among the eight or so entrees, you might enjoy the grilled Rowe farm filet mignon with a deliciously rich red-wine glaze or the hickory-smoked and grilled salmon with fresh horseradish white-wine sauce. You can always select from the pasta-bar menu, which offers similar appetizers and excitingly prepared fettuccine, linguine, lasagna, and cannelloni. The desserts are equally celebrated—coconut cream pie with white chocolate shavings and dark chocolate sauce or the warm, flourless chocolate cake on espresso shortbread with white-chocolate banana sauce are particularly good. The wine list includes some great French and American selections.

## EXPENSIVE

**Coppi.** 3363 Yonge St. ☎ **416/484-4464.** Reservations recommended at dinner. Main courses C$15–$24 (U.S.$11–$17). AE, ER, MC, V. Mon–Fri noon–2pm, Sat 5:30–10:30pm. Subway: Lawrence. ITALIAN.

Named after Fausto Coppi, the legendary Italian cyclist who won virtually every event from 1940 to 1959 before dying of malaria, this restaurant features poster-size photographs of Coppi at various stages of his career. It's a lively, modern, low-lit room, which attracts a knowing clientele that appreciates inexpensive but well-prepared cuisine. The kitchen turns out grilled dishes—calf's liver, chicken breast, salmon, and red snapper—along with 10 or so pastas and risottos, including pappardelle zebra made with porcini mushrooms, shrimps, tomatoes, and white wine. There's a well-priced but predominantly Italian wine list and typical favorite Italian desserts—zabaglione, tiramisu, and gelato.

**Herbs.** 3187 Yonge St. (north of Lawrence). ☎ **416/322-0487.** Reservations recommended. Main courses C$15–$22 (U.S.$11–$16). AE, DC, ER, MC, V. Mon–Fri 11:30am–2pm; Sun–Thurs 5:30–10pm, Fri–Sat 5:30–11pm. Subway: Lawrence. CONTINENTAL.

Brilliant colors and designs inspired by nature are the hallmarks of this appealing restaurant, which attracts a loyal, well-off Lawrence Park crowd. Walls of brilliant yellow, burnt orange, and crimson serve as backdrops for paintings, which are actually for sale. Tables sport floral-design tablecloths of brilliant pink, mauve, and turquoise topped with butcher paper.

The food is eclectically continental. Among the 12 or so main courses, you might find pan-roasted Atlantic salmon on a chiffonade of fennel with citrus dressing; roasted pork tenderloin marinated in ginger, soya, and sesame oil and served with grilled pineapple; or calf's liver with honey-pommery mustard sauce. The desserts are sublime. You'll succumb to the lemon tart, served on a huge Villeroy & Boch china plate and artistically presented with figs, strawberries, and an intense raspberry and crème sorbet.

✪ **Pronto.** 692 Mount Pleasant Rd. ☎ **416/486-1111.** Reservations required. Main courses C$18–$29 (U.S.$13–$21). AE, DC, MC, V. Daily 5–10:30pm. Subway: Eglinton. ITALIAN.

Behind its stucco facade, Pronto, just south of Eglinton Avenue, presents a striking and lovely low-ceilinged dining room that is vibrantly alive and attracts a suitably well-heeled and well-dressed crowd. In the back, behind a tiled counter, you can see the chefs in their crisp white toques preparing the food. At the center of the room, there's always a lavish fresh-flower arrangement. A pianist adds to the atmosphere.

The cuisine matches the decor. The menu changes monthly, but among the appetizers you might find warm portobello mushrooms with asiago cheese on grilled radicchio, arugula with balsamic vinaigrette, or Prince Edward Island mussels steamed in lemongrass ginger broth with leeks and fresh tomato. For a main course, try the rack of lamb crusted with grain mustard on wild mushroom ragout with homemade dumplings, or the grilled Bay of Fundy salmon on lobster potato and steamed sea asparagus with salsa verde. To finish, even the simple shortbread and lemon curd with blueberry sorbetto is sublime.

**Trapper's.** 3479 Yonge St. ☎ **416/482-6211.** Reservations recommended. Main courses C$14–$26 (U.S.$10–$19) at dinner. AE, MC, V. Mon–Fri 11:30am–2:30pm; Mon–Sat 5–10pm, Sun 5–9:30pm. Subway: Lawrence. CONTINENTAL.

Trapper's, between Lawrence Avenue and York Mills Road, draws the moneyed with a seasonal menu that features only the best Canadian ingredients. Start with the Prince Edward Island mussels steamed in Cave Spring chardonnay, with garlic, Kalamata olives, and fresh herbs; or the fresh smoked salmon on fennel with Osaka mustard and a dill yogurt sauce. Follow with grilled Ontario pork tenderloin with a maple syrup, apricot, and ginger sauce, or fillet of Muskoka trout seared in Acadian spices and served with a fruit salsa of mangoes, pineapples, grapefruits, and oranges finished with toasted almonds. Pasta dishes are also offered. The wine list is extensive.

## MODERATE

**Brownes Bistro.** 4 Woodlawn Ave. E. ☎ **416/924-8132.** Reservations recommended. Main courses C$13–$23 (U.S.$9–$16). AE, MC, V. Mon–Fri noon–2pm; daily 5:30–10:30pm. Subway: St. Clair. FRENCH.

Just south of St. Clair Avenue in the heart of Rosedale, Brownes Bistro attracts the mink-wrapped and suited crowd. The decor is low key—mahogany combined with pale gray walls supporting black-and-white photographs of the French countryside. The bistro fare includes such comforting dishes as braised lamb shank with garlic mashed potatoes, and New York strip loin with roasted garlic-shallot butter and frites. There are several fine pizzas and pasta dishes, too.

**Grano.** 2035 Yonge St. ☎ **416/440-1986.** Reservations accepted for parties of 6 or more. Main courses C$9–$20 (U.S.$6–$14). AE, DC, MC, V. Mon–Fri 10am–10:30pm, Sat 10am–11pm. Subway: Davisville or Eglinton. ITALIAN.

Grano is a wild Italian celebration—a celebration of down-to-earth food served in an atmosphere of washed Mediterranean pastels. It's casual and fun. The wine is served in tumblers, there's a courtyard out back, and the tables are painted in brilliant colors of mustard and cherry. The latest Italian art posters decorate the walls, large colorful majolica vessels abound, and arias waft over the whole scene. At the entrance, the display counters are filled with more than 50 different antipasti, and any three, five, or seven of these can be ordered for C$12 (U.S.$9), C$17 (U.S.$12), and C$24 (U.S.$17), respectively. In addition, there are several pasta dishes, like the rigatoni semi-freddo with a sauce made from tomato, prosciutto, arugula, garlic, and shaved Parmesan, and the linguine with squid and octopus in a squid ink sauce. The meat or fish entrees change daily. To finish, there's tiramisu, biscotti, and a variety of Italian custard-cream desserts.

**Le Paradis.** 166 Bedford Rd. (north of Davenport). ☎ **416/921-0995.** Reservations recommended. Main courses C$10–$16.50 (U.S.$7–$12); 3–course prix fixe C$16 (U.S.$11). AE, MC, V. Tues–Fri noon–3pm; Tues–Sat 6–11pm, Sun, Mon 5:30–10pm. Subway: Dupont, then 4 blocks east. FRENCH.

At night when the French doors are flung open to the street and Le Paradis is filled with chattering diners being served by aproned waiters, you could swear that you're in a residential area of Paris. The room is long and narrow, with banquettes and tables stretching alongside one wall, facing the bar opposite. European posters and photographs only add to the atmosphere. The offerings are typical bistro fare—trout amandine, chicken roasted with tarragon, or flank steak with fries—with some regional specialties, such as braised rabbit with onion, fennel, tomato, and garlic in white wine; or lamb and beef sausage, served on couscous. Many of the dishes, especially the seafood offerings, change daily and are listed on a blackboard. Desserts are traditionally French—mousses, tartes, and ice-cream concoctions.

**Thai Magic.** 1118 Yonge St. ☎ **416/968-7366.** Reservations recommended. Main courses C$11–$17 (U.S.$8–$12); complete dinners C$29–$30 (U.S.$21–$21.50) per person. AE, MC, V. Mon–Sat 5:30–11pm. Subway: Summerhill, then walk south. THAI.

Magical, indeed, is this long, narrow restaurant filled with orchids, Thai statuary, and artifacts. Warm mauves and greens make it even more inviting—the perfect backdrop for the cuisine. Start with a combination plate of appetizers, *tom yum kai* (a really spicy soup flavored with lemongrass and containing succulent shrimp), or the familiar noodle dish, pad Thai. For main courses, there are stir-frys and curries (like the flavorsome chicken green curry or shrimp red curry with okra) as well as such dishes as chicken with basil, tamarind fish, coriander lobster, or shrimp lemongrass—the last a specialty that uses a unique family recipe.

## INEXPENSIVE

**Jerusalem.** 955 Eglinton Ave. W. ☎ **416/783-6494.** Reservations not accepted. Main courses C$9–$15 (U.S.$6–$11). AE, MC, V. Mon–Thurs noon–11pm, Fri–Sat noon–midnight, Sun noon–10pm. Subway: Eglinton. MIDDLE EASTERN.

At Jerusalem, just west of Bathurst Street, it's the food and the prices that count. The decor is simple—just some hammered-brass tabletops on the walls—but the atmosphere is extremely warm, and the service friendly and unhurried. All the appetizers are less than C$4 (U.S.$2.85)—falafel, *kibbeh* (a cracked-wheat roll stuffed with ground meat, onions, and pine nuts), various styles of hummus, tahini, and *tabbouleh* (a delicious blend of cracked wheat with chopped tomatoes, onions, parsley, mint, lemon, and olive oil). You can follow them with liver fried in garlic and hot-pepper sauce, *siniyeh* (mixed ground lamb and beef with onions, parsley, and pine nuts, oven baked with tahini sauce), and lamb or beef shish kebab. Finish with a cup of thick, luxurious Turkish coffee.

## 8 Cafes & Java Joints

Toronto has plenty of these to choose from. It even has several dessert chains. **Just Desserts,** 137 John St. at Richmond (☎ 416/599-0655), is one and stays open practically around the clock on weekends for those in need of a sugar fix. Around 40 desserts are available—as many as 12 different cheesecakes, 10 or so assorted pies, plus a whole array of gâteaux, tortes, and meringues, all around C$6 (U.S.$4.30). Open Sunday to Thursday noon to 3am; Friday and Saturday noon to 5am.

    **Dufflet Pastries,** 787 Queen St. W. (☎ 416/504-2870), has extraordinarily beautiful and wonderful-tasting tarts and pastries that can be accompanied by a full range of coffees.

**Demetre,** 400 Danforth Ave. (☎ **416/778-6654**), has been modernized after a recent fire. Although it's changed, the wonderful old-fashioned atmosphere, the Belgian waffles and outrageous sundaes as well as cakes, tortes, and baklava are still great, and families flock here on weekends to enjoy the sweet feast.

Many Torontonians swear that the best ice cream is found at the **Sicilian Ice Cream Company,** 710–712 College St. (☎ **416/531-7716**).

Long before Starbucks arrived on the North American scene, Torontonians were sipping fine coffees at a variety of small coffee chains as well as at many independent and characterful cafes. Today, even though Starbucks has opened in Toronto and there now seems to be one on every street corner, many of the citizens remain loyal to their own coffee bars.

The two biggest chains are the **Second Cup** (about 30 branches), which offers a full range of different flavored coffees and espresso varieties plus cakes, muffins, croissants, and gift items, and **Timothy's** (about 20 branches), which invites you to pour your own selection from about eight to 10 varieties. **The Croissant Tree,** with six or so branches, sells a variety of coffees plus a full range of pastry items. **Future Bakery & Cafes,** 739 Queen St. W. (☎ **416/368-4235**) and 483 Bloor St. W. (☎ **416/922-5875**), attracts an artsy, literate crowd with its great breads. **Lettieri Espresso Bar-Cafe,** 94 Cumberland St. (☎ **416/515-8764**) and 441 Queen St. W. (☎ **416/592-1360**), has all kinds of coffees—lattés, mochas, the works—plus focaccia sandwiches and a full range of tarts, cookies, and pastries.

Some of the best authentic cafes are found in Little Italy along College Street. Among the oldest (and one of the few that has not been "modernized") is **Cafe Diplomatico,** 594 College St. (☎ **416/534-4637**), which has traditional mosaic marble floors, wrought-iron chairs, and an extra-large sidewalk patio. Old Italians, artists, and students all hang out here as they have since the place opened in 1968. The young, beautiful, and hip gather at **Bar Italia,** 582 College St. (☎ **416/535-3621**), and also at the **College Street Bar,** 574 College St. (☎ **416/533-2417**), while an older and more sophisticated crowd comes together at **Sottovoce,** 595 College St. (☎ **416/536-4564**), the modern Italian cafe par excellence with ritzy Milan-style decor and music to match. Another small, intimate cafe-bar is **Wild Indigo,** 607 College St. (☎ **416/536-8797**), which has a tiny patio in the back.

On Queen Street, an artsy intellectual crowd enjoys the **Epicure Cafe,** 512 Queen St. (☎ **416/504-8942**), which also serves full lunch and dinner menus. Posters, marble tables, and jazz create a certain European ambiance. Farther west along Queen, the **Gypsy Coop,** at no. 817 (☎ **416/703-5069**), has a 1960s hippies air. Coffee is not the only king here. Instead, many different teas and infusions are available, which you can take with one of the super-rich and satisfying brownies.

Cafes also line Bloor Street West in the Annex neighborhood. Among the more interesting is the **Daily Express Cafe,** 280 Bloor St. W. (☎ **416/944-3225**), which is atmospheric and draws mainly a student crowd.

# 6

# What to See & Do in Toronto

It takes 5 or 6 days to really see Toronto's highlights. Although most major sights are located downtown, a few range outside the downtown core and take extra time and effort to reach. Ideally, you should spend 1 day each at Ontario Place, the Ontario Science Centre, Canada's Wonderland, and Harbourfront. In fact, that's what the kids will definitely want to do. Then there's also the zoo, which could take a whole day, complete with a picnic.

The Art Gallery of Ontario, Chinatown, and the Royal Ontario Museum (ROM), could be combined in a pinch, but the day might be too museum-oriented for some. Ontario Place could conceivably be combined with Fort York and Exhibition Place. En route to Canada's Wonderland, you could stop in at Black Creek Pioneer Village, but I don't recommend it since it will cut into your time at Canada's Wonderland, which really requires a full day.

As you can see, there are numerous major attractions in Toronto worthy of a whole day's visit. There are also many other downtown sights and neighborhoods—the CN Tower, Eaton Centre, Yorkville, Queen Street, City Hall, and Casa Loma—that you may want to explore. Depending on your interests and whether you have children, there's enough to keep you going for several weeks in Toronto.

## SUGGESTED ITINERARIES

It's hard to prescribe itineraries because travelers will want to make their own choices based on personal interests and other contingencies that range from whether or not they have kids in tow, what time of year it is, and what's on in town. Pick and choose, combine elements, and don't be afraid to go with your gut instincts.

### If You Have 2 Days

**Day 1**    Get to the Ontario Science Centre the minute it opens and then come back into town to spend the late afternoon/early evening at Harbourfront or Ontario Place.

**Day 2**    Start early at the Kensington Market and from there walk up to College Street and through the university area to the Bata Shoe Museum and then to the Royal Ontario Museum. Leave enough time to wander through Yorkville and browse in some of the stores and galleries before most of them close at 5pm.

### If You Have 3 Days

**Days 1–2**  Spend the first 2 days as outlined above.

**Day 3**  Explore Chinatown and stop at the Art Gallery. Then pop over to Eaton Centre and head down to Queen Street to explore Queen Street West in the early evening.

### If You Have 5 Days

**Days 1–3**  Spend days 1–3 as above.

**Day 4**  Visit either Canada's Wonderland (if the family's in tow) or the McMichael Collection in Kleinburg. Black Creek Pioneer Village could even be squeezed in, too.

**Day 5**  Take a trip to the Toronto Islands and while away the day among the lagoons—picnicking, relaxing, or bicycling.

## 1 The Top Attractions

### ON THE LAKEFRONT

**Ontario Place.** 955 Lakeshore Blvd. W. ☎ **416/314-9811,** or 416/314-9900 for a recording. Free admission, with some exceptions (like the CNE). Gate admission C$10 (U.S.$7); play all day pass C$20 (U.S.$14) adults, C$10 (U.S.$7) children 3–5. IMAX movies after Labour Day (included in the summer pass) C$9 (U.S.$6) adults, C$4.50 (U.S.$3.20) seniors and children 12 and under. Mid-May to Labour Day, daily from 10am with most attractions closing at dusk except evening events and dining spots. Parking C$9 (U.S.$6). Take the subway to Bathurst or Dufferin and buses south from there to Exhibition. Call TTC Information (☎ 416/393-4636) for special bus service details.

When this 96-acre recreation complex on Lake Ontario opened in 1971, it seemed futuristic—and 27 years later, it still does (the 1989 renovation no doubt helped). From a distance, you'll see five steel-and-glass pods suspended on columns 105 feet above the lake, three artificial islands, and, alongside, a huge geodesic dome. The five pods contain a multimedia theater, a live children's theater, a high-technology exhibit, and displays that tell the story of Ontario in vivid kaleidoscopic detail. The dome houses Cinesphere, where a 60- by 80-foot screen shows specially made IMAX movies.

Located under an enormous orange canopy, the Children's Village is the most creative playground you'll find anywhere in the world. Here, in a well-supervised area, children aged 12 and under can scramble over rope bridges, bounce on an enormous trampoline, explore the foam forest, slide down a twisting chute, or, most popular of all, squirt water pistols and garden hoses, swim, and generally drench one another in the water-play section. Afterward, parents can just pop them in the convenient dryers before moving on to other kids' amusements.

A stroll around the complex reveals two marinas full of yachts and other craft, the HMCS *Haida* (a destroyer, open for touring, that served in both World War II and the Korean War), a miniature 18-hole golf course, plenty of grassland for picnicking and general cavorting, and a wide variety of restaurants and snack bars serving everything from Chinese, Irish, German, and Canadian food to hot dogs and hamburgers. And don't miss the wildest rides in town—the Hydrofuge, a tube slide that allows folks to reach speeds over 30 m.p.h.; the Rush River Raft Ride, which carries you along a lengthy flume in an inflatable raft; the pink twister and purple pipeline (water slides); plus bumper boats and go-karts. For something more peaceful, you can navigate pedal boats or remote-control boats between the artificial islands.

At night, the outdoor Molson Amphitheatre accommodates 16,000 under a copper canopy and outside on the grass. It features top-line entertainers—Kenny G,

# Downtown Toronto Attractions

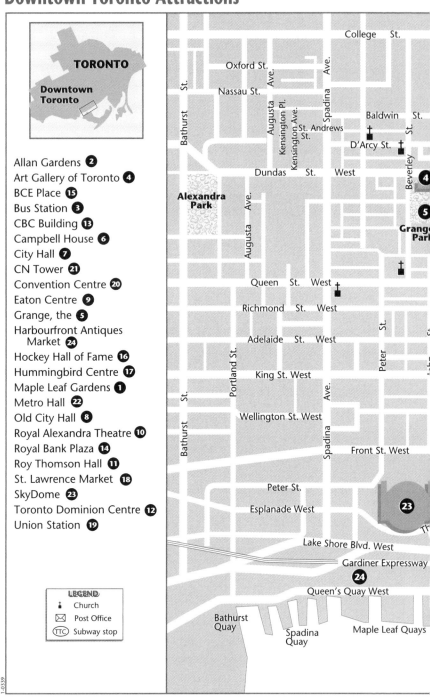

Allan Gardens ❷
Art Gallery of Toronto ❹
BCE Place ⓯
Bus Station ❸
CBC Building ⓭
Campbell House ❻
City Hall ❼
CN Tower ㉑
Convention Centre ⓴
Eaton Centre ❾
Grange, the ❺
Harbourfront Antiques
    Market ㉔
Hockey Hall of Fame ⓰
Hummingbird Centre ⓱
Maple Leaf Gardens ❶
Metro Hall ㉒
Old City Hall ❽
Royal Alexandra Theatre ❿
Royal Bank Plaza ⓮
Roy Thomson Hall ⓫
St. Lawrence Market ⓲
SkyDome ㉓
Toronto Dominion Centre ⓬
Union Station ⓳

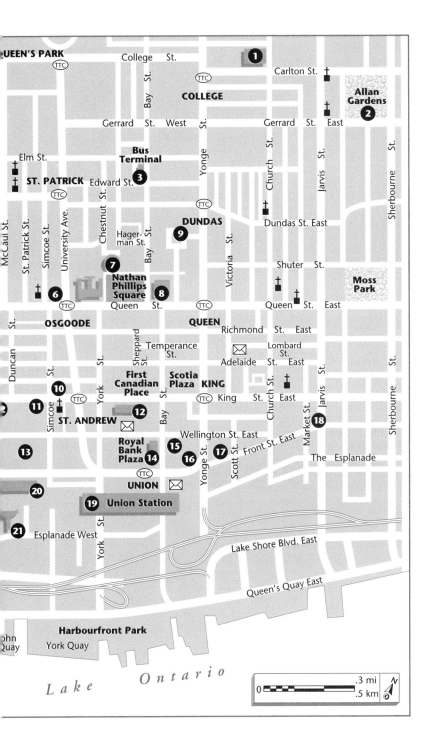

QUEEN'S PARK
College St.
Carlton St. †
COLLEGE
Bay St.
Gerrard St. West
Gerrard St. East
Allan Gardens
Bus Terminal
Elm St.
ST. PATRICK
Edward St.
Yonge
Church St.
Jarvis St.
Sherbourne St.
McCaul St.
St. Patrick St.
Simcoe St.
University Ave.
Chestnut St.
Hager-man St.
DUNDAS
Dundas St. East
Bay St.
Victoria St.
Shuter St. †
Moss Park
Nathan Phillips Square
Queen St.
Queen St. East
OSGOODE
QUEEN
Richmond St. East
Duncan St.
Temperance St.
Sheppard St.
Lombard St.
Adelaide St. East
First Canadian Place
Scotia Plaza
KING
York St.
Bay St.
Church St.
King St. East
Jarvis St.
Sherbourne St.
Simcoe
ST. ANDREW
Royal Bank Plaza
Wellington St. East
Yonge St.
Scott St.
Front St. East
Market St.
The Esplanade
UNION
Union Station
Esplanade West
York St.
Lake Shore Blvd. East
Queen's Quay East
Harbourfront Park
John Quay
York Quay
Lake Ontario
0 .3 mi / .5 km

103

James Taylor, The Who, Hank Williams, Lord of the Dance, and more. For information, call ☎ **416/260-5600.** For tickets, call **Ticketmaster** at ☎ **416/870-8000.**

*Note:* An C$80 million aquarium is being added to the complex, but an opening date has not yet been set.

✪ **Harbourfront Centre.** Queen's Quay W. ☎ **416/973-3000** for information on special events, or 416/973-4000 for the box office. Take the LRT from Union Station.

In 1972, the federal government took over a 96-acre strip of prime waterfront land to preserve the waterfront vista—and since then Torontonians have rediscovered their lakeshore. Abandoned warehouses, shabby depots, and crumbling factories were refurbished, and a tremendous urban park now stretches on and around the old piers. Today it's one of the most popular hangouts for Torontonians and visitors—a great place to spend a day sunbathing, picnicking, biking, shopping, and sailing.

**Queen's Quay,** at the foot of York Street, is the closest quay to town, and it's the first one you'll encounter as you approach from the Westin Harbour Castle. From here, boats depart for tours of the harbor and islands. Here in this renovated warehouse you'll find a dance theater, plus two floors of shops, restaurants, and waterfront cafes.

After exploring Queen's Quay, walk west along the glorious waterfront promenade to **York Quay,** passing the Power Plant, a contemporary art gallery, and behind it, the Du Maurier Theatre Centre. At York Quay Centre you can secure a lot of information on programming as well as entertain yourself in several galleries, including The Craft Studio, where you can watch artisans blow glass, throw pots, and make silk-screen prints. On the other side of the center, you can attend a free Molson Dry Front Music outdoor concert, held all summer long at Molson Place. Also on the quay in the center is the Water's Edge Cafe, overlooking a small pond for electric model boats (there's skating here in winter) and a children's play area.

From here, take the footbridge to John Quay, crossing over the sailboats moored below, to the stores and restaurants on **Pier 4**—Wallymagoo's Marine Bar and the Pier 4 Storehouse. Beyond on Maple Leaf Quay lies the Nautical Centre.

At the **Harbourside Boating Centre,** 283 Queen's Quay W. (☎ **416/203-3000**), you can rent sail- and powerboats or sign up for sailing lessons. A 3-hour sailboat rental costs C$55 (U.S.$39) to C$495 (U.S.$354), depending on the size of boat. Powerboats cost C$85 to C$180 (U.S.$61 to U.S.$129). Week-long and weekend sailing courses are also offered.

The **Harbourfront Antiques Market,** at 390 Queen's Quay W., at the foot of Spadina Avenue (☎ **416/260-2626**), will keep antique-lovers busy browsing for hours. More than 100 antique dealers spread out their wares—jewelry, china, furniture, toys, and books. Indoor parking is adjacent to the market, and a cafeteria serves fresh salads, sandwiches, and desserts. It's open May to October, Tuesday to Saturday from 10am to 6pm and Sunday from 8am to 6pm; November to April, Tuesday to Friday from 11am to 5pm, Saturday and Sunday from 10am to 6pm.

At the west end of the park stands **Bathurst Pier,** with a large sports field for romping around, plus two adventure playgrounds, one for older kids and the other (supervised) for 3- to 7-year-olds.

More than 4,000 events take place annually at Harbourfront, including a **Harbourfront Reading Festival,** held every Tuesday on York Quay, which attracts some very eminent writers. Other happenings include films, dance, theater, music, children's events, multicultural festivals, and marine events. Two of the most important events are the annual Children's Festival and the International Festival of Authors. Most activities are free.

✪ **The Toronto Islands.** ☎ **416/392-8193,** for ferry schedules. Round-trip fare C$4 (U.S.$2.85) adults, C$2 (U.S.$1.45) seniors and ages 15–19, C$1 (U.S.70¢) for children 14 and under. Ferries operate all day, leaving from the docks at the bottom of Bay St. To get there, take a subway to Union Station and the LRT south.

In only 7 minutes, an 800-passenger ferry will take you across to 612 acres of island park crisscrossed by shady paths and quiet waterways—a glorious spot to walk, play tennis, bike, feed the ducks, putter around in boats, picnic, or just sit. There are 14 islands in total, but the three major islands are **Centre, Ward's,** and **Algonquin.** The first is the busiest; the other two are home to about 600 people who live in modest cottages. Originally, the land was a peninsula, but in the mid-1800s a series of storms shattered the finger of land into islands.

On Centre Island, families enjoy **Centreville** (☎ **416/203-0405**), a 19-acre old-time amusement park, built and designed especially for them. But you won't find the usual neon signs, shrill hawkers, and the aroma of greasy hot-dog stands. Instead you'll find a turn-of-the-century village complete with a Main Street, tiny shops, a firehouse, and even a small working farm where the kids can pet lambs and chicks and enjoy pony rides. They'll also love trying out the antique cars, fire engines, old-fashioned train, authentic 1890s carousel, flume ride, and the aerial cars. Individual rides (19 of them) cost anywhere from C$1.10 to C$3.30 (U.S.80¢ to U.S.$2.35). An all-day ride pass costs C$11.45 (U.S.$8) for those 4 feet tall and under and C$16.35 (U.S.$12) for those over 4 feet. Open daily from mid-May to Labour Day, 10:30am to 6pm (and weekends in early May and September).

## DOWNTOWN

**CN Tower.** 301 Front St. W. ☎ **416/360-8500.** Admission C$13 (U.S.$9) adults, C$11 (U.S.$8) seniors, C$9 (U.S.$6) children 5–12. Cosmic Pinball, Q-Zar, and Virtual World C$6 (U.S.$4.30) adults and seniors, C$5 (U.S.$3.55) children 4–12. Combination tickets are available from C$22 (U.S.$16). May–Sept daily 8am–11pm; Oct–Apr 9am–10pm.

As you approach the city, the first thing you'll notice is this slender needlelike structure. Tiny glass-walled elevators that look like jumping beans glide to the top of its 1,815-foot-high tower—the tallest freestanding structure in the world.

They whisk you to the 1,136-foot-high, seven-level sky pod in just under a minute. From here, on a clear day you can't quite see forever, but you can see, I'm told, all the way to Niagara Falls, or even Buffalo, if you wish.

Attractions are often revamped at the tower. Among the most recent new draws are the IMAX theater, which shows a film of a cross-Canada journey; two simulator airplane trips, one that is gentle and calm, the other in which the rider rockets through caves and over mountains; and a series of interactive displays that showcase the CN Tower along with such forerunners as the Eiffel Tower and the Empire State Building. The pod also contains broadcasting facilities, a nightclub, and **360,** a revolving restaurant reviewed in chapter 5. For lunch, dinner, or Sunday brunch reservations, call ☎ **416/362-5411.**

Atop the tower sits a 335-foot antenna mast that took 31 weeks to erect with the aid of a giant Sikorsky helicopter. It took 55 lifts to complete the operation. Above the sky pod is the world's highest public observation gallery, the Space Deck, 1,465

## Impressions

*A global psychiatrist, if asked to take a look at Toronto's rather unhealthy obsession with the CN Tower, would advise the city to take a cold shower and lie down on the couch for a spell.*

—Allan Fotheringham, *Maclean's* (1975)

feet above the ground (C$3/U.S.$2.15 additional charge). The Observation deck one floor below has a glass floor that makes for wobbly knees and a turbulent gut. But don't worry about the elements sweeping the tower into the lake: It's built of contoured reinforced concrete covered with thick glass-reinforced plastic and designed to keep ice accumulation to a minimum. The structure can withstand high winds, snow, ice, lightning, and earth tremors.

**SkyDome.** 1 Blue Jays Way. ☎ **416/341-2770.** Tours C$9.50 (U.S.$7) adults, C$7 (U.S.$5) students 16 and under and seniors, C$6 (U.S.$4.30) children 4–11, free for children under 3. Tour schedule depends on events/sports schedule, so call ahead (tours usually begin on the hour). Subway: Union.

In 1989, the opening of the 53,000-seat SkyDome, home to the Toronto Blue Jays baseball team and the Toronto Argonauts football team, was a gala event. In 1992, SkyDome became the first Canadian stadium to host the World Series, with the Blue Jays grabbing the crown for the first of two consecutive years. The stadium itself represents an engineering feat, featuring the world's first fully retractable roof, spanning more than 8 acres, and a gigantic video scoreboard. So large is it that you could fit a 31-story building inside the complex when the roof is closed. Indeed, there's already a spectacular 11-story hotel with 70 rooms facing directly onto the field.

✪ **Art Gallery of Ontario.** 317 Dundas St. W., between McCaul and Beverley sts. ☎ **416/977-0414.** Admission by donation with suggestion of C$5 (U.S.$3.55) per adult. A fee as high as C$11 (U.S.$8) is charged for special exhibits. Tues–Fri noon–9pm, Sat–Sun 10am–5:30pm. Grange House: Tues–Sun noon–4pm, Wed noon–9pm. Closed Dec 25 and Jan 1. Subway: St. Patrick.

The exterior gives no hint of the light and openness inside this beautifully designed gallery. The recently refurbished and expanded space is dramatic, and the paintings are imaginatively displayed. Throughout there are audiovisual presentations and interactive computer presentations that provide information on particular paintings or schools of painters.

Although the European collections are fine, I would concentrate on the Canadian galleries. The galleries displaying the Group of Seven—Tom Thomson, F.H. Varley, Lawren Harris, and others—are extraordinary. In addition, other galleries show the genesis of Canadian art from earlier to more modern artists. Don't miss the galleries featuring Inuit art.

The Henry Moore Sculpture Centre, with over 800 pieces (original plasters, bronzes, maquettes, woodcuts, lithographs, etchings, and drawings), is the largest public collection of his works. They were given to Toronto by the artist because he was so moved by the citizens' enthusiasm for his work (public donations bought his sculpture *The Archer* to decorate Nathan Phillips Square at City Hall after politicians refused to free up money for it). In one room, under a glass ceiling, 20 or so of his large works stand like silent prehistoric rock formations. Along the walls flanking a ramp are color photographs showing Moore's major sculptures in their natural locations, which fully reveal their magnificent dimensions.

The collection of European old masters ranges from the 14th century to the French impressionists and beyond. An octagonal room is filled with works by Pissarro, Monet, Boudin, Sisley, and Renoir. De Kooning's *Two Women on a Wharf* and Karel Appel's *Black Landscape* are just two of the more modern examples. Among the sculptures, you'll find Picaso's *Poupée* and Brancusi's *First Cry*, two beauties.

Behind the gallery and connected by an arcade stands The Grange (1817), Toronto's oldest surviving brick house, which was the gallery's first permanent space. Originally the home of the Boulton family, it was a gathering place for many of the city's social and political leaders as well as for such eminent guests as Matthew Arnold,

Prince Kropotkin, and Winston Churchill. Today it's a living museum of mid-19th-century Toronto life, having been meticulously restored and furnished to reflect the 1830s. Entrance is free with admission to the art gallery.

The gallery has an attractive restaurant/atrium bar open for lunch and dinner, as well as a cafeteria, a gallery shop, plus a full program of films, concerts, and lectures.

## MIDTOWN

✪ **Royal Ontario Museum.** 100 Queen's Park Crescent. ☎ **416/586-5549.** Admission C$10 (U.S.$7.15) adults; C$5 (U.S.$3.55) seniors, students, and children 5–14; C$16 families; free for children under 5; free for seniors all day on Tues; free for all Tues 4:30–8pm. Mon–Sat 10am–6pm (until 8pm on Tues), Sun 11am–6pm. Closed Dec 25 and Jan 1. Subway: Museum.

The ROM, as it's affectionately called, is Canada's largest museum, with more than six million objects in its collections.

Among the many highlights is the world-renowned **Chinese collection,** to which a new suite of galleries was added in 1996, enabling the museum to display 1,200 additional works. One of the collection's treasures is the procession of 100 earthenware figures including ox-drawn carts, soldiers, musicians, officials, and attendants dating from the early 6th to the late 7th century. Another is the collection of 14 monumental Buddhist sculptures dating from the 12th to the 16th century. Visitors can also see outstanding examples of early weapons and tools, oracle bones, bronzes and jades, ceramic vessels, human and animal figures, and jewelry and fashion ornaments.

The **Sigmund Samuel Canadiana galleries** display a premier collection of early Canadian decorative arts and historical paintings. More than 1,200 objects showcased in elaborate period room settings reveal in a very concrete way the French and English contributions to Canadian culture.

Other highlights include the Ancient Egypt Gallery, featuring several mummies, the Roman Gallery (the most extensive collection in Canada), the world-class textile collection, nine life-science galleries (devoted to evolution, mammals, reptiles, and botany), and The Gallery of Indigenous Peoples, featuring changing exhibitions exploring the past and present cultures of Canada's indigenous peoples.

A favorite with kids is the **Bat Cave Gallery,** a miniature replica of the St. Clair bat cave in Jamaica, complete with more than 3,000 very lifelike bats roosting and flying through the air amid realistic spiders, crabs, a wildcat, and snakes. Kids also enjoy the spectacular **Dinosaur Gallery,** featuring 13 dinosaur skeletons displayed very realistically, and the **Discovery Gallery,** a minimuseum where kids and adults alike can touch authentic artifacts from Egyptian scarabs to English military helmets.

The latest gallery to open is the **Joey and Toby Tanenbaum Gallery,** which is devoted to Byzantine art and has over 300 objects—icons, frescoes, mosaics, gold jewelry, coins, and glassware.

The ROM's light and airy cafeteria and dining lounge, with a small terrace for outdoor dining, is under the expert supervision of Jamie Kennedy, one of Canada's top chefs. It's well worth stopping in for lunch or dinner.

✪ **George R. Gardiner Museum of Ceramic Art.** 111 Queen's Park. ☎ **416/586-8080.** Suggested donation C$5 (U.S.$3.55). Mon–Sat 10am–5pm (Tues until 8pm), Sun 11am–5pm. Closed Dec 25 and Jan 1. Subway: Museum or St. George.

Across the street from the ROM, the George R. Gardiner Museum, North America's only specialized ceramics museum, houses a great collection of 15th- to 18th-century European ceramics in four galleries. The pre-Columbian gallery contains fantastic Olmec and Maya figures, and objects from Ecuador, Colombia, and Peru. The majolica gallery displays spectacular 16th- and 17th-century salvers and other pieces from

# Midtown Toronto Attractions

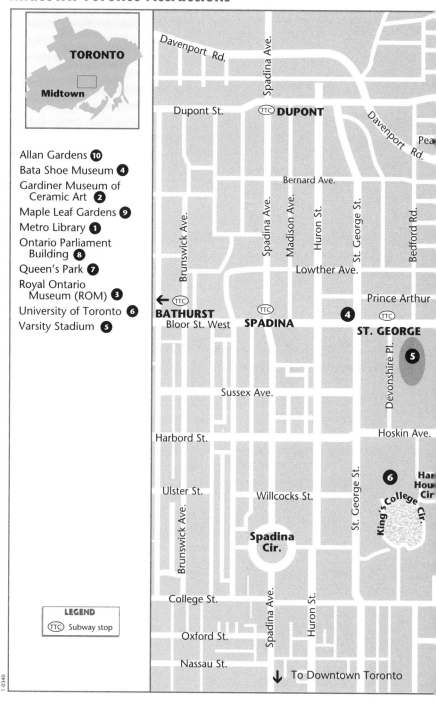

Allan Gardens ⑩
Bata Shoe Museum ④
Gardiner Museum of
  Ceramic Art ②
Maple Leaf Gardens ⑨
Metro Library ①
Ontario Parliament
  Building ⑧
Queen's Park ⑦
Royal Ontario
  Museum (ROM) ③
University of Toronto ⑥
Varsity Stadium ⑤

TORONTO
Midtown

Davenport Rd.
Spadina Ave.
Dupont St.   ⓉⓉⒸ DUPONT
Davenport Rd.
Pea

Bernard Ave.
Brunswick Ave.
Spadina Ave.
Madison Ave.
Huron St.
St. George St.
Bedford Rd.
Lowther Ave.

Prince Arthur
← ⓉⓉⒸ
BATHURST   ⓉⓉⒸ   ④   ⓉⓉⒸ
Bloor St. West   SPADINA   ST. GEORGE
Devonshire Pl.   ⑤

Sussex Ave.

Harbord St.
Hoskin Ave.

Ulster St.   Willcocks St.   St. George St.   ⑥   Har
                                                    Hou
Brunswick Ave.                        King's College Cir.   Cir

Spadina
Cir.

College St.
Spadina Ave.
Huron St.

Oxford St.

Nassau St.
↓ To Downtown Toronto

LEGEND
ⓉⓉⒸ  Subway stop

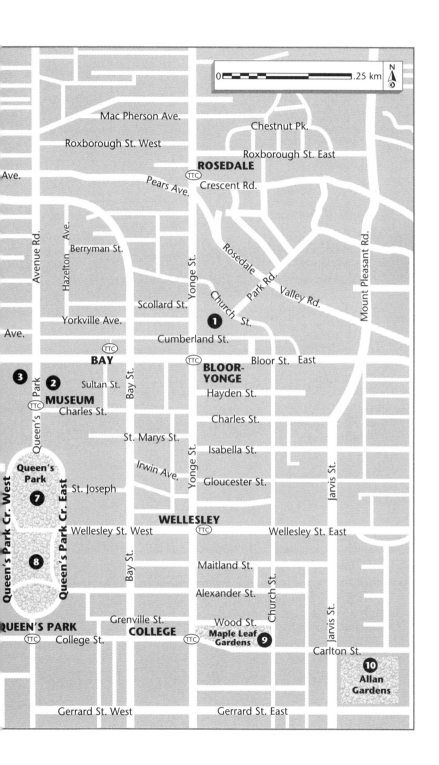

MacPherson Ave.

Chestnut Pk.

Roxborough St. West

Roxborough St. East

Ave.

**ROSEDALE**

Pears Ave.

Crescent Rd.

Avenue Rd.

Hazelton Ave.

Berryman St.

Rosedale Valley Rd.

Park Rd.

Mount Pleasant Rd.

Yonge St.

Scollard St.

Church St.

❶

Yorkville Ave.

Ave.

Cumberland St.

**BAY**

**BLOOR-YONGE**

Bloor St. East

❸

❷ Sultan St.

**MUSEUM**

Charles St.

Hayden St.

Queen's Park

Bay St.

Charles St.

St. Marys St.

Isabella St.

Irwin Ave.

Jarvis St.

Yonge St.

Gloucester St.

**Queen's Park**

St. Joseph

❼

**Queen's Park Cr. West**

**Queen's Park Cr. East**

**WELLESLEY**

Wellesley St. West

Wellesley St. East

❽

Bay St.

Maitland St.

Alexander St.

Church St.

Jarvis St.

**QUEEN'S PARK**

Grenville St.

**COLLEGE**

Wood St.

**Maple Leaf Gardens** ❾

Carlton St.

College St.

❿
**Allan Gardens**

Gerrard St. West

Gerrard St. East

0 ━━━━━ .25 km

N

Florence, Faenza, and Venice, and a Delftware collection of fine 17th-century chargers and other examples.

Upstairs, the galleries are given over to 18th-century continental and English porcelain—Meissen, Sèvres, Worcester, Chelsea, Derby, and other great names. All are spectacular. Among the highlights are pieces from the Swan Service—a 2,200-piece set that took 4 years (1737–41) to make—and an extraordinary collection of Commedia dell'Arte figures.

## ON THE OUTSKIRTS

✪ **Ontario Science Centre.** 770 Don Mills Rd. (at Eglinton Ave. E.). ☎ **416/696-3127,** or 416/696-1000 for Omnimax tickets. Admission C$8 (U.S.$6) adults, C$5 (U.S.$3.60) seniors and children 5–16, C$21 (U.S.$15) families; children under 4 free. Omnimax admission is the same respectively. Special discounts apply if you attend both. July–Aug daily 10am–8pm, otherwise Sun–Tues and Thurs–Sat 10am–5pm, Wed 10am–8pm, Fri 10am–9pm. Closed Dec 25. Parking C$5 (U.S.$3.55). Take the Yonge St. subway to Eglinton, then the Eglinton bus going east; get off at Don Mills Rd. If you're driving from downtown, take the Don Valley Pkwy. and follow the signs from Don Mills Rd. north.

Described as everything from the world's most technical fun fair to a hands-on museum for the 21st century, the Science Centre really does hold a series of wonders for adult and child—800 interactive exhibits in 10 cavernous exhibit halls. With more than a million people visiting every year, it's best to arrive promptly at 10am—that way, you'll be able to get around with less hassle.

Wherever you look, there are things to touch, push, pull, or crank. Test your reflexes, balance, heart rate, and grip strength; surf the Internet; walk through a tropical rain forest; watch frozen-solid liquid nitrogen shatter into thousands of icy shards; study slides of butterfly wings, bedbugs, fish scales, or feathers under the microscope; tease your brain with a variety of optical illusions; land a spaceship on the moon; watch bees making honey; see how many lights you can light or how high you can elevate a balloon with your own pedal power. The fun goes on and on in 10 separate, themed exhibit halls.

Throughout, there are small theaters showing film and slide shows, plus regular 20-minute demonstrations of lasers, metal casting, and high-voltage electricity (watch your friend's hair stand on end). Another draw is the Omnimax Theatre, featuring a 24-meter domed screen that creates spectacular effects. Facilities include a licensed restaurant and lounge, cafeteria, and science shop.

✪ **The Metropolitan Zoo.** Meadowvale Rd. (north of Hwy. 401 and Sheppard Ave.), Scarborough. ☎ **416/392-5900.** Admission C$12 (U.S.$9) adults, C$9 (U.S.$6) seniors and children 12–17, C$7 (U.S.$5) children 4–11, free for children under 3. Summer, daily 9am–7:30pm; spring/fall 9am–5:30pm; winter, daily 9:30am–4:30pm. Last admission is 1 hour before closing. Closed Dec 25. Take the subway to Kennedy on the Bloor–Danforth line. Then take bus no. 86A north. Check with the TTC for schedules (☎ **416/393-4636**). Driving from downtown, take the Don Valley Pkwy. to Hwy. 401 east and exit on Meadowvale Rd.

Covering 710 acres of parkland in Scarborough is a unique zoological garden containing some 5,000 animals, plus an extensive botanical collection. The plants and animals are housed either in pavilions—including Africa, Indo-Malaya, Australasia, and the Americas—or in outdoor paddocks. It's a photographer's dream.

The latest excitement at the zoo is at the African Savannah project, which re-creates an African market bazaar and safari through Kesho (meaning "tomorrow") National Park past such special features as a bush camp, rhino midden, elephant highway, and several watering holes.

Six miles of walkways offer access to all areas of the zoo. During the warmer months, the Zoomobile takes visitors around the major walkways to view the animals contained in the outdoor paddocks. Facilities include restaurants, a gift shop, first-aid, and a family center; strollers, wagons, and wheelchairs are also available. The zoo is equipped with ramps and washrooms for those with disabilities. The African pavilion is also equipped with an elevator for strollers and wheelchairs. There's ample parking and plenty of picnic areas with tables.

✪ **The McMichael Canadian Art Collection.** 10365 Islington Ave., Kleinburg. ☎ **905/ 893-1121.** Admission C$7 (U.S.$5) adults, C$5 (U.S.$ 3.55) seniors and students; children under 5 free. May–Oct daily 10am–5pm; Nov–Apr Tues–Sat 10am–4pm, Sun 10am–5pm. From downtown, take the Gardiner Expwy. to Hwy. 427 north, following it to Hwy. 7. Go east at Hwy. 7 and turn left (north) at the first light onto Hwy. 27. Turn right (east) at Major Mackenzie Dr. and left (north) at the first set of traffic lights to Islington Ave. and the village of Kleinburg. Or take the 401 to Hwy. 400 north. At Major Mackenzie Dr., go west to Islington Ave. and take a right to get to the gallery. Buses travel to the Gallery from Bay and Dundas station and the Yorkdale GO station. Trolley service for C$19 (U.S.$14 adult), C$17 (U.S.$12) children, under 4 free, is also available from key downtown hotels.

Located in Kleinburg, 25 miles north of the city, the McMichael is worth a visit—for the setting as well as the art. The collection is displayed in a log-and-stone gallery that sits amid quiet stands of trees on 100 acres of conservation land. Specially designed for the landscape paintings it houses, the gallery is a work of art itself: The lobby has a pitched roof that soars to a height of 27 feet on massive rafters of Douglas fir; and throughout the gallery, panoramic windows look south over white pine, cedar, ash, and birch.

The work of Canada's famous group of landscape painters, the "Group of Seven," as well as Tom Thomson, David Milne, Emily Carr, and their contemporaries, is displayed here. These artists, inspired by the turn-of-the-century Canadian wilderness, particularly in Algonquin Park and northern Ontario, recorded its rugged landscape in highly individualistic styles. An impressive collection of Inuit and contemporary Native Canadian art and sculpture is also on display. In addition, four galleries are dedicated to changing exhibitions of works by contemporary artists.

Founded by Robert and Signe McMichael, the gallery began in 1965 when they donated their property, home, and collection to the Province of Ontario. Since then, the collection has expanded to include more than 6,000 works.

The museum has a good book and gift store and also an excellent restaurant featuring Canadian cuisine.

**Paramount Canada's Wonderland.** 9580 Jane St., Vaughan. ☎ **905/832-7000,** or 905/ 832-8131 for concert information at the Kingswood Music Theatre. Pay-One-Price Passport, including a day's unlimited rides and shows (excluding parking, special attractions, and the Kingswood Music Theater) C$36 (U.S.$26) adults, C$18 (U.S.$13) seniors and children 3–6, free for children under 2. Grounds admission only (no rides) C$20 (U.S.$14). June 1–25 Mon–Fri 10am–8pm, Fri–Sat 10am–10pm. June 26–Labour Day daily 10am–10pm; May and Labour Day– Oct weekends only 10am–8pm. Closed early Oct to early May. Parking C$6.50 (U.S.$4.65). Take subway to Yorkdale or York Mills, then GO Express Bus directly to Wonderland. If you're driving, take Yonge St. north to Hwy. 401 and travel west to Hwy. 400. Go north on Hwy. 400 to the Rutherford Rd. exit and follow the signs. Exit at Major Mackenzie, if you're going south.

Thirty minutes north of Toronto lies Canada's answer to Disney World. The 300-acre park features more than 140 attractions, including 50 rides, a 20-acre water park called Splash Works, a participatory play area called Kid's Kingdom, and live shows.

Adults and kids alike come for the thriller rides. Because the park relies on the local audience, new rides are introduced every year. The latest stomach churner is the Drop Zone, in which riders free-fall 230 feet in an open cockpit. Another terrifying experience can be had aboard the Xtreme Skyflyer—a cross between hang gliding and skydiving—plunging riders 150 feet in a free fall. The most popular rides are the nine roller coasters, which range from a nostalgic, relatively tame wooden version to the looping inverted Top Gun, the stand-up looping Sky Rider, and the Vortex, a suspended roller coaster. Splash Works offers a huge wave pool, plus 16 water rides from speed slides and tube rides to special scaled-down slides and a kids' water-play area. To add to the thrills for kids and adults, Klingons, Vulcans, Romulans, and Bajorans (along with Hanna-Barbera characters) stroll around the park. Additional attractions include Speedcity Raceway, featuring two-seater go-karts, minigolf, batting cages, restaurants, shops, and the Kingswood Theatre, which hosts top-name entertainers.

You'll probably need 8 hours to see everything. If you picnic on the grounds and forgo buying souvenirs, a family of four can do the park for about C$110 to C$150 (U.S.$79 to U.S.$107), depending on the age of the kids. Watch out, though, for the extra attractions not included in the admission pass, particularly the many "games of skill," which the kids love, but the purse hates.

## 2 More Museums

**The Art Gallery of North York.** 5040 Yonge St., Ford Centre for the Performing Arts, North York. ☎ **416/395-0067.** Free admission. Tues–Sun noon–5pm. Subway: North York Centre.

This 3-year-old gallery is charged with collecting and exhibiting the best contemporary Canadian art created since 1985. Currently, the collection includes works by Stephen Andrews, Genevieve Cadieux, Ivan Eyre, Betty Goodwin, Micah Lexier, Arnaud Maggs, and Roland Poulin.

✪ **The Bata Shoe Museum.** 327 Bloor St. W., at the corner of St. George. ☎ **416/979-7799.** Admission C$6 (U.S.$4.30) adults, C$4 (U.S.$2.85) seniors/students, C$2 (U.S.$1.45) children 5–14, first Tues of the month free. Tues–Wed and Fri–Sat 10am–5pm, Thurs 10am–8pm, Sun noon–5pm. Subway: St. George.

Imelda Marcos—or anyone else obsessed with shoes—will love this museum, housing the 10,000-item personal collection of the Bata family. The building, which was designed by Raymond Moriyama, is spectacular. The main gallery, All About Shoes, traces the history of footwear. It begins with a plaster cast of the first human footprints discovered in Africa by anthropologist Mary Leakey, dating back to 4 million B.C., then wanders through the fads and fashions of every era.

You'll come across such specialty shoes as spiked clogs used to crush chestnuts in 17th-century France, which contend for space with Elton John's 12-inch-plus platforms as well as the well-worn sandals of Pierre Trudeau. In addition to the general historic exhibition, one display focuses on Canadian footwear fashioned by the Inuit, while another highlights 19th-century ladies' footwear. Another smaller gallery houses changing exhibits.

**Black Creek Pioneer Village.** 1000 Murray Ross Pkwy., Downsview, at Steeles Ave. and Jane St. ☎ **416/736-1733.** Admission C$8 (U.S.$6) adults, C$6 (U.S.$4.30) seniors, C$4 (U.S.$2.85) children and students; children under 4 free. May–June weekdays 9:30am–4:30pm, weekends and holidays 10am–5pm; July–Sept daily 10am–5pm; Oct–Dec weekdays 9:30am–4pm, weekends and holidays 10am–4:30pm. Closed Dec 25 and Jan 1–Apr 30. Subway: Finch; then take bus no. 60 to Jane St.

Life here moves at the gentle pace of rural Ontario as it was a hundred years ago. You can watch the authentically dressed villagers going about their chores, spinning, sewing, rail splitting, sheepshearing, and threshing; enjoy their cooking; wander through the cozily furnished homesteads; visit the working mill; shop at the general store; or rumble past the farm animals in a horse-drawn wagon. There are more than 30 restored buildings to explore in this beautifully landscaped village. Special events are offered throughout the year, from a great Easter egg hunt to Christmas by lamplight.

For your convenience, there's a dining room serving lunch and afternoon tea (open May to Thanksgiving and December).

**Canada Sports Hall of Fame.** Exhibition Place. ☎ **416/260-6789.** Free admission. Mon–Fri 10am–4:30pm. Subway: Bathurst; then take streetcar no. 511 south to the end of the line.

Located in the center of Exhibition Place, this three-floor sports hall is devoted to the country's greatest athletes in all major sports. It offers displays complemented by touch-screen computers that tell you everything you could want to know about particular sports personalities and Canada's sport heritage.

**Design Exchange.** 234 Bay St. ☎ **416/363-6121.** Admission C$5 (U.S.$3.55) adults, C$3.50 (U.S.$2.50) students and seniors, free for children 12 and under. Mon–Fri 10am–6pm, Sat–Sun noon–5pm. Subway: King.

Located in the old Stock Exchange Building, this has become Toronto's design center. It showcases the work of design professionals, but the main purpose of the institution is to nurture designers of all types—graphic, industrial, interior, landscape, and urban—and serve as a clearinghouse and resource center for the design community. Small exhibitions on the first floor are open daily and free of charge, while those in the upstairs Exhibition Hall are generally on view for 3 to 6 months and require admission. There's also a good bookstore and Cafe Deco, a cool cafe open Monday through Friday 7:30am to 5pm.

**✪ Hockey Hall of Fame.** 30 Yonge St. at Front in BCE Place. ☎ **416/360-7765.** Admission C$10 (U.S.$7) adults, C$5.50 (U.S.$4) seniors and children 3–13; children under 2 free. Summer: Mon–Sat 9:30am–6pm, Sun 10am–6pm; winter: Mon–Fri 10am–5pm, Sat 9:30am–6pm, Sun 10:30am–5pm. Closed Dec 25 and Jan 1. Subway: Union.

Ice-hockey fans will be thrilled to see the original Stanley Cup (donated in 1893 by Lord Stanley of Preston), a replica of the Montréal Canadiens' locker room, Terry Sawchuck's goalie gear, Newsy Lalonde's skates, and the stick that Max Bentley used, along with photographs of the personalities and great moments in hockey history. The best fun is had at the shooting and goalkeeping interactive displays, where you can take a whack at targets with a puck or don goalie gear and face down flying video pucks or sponge pucks.

**Marine Museum.** Exhibition Place. ☎ **416/392-1765.** Admission C$3.50 (U.S.$2.50) adults, C$2.75 (U.S.$2) seniors and teenagers 13–18, C$2.50 (U.S.$1.80) children under 12; free for children under 6. Tues–Fri 10am–4pm, Sat–Sun noon–5pm. Subway: Bathurst; then take streetcar no. 511 south to the end of the line.

This museum on the grounds of Exhibition Place interprets the history of Toronto Harbour and its relation to the Great Lakes. In summer, visitors can also board the fully restored 1932 *Ned Hanlan,* the last steam tugboat to sail on Lake Ontario. The museum displays marine paintings, ship's models, and memorabilia and artifacts relating to the shipping and naval history of the region.

*Note:* At press time, the museum is closed for renovation, and the collections will be displayed in a more exciting interactive way when it reopens in July 1998 in a new location on the Harbourfront at **The Pier,** 245 Queen's Quay W.

**✪ The Museum for Textiles.** 55 Centre Ave. ☎ **416/599-5321,** or 416/599-5515 for taped information. Admission C$5 (U.S.$3.55) adults, C$4 (U.S.$2.85) students and seniors. Tues–Fri 11am–5pm (Wed until 8pm), Sat–Sun noon–5pm. Subway: St. Patrick.

This fascinating museum is internationally recognized for its collection of more than 8,000 historic and ethnographic textiles and related artifacts. Here you'll find fine Oriental rugs and cloth and tapestries from all over the world. The contemporary gallery also presents the work of contemporary artists. The museum is small so only a tiny portion of the collection is on display, but you'll always find a vibrant, interesting show on view.

## 3  Exploring the Neighborhoods

A city is a patchwork of neighborhoods and the best way to discover the soul and flavor of any place is to walk through the streets looking at the buildings and blending into the street life. Even though Toronto is a sprawling place, it still has distinct neighborhoods. These are among the best.

**THE BEACHES**    This is one of the neighborhoods that makes Toronto a unique city. Here, near the terminus of the Queen Street East tram line, you can stroll or cycle along the lakefront boardwalk. Because of its natural assets, it has become a much sought-after residential neighborhood for young boomers and their families, and there are plenty of well-stocked and eminently browsable stores along Queen Street. Just beyond Waverley Road, you can turn down through Kew Gardens to the boardwalk and walk all the way past the Olympic Pool (jam-packed in summer) to Ashbridge's Bay Park.

**✪ CHINATOWN**    Stretching along Dundas Street west from Bay Street to Spadina Avenue and north and south along Spadina Avenue, Chinatown, home to some of Toronto's 350,000 Chinese citizens, is packed with fascinating shops and restaurants. Even the street signs are in Chinese here.

In **Dragon City,** a large shopping mall at Spadina and Dundas that's staffed by and patronized by Chinese, you'll find all kinds of stores, some selling exotic Chinese preserves like cuttlefish, lemon ginger, whole mango, ginseng, and antler, and others specializing in Asian books, tapes, and records, as well as fashions and foods. Downstairs, a fast-food court features Korean, Indonesian, Chinese, and Japanese cuisines.

As you stroll through Chinatown, stop at the **Kim Moon Bakery** on Dundas Street West (☎ **416/977-1933**) for Chinese pastries and a pork bun or go to one of the tea stores. A walk through Chinatown at night is especially exciting—the sidewalks are filled with people and neon lights shimmer everywhere. You'll pass windows where ducks hang, gleaming noodle houses, record stores selling the Top 10 in Chinese, and trading companies filled with all kinds of Asian produce. Another stopping place might be the **New Asia Supermarket,** around the corner from Dundas Street at 299 Spadina Ave.

For details, see the "Chinatown & Kensington Market" walking tour in chapter 7.

**THE DANFORTH—THE EAST END**    This area stretching along the Danforth east of the Don River is hot, hot, hot and swings until the early hours when the restaurants and bars are still crowded and frenetic. During the day visitors can browse the traditional Greek stores—like **Akropol,** a Greek bakery that displays stunning multitiered wedding cakes in the window. It's an eclectic neighborhood. Along with the Greek food vendors and travel agents, you'll also find stores like the **Scandinavian Shoppe,** at no. 364, which sells great glass and ceramics; **Big Kids Hafta Play Too** (at no. 464), which has some really cool T-shirts; and some New Age and alternative stores.

**LITTLE ITALY**    This vies with Queen Street for the hottest spot in the city. The street hums at night as people crowd the coffee bars, pool lounges, social clubs, and trattorias. It stretches along College Street between Euclid and Shaw.

**MIRVISH VILLAGE**    One of the city's most famous characters is Honest Ed Mirvish, who started his career in the 1950s with his no-frills store at the corner of

Markham and Bloor streets (1 block west of Bathurst). Even from blocks away, neon signs race and advertisements screaming bargains hit you from every direction. Among other things, Ed Mirvish rose to save the Royal Alexandra Theatre on King Street from demolition, established a whole row of adjacent restaurants for theater patrons, and finally developed this block-long area with art galleries, restaurants, and bookstores. He was, of course, responsible for saving and renovating London's Old Vic, although recently he has announced that it is for sale.

Stop by and browse, and don't forget to step into **Honest Ed's** on the corner. (See "Discount" in chapter 8 for a review.)

**QUEEN STREET WEST**   This street has over the years been known as the heart of Toronto's funky, avant-garde scene. Along this street are several clubs—**Bamboo** and the **Rivoli,** in particular—where major Canadian artists/singers have launched their careers. The street is lined with an eclectic mix of stores and businesses. Although recent trends have brought such mainstream stores as the Gap to the street, it still retains a raw, authentic neighborhood edge. There's a broad selection of good-value bistro-style restaurants, a number of fine secondhand antiquarian bookstores, and a lot of funky fashion stores as well as outright junk shops, nostalgic record emporiums, kitchen supply stores, and discount fabric houses. East of Bathurst the street is being slowly gentrified, but beyond Bathurst it still retains its rough-and-ready energy.

For details, see our shopping tour at the end of chapter 8.

**YORKVILLE**   This is the name given to the area that stretches north of Bloor Street, between Avenue Road and Bay Street. Since its founding in 1853 as a village outside the city proper, Yorkville has experienced many transformations. In the 1960s it became Toronto's Haight-Ashbury, the mecca for young suburban runaways otherwise known as hippies. It was the neighborhood of the counterculture. In the 1980s it became the shopping ground of the chic, who dropped their money liberally at such designer-name boutiques as Hermès, Courrèges, Gianni Versace, Cartier, and Turnbull & Asser, as well as at the neighborhood's many fine art galleries. In the early 1990s, the recession left its mark on the area—a fact that became glaringly obvious when Creeds, a Toronto institution, shut its doors. The restored town houses began to look a little forlorn, but today the energy is back and Bloor Street and Hazelton Lanes continue to attract high-style stores, including a branch of Tiffany's.

Stroll around and browse—or sit out and have an iced coffee in the sun at one of the cafes on Yorkville or Cumberland Avenue and watch the parade go by. Some good vantage points can be had at Hemingway's or at any one of many cafes along Yorkville Avenue. Most of these cafes have happy hours from 4 to 7 or 8pm.

Make sure you wander through the labyrinths of Hazelton Lanes between Avenue Road and Hazelton Avenue. There you'll find a maze of shops and offices clustered around an outdoor court in the center of a building that is topped with apartments—one of the most sought-after addresses in the city. In summer, the courtyard is used for outdoor dining; in winter, for skating.

And while you're in the neighborhood (especially if you're an architecture buff), take a look at the redbrick building on Bloor Street at the end of Yorkville Avenue that houses the **Metro Library.** If more libraries had been built like this one in the past, then perhaps study and learning would have come out of the dim and musty closets and into the world where they belong. Step inside—a pool and a waterfall gently screen out the street noise, and pine fencelike partitions undulate through the area like those you find along the sand dunes. Step farther inside and the space opens dramatically to the sky. Every corner is flooded with light and air.

## 4 Architectural Highlights

✪ **Casa Loma.** 1 Austin Terrace. ☎ **416/923-1171.** Admission C$8 (U.S.$6) adults, C$5 (U.S.$3.55) seniors and youths, C$4.50 (U.S.$3.20) children 4–13. Daily 9:30am–4pm. Subway: Dupont; then walk 2 blocks north.

Every city has its folly, and Toronto has a charming one—complete with Elizabethan-style chimneys, Rhineland turrets, secret passageways, an 800-foot underground tunnel, and a mellifluous-sounding name: Casa Loma.

Sir Henry Pellatt, who built it between 1911 and 1914 at a cost of $3.5 million (plus $1.5 million for furnishings), had a lifelong and incurably romantic fascination with medieval castles—so he decided to build his own. He studied European medieval castles and gathered materials and furnishings, bringing marble, glass, and paneling from Europe, teak from Asia, and oak and walnut from prime areas of North America. He imported Scottish stonemasons to build the massive walls that surround the 6-acre site.

It's a fascinating place to explore: the majestic Great Hall, with its 60-foot-high hammer-beam ceiling; the Oak Room, where three artisans took 3 years to fashion the paneling; the Conservatory, with its elegant bronze doors, stained-glass dome, and pink-and-green marble; the battlements and tower; Peacock Alley, designed after Windsor Castle; Sir Henry's suite, containing a shower with an 18-inch-diameter shower head; the 1,700-bottle wine cellar; and the 800-foot tunnel to the stables, where horses were quartered amid the luxury of Spanish tile and mahogany. The tour is self-guided; you'll be given an audio cassette on arrival. From May to October, the gardens are open, too.

**City Hall.** Queen St. W. ☎ **416/392-7341.** Free admission. Self-guided tours Mon–Fri 8:30am–4:30pm. Subway: Queen; then walk west to Bay or take the Queen St. streetcar west 1 stop.

An architectural spectacle, City Hall houses the mayor's office and the city's administrative offices. Daringly designed in the late 1950s by Finnish architect Viljo Revell, it consists of a low podium topped by the flying-saucer-shaped Council Chamber, enfolded between two curved towers. Its interior is as dramatic as its exterior. A cafeteria and dining room are located in the basement.

In front stretches **Nathan Phillips Square** (named after the mayor who initiated the project), where in summer you can sit and contemplate the flower gardens, fountains, and reflecting pool (which doubles as a skating rink in winter), as well as listen to concerts. Here also stands Henry Moore's *Three-Way Piece No. 2,* locally referred to as *The Archer,* purchased through a public subscription fund, and the Peace Garden, commemorating Toronto's sesquicentennial in 1984. In contrast, to the east stands the **Old City Hall,** a green-copper-roofed Victorian Romanesque-style building.

**Eaton Centre.** Dundas and Yonge sts. ☎ **416/598-8700.** Free admission. Mon–Fri 10am–9pm, Sat 9:30am–6pm, Sun noon–5pm. Subway: Dundas or Queen.

Buttressed at both ends by 30-story skyscrapers, this high-tech center, which cost over C$250 million to build, stretches from Dundas Street and Yonge Street south to Queen Street, an area that encompasses six million square feet. **Eaton's Department Store** takes up one million square feet, and the rest is filled with more than 320 stores and restaurants and two garages. Some 20 million people shop here annually.

Inside, the structure opens into the impressive **Galleria,** an 866-foot-long glass-domed arcade dotted with benches, orchids, palm trees, and fountains; it's further adorned by Michael Snow's 60 soaring Canada geese, entitled *Step Flight.* The birds

## Impressions

*It is impossible to give it anything but commendation. It is not squalid like Birming-
ham, or cramped like Canton, or hellish like New York, or tiresome like Nice. It is all
right. . . .*

—Rupert Brooke, *Letters from America* (1913)

*O for a half hour of Europe after this sanctimonious icebox!*

—Wyndham Lewis *(The Letters of Wyndham Lewis)*

are made from black-and-white photos mounted on cast fiberglass frames. Three tiers
rise above, reached by escalator and glass elevators, giving glorious views over this
Crystal Palace and Milan–style masterpiece designed by Eb Zeidler (who also
designed Ontario Place). Here, rain or shine, you can enjoy the sights, sounds, and
aromas in comfort—don't be surprised by the twittering of the sparrows, some of
whom have decided that this environment is as pleasant as the outdoors.

One more amazing fact about this construction: It was built around two of
Toronto's oldest landmarks—**Trinity Church** (1847) and **Scadding House**
(☎ **416/598-4521**), home of Trinity's rector, Dr. Scadding—because the public demanded that the developers allow the sun to continue to shine on the church's twin
towers. It does!

**Metropolitan Toronto Reference Library.** 789 Yonge St. ☎ **416/393-7000.** Free admission. Mon–Thurs 10am–8pm, Fri–Sat 10am–5pm, Sun 1:30–5pm (closed Sunday May–
Thanksgiving). Subway: Bloor.

If more libraries were built like this one, perhaps academia would be a more attractive profession. Step inside—a pool and a waterfall gently screen out the street
noise—and the space opens dramatically to the sky. Every corner is flooded with light
and air. I envy the citizens of Toronto for their architect Raymond Moriyama, who
designed this incredible structure.

✪ **Ontario Legislature.** 111 Wellesley St. W. at University Ave. ☎ **416/325-7500.** Free admission. Mon–Fri and weekends from Victoria Day to Labour Day. On weekends, tours are given
every half hour 9–11:30am and 1–4pm; call ahead at other times. Subway: Queen's Park.

East of the university, at the northern end of University Avenue, lies Queen's Park,
surrounding the rose-tinted sandstone-and-granite Ontario Parliament Buildings,
with stately domes, arches, and porte cocheres. At any time of year other than summer, drop in around 2pm—when the legislature is in session—for some pithy com-
ments during the question period, or take one of the regular tours. It's best to call
ahead to check times.

**Royal Bank Plaza.** Front and Bay sts. Free admission. Year-round. Subway: Union.

Shimmering in the sun, Royal Bank Plaza looks like a pillar of gold, and with good
reason. During its construction, 2,500 ounces of gold were used as a coloring agent
in the building's 14,000 windows. More importantly, it's a masterpiece of architectural design. Two triangular towers of bronze mirror glass flank a 130-foot-high
glass-walled banking hall. The external walls of the towers are built in a serrated con-
figuration so that they reflect a phenomenal mosaic of color from the skies and surrounding buildings.

In the banking hall, hundreds of aluminum cylinders hang from the ceiling, the
work of Venezuelan sculptor Jésus Raphael Soto. Two levels below, there's a waterfall and pine-tree setting that's naturally illuminated from the hall above.

## 5 Historic Buildings

**Campbell House.** 160 Queen St. W. ☎ **416/597-0227.** Admission C$3.50 (U.S.$2.50) adults; C$2.50 (U.S.$1.80) seniors, students, and children. Mon–Fri 9:30am–4:30pm; Sat–Sun noon–4:30pm (late May to mid-Oct). Subway: Osgoode.

Just across from Osgoode Hall, at the corner of University Avenue, sits the 1822 mansion of Loyalist and sixth chief justice of Upper Canada Sir William Campbell. In 1829, he retired to this mansion, where he resided until his death in 1834. It was moved from its original location in 1972 and has been beautifully restored and features a collection of period furniture. Costumed interpreters conduct guided tours that provide insight into Toronto's early history.

**Colborne Lodge.** High Park. ☎ **416/392-6916.** Admission C$3.50 (U.S.$2.50) adults, C$2.75 (U.S.$1.95) seniors and children 13–18, C$2.50 (U.S.$1.80) children 12 and under. Tues–Sun noon–5pm. Call ahead; hours do change. Subway: High Park.

This charming, English-style Regency cottage with a three-sided veranda was built in 1836–37 to take advantage of the view of Lake Ontario and the Humber River. When it was built, it was considered to be way out in the country and a bother to travel to during the harsh winters. In 1873, the owner, a Toronto surveyor and architect named John Howard, donated the house and surrounding land to the city in return for an annual salary, thus creating High Park—a great recreational area.

**Fort York.** Garrison Rd., off Fleet St. ☎ **416/392-6907.** Admission C$5 (U.S.$3.55) adults, C$3.25 ($2.30) ages 13–18 and seniors, C$3 (U.S.$2.15) children 6–12. Summer (June–Oct): Mon–Wed and Fri 10am–5pm, Thurs 10am–7pm, Sat–Sun noon–5pm; winter: Tues–Fri 10am–5pm, Sat–Sun noon–5pm. Subway: Bathurst; then streetcar no. 511 south.

Established by Lieutenant Governor Simcoe in 1793 to defend "little muddy York," as Toronto was then known, Fort York, between Bathurst Street and Strachan Avenue, was sacked by Americans in 1813. You can tour the soldiers' and officers' quarters and clamber over the ramparts, as well as view demonstrations. In summer, the fort really comes to life with daily demonstrations of drill, music, and cooking. The fort is a few blocks west of the CN Tower and 2 blocks east of Exhibition Place.

**Mackenzie House.** 82 Bond St. ☎ **416/392-6915.** Admission C$3.50 (U.S.$2.50) adults, C$2.75 (U.S.$2) seniors and ages 13–18, C$2.50 (U.S.$1.80) children 5–12. May–Dec Tues–Sun noon–4pm. Sat–Sun noon–5pm the rest of the year. Subway: Dundas.

This typical mid-19th-century brick row house, 2 blocks east of Yonge and south of Dundas, gives some idea of what Toronto must have looked like then, when the streets were lined with similar buildings. It was purchased for William Lyon Mackenzie, leader of the 1837 rebellion, by concerned friends and fund-raisers, and he lived here from 1859 to 1861. It's furnished in 1850s style, and in the back there's a print shop designed after Mackenzie's own.

**Osgoode Hall.** 130 Queen St. W. ☎ **416/947-3300.** Free admission. Tours given Mon–Fri at 1:15pm July–Aug only. Subway: Osgoode.

To the west of City Hall extends an impressive, elegant wrought-iron fence in front of an equally gracious public building, Osgoode Hall, currently the home of the Law Society of Upper Canada and the Court of Appeal for Ontario. Folklore has it that the fence was originally built to keep cows from trampling the flower beds. Tours of the interior will show you the splendor of the grand staircase, the rotunda, the Great Library, and the fine portrait and sculpture collection. Building began in 1829 on this structure, troops were billeted here after the Rebellion of 1837, and the buildings now house the headquarters of Ontario's legal profession and several

---

**❓ Did You Know?**

- The first singing commercial was supposedly created by Torontonian Ernie Bushnell in 1926 for the local Jehovah's Witness radio station.
- The Ontario Legislature sits on land that was originally occupied (appropriately, some say) by a lunatic asylum.
- The population of York (Toronto) in 1812 was a mere 703.
- It takes an average fit person 20 minutes just to descend the 2,570 steps of the CN Tower.
- Ernest Hemingway was hired by the Toronto Star at age 19 and was paid $150 a year.
- Before breaking into the major leagues, Babe Ruth hit his first home run as a professional ball player during a game at Hanlan's Point Stadium on the Toronto Islands in September, 1914. He also managed to pitch a shutout.
- 2500 ounces of gold were used as a coloring agent in the 14,000 windows of the Royal Bank Building.
- Yonge Street is the longest street in the world, stretching 1,900km (1,190 miles) north from downtown Toronto.
- Toronto is home to more than 80 different ethnic groups speaking 100 different languages.

---

magnificent courtrooms—including one built with materials from London's Old Bailey. The courts are open to the public.

**Spadina.** 285 Spadina Rd. ☎ **416/392-6910.** Admission C$5 (U.S.$3.55) adults, C$3.25 (U.S.$2.30) seniors and youth, C$2.15 (U.S.$1.55) children 12 and under. Tues–Fri noon–4pm, Sat–Sun noon–5pm. Subway: Dupont.

If you want to know how the leaders of the Family Compact lived, visit this historic home of financier James Austin. The exterior of the house is not that imposing but the interior contains a remarkable collection of art, furniture, and decorative objects. The same family, the Austins, occupied the house from 1866 to 1980, which accounts for the richness of the collections. Tours are mandatory. In summer, the gardens can also be toured; during the Christmas season the house is decorated authentically too. It's next door to Casa Loma.

# 6 Markets

✪ **Kensington Market.** Bounded by Dundas St., Spadina Ave., Baldwin St., and Augusta Ave. Most stores are open Mon–Sat. Subway: St. Patrick, then take the streetcar west.

This is a colorful and lively tapestry that should not be missed. If you can struggle out of bed to get here around 5am, you'll see the squawking chickens being carried from their trucks to the stalls. You'll hear the accents of Caribbean Islanders, Portuguese, Italians, and merchants of other nationalities, who spread their wares before them—squid and crabs in pails, chickens, pigeons, bread, cheese, apples, pears, peppers, ginger, and mangoes from the West Indies, salted fish from Portuguese dories, lace, fabrics, and other colorful remnants. There's no market on Sunday.

✪ **St. Lawrence Market.** 92 Front St. E. ☎ **416/392-7219.** Tues–Thurs 9am–7pm, Fri 8am–8pm, Sat 5am–5pm. Subway: Union.

This handsome food market is housed in a vast building constructed around the facade of the second city hall, built in 1850. Vendors sell fresh meat, fish, fruit, vegetables, and dairy products as well as other foodstuffs. The best time to visit is early Saturday morning, shortly after the farmers have brought their wares into town.

## 7 Parks & Gardens

**Allan Gardens.** Stretching between Jarvis, Sherbourne, Dundas, and Gerrard sts. ☎ **416/392-7259.** Free admission. Daily dawn–dusk. Subway: Dundas.

These gardens were given to the city by George William Allan, who was born in 1822 to wealthy merchant and banker William Allan. His father gave him a vast estate stretching from Carlton Street to Bloor Street between Jarvis and Sherbourne. George married into the Family Compact when he married John Beverley Robinson's daughter. A lawyer by training, he became a city councilor, mayor, senator, and philanthropist. The lovely old concert pavilion was demolished, but the glass-domed Palm House still stands in all its radiant Victorian glory. Today it's rather seedy and certainly should be avoided after dark.

**Edwards Garden.** Lawrence Ave. and Leslie St. ☎ **416/397-1340.** Free admission. Daily dawn–dusk. Subway: Eglinton, then take the Leslie or Lawrence bus.

This quiet, formal garden with a creek cutting through it is part of a series of parks. Gracious bridges arch over the creek, rock gardens abound, and rose and other seasonal flower beds add color and scent to the landscape. The garden is famous for its rhododendrons. The Civic Garden Centre operates a gift shop and gives walking tours on Tuesday and Thursday at 11am and 2pm. The Centre also boasts a very fine horticultural library.

**High Park.** In the West End, extending south of Bloor St. to the Gardiner Expwy. Free admission. Daily dawn to dusk. Subway: High Park.

This 400-acre park was John G. Howard's great gift to the city. He lived in Colborne Lodge, which still stands in the park. The park contains a large lake called Grenadier Pond (great for skating in winter), a small zoo, a swimming pool, tennis courts, sports fields, bowling greens, and vast expanses of green for baseball, jogging, picnicking, bicycling, and more.

## 8 Cemeteries

✪ **Mount Pleasant Cemetery.** 1643 Yonge St. or 375 Mount Pleasant Rd., north of St. Clair Ave. ☎ **416/485-9129.** Free admission. Daily 8am–dusk. Subway: St. Clair.

Home to one of the finest tree collections in North America, this cemetery is also the final resting place of many fascinating people. Of particular note are **Glenn Gould,** the celebrated classical pianist; **Drs. Banting** and **Best,** the codiscoverers of insulin; golfer **George Knudson;** and the **Massey** and **Eaton** families, whose mausoleums are impressive architectural monuments. Prime Minister **William Lyon Mackenzie King;** Canada's greatest war hero, Lt. Col. **William Barker;** and 52 victims of Air Canada Flight 621, which crashed en route to Los Angeles in 1970, were also laid to rest here.

**Necropolis.** 200 Winchester St. at Sumach St. ☎ **416/923-7911.** Free admission. Daily 8am–dusk. Subway: Parliament.

This is one of the city's oldest cemeteries (1850). Many of the remains that are buried here, though, were originally buried in Potters Field, where Yorkville stands today.

Before strolling through the cemetery, pick up a History Tour at the office. You'll find the graves of **William Lyon Mackenzie,** leader of the 1837 rebellion, as well as those of his followers, **Samuel Lount** and **Peter Matthews,** who were hanged for their part in the rebellion. **Anderson Abbot,** the first Canadian-born black surgeon; **Joseph Tyrrell,** who discovered dinosaurs in Alberta; **Ned Hanlan,** world-champion oarsman; and many more notable Torontonians can be found in this 15-acre cemetery, beyond the porte cochere and Gothic Revival chapel, designed by **Henry Langley,** who is also buried in the cemetery.

## 9 Especially for Kids

The city puts on a fabulous array of special events for children at **Harbourfront.** In March, the **Children's Film Festival** screens 40 films from 15 countries. In April, **Spring Fever** celebrates the season with egg decorating, puppet shows, and more; on Saturday mornings in April, **cushion concerts** are given for the 5 to 12 set. In May, the **Milk International Children's Festival** brings 100 international children's performers to the city for a week of great entertainment. For additional information, call ☎ **416/973-3000.**

For the last 30 years, the **Young Peoples Theatre,** at 165 Front St. E., at Sherbourne Street (☎ **416/862-2222** box office or 416/363-5131 administration), has been entertaining young people. Its season runs from August to May.

Look in the sections above for the following Toronto-area attractions that have major appeal for kids of all ages. I've summarized the top attractions for kids in what I think is the most logical order, at least from a kid's point of view (the first five, though, really belong in a dead heat).

- **Ontario Science Centre** (*see p. 110*)   Kids race to be the first at this paradise of fun hands-on games, experiments, and push-button demonstrations—800 of 'em.
- **Paramount Canada's Wonderland** (*see p. 111*)   The kids can't wait to get on the roller coasters and daredevil rides in this theme park. But watch out for those video games, which they also love—an unanticipated extra cost.
- **Harbourfront** (*see p. 104*)   Kaleidoscope is an ongoing program of creative crafts, active games, and special events on weekends and holidays. There's also a summer pond, winter ice-skating, and a crafts studio.
- **Ontario Place** (*see p. 101*)   The Children's Village, water slides, a huge Cinesphere, a futuristic pod, and other entertainments are the big hits at this recreational/cultural park on three artificial islands on the edge of Lake Ontario. In the Children's Village, kids 12 and under can scramble over rope bridges, bounce on an enormous trampoline, or drench one another in the water-play section.
- **Metro Zoo** (*see p. 110*)   One of the best in the world, modeled after San Diego's—the animals in this 710-acre park really do live in a natural environment.
- **Toronto Islands—Centreville** (*see p. 105*)   Riding a ferry to this turn-of-the-century amusement park is part of the fun.
- **CN Tower** (*see p. 105*)   Especially for the interactive simulator games and the terror of the glass floor.
- **Royal Ontario Museum** (*see p. 107*)   The top hit is always the dinosaurs and the spooky bat cave.
- **Fort York** (*see p. 118*)   For its reenactments of battle drills, musket and cannon firing, and musical marches with fife and drum.

- **The Hockey Hall of Fame** (*see p. 113*) Who wouldn't want the chance to goalkeep against Mark Messier and Wayne Gretzky (with a sponge puck) and to practice scoring and keeping with the fun and challenging video pucks?
- **Black Creek Pioneer Village** (*see p. 112*) For craft and other demonstrations.
- **Casa Loma** (*see p. 116*) The stables, secret passageway, and fantasy rooms really capture children's imaginations.
- **Art Gallery of Ontario** (*see p. 106*) For its hands-on kids' exhibit.

**Chudleigh's.** 9528 Hwy. 25 (3km north of Hwy. 401), Milton. ☎ **905/826-1252.** Orchard admission C$3 (U.S.$2.15) ages 4 and older, applied to purchases. July 1–Oct 31 daily 9am–7pm, Nov–June Fri–Sun 10am–5pm.

A day here will introduce the kids to life on a farm. They'll enjoy the hay rides, pony rides, and, in season, the apple picking as well as the playground, straw maze, and more. The store sells pies, cider, and other produce.

**Cullen Gardens & Miniature Village.** Taunton Rd., Whitby. ☎ **905/668-6606.** Admission C$10 (U.S.$7) adults, C$8 (U.S.$6) seniors, C$4 (U.S.$2.85) children 3–12. Daily in summer 9am–8pm, daily 10am–5pm spring and fall. Closed early Jan to mid-Apr.

The miniature village made to $^1/_{12}$ scale has great appeal. The 27 acres of gardens, the children's playground with two splash ponds, the shopping, and the live entertainment only add to the fun.

**Playdium.** 99 Rathburn Rd. W., Mississauga. ☎ **905/273-9000.** C50¢–$5.50 (U.S.35¢–$4) per game or attraction. Mon–Wed 11am–10pm, Thurs–Fri 11am–midnight, Sat 9am–midnight, Sun 9am–10pm. Take Hwy. 401 west to Hwy. 403 west, taking the exit south at Hurontario and an immediate right on Rathburn. Or from downtown, take the QEW west to Hurontario Rd., then drive north for 15 min., take a left on Robert Speck Pkwy., then a right on City Center Dr. and continue to Rathburn, taking a left.

The Playdium is an up-to-the-minute interactive pleasure palace filled with 180 games and simulators like Speedzone, an IndyCar race. In addition, there are rock-climbing walls, a go-kart track, an IMAX theater, batting cages, and minigolf, too. When you need a break, there's a lounge-restaurant. Beyond the sliding steel door activated by an infrared sensor, you'll discover a surreal scene of huge TV screens, circuit boards, and neon and strobe-lit "alien squid mushrooms."

**Riverdale Farm.** 201 Winchester St., off Parliament, 1 block north of Carlton. ☎ **416/392-6794.** Free admission. Daily 9am–5pm.

Idyllically situated on the edge of the Don Valley Ravine, this working farm right in the city is a favorite with small tots who enjoy watching the cows and pigs and petting the other farm animals.

**Wildwater Kingdom.** Finch Ave., 1 mile west of Hwy. 427, Brampton. ☎ **416/369-0774** or 905/794-0565. Admission C$18 (U.S.$13) adults, C$14 (U.S.$10) children 4–9. May 31 to mid-June weekends only 10am–6pm, July–Labour Day daily 10am–8pm. Note that openings are weather-dependent.

A huge water theme park complete with a 20,000-square-foot wave pool, tube slides, speed slides, giant hot tubs, and the super-thrilling Cyclone water ride. There are bumper boats, pedal boats, canoes, batting cages, and minigolf, too.

# 10 Tours

## INDUSTRIAL TOURS

✪ **Canadian Broadcasting Centre.** 250 Front St. W. Free tours of the facilities are given daily; reservations are required. ☎ **416/205-3700** for times and reservations. Subway: Union.

The headquarters for the English Networks of the CBC, this building was designed by Bregman and Hamann and Scott with John Burgee and Philip Johnson as consultants. It's one of the most modern broadcasting facilities in North America. From the minute visitors enter, they know they're in a studio facility because there's even a lobby viewing studio. Check out the **CBC Museum,** an often-nostalgic series of interactive exhibits and film clips showcasing CBC's broadcast history (open weekdays 9am to 5pm; free).

✪ **ChumCity.** 299 Queen St. W. ☎ **416/591-5757** to arrange a tour. Subway: Osgoode.

This innovative television station contrasts dramatically with the formality of the CBC. In the ChumCity building at the corner of John and Queen streets, visitors will discover a television factory where cameras are not hard-wired to studios or control rooms, but can be plugged into any one of 35 hydrants that allow them to go on-air in minutes. Instead of formal shows confined to studios, programs can virtually flow minute by minute from any working area in the building, including the hallways and rooftop. From this location, the cutting-edge company operates three channels—**Citytv,** a popular local TV station, **MuchMusic,** which is similar to MTV, and **Bravo,** a 24-hour arts channel. The staff is young and cutting-edge, with an impressive, fast-response news team. They have 100 permanently fixed remote-control cameras, 25 mobile news cruisers, plus remote terminals at key locations such as City Hall, Metro Hall, the TTC, and police headquarters. The results can be seen on CityPulse at noon, 6, and 11pm.

This futuristic, truly interactive TV station even invites casual visitors to air their opinions and grievances. Simply enter **Speakers Corner,** a video booth at the corner of John and Queen streets, and bare your soul before the camera. If you're compelling or bizarre enough, you'll get your 15 seconds of fame on a weekly half-hour show, or in short blurbs run on Citytv and MuchMusic.

**Toronto Stock Exchange.** Exchange Tower, 2 First Canadian Place, at the northeast corner of King and York sts. ☎ **416/947-4670.** Free admission. Mon–Fri 9am–4:30pm. Subway: St. Andrew.

With C$1 billion dollars of stock being traded every business day, this is Canada's premier marketplace and the second-largest stock exchange in North America. The public gallery is currently being redesigned and will reopen in May 1998.

## ORGANIZED TOURS

**BUS TOURS**   If you enjoy hop-on, hop-off bus tours, try the one offered by **Olde Town Toronto Tours Ltd.,** 900 Dixon Rd., Etobicoke, ON, M9W 1J7 (☎ **416/368-6877**). Tickets—C$25 (U.S.$18) for adults, C$23 (U.S.$16) children over 12, C$12 (U.S.$9) for children 4–11—are valid for 24 hours, allowing you to disembark from the double-decker bus whenever and wherever you wish. Tours operate year-round from 9am to 9pm in summer and from 9am to 4pm in winter.

**Grayline Tours,** 184 Front St. E. (☎ **416/594-3310**), operates similar tours, going past such major sights as Eaton Centre, City Hall, the university, Yorkville, Casa Loma, Chinatown, Harbourfront, and the CN Tower. These tours are operated between early May and the end of October, and cost C$25 (U.S.$18) adults, C$22 (U.S.$16) seniors, and C$16 (U.S.$11) for children 2 to 12.

**HARBOR & ISLAND TOURS**   **Toronto Tours** (☎ **416/869-1372**) operates 1-hour tours of the port and the islands from May to the end of October every hour on the hour between 10am and 5pm (until 8pm in July and August) for C$14.75 (U.S.$11) adults, C$11.75 (U.S.$8) seniors, and C$8.75 (U.S.$6) for children 12 and under. Tours leave from 145 Queen's Quay W. at the foot of York Street.

For a real thrill, board the three-masted, 96-foot schooner *The Challenge* for a 1- or 2-hour cruise at 12:15, 1:15, 3:45, and 5pm on weekdays, and 11am, 1, 2, 4, and 5pm on weekends. Prices for the 1-hour cruise are C$12 (U.S.$9) adults, C$10 (U.S.$7) seniors and students, and C$7 (U.S.$5) children 5 to 14; for 2 hours, it's C$17 (U.S.$12), C$14 (U.S.$10), and C$11 (U.S.$8), respectively. For more information, call the **Great Lakes Schooner Company,** 249 Queens Quay W., Suite 111 (☎ **416/260-6355**).

**HELICOPTER TOURS**    For an aerial view of the city, contact **National Helicopters,** Toronto City Centre Airport, Toronto ON, M5V 1A1 (☎ **416/361-1100**), whose helicopters take off from the Island airport. The charge is C$50 (U.S.$36) per person for 8 minutes.

**WALKING/BIKING TOURS**    Among the many available walking tours, some of the very best are led by the youthful, energetic, and enthusiastic Shirley Lum, a self-confessed foodie. Shirley was born in Toronto and loves her city. She is a graduate in politics, philosophy, and sociology and brings all of her expertise and enthusiasm to bear on the history and social life of whichever area she is exploring. She leads a wonderful tour through Old Chinatown that focuses on the history and personalities of the neighborhood and also includes stops at a variety of stores, including a tofu manufacturing store, an herbalist, a tea store, a bakery, and a Taoist temple. The highlight of the tour is a leisurely dim sum lunch at one of the best such emporiums in the community. It's great fun, and you'll never look at Chinatown in quite the same way again. Shirley also offers tours of Rosedale and Yorkville, Kensington Market, the East End, and the St. Lawrence Market, as well as bike tours. Two-hour tours cost C$12 (U.S.$9) adults, C$10 (U.S.$7) seniors and students, C$6 (U.S.$4) children under 12; 3-hour tours, including meals and tasting samples, cost C$25 (U.S.$18), C$20 (U.S.$14), and C$12 (U.S.$9), respectively. Bike tours, which include a light lunch and afternoon snack, are C$35 (U.S.$25), C$30 (U.S.$21), and C$25 (U.S.$18), respectively. For information and reservations, call ☎ **416/463-9233.**

During the summer, the **Toronto Historical Board** offers free walking tours of several different neighborhoods, including Cabbagetown and Rosedale. Call ☎ **416/392-6827** for details.

## 11  Outdoor Activities

For additional information on facilities in the parks, golf courses, tennis courts, swimming pools, beaches, and picnic areas, call **Metro Parks** (☎ **416/392-8186**) or **City Parks** (☎ **416/392-1111**). Also see "Parks & Gardens," above.

**BIKING**    *Bicycling* magazine recently named Toronto the number one cycling city in North America because of its large number of bike paths and local pedalers (7% of the population). And indeed the city is great for biking. Bikes can be rented from **Wheel Excitement,** 5 Rees St. south of Skydome (☎ **416/260-9000**), for C$14 (U.S.$10) for the first 2 hours, plus C$2 (U.S.$1.45) for each additional hour, or C$24 (U.S.$17) a day. You can also rent bicycles from **McBride Cycle,** 180 Queens Quay W. at York on Harbourfront (☎ **416/203-5651**); **Toronto Island Bicycle Rental** (☎ **416/203-0009**) on Centre Island; and from **High Park Cycle and Sports,** 24 Ronson Dr. (☎ **416/614-6689**).

The Martin Goodman Trail, which runs from the Beaches to the Humber River along the waterfront, is ideal for biking. There's also a Lower Don Valley bike trail that starts in the east end of the city at Front Street and runs north to Riverdale Park.

*Toronto is New York . . . run by the Swiss.*

—Peter Ustinov

High Park is another good venue, along with the parks along the ravines. Official bike lanes are marked on College/Carlton streets, the Bloor Street Viaduct leading to the Danforth, Beverly/St. George, and Davenport Road. The Convention and Visitors Association has more detailed information on these bike lanes. **The Toronto Bicycling Network (☎ 416/766-1985)** offers day and weekend trips.

**BOATING/CANOEING**  At the **Harbourside Boating Centre,** 283 Queen's Quay W. (☎ 416/203-3000), you can rent sail- and powerboats and take sailing lessons. For 3 hours, depending on the boat's size, sailboats cost from C$55 (U.S.$39) to C$495 (U.S.$354). Powerboats cost C$85 to C$180 (U.S.$61 to U.S.$129). Week-long and weekend sailing courses are also offered.

**Harbourfront Canoe and Kayak School,** 283A Queens Quay W. (☎ 416/203-2277), rents kayaks for C$50 (U.S.$36) weekends, C$35 (U.S.$25) a day, or C$15 (U.S.$11) an hour; canoes for C$45 (U.S.$32) on weekends, C$30 (U.S.$21) a day, and C$10 (U.S.$7) an hour. Open daily in summer mid-June to Labour Day; weekdays only spring and fall, weather permitting.

Canoes, rowboats, and pedal boats can also be rented on the Toronto Islands just south of Centreville.

**CROSS-COUNTRY SKIING**  You can ski in Toronto's parks when snow is on the ground. Best bets are Sunnybrook Park and Ross Lord Park, both in North York. For more information, call **Metro Parks** (☎ 416/392-8186).

**GOLF**  Among the city's half-dozen metro public golf courses the following stand out:

**Don Valley,** at Yonge Street south of Highway 401 (☎ 416/392-2465), designed by Howard Watson, is a scenic course with some challenging elevated tees and a par-5 12th hole. It's a good place to start your kids. Greens fees are C$26 to C$33 (U.S.$19 to U.S.$24).

**Humber Valley** (☎ 416/392-2488) is a par-70 links and valleyland course that has three final holes requiring major concentration. Greens fees are C$25 to C$28 (U.S.$18 to U.S.$20).

The moderately difficult **Tam O'Shanter** course, Birchmount Avenue, north of Sheppard (☎ 416/392-2547), features links holes and water hazards among its challenges. Greens fees are C$25 to C$28 (U.S.$18 to U.S.$20).

There are several outstanding championship courses in the Toronto area. The most famous is the Jack Nicklaus-designed **Glen Abbey Golf Club** in Oakville (☎ 905/844-1800), the course where the Canadian Open is most often played. Greens fees at Glen Abbey are C$145 (U.S.$104). **The Lionhead Golf Club** in Brampton (☎ 905/455-4900) has two 18-hole par-72 courses, charging C$145 (U.S.$104) for the tougher course and C$130 (U.S.$93) for the other course. In Markham, the **Angus Glen Golf Club** (☎ 905/887-5157) has a Doug Carrick–designed par-72 course and charges a C$120 (U.S.$86) greens fee.

**FITNESS CENTERS**  **Metro Central YMCA,** 20 Grosvenor St. (☎ 416/975-9622), has excellent facilities, including a 25-meter swimming pool, all kinds of cardiovascular machines, Nautilus equipment, an indoor track, squash and racquetball courts, and aerobics classes. A reasonably priced day pass is available.

**ICE-SKATING**    Nathan Phillips Square in front of City Hall becomes a free ice rink in winter, as does an area at Harbourfront Centre. Rentals are available. Artificial rinks are also found in more than 25 parks, including Grenadier Pond in High Park—a romantic spot with its bonfire and vendors selling roasted chestnuts. They're open from November to March.

**IN-LINE SKATING**    In-line skates can be rented from **Wheel Excitement** (see "Biking," above).

**JOGGING**    Downtown sites might include Harbourfront and along the lakefront, or through Queen's Park and the University. The Martin Goodman Trail runs 20 kilometers (12.4 miles) along the waterfront from the Beaches in the east to the Humber River in the west, and it's ideal for jogging, walking, or cycling. It links to the Tommy Thompson Trail, which travels the parks stretching from the lakefront along the Humber River. Near the Ontario Science Centre in the Central Don Valley, Ernest Thompson Seton Park is also good for jogging. Parking is available at the Thorncliffe Drive and Wilket Creek entrances.

**SWIMMING**    There are a dozen or so outdoor pools (open June to September) in the municipal parks, including High and Rosedale parks, plus indoor pools at several community recreation centers. For **pool information,** call ☎ **416/392-1111.**

The **University of Toronto Athletic Centre,** 55 Harbord St. at Spadina Avenue (☎ **416/978-4680**), opens its swimming pool free to the public on Sunday from noon to 4pm. The pool at the **YMCA,** 20 Grosvenor St. (☎ **416/975-9622**), can be used on a day pass, which costs C$12.84 (U.S.$9).

There are public beaches on the Toronto Islands (off Hanlan's Point), and at Woodbine Beach in the Beaches neighborhood, but quite frankly, the waters of Lake Ontario are polluted, and although people do swim in them, they do so at their own risk. Signs are posted when a beach is deemed unsafe, usually after a heavy rainfall.

**TENNIS**    There are tennis facilities in more than 30 municipal parks. The most convenient locations are the courts in High Park, Rosedale, and Jonathan Ashridge parks. They are open in summer only. At Eglinton Flats Park, west of Keele Street at Eglinton, six of the courts can be used in winter. Call the city at ☎ **416/392-1111** or Metro Parks at ☎ **416/392-8186** for additional information.

# 12  Spectator Sports

**AUTO RACING**    **The Molson Indy** is run at the Exhibition Place Street circuit, usually on the third weekend in July. For information, call ☎ **416/872-4639.**

**BASEBALL**    The **SkyDome,** on Front Street beside the CN Tower, is the home of the **Toronto Blue Jays** (World Series champs in 1992 and 1993). For information, contact the Toronto Blue Jays, P.O. Box 7777, Adelaide St., Toronto, ON, M5C 2K7 (☎ **416/341-1000**). For tickets, which run from C$4 to C$35 (U.S.$2.85 to U.S.$25), call ☎ **888/654-6529** or 416/341-1234.

**BASKETBALL**    Toronto's basketball team, the Raptors, has generated an urban fever. Currently, the team is playing at the SkyDome in a 45-game schedule from October to April. When the brand-new Air Canada Centre stadium opens in February 1999, the team will move there. For information, contact the **Raptors Basketball Club,** 20 Bay St., Suite 1702 (☎ **416/214-2255**). For tickets, C$13 to C$108 (U.S.$9 to U.S.$77), call **Ticketmaster** at ☎ **416/872-5000.**

**FOOTBALL**    SkyDome is also home to the Argonauts football team, which plays in the Canadian Football League between June and November. For information, contact the club at SkyDome, Gate 3, Suite 1300, Toronto, ON, M5V 1J3 (☎ **416/ 341-5151**). Argos tickets cost C$10 to C$35 (U.S.$7 to U.S.$25); call ☎ **888/ 654-6529** or 416/341-1234.

**GOLF TOURNAMENTS**  Canada's national golf tournament, the **Bell Canadian Open,** is usually held at the **Glen Abbey Golf Club** in Oakville, about 40 minutes from the city (☎ **905/844-1800**). Most years, it's played over the Labour Day weekend.

**HOCKEY**  Some wag once said there's really only one religious place in Toronto, and that's **Maple Leaf Gardens,** 60 Carlton St. (☎ **416/977-1641**), where the city's ice-hockey team, the Maple Leafs, wield their sticks to the delight and screaming enthusiasm of fans. Tickets are nigh impossible to attain because many are sold by subscription; as soon as the remainder go on sale, there are lines around the block. The only way to secure tickets is to harass your concierge or pay a scalper. If by boon of God you do find legitimate tickets, they should cost C$24.50 to C$95 (U.S.$17.50 to U.S.$68). Try calling **Ticketmaster** at ☎ **416/872-5000.**

Rumors about relocating the Leafs to another stadium have sparked major— I mean major—discussion and shock, not to mention rage, horror, and sadness. At press time, negotiations were in the works.

**HORSE RACING**  Horse racing takes place at **Woodbine Racetrack,** Rexdale Boulevard and Highway 427 in Etobicoke (☎ **416/675-6110** or 416/675-7223), famous for the Queen's Plate (contested in June/July); the Canadian International, a world classic turf race (contested in September or October); and the North America Cup (mid-June). Woodbine also hosts harness racing in spring and fall.

About 100 miles outside Toronto, **Fort Erie Race Track** (☎ **905/871-3200**) is another beautiful racing venue and the host of the Prince of Wales Stakes in July or August. Harness racing takes place at **Mohawk Raceway,** 30 miles west of the city at Highway 410, and Guelph Line hosts the Breeder's Crown in October (☎ **416/ 675-7223**).

**TENNIS TOURNAMENTS**  Canada's international tennis championship, the **Du Maurier Ltd. Open,** is an important stop on the pro-tennis tour, attracting stars like Sampras, Agassi, and Sanchez Vicario. It's played in Toronto at the National Tennis Centre at York University, and in Montréal in late July, with the men's and women's championship alternating between the two cities. In 1998, women play in Montréal; men play in Toronto. In 1999, they alternate, and so on in subsequent years. For information, call ☎ **416/665-9777.**

# 7

# City Strolls

Toronto is a huge, sprawling city, and it's difficult to imagine walking everywhere. But its different neighborhoods are quite compact, making it possible to explore parts of Toronto on foot, and the city is blessed with a super-efficient public transportation system.

The walking tours in this chapter aren't designed to give you an overview; instead, they'll give you an entry to the most colorful, exciting neighborhoods in the city, as well as those areas that are packed with sights on almost every corner.

## WALKING TOUR 1
## Harbourfront

**Start:** Union Station.
**Finish:** Harbourfront Antiques Market.
**Time:** Anywhere from 2 to 4 hours, depending on how much time you spend shopping, eating, and daydreaming.
**Best Time:** Sunday, when the Harbourfront Antiques Market is bustling.
**Worst Times:** Monday to Thursday, when the Waterfront is quiet.

As you start your tour, pause to look at the beaux arts interior of Union Station. From here, either take the LRT to York Quay or walk down York Street to Queen's Quay West. Directly ahead, across the street, is the:

1. **Queen's Quay Terminal,** a large complex that houses more than 100 shops and restaurants and, on the third floor, a theater specially designed for dance. Built in 1927 when lake and railroad trade flourished, this eight-story concrete warehouse has been attractively renovated and turned into a light and airy two-story marketplace with garden courts, skylights, and waterfalls. The floors above are occupied by condominium apartments.

Although you'll find few bargains here, some of my favorite stores on the street level are **Rainmakers,** selling zillions of whimsical umbrellas and parasol hats, plus terrific insulated rainwear, including rain slickers featuring cartoon characters; **Touch the Sky,** displaying colorful kites of all shapes and sizes; **Crabtree & Evelyn,** for soaps and other products to care for the body and appeal to the senses; and **Suitables,** for reasonably priced silk fashions.

On the upper level, there's also plenty to choose from: the classic Canadian **Tilley Endurables,** founded by Torontonian Alex Tilley (who invented the world's most endurable and adaptable hat as well as multipocketed jackets); **First Hand Canadian Crafts,** representing more than 200 contemporary folk artists who make both decorative and functional pieces; and **Table of Contents,** selling all kinds of kitchen gear, napkins, tablecloths, and utensils.

☕ **TAKE A BREAK**   If you want to sit out and watch the lakefront traffic—boat and human—go to **Spinnakers,** or the **Boathouse Cafe,** on the ground floor of Queen's Quay. Otherwise, go upstairs and dine at **Pink Pearl** (Chinese) or more casually at **La Bouchée.**

From Queen's Quay Terminal, walk along the water to:

2. **The Power Plant Contemporary Art Gallery,** a former power plant that has been converted to display modern art. The same building also houses the Du Maurier Theatre Centre, which presents works in French.

    Behind this building, adjacent to Queen's Quay West, is the **Tent in the Park,** which shelters different events during the summer season. Walk west into the:

3. **York Quay Centre,** a complex converted from a 1940 trucking warehouse that now contains a number of interesting restaurants and galleries. Spend some time in the Craft Studio watching the glassblowers, potters, jewelry makers, and other artisans at work and browse in the store that sells their work.

    On the waterfront side in front of York Quay, there's a pond where kids operate model boats in summer; in winter it turns into an ice-skating rink.

    From York Quay, cross the Amsterdam Bridge above Marina 4, checking out the wealth that's bobbing down below. You'll arrive on:

4. **John Quay.** The first building you'll come to contains four restaurants, beyond which are the towers of the:

5. **Radisson Plaza Hotel Admiral and Admiralty Point Condominiums,** and, across Queen's Quay West, the HarbourPoint Condominiums. On the ground level of the Admiralty Point Condos are a few interesting stores: **The Nautical Mind,** which sells marine books, photographs, navigational charts, and boating videos; and the **Dock Shoppe,** filled with all kinds of sailing gear and fashions.

☕ **TAKE A BREAK**   Pop into the **Radisson Plaza Hotel Admiral,** 249 Queen's Quay W., which has a couple of dining rooms, plus a pleasant poolside terrace if it's a sunny day. Or try something fresh from **Wallymagoo's** marine bar.

Continue west along Queen's Quay West past:

6. **Maple Leaf Quay** (unless you want to stop at the Nautical Centre to sign up for sailing classes and the like). Continue west and you'll see the Maple Leaf Quay Apartments on your right and the Harbour Terrace Condominiums farther along on your left on the waterfront. Next door to the westernmost tower of the Maple Leaf Quay Apartments is the:

7. **Harbourfront Antiques Market,** a terrific market in which more than 150 dealers sell fine furniture, jewelry, books, clocks, and art deco items. On Sunday, there's also an outdoor market featuring less established dealers. Go on Sunday—few dealers are open during the week.

☕ **WINDING DOWN**   In the Harbourfront Antiques Market, **Sophie's** has great fresh salads, sandwiches, quiches, and desserts.

To return to downtown, board the LRT and head back to Union Station.

# Walking Tour—Harbourfront

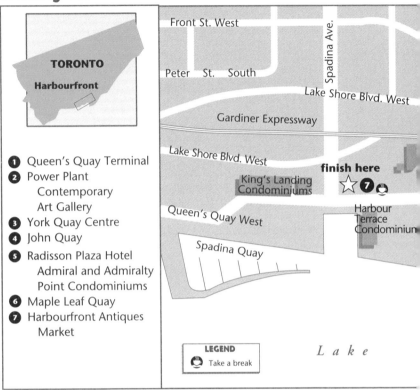

1. Queen's Quay Terminal
2. Power Plant Contemporary Art Gallery
3. York Quay Centre
4. John Quay
5. Radisson Plaza Hotel Admiral and Admiralty Point Condominiums
6. Maple Leaf Quay
7. Harbourfront Antiques Market

TORONTO
Harbourfront

Front St. West
Peter St. South
Spadina Ave.
Lake Shore Blvd. West
Gardiner Expressway
Lake Shore Blvd. West
King's Landing Condominiums
**finish here**
Queen's Quay West
Spadina Quay
Harbour Terrace Condominium

LEGEND
Take a break

*Lake*

1-0342

## WALKING TOUR 2
## The Financial District

This is the Wall Street of Toronto, the financial engine that has made Ontario the nation's strongest and wealthiest economy. For more insight into the major sights mentioned below, see the listings in chapter 6.

**Start:** The CN Tower, near the corner of John and Front streets.
**Finish:** At one of Queen Street West's watering holes.
**Time:** 4 to 6 hours, depending on how long you take to browse.
**Best Time:** Weekdays during business hours.
**Worst Times:** Weekends when the Stock Market is closed and the Financial District is dead.

Start by going up the:

1. **CN Tower,** which is the tallest freestanding structure in the world. Although it has become a symbol of the city, the CN Tower was castigated by many when it was built. For example, Allan Fotheringham blamed its creation on the city's lack of any topographical contours and railed in *Maclean's* that "It is completely understandable . . . that when you have a city that is virtually sterile, there is a need to erect a phallic symbol as an attempt at mechanical machismo. The rationale is obvious. A global psychiatrist, if asked to take a look at Toronto's rather unhealthy obsession with the CN Tower would advise the city to take a cold shower and lie down on the couch for a spell." Ponder this, if you will, on your way up.

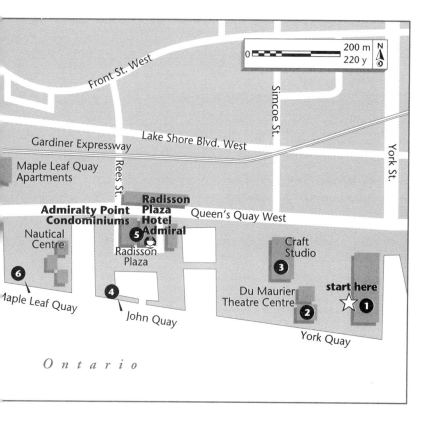

Once you're back down at the base, exit at the corner of John and Front streets. From here, look east along Front Street to see the glistening golden Royal Bank towers. The CBC Center stretches along the north side of Front Street for a whole long block. Go in and peek at the lobby radio studios and take a nostalgic radio-TV trip in the free museum.

Walk north on John Street, cross Wellington, and continue up to King Street. Turn right. On the northeast corner of King Street, sports fans will want to stop in at **Legends of the Game.** Doors with baseball-shaped handles open onto an emporium that features the Wall of Fame and every conceivable sports collectible.

Continue walking along the north side of King Street to:

2. **The Princess of Wales Theatre,** which was opened in 1993 by the Princess herself, and was the brainchild of son and father David and Ed Mirvish. If you can, go inside and get a look at the 10,000 square feet of murals created by Frank Stella. There's even one on the exterior back of the building worth walking around to see. Immediately after the death of Princess Diana, the theater became the shrine to which mourning Torontonians came to place thousands of floral tributes to the princess and her memory. Exit the theater and continue along King Street past a cluster of Ed Mirvish restaurant creations (drop into one just to check out the larger-than-life decor purchased by Ed at antiques closeouts) and a wall of newspaper clippings about this gutsy, quintessential Torontonian who, with his great love and boostering of the city, seems a shyer version of New York's former mayor Ed Koch.

Booster and benefactor of the city, he started out in bleak circumstances when he was left in possession of a bankrupt store during the Depression. Somehow he managed to pay off the debt and launch **Honest Ed's,** a discount store at Bloor and Bathurst that brought him fame and fortune. He saved the Royal Alex from demolition, and he and his son have become legendary theater impresarios even in London, where Ed outbid Andrew Lloyd Webber in 1982 for the Old Vic. For this he was named a Commander of the order of the British Empire (CBE). (For a review of the eyeful that is Honest Ed's, see page 156.)

Next you'll come to:

**3. The Royal Alex.** This beloved theater, named after the king's consort, was built in 1906 and 1907 by John M. Lyle in a magnificent beaux-arts style that cost C\$750,000. In 1963, it was scheduled for demolition to make way for a parking lot, but Ed Mirvish purchased it for a mere C\$200,000 and refurbished it. Named after Queen Alexandra, wife of Edward VII, it's Edwardian to a tee, loaded with gilt and velvet, and sporting an entrance foyer lined with green marble.

Across the street from these two theaters stands the new **Metro Hall,** designed by Brisbin Brook Beynon. Go in to see the interior art installations, especially the animal sculptures by Cynthia Short. Tours are given of the first three floors. Call ☎ **416/392-8000.**

Also on the south side of the street, at the corner of King and Simcoe streets, is:

**4. Roy Thomson Hall,** named after newspaper magnate Lord Thomson of Fleet. Built between 1972 and 1982 and designed by Arthur Erickson, the building's exterior looks very space-age, and inside, the mirrored effects are dramatic. Tours are usually given of this fabulous concert hall at 12:30pm, but call ahead at ☎ **416/593-4828** to confirm the schedule. If you don't want to take a tour, at least go in for a look.

Continue walking east. You'll be walking through the heart of the financial district, surrounded by the many towers owned and operated by banks and brokerage, trust, and insurance companies. Cross Simcoe Street. On the northeast corner of King and Simcoe rises the first of the towers that makes up the Sun Life Centre; on the southeast corner stands:

**5. St. Andrew's Presbyterian Church,** a quietly inviting retreat from the city's pace and noise. It was built in 1874–75 and designed by the city's premier architect of the time, W.G. Storm, in an inspired picturesque Scottish Romanesque style. That Sun Life paid \$4.3 million for the church's "air rights" doubtless contributed to its survival. Continue along the block to University Avenue. Opposite, on the northeast corner, is the:

**6. Sun Life Centre's second tower,** marked by a sculpture by Sorel Etrog. Farther along the block you'll find another sculpture, *Parent I,* by British sculptor Barbara Hepworth, in a courtyard setting complete with splashing fountain at the northwest corner of York Street. On the northeast corner stands:

**7. 2 First Canadian Place,** and north of it **the Toronto Exchange Tower,** at the corner of Adelaide and York streets. The first contains the Sculptor's Society Gallery, which always has an interesting free show. Then head up to the Stock Exchange's public gallery, which is currently being renovated. When it opens, it should be worth visiting to see the action on the floor and to see a presentation explaining how today's cyber trading works. Also on the ground floor in the building, stop in to see the fabulous glass sculptures and other glass pieces in the Sandra Ainsley gallery.

Continue along King Street past:

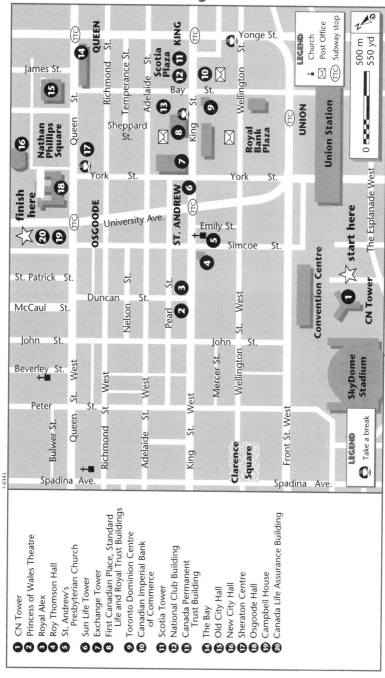

QUEEN

KING

Yonge St.

Scotia
Plaza

James St.

Bay St.

Nathan
Phillips
Square

Sheppard
St.

Royal
Bank
Plaza

UNION

Union Station

finish
here

OSGOODE

ST. ANDREW

York St.

University Ave.

Emily St.

Simcoe St.

start here

The Esplanade West

St. Patrick St.

Convention Centre

CN Tower

McCaul St.

Duncan St.

Nelson St.

Pearl St.

St. West

John St.

John St.

Mercer St.

Wellington St.

SkyDome
Stadium

Beverley St. West

Peter St.

Bulwer St.

Queen St. West

Richmond St. West

Adelaide St. West

King St. West

Front St. West

Clarence
Square

Spadina Ave.

Spadina Ave.

1-0343

1 CN Tower
2 Princess of Wales Theatre
3 Royal Alex
4 Roy Thomson Hall
5 St. Andrew's
  Presbyterian Church
6 Sun Life Tower
7 Exchange Tower
8 First Canadian Place, Standard
  Life and Royal Trust Buildings
9 Toronto Dominion Centre
10 Canadian Imperial Bank
  of Commerce
11 Scotia Tower
12 National Club Building
13 Canada Permanent
  Trust Building
14 The Bay
15 Old City Hall
16 New City Hall
17 Sheraton Centre
18 Osgoode Hall
19 Campbell House
20 Canada Life Assurance Building

133

8. **First Canadian Place** on the north side and the **Standard Life** and **Royal Trust buildings** (part of the Toronto Dominion Center) on the south, until you reach Bay Street. The first was designed by New York architect Edward Durell Stone with Bregman & Hamann and is faced with marble in contrast to the TD Centre, which is black. Again, there are views of the magnificent Royal Bank towers from here.

   The intersection of Bay and King streets was once considered the precise geographical center of Toronto's financial power, and during the mining booms in the 1920s and 1950s, Bay Street was lined with offices that were filled with commission salesmen peddling stocks to the equivalent of the little ol' lady from Dubuque. This is the hub that gave Torontonians their reputation as a voracious band of money-grubbing folks that Hugh McLennan portrayed in his marvelous novel about Québec, *Two Solitudes.* Today it's called Mint Corner because each corner is occupied by a major bank.

   If it's near lunchtime and your stomach is rumbling, this isn't a bad place to:

☕ **TAKE A BREAK**   Your best bet for a leisurely lunch in this neighborhood is **Jump Cafe and Bar,** a block south at 1 Wellington St. W. (For a review of Jump, see page 70.) For a quick and easy snack, seek out one of the casual dining spots in the concourse of **First Canadian Place.**

   Our next stop at King and Bay is the:

9. **Toronto Dominion Centre,** built between 1963 and 1969 and designed by Mies van der Rohe in his sleek trademark style. The black steel and dark-bronze-tinted glass tower rises from a gray granite base launching pad. Go through the Royal Trust and Toronto Dominion Towers. Cross Wellington Street and go into the Aetna Tower. Stop to browse through the Toronto Dominion Gallery of Inuit Art, 79 Wellington St. W. (☎ **416/982-8473**), on the ground floor and mezzanine. Here there are close to 100 marvelous soapstone sculptures on display. Double back across Wellington and go up a short staircase to the Courtyard between the Commercial Union Tower and the Toronto Dominion Bank Tower. Here in this open space you'll find a patch of grass where half a dozen bronze cows are lazing, artist Joe Fafard's *Pasture,* a reminder to the bankers and stockbrokers that Toronto's wealth was derived from other stock, too.

   Exit onto King Street and continue east. Cross Bay Street. On the south side of King Street, you'll come first to the entrance to Commerce Court. Architecture buffs will also want to go into the:

10. **Canadian Imperial Bank of Commerce** (1929–31), if only to see the massive banking hall—145 feet long, 85 feet wide, and 65 feet high—with its coffered ceiling, gilt moldings, and decorative sculpted friezes. The main entrance is decorated, for instance, with squirrels, roosters, bees, bears, and figures representing Industry, Commerce, and Mercury. For years, this 34-story building dominated the Toronto skyline. It was designed by New Yorkers York and Sawyer, with Darling and Pearson. Note the carved heads on the top of the building depicting courage, observation, foresight, and enterprise. In the early 1970s I.M. Pei was asked to design a new complex while preserving the old building. He set the new stainless-steel bank tower that glistens (thanks to its mercury lamination) back from King Street, creating Commerce Court.

   Opposite, on the north side of King Street, note:

11. **Scotia Tower,** the red-granite building, designed by Webb Zerafa Menkes Housden between 1985 and 1988.

Walk back to Bay Street and turn right going north. At no. 303 on the east side is the:

12. **National Club Building.** In 1874 the Canada First Movement, which had been started in Ottawa in 1868, became centered in Toronto. As its name suggests, the members were fervent nationalists. It established a weekly, *The Nation,* and entered politics as the Canadian National Association and founded the National Club. The club moved to these premises in 1907. Today, it's a prestigious private club.

Across the street on the west side, at the corner of Bay and Adelaide streets, stands the:

13. **Canada Permanent Trust Building** (1928). Go in to view the beautifully worked art deco brass and bronze, particularly the elevator doors, which are chased and engraved with foliage and flowers.

Cross Adelaide Street. As you walk up Bay Street, the magnificently solid Old City Hall is clearly in view, but first, on the east side of Bay between Richmond and Queen, look at, or, if you like, stop into:

14. **The Bay,** one of Canada's venerable retailers. The Bay (formerly Simpson's), along with arch rival Eaton's, has influenced the development of the downtown areas of most major Canadian cities. If you like, go in and check out the art deco bar in the SRO bar on the ground floor.

Across Queen Street looms the:

15. **Old City Hall,** reflected dramatically in the Cadillac Fairview Office Tower at the corner of James and Queen streets. This solid, impressive building, designed by Edward James Lennox, is built out of Credit River Valley sandstone in a magnificent Romanesque Revival style that is obviously influenced by H.H. Richardson. Begun in 1885, it was opened in 1899, and for years its clock tower was a familiar skyline landmark. Today, the building houses the provincial criminal courts. Go in to see the impressive staircase, columns with decorative capitals, mosaic floor, and stained-glass window (1898) by Robert McCausland depicting the union of Commerce and Industry watched over by Britannia. Note the carved heads on the exterior entrance pillars—supposedly portraits of the political figures and citizens of the period, including the architect himself.

Pause on your way out to look down the canyon of Bay Street, the city's equivalent of New York's Wall Street. Bay Street curves around, and to your left there is suddenly the:

16. **New City Hall,** the city's fourth, built between 1958 and 1965 in modern sculptural style; it's the symbol of Toronto's post-war dynamism, although not everyone felt that way when it was built. According to Pierre Berton, Frank Lloyd Wright said of it "Every graveyard in Canada, if it could speak, would say 'amen' to the slab. Well, that's what this building says for Toronto. You've got a headmarker for a grave and future generations will look at it and say: 'This marks the spot where Toronto fell.'" Heady stuff, but not proven true to date. Designed by Finnish architect Viljo Revell, who won the competition that was entered by 510 architects from 42 countries, including I.M. Pei, it has a great square in front with a fountain and pool to which office workers flock in summer to relax, and in winter to skate. The square is named after Nathan Phillips, Toronto's first Jewish mayor, who helped push the project through. The Council Chamber, supported on a two-tier podium, looks like a flying saucer, but the glass walls make it seem open and accessible, which indeed it is. Take the elevator up and enter the public galleries of this circular chamber; it feels too open for a place of government.

City Hall also has some art worth viewing. Look just inside the entrance for *Metropolis,* which local artist David Partridge fashioned from more than 100,000 common nails. You'll need to stand well back to enjoy the effect. Henry Moore's sculpture *The Archer* stands in front of the building—thanks to Mayor Phil Givens, who raised the money to buy it through public subscription after the city authorities refused to purchase it. This gesture encouraged Henry Moore to bestow a major collection of his works on the Art Gallery. The Council Chamber is flanked by two curved concrete towers that house the bureaucracy. From the air, the whole complex supposedly looks like an eye peering up at the heavens.

For the best view of City Hall, enter the:

**17. Sheraton Centre,** on the south side of Queen Street, and go up to the second-floor Long Bar, which overlooks the square.

🕑 **TAKE A BREAK**　For some light refreshment, stop in at one of several dining spots in the **Sheraton Centre,** 123 Queen St. W., among them the pub **The Good Queen Bess**.

From City Hall, walk west along Queen Street. On your right, behind an ornate wrought-iron fence that once kept out the cows, you'll see:

**18. Osgoode Hall,** since the 1830s headquarters of the Law Society of Upper Canada, a kind of professional trade union. Named after the first chief justice of Upper Canada, the building was constructed in stages, starting with the East Wing in 1831 to 1832, the West Wing in 1844 to 1845, and the center block in 1856 to 1860. The last, designed by W.G. Storm, with its Palladian portico, is the most impressive. Inside is the **Great Library**—112 feet long, 40 feet wide, and 40 feet high—with stucco decoration and coved domed ceiling. The Ontario Supreme Court is across the street on the south side of Queen Street.

Keep walking west to University Avenue. On the northwest corner you can visit:

**19. Campbell House,** the elegant Georgian residence of Sir William Campbell, a Scot who moved to York in 1811 and rose to become chief justice of Upper Canada. A handsome piece of Georgian architecture, it was moved to this location from a few miles farther east.

Stretching northward behind Campbell House, on the northwest side of University Avenue, is the:

**20. Canada Life Assurance Building.** Atop the tower a neon sign provides weather reports—white flashes for snow, red flashes for rain, green beacon for clement weather, or red beacon for cloudy weather. If the flashes move upward, the temperature is headed that way, and vice versa.

At University Avenue and Queen Street, you can end the tour by boarding the subway at Osgoode to your next destination, or you can continue walking west along Queen Street to explore its many delights. (For a shopping tour of Queen Street West, see chapter 8.)

# WALKING TOUR 3
## St. Lawrence & Downtown East

**Start:** Union Station.

**Finish:** King subway station.

**Time:** 2 to 3 hours, allowing for browsing time.

**Best Time:** Saturday (when the St. Lawrence Market is in full swing).

**Worst Time:** Sunday (when it's closed).

# Walking Tour—St. Lawrence & Downtown East

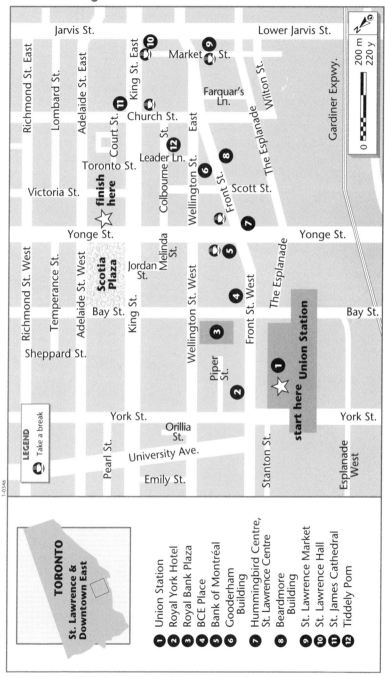

**Jarvis St.** **Lower Jarvis St.**

Richmond St. East
Lombard St.
Adelaide St. East
King St. East — 🔟
Market — 9️⃣ St.
Wilton St.

Farquar's Ln.

Victoria St.
Toronto St.
Court St.
1️⃣1️⃣
Church St.
East
St.
1️⃣2️⃣
Leader Ln.
Colbourne St.
Wellington St.
8️⃣
6️⃣
Front St.
Scott St.
Gardiner Expwy.
The Esplanade

⭐ finish here

**Yonge St.** 7️⃣ **Yonge St.**

Richmond St. West
Temperance St.
Adelaide St. West
Bay St.
King St.
**Scotia Plaza**
Jordan St.
Melinda St.
Wellington St. West
Jordan St.
5️⃣
4️⃣
Front St. West
The Esplanade
Bay St.

Sheppard St.
3️⃣
Piper St.
2️⃣
1️⃣
⭐ start here  **Union Station**

**York St.** **York St.**

Orillia St.
Pearl St.
University Ave.
Stanton St.
Esplanade West

Emily St.

1-0346

**LEGEND**
Take a break

**TORONTO**
**St. Lawrence & Downtown East**

1. Union Station
2. Royal York Hotel
3. Royal Bank Plaza
4. BCE Place
5. Bank of Montréal
6. Gooderham Building
7. Hummingbird Centre, St. Lawrence Centre
8. Beardmore Building
9. St. Lawrence Market
10. St. Lawrence Hall
11. St. James Cathedral
12. Tiddely Pom

200 m
220 y
0

At one time, this area was at the center of city life. Today it's a little off-center, and yet it has some historic and modern architectural treasures and a wealth of history in and around the St. Lawrence Market. Begin at:

1. **Union Station.** Check out the interior of this classical revival beauty, which opened in 1927 as a temple to and for the railroad. Look up and marvel at the shimmering ceiling faced with vitrified Guastavino tile. It soars 88 feet above the 260-foot-long concourse.

    Across the street, at York and Front streets, stands the:

2. **Royal York Hotel,** a venerable railroad hotel, longtime gathering place for Torontonians, and home of the famous Imperial Room cabaret/nightclub, which used to be one of Eartha Kitt's favorite venues (it's still there, but for dining and dancing only). The hotel was once the tallest building in Toronto and the largest hotel in the British Commonwealth. Check out the lobby with its coffered ceiling and opulent furnishings, and the meeting rooms where so many of the city's banquets and other events have taken place.

    Walk east on Front Street and, at the corner of Bay and Front, look up at the shimmering and absolutely stunning:

3. **Royal Bank Plaza,** two triangular gold-sheathed towers, one 41 floors, the other 26, joined by a 130-foot-high atrium. The mirrored glass is enhanced by 150 pounds of gold. It was designed by Webb Zerafa Menkes Housden and built between 1973 and 1977.

    Cross Bay and continue east on Front Street. On the south side of the street is the impressive sweep of **One Front Street,** the main post office building, which for some reason reminds me of Buckingham Palace. On the north side of the street is the city's latest financial palace and most impressive architectural triumph, Bell Canada Enterprises's:

4. **BCE Place.** Go inside to view the soaring galleria. It was designed by Skidmore, Owings, and Merrill with Bregman & Hamann in 1993. The twin office towers are connected by a huge glass-covered galleria five stories high, spanning the block between Bay and Yonge. It connects the old Midland Bank building to the twin towers and was designed by artist-architect Santiago Calatrava with Bregman & Hamann.

🍵 **TAKE A BREAK**    For a unique dining experience, stop in at **BCE Place's Movenpick Marché,** which simulates a market dining experience (see page 79 for a review). Across the courtyard, for fine dining, try the dramatically designed **Acqua** (see page 68). Downstairs, there's also a food court with a variety of fast-food and casual dining choices; or if you prefer a deli sandwich, head for **Shopsy's** at 33 Yonge St. (see page 84).

Back out on Front Street, continue to the northwest corner of Yonge and Front, stopping to admire the:

5. **Bank of Montréal** (1885–86), a suitably ornate building for the most powerful Canadian bank in the 19th century, banker to the colonial and federal governments. Inside, the banking hall rises to a beamed coffered ceiling with domed skylights of stained glass. It now houses the Stanley Cup and other hockey trophies plus the **Hockey Hall of Fame** (see page 113), another example of the city's genius for architectural adaptation. The exterior, embellished with carvings, porthole windows, and a balustrade, is a sight in itself.

From here, you can look along Front Street and see the weird mural by Derek M. Besant that adorns the famous and highly photogenic:

6. **Flatiron or Gooderham Building** (1892), which was built as the headquarters of George Gooderham, who had expanded his distilling business into railroads, insurance, and philanthropy. At one time his liquor business was the biggest in the British Empire and he was also the President of the Bank of Toronto. The building occupies a triangular site and the western tip of the five-story structure is beautifully curved—the windows as well—and topped with a semicircular tower. The design is by David Roberts.

At the southwest corner of Yonge and Front, you can stop in at:

7. **The Hummingbird Centre** and, across Scott Street, the neighboring **St. Lawrence Centre.** The former is home to the National Ballet of Canada and the Canadian Opera Company.

Continue east along Front Street to:

8. **The Beardmore Building** (1872), at 35–39 Front St. E. This and the many other cast-iron buildings that line the street were the heart of the warehouse district in the late 19th century, close to the lakefront and railheads. Now they're occupied by stores like **Frida Crafts,** which sells imports from Guatemala, India, and Bangladesh, as well as jewelry, bags, candles, and other knickknacks; and **Mountain Equipment Co-op,** stocked with highly durable outdoor adventure goods. At nos. 41–43, note the **Perkins Building,** and at 45–49, look for the building with a totally cast-iron facade. Continue to Church Street, browsing in the stores.

Cross Church Street. More browsing follows. At no. 83, **Wonderful Whites** features everything that is indeed white and wonderful—Victorian linens, lace, pillows—as well as china and glass. Next door, **Ra** offers an array of Indian and other decorative accents—Indian bedspreads and pillows, along with apparel and jewelry.

Now cross Market Street to the:

9. **St. Lawrence Market,** in the old market building on the right. Enter this great market hall, which was constructed around the city's second city hall (1844–45). The elegant pedimented facade that you see as you stand in the center of the hall was originally the center block of the city hall. Today the market is filled with all kinds of vendors selling fresh eggs, Mennonite sausage, seafood, meats, cheeses, and baked goods. From Thursday to Saturday the north building across the street hosts a farmers' market exhibiting fresh produce starting at 5am.

The delicious smells here make this an obvious place to:

☕ **TAKE A BREAK**   The most fun place to stop is at one of the stands offering fresh produce in the market itself. Other choices, though, are **Le Papillon** (see page 84), around the corner on Church Street, which features a raft of savory and dessert crepes, or **Pizzeria Uno** on Front Street.

Exit the market where you came in. Cross the street and cut through Market Lane Park and the shops at Market Square past the north market building. Turn right onto King Street to:

10. **St. Lawrence Hall** (1850–51), the focal point of the community in the mid–19th century. This hall was the site of grand city occasions, political rallies, balls, and entertainment. Frederick Douglass delivered an antislavery lecture here; Jenny Lind and Adelina Patti sang here in 1851 and 1860, respectively; General Tom Thumb

appeared here in 1862; and George Brown campaigned for Confederation here in this most elegant Palladian-style building with its domed cupola, which was designed by William Thomas.

Cross the street and enter the 19th-century garden with a cast-iron drinking fountain for people, horses, and dogs, and neatly trimmed flower beds that are filled with seasonal flowers. If you like, you can sit on a bench and rest while you admire the handsome proportions of St. Lawrence Hall and listen to the chimes of:

11. **St. James Cathedral,** which is adjacent to the garden on the north side of King Street. York's first church and first Anglican church was built here from 1803 to 1807. Originally a frame building, it was enlarged in 1818 and 1819 and replaced in 1831.

The first incumbent was the Rev. George O'Kill Stuart, followed by John Strachan (pronounced *Strawn*), later the first bishop of Toronto, who conducted himself with great pomp from his mansion on Jarvis Street and wielded great temporal as well as spiritual power in the city. For 50 years until his death in 1867, he was an indomitable spirit, the man who threatened the Americans with the vengeance of the British Navy after they occupied York (Toronto), the man who defied the British prelates by keeping King's College open over their objections that the Charter was too liberal, and the man who dismissed Thomas Jefferson as "a mischief maker." He revered British institutions and abhorred anything Yankee; thus he has become, ironically, the patron saint of Yankee baiters.

The second church was burned in 1839 and the first cathedral was erected, but this, too, was destroyed by fire, in the great fire of 1849. The present building was begun in 1850 and finished in 1874. Inside, there's a Tiffany window in memory of William Jarvis at the northern end of the east aisle. It also boasts the tallest steeple in Canada.

From here, you can also view one of the early retail store buildings that were built when King Street was the main commercial street. **Nos. 129–35** were originally built as an Army and Navy Store, using cast iron, plate glass, and arched windows so that the shopper could see what was available in the store. Sandwiched between the Toronto Sculpture Garden, note, too, nos. 111 and 125. **The Sculpture Garden (☎ 416/485-9658)** at 115 King is a quiet corner for contemplation.

☕ **TAKE A BREAK** From St. James, the venerable **King Edward Hotel** is only a block away if you need refreshment. Afternoon tea is served or you can stop for light fare or lunch in the **Café Victoria.** Both **La Maquette,** 111 King St. E., and **Biagio,** 157 King St. E., have very appealing outdoor dining courtyards. See page 81 for reviews of the last two establishments.

From St. James, go south on Church Street and turn right into Colbourne Street. If you have kids, you might enjoy browsing at:

12. **Tiddely Pom,** which is devoted exclusively to children's books. Wine enthusiasts might want to check out **Wine Not,** an establishment that sells everything you need to make beer and wine—from corks and labels to glucose and vats.

From Colbourne, turn left down Leader Lane to Wellington, where you can enjoy a fine view of the mural on the Flatiron Building and also of the rhythmic flow of mansard rooflines along the south side of Front Street.

Turn right and proceed to Yonge, then turn right and walk to King Street to catch the subway to your next destination.

# WALKING TOUR 4
## Chinatown & Kensington Market

**Start:** Osgoode subway station.
**Finish:** Toronto Public Reference Library.
**Time:** 6 to 8 hours, depending on whether or not you linger at the various stops.
**Best Times:** Tuesday to Saturday during the day.
**Worst Times:** Sunday, when many of the stores in Kensington Market close, and Monday, when the Art Gallery is closed.

This walk will take you through the oldest of Toronto's several Chinatowns. The original Chinatown was on York Street between King and Queen, but it has long since been replaced by skyscrapers and the community has moved north and west. Although today there are at least four Chinatowns and most Chinese live in the suburbs, Dundas/Spadina is still a major shopping and dining area for the Asian community. As a new wave of Asian immigrants to Canada has arrived from Southeast Asian countries like Thailand and Vietnam in particular, this old, original Chinatown has taken them in; and today many of the businesses are in fact Vietnamese or Thai.

Successive waves of immigration have also changed the face of the nearby Kensington Market over the years. At the turn of the century and right up until the 1950s it was the heart of the Jewish community before it dispersed to the suburbs. In the 1950s, the Portuguese arrived to work in the food-processing and meatpacking industries and made it their home. In the '60s, a Caribbean presence was established. Today traces of all these communities remain in the vibrant life of the market.

From the Osgoode subway station, walk west on Queen Street. Turn right onto McCaul Street. If you're interested in crafts, you'll want to stop on the left side of McCaul at the:

1. **Prime Gallery,** at no. 52, which sells ceramics, jewelry, fabrics, and other art objects crafted by contemporary artisans.

   On the right is:

2. **Village by the Grange,** an apartment/shopping complex that's laid out in a series of courtyards (one even contains a small ice-skating rink). Go into the complex at the southern end and stroll through, emerging from the food market. En route you'll come across some small fashion boutiques and **18 Karat,** where the proprietors design and craft jewelry behind the counter (show them what you have in mind and they will craft it for you beautifully).

☕ **TAKE A BREAK**   Also in Village by the Grange is one of the city's oldest and most popular Chinese restaurants—**Sun Lok.** The **Food Market** contains stalls selling everything—12 varieties of freshly brewed coffee, schnitzels, satay, Japanese noodles, salads, falafel, hot dogs, Chinese food, kebabs, pizza, and fried chicken.

Continue north along McCaul, passing the Ontario College of Art on the left side of the street, until you reach Dundas Street, where on the left you'll encounter a large Henry Moore sculpture entitled *Large Two Forms,* which describes precisely what it is.

Turn left. On the left is the entrance to the:

3. **Art Gallery of Ontario.** If you don't want to go in to see the collections, you can browse the gallery stores without paying admission.

Cross to the north side of Dundas, opposite the Art Gallery. It's worth stopping in at the:

4. **Bau-Xi,** a gallery representing modern Canadian artists. From here, continue to Beverly and turn right, walking to Baldwin Street, a short street containing so many ethnic restaurants that you can virtually dine around the world from China and Japan to France and Mexico. On the corner of Baldwin and Beverley is the:

5. **George Brown House,** at 50 Baldwin. This is the home of the founder of the reform newspaper, the *Globe* (1844), and a prominent politician. Brown's house was built in 1877 and even featured such a modern amenity as a shower.

Backtrack to Dundas, taking a right. You're now walking into the heart of Chinatown, with an abundance of grocery stores, bakeries, bookstalls, and other emporiums selling foods, handcrafts, and other items from Asia.

What follows are some of my favorite browsing stops along the stretch of Dundas Street between Beverley Street and Spadina Avenue. On the south or left side as you go west is:

6. **Tai Sun Co.,** at nos. 407–09, a supermarket displaying dozens of different mushrooms, all clearly labeled in English, as well as all kinds of fresh Chinese vegetables, meats, fish, and canned goods. **Melewa Bakery,** at no. 433, has a wide selection of pastries, like mung-bean and lotus-paste buns. Outside **Kiu Shun Trading,** at no. 441, dried fish are displayed, while inside you'll find numerous varieties of ginseng and such miracle remedies as "Stop Smoking Tea" and delicacies such as swallows' nests.

On the north side of the street:

7. **J & S Arts and Crafts,** at no. 430, is a good place to pick up souvenirs, including kimonos and happy coats, kung-fu suits, address books, cushion covers, and all-cotton Chinatown T-shirts. **New World Book Store,** at no. 442, has a good selection of Chinese and other Asian-language dictionaries as well as Chinese cards.

At the corner of Huron Street, on the north side of Dundas, is:

8. **Ten Ren Tea,** no. 454, which sells all kinds of teas—black, oolong, and so forth—stored in large canisters in the back of the store, as well as charming small ceramic teapots priced from $25 to $70. Most likely, you will be asked to sample some tea in a tiny cup. A large variety of gnarled ginseng root is also displayed for sale. Next door, **W Y Trading Co., Inc.,** has a great selection of records, CDs, and tapes—everything from Chinese folk songs and cantatas to current hit albums from Hong Kong and Taiwan. This is one place a non-Chinese-speaking visitor can read what the recording contains. **Furuya,** at no. 460, stocks Japanese food and other specialties. At no 482A, **Po Chi Tong** is a fun store to go in to view the exotic remedies available, like deer-tail extract and liquid-gold ginseng or royal jelly. The best remedy of all time is the "slimming tea." Watch them weigh each item out and total the bill with a fast-clicking abacus.

**TAKE A BREAK** Right in Chinatown, **Champion House** at 480 Dundas St. W. is a good lunch stop that offers comfortable, elegant surroundings (in contrast to the strictly functional look that prevails in Chinatown) and good Chinese cuisine. The specialty is Peking duck, and a gong is sounded when it comes out of the kitchen. They have other dishes, too, like beef with ginger and green onions and also orange chicken, priced from C$9 to C$13 (U.S.$6 to U.S.$9). For terrific dim sum, another good bet is the **Chinatown International** on the third floor at no. 421 Dundas.

At Spadina, cross over to the southwest corner to:

# Walking Tour—Chinatown & Kensington Market

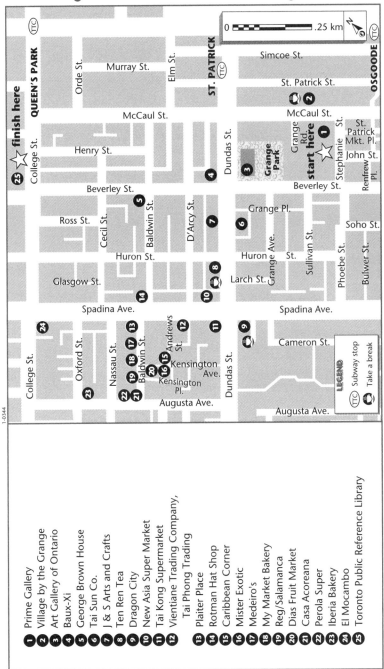

- 1 Prime Gallery
- 2 Village by the Grange
- 3 Art Gallery of Ontario
- 4 Baux-Xi
- 5 George Brown House
- 6 Tai Sun Co.
- 7 J & S Arts and Crafts
- 8 Ten Ren Tea
- 9 Dragon City
- 10 New Asia Super Market
- 11 Tai Kong Supermarket
- 12 Vientiane Trading Company, Tai Phong Trading
- 13 Plaiter Place
- 14 Rotman Hat Shop
- 15 Caribbean Corner
- 16 Mister Exotic
- 17 Medeiro's
- 18 My Market Bakery
- 19 Reg/Salamanca
- 20 Dias Fruit Market
- 21 Casa Acoreana
- 22 Perola Super
- 23 Iberia Bakery
- 24 El Mocambo
- 25 Toronto Public Reference Library

**9. Dragon City,** an Asian-style shopping complex complete with a food court on the west side of Spadina at no. 280.

☕ **TAKE A BREAK**   Join the Chinese at the food court serving all kinds of Asian cuisine downstairs at **Dragon City.** The stalls sell dim sum, noodles, curry, and all kinds of good Asian fare at low prices.

Spadina Avenue is the widest street in the city because the wealthy Baldwin family had a 132-foot swath cut through the forest from Queen Street to Bloor Street so that they could view the lake from their new home on the top of Spadina Hill. Later, in the early 20th century, Spadina became Toronto's garment center, the equivalent of New York's Seventh Avenue and the focal point of the city's Jewish community.

Although it's still the garment center, with wholesale and discount fashion houses, as well as the fur district (farther south around Adelaide), today Spadina has become more Asian than Jewish.

If you enjoy strolling through supermarkets filled with exotic Asian delights, including such fruits as durian in season, then go into the:

**10. New Asia Supermarket,** at nos. 295–97, or cross the street and explore the:

**11. Tai Kong Supermarket.** Look at all the different provisions—chili and fish sauces, fresh meat and fish (including live tilapia in tanks), preserved plums, chrysanthemum tea and other kinds of infusions, moon cakes, and large sacks of rice.

As the Asian community in Toronto has grown, other Chinatowns have been developed elsewhere, and much of the old original Chinatown now offers Thai, Vietnamese, and other Asian specialty stores. For example, there's the:

**12. Vientiane Trading Company,** at no. 334, where they label some vegetables in English, like lotus root, bamboo, and coriander.

Continuing north, cross St. Andrews Street to no. 360, **Tap Phong Trading,** which has some terrific wicker baskets of all shapes and sizes, as well as woks and ceramic cookware; heavy, attractive mortars and pestles; and other household items. Cross Baldwin Street to:

**13. Plaiter Place,** at no. 384, which has a huge selection of finely crafted wicker baskets, birdcages, woven blinds, bamboo steamers, hats, and other fun items. Stop, too, at **Fortune Housewares,** no. 388, to shop for kitchen and household items— including all the good brand names—for at least 20% off prices elsewhere in the city.

Across the street is the:

**14. Rotman Hat Shop,** at no. 345 just north of Baldwin, selling Panama hats that are as light as feathers and woven from the finest-quality Ecuadorian plants. The store, which has been in business here for over 42 years, also stocks grouser hats and other fun headgear.

Now cross Spadina and double back to St. Andrews. Turn onto St. Andrews and note the synagogue on the north side of the street.

Walk along St. Andrews to Kensington Avenue and turn right. Here you'll be in the heart of the **Kensington Market** area, which has always reflected the current ethnic scene that exists in the city. Once it was primarily a Jewish market; later it became more Portuguese; today, it is a blend of Portuguese, Jewish, Caribbean, and Asian.

Walk north on Kensington Avenue. There are several West Indian grocery stores on this street, like:

**15. Caribbean Corner,** on the east side of the street, selling such items as plantains, yuca, sugarcane, papaya, mangoes, and other tropical products.

On the west side is:

16. **Mister Exotic,** at no. 70, which displays Caribbean specialties, while next door **Mendel's Creamery** sells smoked fish, herring, cheeses, and fine dill pickles. One more door down, **Global Cheese** offers an enormous selection at good prices.

  Continue along Kensington Avenue to Baldwin Street, another prime food shopping street. On the opposite side of Baldwin, you'll find:

17. **Medeiro's Fish Market, Seven Seas, and Coral Sea,** which are just several fish stores on the north side of the street where folks come to purchase their supplies of salt cod.

  Nearby, stick your nose in the air and sniff the comforting aromas wafting out of:

18. **My Market Bakery** and the **Baldwin Street Bakery,** which will doubtless lure you in to buy some bread—foccacia, sourdough, you name it, they have it.

  From here to the corner, the street is lined with stores like:

19. **Reg** and **Salamanca,** selling an array of nuts, fruits, and grains. Pick up some dried papaya, mango, pineapple, or apricots as a snack.

  On the south side of Baldwin, you'll pass:

20. **Dias Fruit Market,** selling all manner of fresh fruits and vegetables; **Abyssinia,** which specializes in African and West Indian products; **Patty King,** selling Jamaican breads and other West Indian goods including roti, bread pudding, and tamarind balls; several **seafood stores** displaying infinite varieties of fresh fish and salted cod piled up in boxes out on the sidewalk; and the **Royal Food Centre,** which sells a variety of Jamaican specialties, including goat meat.

  At the corner of Augusta Avenue and Baldwin Street is:

21. **Casa Acoreana,** an old-fashioned store stocking a full range of fresh coffees as well as some great pecans and filberts.

  At the end of Baldwin, turn right onto Augusta Avenue into the heart of the old Portuguese neighborhood. In addition to the discount and used-clothing emporiums on the west side of the street, there are several Latino stores, such as:

22. **Perola Super** at no. 247, which displays cassava and strings of peppers hung up to dry as well as in bins—ancho, arbol, pasilla, plus more exotic fruits and herbs; and **Emporium Latino,** which sells cactus leaves and yuca, and chilies, among many other Latin American items.

  Cross Nassau Street to a couple of Portuguese establishments:

23. **Iberica Bakery,** at 279 Augusta, where you can enjoy some coffee and pastries at a handful of tables, and the **Portuguese Meat Market,** both on the east side of the street. They represent the few remaining traces of the Portuguese presence in the Kensington Market area, along with the Portuguese Radio Station around the corner on Oxford Avenue.

  Turn right down Oxford Avenue and walk over to Spadina Avenue. Turn left to:

24. **El Mocambo,** the rock-and-roll landmark where the Rolling Stones played on March 4 and 5, 1977, and then hop on the trolley traveling east along College Street to the subway. Along the route, you'll pass on the left (north) side of the street what used to be the:

25. **Toronto Public Reference Library,** an attractive classical revival building now occupied by the University of Toronto bookstore and Koffler Student Centre. On the south corner of College Street and University Avenue, you'll see the weird-looking mirrored-glass **Hydro Place.**

# 8 | Shopping

Toronto's major shopping areas are the **Bloor/Yorkville** area, for designer boutiques and top-name galleries; **Queen Street West,** for an edgier mixture of fashion, antiques, and bookstores; and a number of shopping malls/centers, such as **Queen's Quay** on the waterfront, the 2-block-long Eaton Centre, and other smaller complexes like College Park, Royal Bank Plaza, and Village by the Grange. Look for our special tour of Queen Street West at the end of this chapter.

## 1  The Shopping Scene

The two great names in Toronto retailing are **Eaton's** and the **Hudson's Bay Company** (formerly Simpson's), both founded in the mid-19th century. They're still here and thriving. Canadian fashion names to look for are Alfred Sung, Cy Mann, Norma, and a host of younger designer names and boutiques along Queen Street West.

The two major markets are **Kensington Market** and the **St. Lawrence Market.** (See "Markets" in chapter 6 for more information.)

Best buys are mainly Canadian arts and crafts, which can be imported into the United States duty-free.

Store hours are generally Monday to Wednesday from 9:30 or 10am to 6pm, and Saturday and Sunday from 10am to 5pm, with extended hours (8–9:30pm) on Thursday and usually Friday.

Provincial sales tax is 8%, but out-of-province visitors can reclaim it. Nonresidents can also reclaim the 7% goods-and-services tax (GST). See "Fast Facts: Toronto," in chapter 3.

## 2  Shopping A to Z

### ANTIQUES

You'll find the greatest concentration of good-quality antiques at the Harbourfront Antiques Market, best visited Sunday when all the dealers are in residence (during the week many are at their stores). The finest antiques can be found in the Bloor/Yorkville area, with many shops a short walk from the Four Seasons Hotel, and in the Mount Pleasant/St. Clair area along the 500, 600, and 700 blocks of Mount Pleasant Road. The more funky and often more recent collectibles can be found at various stores along Queen Street West. Markham Village also has several antiques stores.

# Shopping Highlights—Bloor/Yorkville

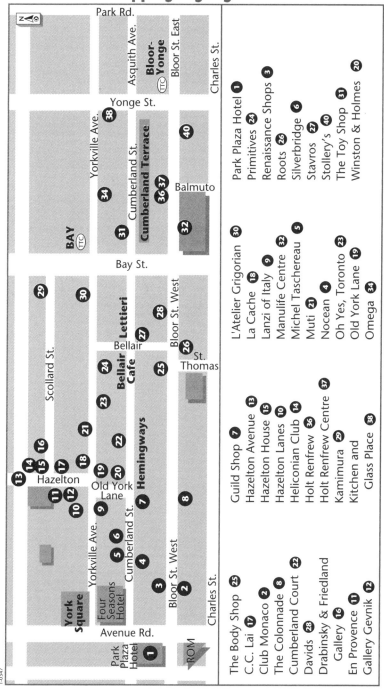

Park Plaza Hotel **1**
Primitives **24**
Renaissance Shops **3**
Roots **26**
Silverbridge **6**
Stavros **27**
Stollery's **40**
The Toy Shop **31**
Winston & Holmes **20**

L'Atelier Grigorian **30**
La Cache **18**
Lanzi of Italy **9**
Manulife Centre **32**
Michel Taschereau **5**
Muti **21**
Nocean **4**
Oh Yes, Toronto **23**
Old York Lane **19**
Omega **34**

Guild Shop **7**
Hazelton Avenue **13**
Hazelton House **15**
Hazelton Lanes **10**
Heliconian Club **14**
Holt Renfrew **36**
Holt Renfrew Centre **37**
Kamimura **29**
Kitchen and
  Glass Place **33**

The Body Shop **25**
C.C. Lai **17**
Club Monaco **2**
The Colonnade **8**
Cumberland Court **22**
Davids **28**
Drabinsky & Friedland
  Gallery **16**
En Provence **11**
Gallery Gevnik **12**

1-0347

**Bernardi Antiques.** 699 Mount Pleasant Rd., south of Eglinton Ave. ☎ **416/483-6471.** Subway: St. Clair, then Mount Pleasant bus, or Davisville, then bus to Mount Pleasant.

Look here for discontinued Doulton figurines, glass art, paintings, carpets, silver, and furniture.

**C. C. Lai.** 9 Hazelton Ave. ☎ **416/928-0662.** Subway: Bay.

This cluttered store has fine Chinese antiques—exquisite inlaid furniture and screens, Buddhas, and jewelry—really beautiful pieces, both large and small.

**Fifty One Antiques Ltd.** 21 Avenue Rd. ☎ **416/968-2416.** Subway: Bay/Museum.

A specialist in 17th- and 18th-century furniture, as well as Empire, Biedermeier, and other later styles, Fifty One Antiques also has lots of accessories, like lamps made from old vases, carvings, European paintings, and more.

**✪ Harbourfront Antiques Market.** 390 Queen's Quay W. ☎ **416/260-2626.** Subway: Union, then take the LRT.

The 100-plus dealers here sell fine-quality antiques. On summer Sundays there's also a market outside featuring less-established dealers. Although it's relatively quiet during the week, it's hopping on weekends, when more than 150 dealers open up; you'll have to get there early. Hours are Tuesday to Friday from 11am to 6pm, Saturday from 10am to 6pm, and Sunday from 8am to 6pm.

**Journeys End.** 612 Markham St. ☎ **416/536-2226.** Subway: Bathurst.

This is an appropriate name for the miscellaneous assortment of estate china, jewelry, silver, and furniture that winds up here in an amorphous display. The store is eminently browsable.

**Mark McLaine.** Hazelton Lanes. ☎ **416/927-7972.** Subway: Bay.

This marvelously eclectic store has unique and wonderful pieces: pine furniture, French sconces, costume jewelry (especially deco), carved wood and stone pieces, silver frames, perfume bottles, and blue-and-white Oriental ware. You'll find reproductions, too. It's a great place to browse. Prices range from C$16 to C$6,000 (U.S.$11 to U.S.$4,286).

**✪ Michel Taschereau Antiques.** 176 Cumberland St. ☎ **416/923-3020.** Subway: Bay.

In this fine store you'll have to thread your way through the dense collection very carefully. You'll find 18th- and 19th-century English and French furniture, including large armoires, and French and English china, like Coalport, Derby, and Worcester. There's Lalique glass and Canadian folk art, also.

**Mostly Movables.** 785 Queen St. W., west of Bathurst St. ☎ **416/504-4455.** Subway: Osgoode, then streetcar west.

A large selection of furniture, mostly purchased at estate sales, is featured here, including wardrobes, dressers, couches, and dining-room sets for as little as C$950 (U.S.$679). Most of the pieces date from the 1920s on and cost C$150 (U.S.$107) and up. Turn-of-the-century Canadian pine plus British oak furniture from the 1920s and 1930s is also available.

**The Paisley Shop Limited.** 77 Yorkville Ave. ☎ **416/923-5830.** Subway: Bay.

A specialist in 18th- and 19th-century English furniture—dining tables, chairs, sideboards, mirrors, and desks—The Paisley Shop Limited also offers such accessories as porcelain, glass, and chandeliers. Downstairs is a selection of floral and other patterned cushions and lamps.

**R.A. O'Neill Antiques.** 100 Avenue Rd. ☎ **416/968-2806.** Subway: Bay.

This is the place for country furniture—pine and butternut from around the world—French, German, English, American, Dutch, and Irish. Along with tables, chairs, chests, and cupboards, the stock includes samplers, baskets, lamps, decoys, and brass and tin objects.

**Red Indian and Empire Antiques.** 536 Queen St. W. ☎ **416/504-7706.** Subway: Osgoode, then streetcar west.

The eclectic mixture of objects here spans the 1930s to the 1950s—fountain pens, Coke memorabilia, neon clocks, Bakelite jewelry, torchére lamps, wall sconces, mirrors, figurines, and other nostalgia. It's open Monday to Saturday from 11:30am to 6pm.

**Showcase Antique Mall.** 610 Queen St. W. ☎ **416/703-6255.** Subway: Osgoode, then streetcar west.

Three hundred dealers display their wares on the four floors of this complex. There's every conceivable collectible from clocks, art deco, coins, and jewelry to jukeboxes, Elvis and Beatle memorabilia, and lunch boxes. This is a good place to start or add to any collection.

**Stanley Wagman Antiques.** 111 Avenue Rd. ☎ **416/964-1047.** Subway: Bay.

A major purveyor of French furniture, both country and formal, as well as art deco, Stanley Wagman also features marble fireplaces, chandeliers, and wall sconces.

**Whim Antiques.** 561 Mount Pleasant Rd. ☎ **416/481-4474.** Subway: St. Clair, then Mount Pleasant bus, or Davisville, then bus to Mount Pleasant.

In this interesting shop, you will find antique and estate jewelry, rare Belleek pieces, silver, and other objets d'art.

## ART

Most of these galleries are open Tuesday to Saturday from 10:30am to 5:30pm, so don't come around on Sunday or Monday. Note that one place to see the latest works by contemporary artists is **80 Spadina Ave.** at King Street, which contains four floors of art galleries.

**Bau-Xi.** 340 Dundas St. W. ☎ **416/977-0600.** Subway: St. Patrick.

This bilevel gallery exhibits paintings, sculpture, drawings, and prints by contemporary Canadian artists—Ted Godwin, Jack Shadbolt, Joseph Plaskett, Claude Breeze, Brian Kipping, Roly Fenwick, Robert Marchessault, and Hugh Mackenzie.

**Bay of Spirits Gallery.** 156 Front St. W. ☎ **416/971-5190.** Subway: Union.

This gallery features the artwork of the Pacific Coast Indians—totem poles, masks, prints, and jewelry.

**Del Bello.** 788 King St. W. ☎ **416/504-2422.** Subway: St. Andrew, then streetcar west.

This gallery specializes in showing international contemporary artists—European, Canadian, and American. It's well known for its annual miniature art show, held in December and January, which features works from 1,500 artists from 40 or more countries.

**Drabinsky and Friedland Gallery.** 122 Scollard St. ☎ **416/324-5766.** Subway: Bay.

Originally called the Marianne Friedland Gallery, this gallery has shown contemporary Canadian and American artists for decades, representing such figures as Alex

Colville, Harold Town, Milton Avery, Philip Pearlstein, Al Held, Hans Hofmann, Margaret Priest, Karen Kulyk, Wolf Kahn, Ronald Boaks, Rafael Goldchain, and Suzanne Olivier.

**Du Verre Glass.** 280 Queen St. W. ☎ **416/593-0182.** Subway: Osgoode.

This store displays the works of some of Canada's finest glass blowers, plus a beautiful selection of ceramics and handcrafted wrought-iron and wood furniture and other design accessories.

**۞ Eskimo Art Gallery.** 12 Queen's Quay W. (opposite Westin Harbour Castle). ☎ **416/366-3000.** Subway: Union, then the LRT.

This gallery carries about 500 small and large high-quality Inuit sculptures, most from Cape Dorset, Lake Harbour, and Iqaluit on Baffin Island. Prices range from C$30 to C$14,000 (U.S.$21 to U.S.$10,000). It's certainly one of the largest collections in the city.

**۞ Feheley Fine Arts.** 14 Hazelton Ave. (2nd floor). ☎ **416/328-1373.** Subway: Bay.

Inuit art is the specialty of this prestigious gallery located in Yorkville. The Feheleys have collected, exhibited, and sold Inuit sculpture, prints, and drawings for over 35 years, and they personally select each artist and work of art. The gallery, therefore, offers a wide selection of the finest-quality sculpture and graphics from the Canadian Arctic; they range from small and primitive bone and ivory carvings to contemporary pieces.

**Gallery Gevik.** 12 Hazelton Ave. ☎ **416/968-0901.** Subway: Bay.

This gallery is operated by a friendly owner who shows a variety of fine contemporary Canadian artists including Henry Wanton Jones, Bob Boyer, Daphne Odjig, Suzanne Charo, Igor Khazanov, Pierre Patry, Richard James Rivet, and many others.

**Gallery Moos.** 622 Richmond St. W. ☎ **416/504-5445.** Subway: Osgoode, then streetcar west.

Another longtime Toronto gallery, in business for more than 30 years, this establishment represents international and Canadian contemporary artists, including Jean-Paul Riopelle.

**Gallery One.** 121 Scollard St. ☎ **416/929-3103.** Subway: Bay.

A fixture on the Toronto art scene for 20-plus years, this gallery is associated with the abstract painters Jack Bush, Kenneth Lochhead, Joseph Drapell, Harold Feist, and Douglas Haynes, as well as with other Canadian artists like Anne Meredith Barry, David Blackwood, Christopher Broadhurst, Brian Burnett, William Goodrige Roberts, and sculptor Alan Reynolds. It also represents American artists Helen Frankenthaler, Kenneth Noland, and Stanley Boxer.

**The Gallery Shop.** In the Art Gallery of Toronto, 317 Dundas St. W. ☎ **416/979-6610.** Subway: St. Patrick.

Adjacent to the bookstore, this shop carries a great selection of reproductions of international and Canadian art, as well as posters and juvenile prints. Framing and laminating services are available.

**۞ Isaacs/Inuit Gallery of Eskimo Art.** 9 Prince Arthur Ave. ☎ **416/921-9985.** Subway: Bay or St. George.

Museum-quality Inuit sculpture, prints, drawings, wall hangings, and antiquities from across the Arctic are featured here. The gallery also specializes in early Native Canadian art and artifacts.

✪ **Jane Corkin.** 179 John St. ☎ **416/979-1980.** Subway: Osgoode.

This gallery specializes in historical and contemporary photographs by international and Canadian photographers. It represents 20 contemporary artists, many of whom are Canadians, and also carries the works of such masters as André Kertesz, Irving Penn, and Horst.

**Kamimura.** 1300 Bay St., at Scollard. ☎ **416/923-7850.** Subway: Bay.

This upstairs gallery specializes in Japanese prints and antiques. It's open Tuesday to Saturday from 11am to 5pm.

**Kaspar Gallery.** 86 Scollard St. ☎ **416/968-2536.** Subway: Bay.

Specializing in Canadian art from the 19th century to the Group of Seven, the Kaspar Gallery features watercolors and contemporary artists, too.

**Kinsman Robinson.** 14 Hazelton Ave. ☎ **416/964-2374.** Subway: Bay.

This bilevel gallery exhibits such contemporary Canadian artists as the brilliant colorist Norval Morrisseau, Henri Masson, Robert Katz, John Newman, and Stanley Cosgrove, plus sculptors Esther Wertheimer, Maryon Kantaroff, and Robert Davidson. Also international paperworks by Braque, Chagall, Grosz, Kollwitz, Manet, Picasso, and Zuniga.

**Mira Godard.** 22 Hazelton Ave. ☎ **416/964-8197.** Subway: Bay.

Another major international player in Toronto, Mira Godard represents, among many others, such famous names as Botero, Robert Motherwell, Frank Stella, Larry Rivers, Jacques Lipchitz, David Hockney, and Jasper Johns, as well as Canadian greats Lawren Harris and Jean-Paul Riopelle.

**Nancy Poole's Studio.** 16 Hazelton Ave. ☎ **416/964-9050.** Subway: Bay.

For over 25 years this gallery has been exhibiting painting, sculpture, and ceramics of a roster of about 25 contemporary artists. It also specializes in Canadian impressionist works. Every 2 weeks the gallery mounts one-artist shows, except during the summer, when group shows take over.

**Sable-Castelli.** 33 Hazelton Ave. ☎ **416/961-0011.** Subway: Bay.

This gallery specializes in contemporary Canadian art, with names like David Craven, among others.

**Sandra Ainsley.** 2 First Canadian Place, at the corner of Adelaide and York. ☎ **416/362-4480.** Subway: Bay.

If you want to view the most beautiful and up-to-the-minute glass being crafted today, this is the place to come to see cast glass sculptures by such internationally famous artists as Ann Wolff. It's absolutely top-notch and occasionally quite affordable—look for paperweights, vases, jewelry, and other beautiful decorative items.

# BOOKS

✪ **Abelard Books.** 519 Queen St. W. ☎ **416/504-2665.** Subway: Osgoode, then streetcar west.

This is one of my favorite rare-book stores in the city. It has a fabulous collection of early editions and other rare books, with every subject clearly cataloged. Armchairs invite leisurely browsing. It's a real book-lover's haven.

**About Books.** 83 Harbord St. ☎ **416/975-2668.** Subway: Spadina, then walk south 1 major block.

At this used-book store, the titles are all well cataloged and the selection is extensive—particularly strong in literature, natural history, mathematics, and science. Out-of-print and antiquarian volumes are available.

✪ **Albert Britnell Book Shop.** 765 Yonge St., north of Bloor St. ☎ **416/924-3321.** Subway: Bloor/Yonge.

A Toronto tradition (in business since 1893), this wonderful store has a great selection of hard- and softcover books displayed handsomely on wooden shelves. The staff is very knowledgeable and helpful.

**Another Man's Poison.** 29 McCaul St. (just north of Queen). ☎ **416/593-6451.** Subway: Osgoode, then walk west.

This store is heaven for any aspiring architect, interior designer, or graphic artist because it's filled with a large worldwide stock of books on graphics, architecture, 20th-century design, antiques, and collectibles—all aspects of design.

**Atticus Books.** 84 Harbord St. ☎ **416/922-6045.** Subway: Spadina, then walk south 1 major block.

The preeminent Toronto dealer in scholarly used books, especially philosophy, psychoanalysis, history and philosophy of science, and classics. It also stocks antiquarian books and illuminated manuscripts and has an art room in the back.

**Bakka Science Fiction Book Shoppe.** 282 Queen St. W. ☎ **416/596-8161.** Subway: Osgoode.

This store is the answer to a science-fiction buff's dreams. It stocks paperback and hardcover versions of both new and used science fiction and fantasy.

**Ballenford Books on Architecture.** 600 Markham St. ☎ **416/588-0800.** Subway: Bathurst.

For interior designers and others interested in architecture, landscaping, urban planning, and design of any sort, this store is a treasure trove.

**Bob Miller Book Room.** 180 Bloor St. W. (Lower Concourse). ☎ **416/922-3557.** Subway: St. George.

This academic bookstore carries a wide selection of titles in the humanities and social sciences. Look for the fiction titles listed under "Recommended Books & Films" in chapter 1—you're likely to find them here.

**Book Cellar Yorkville.** 142 Yorkville Ave. ☎ **416/925-9955.** Subway: Bay.

This store is well stocked with art, travel, history, and fiction and also has a large selection of domestic and foreign magazines in the back room. It also stays open late—until 11pm during the week and until midnight on weekends.

**Book City.** 501 Bloor St. W. ☎ **416/961-4496.** Subway: Spadina/Bathurst.

This store offers good discounts (10% to 25%) on new books as well as a large selection of remainders. It's a well-stocked general bookstore with large philosophy and religion sections. It's open late daily.

There are other branches at 348 Danforth Ave., 2350 Bloor St. W., and 1950 Queen St. E.

**Children's Book Store.** 2532 Yonge St., north of Eglinton. ☎ **416/480-0233.** Subway: Eglinton.

Here you'll find books, cassettes, and videos for kids from birth to age 14. A staff of librarians and teachers assists selection. It's the ultimate choice of book-loving kids. There are special events, too, on Saturday and Sunday afternoons in the fall.

**Coles The World's Biggest Bookstore.** 20 Edward St. ☎ **416/977-7009.** Subway: Dundas.

With 17 miles of bookshelves and more than a million books categorized into more than 50 specialty departments, Coles boasts that if you can't get it here, it doesn't exist, although to be honest there are a lot of books here that you wouldn't want to own. The store also stocks software, videos, magazines, and cassettes. Coles has smaller locations in **Commerce Court Concourse** (☎ **416/868-1782**), in the **Eaton Centre** (☎ **416/979-9348**), and at various other locations in the city and in the suburbs. It's open late.

**The Cookbook Store.** 850 Yonge St., at Yorkville Ave. ☎ **416/920-2665.** Subway: Bloor/Yonge.

Everything's here for the cook and food lover, including international cookbooks organized by cuisine, wine books, professional books for restaurateurs, dessert books, health books, and cooking and wine magazines.

✪ **David Mason.** 342 Queen St. W. ☎ **416/598-1015.** Subway: Osgoode.

Another fine used-book store with plenty of first and collector's editions of Canadian, English, and American literature. The store has a huge selection on all subjects, with especially good travel and women's sections. There's a great bookish atmosphere.

✪ **David Mirvish Books and Books on Art.** 596 Markham St. ☎ **416/531-9975.** Subway: Bathurst.

This is a fabulous large store specializing in current books on the visual arts—ceramics, sculpture, photography, art history, architecture, and other related subjects. Some out-of-print and rare titles are here, too. Good discounts are offered. Open Thursday and Friday until 7pm.

**Dragon Lady Comic Shop.** 200 Queen St. W., at University. ☎ **416/596-1602.** Subway: Osgoode.

Comic aficionados will find old and new comics here from 1950 to the present, as well as books related to comics. There are also posters and such collectibles as *Life* magazines (from 1915 on).

**Glad Day Bookshop.** 598A Yonge St., 2nd floor. ☎ **416/961-4161.** Subway: Wellesley.

This store serves the community, offering gay fiction, biography, and other nonfiction of interest to the gay community. It also stocks calendars, journals, magazines, and other items for its gay clients.

**Old Favourites Book Shop.** Hwy. 7, east of Markham. ☎ **905/294-3865.**

This is possibly the largest collection of used books in the country—about 300,000 to 400,000 paperbacks and hardbacks. Among the rare-book specialties are equestrian titles focusing on carriages, coaches, and horses.

**Open Air Books & Maps.** 25 Toronto St. ☎ **416/363-0719.** Subway: King.

This is the place to go for travel guidebooks, maps, and other books relating to the outdoors and ecology.

**Pages.** 256 Queen St. W. ☎ **416/598-1447.** Subway: Osgoode.

This large store is a fine, well-stocked general bookstore, with an extensive selection of foreign, literary, and other magazines.

**Seekers Books.** 509 Bloor St. W., at Borden. ☎ **416/925-1982.** Subway: Bathurst.

This store offers an eclectic assortment of new and used books, with an emphasis on Eastern religions, the occult, meditation, and other New Age titles, as well as literature and general books.

**Smithbooks.** Toronto Dominion Centre. ☎ **416/362-5967.** Subway: King.

This chain merged with Coles but has retained its name. It's a decent general bookstore, with plenty of titles on Toronto, along with best-sellers and a good selection of newspapers and magazines.

There are many locations in the metro area, including the **Eaton Centre** (☎ 416/979-9376), **Hudson's Bay Centre** (☎ 416/967-7177), **Scotia Plaza** (☎ 416/366-7536), the **Royal Bank Plaza** (☎ 416/865-0090), **Queen's Quay** (☎ 416/203-0527), and most of the **airport terminals.**

**Steven Temple Books.** 489 Queen St. W., 2nd floor. ☎ **416/703-9908.** Subway: Osgoode, then streetcar west.

This rare-book store specializes in 19th- and 20th-century literary first editions, with a large stock of Canadian literature. There's also a broad selection of good-condition used volumes in various fields.

**Theatrebooks.** 11 St. Thomas St. ☎ **416/922-7175.** Subway: Bay.

The ultimate performing-arts bookstore carries books and magazines on all aspects of theater, film, opera, and dance, including plays, film scripts, criticism, history, and cultural studies.

**Toronto Women's Bookstore.** 73 Harbord St. ☎ **416/922-8744.** Subway: Spadina, then walk 1 major block south.

This feminist bookstore has sections for lesbians, books by and about women of color, literary criticism, fiction, and titles that deal with violence against women and children.

**Ulysses.** 101 Yorkville Ave., between Bay St. and Avenue Rd. ☎ **416/323-3609.** Subway: Bay.

A travel-book specialist, the store is well stocked with travel guidebooks, maps, travel literature, and other travel accessories.

**The University of Toronto Bookstore.** 214 College St. ☎ **416/978-7907.** Subway: Queen's Park, then streetcar west.

With much more than just textbooks, this academic and general bookstore also features medical, computer, and children's books, plus U of T–crested gifts and clothes.

**Writers & Co.** 2005 Yonge St. ☎ **416/481-8432.** Subway: Davisville.

This cutting-edge literary bookstore carries a broad selection of international fiction and poetry titles as well as children's books, travel narratives, and books on jazz.

# CHINA, SILVER & GLASS

✪ **Ashley China.** 55 Bloor St. W. ☎ **416/964-2900.** Subway: Bloor/Yonge.

The ultimate store for fine china, crystal, and silver. It stocks all of the very best names in tableware, from Baccarat and Orrefors to Lenox, Royal Worcester, Spode, and Waterford.

✪ **Birks.** Manulife Centre. 55 Bloor St. W. ☎ **416/922-2266.** Subway: Bloor/Yonge.

A quintessential, reliable Canadian store known for its jewelry, watches, and gifts. It carries the top names in desk accessories, too. There are more stores at the **Eaton Centre** (☎ **416/979-9311**), **First Canadian Place** (☎ **416/363-5663**), and other in-town and suburban locations.

# CRAFTS

✪ **The Algonquians Sweet Grass Gallery.** 668 Queen St. W., near Bathurst St. ☎ **416/703-1336.** Subway: Osgoode, then streetcar west.

This store, owned by an Ojibwa, has been in business for 25 years or so, specializing in Native Canadian arts and crafts—Iroquois masks, porcupine quill boxes, soapstone sculpture, antler carvings, prints, tamarack decoys, as well as moccasins.

**The Arctic Bear.** 125 Yorkville Ave. ☎ **416/967-7885.** Subway: Bay.

This store has an eclectic assortment of Inuit soapstone sculpture, fur and beaver hats, and some Native Canadian clothes and jewelry. You'll need to know precisely what you're looking for.

**Arts on King.** 169 King St. E. ☎ **416/777-9617.** Subway: King.

This is a very large complex in a landmark building housing crafts and fine art galleries.

**Art Zone.** 592 Markham St., at Bloor and Bathurst sts. ☎ **416/534-1892.** Subway: Bathurst.

Here you'll find a variety of glass art—stained glass, sandcarved, beveled, etched, and slumped glass (bent into marvelous shapes), as well as fused glass, in which the colors have been melted together. Some glass jewelry sells for C$10 to C$15 (U.S.$7 to U.S.$11), but prices can rise into the thousands for custom work. The studio where the Irwin sisters work is adjacent.

**Five Potters Studio.** 131A Pears Ave., between Avenue and Bedford rds. ☎ **416/924-6992.** Subway: St. George.

Located upstairs, this studio displays and sells the work of five women ceramists who have worked together for many years. Their work varies: Some pieces are functional, others sculptural; some are hand-worked, other pieces fashioned on the wheel. Feel free to observe the potters at work, but call ahead for an appointment.

**Frida Craft Stores.** 39 Front St. E. ☎ **416/366-3169.** Subway: Union.

Canadian crafts plus items and artifacts from Africa, Asia, and Latin America are aesthetically displayed in a handsome high-ceilinged space. Everything from rugs, fabrics, and bags to costume jewelry, clothes, candles, and knickknacks is here. Open daily.

✪ **Guild Shop.** 118 Cumberland St. ☎ **416/921-1721.** Subway: Bay.

Famous for Native Canadian crafts. This store has a wonderful selection of the best contemporary Canadian ceramics, glass, woodwork, jewelry, textiles, and more. The store also sells Inuit and Native Canadian art.

**Lynn Robinson.** 709 Queen St. W. ☎ **416/703-2467.** Subway: Osgoode, then streetcar west.

The raku and bronze items are made by Lynn Robinson, who works right in the store along with three jewelers who fashion precious metals. Also featured are glass, clay, wood, fiber, and leather items crafted by Canadians as well as furniture and carved stones.

**Prime Gallery.** 52 McCaul St. ☎ **416/593-5750.** Subway: St. Patrick.

This gallery displays contemporary crafts in all materials—ceramics, clay, fabric, metal (jewelry), and paper. Prices range anywhere from C$50 (U.S.$36) for a ceramic teapot to C$8,000 (U.S.$5,714) for a brilliantly colored ceramic sculpture by Montréaler Paul Mathieu.

**Snow Lion Interiors**. 575 Mount Pleasant Rd. ☎ **416/484-8859.** Subway: St. Clair, then Mount Pleasant bus, or Davisville, then bus to Mount Pleasant.

If you're looking for exceptional Oriental craft items, head north to this store, which stocks screens, porcelains, howdahs, lamps, Tibetan paintings, and hand-knotted Tibetan carpets. Silver jewelry and Buddhist books and accessories are also available.

## DEPARTMENT STORES

**Eaton's**. Eaton Centre. 290 Yonge St. ☎ **416/349-7111.** Subway: Dundas.

There are numerous Eaton's in metro Toronto. The flagship store is in the four-level Eaton Centre, which stretches 2 blocks from Dundas Street to Queen Street.

**The Hudson's Bay Company**. Queen and Yonge sts. ☎ **416/861-9111.** Subway: Queen.

Arch rival to Eaton's, this downtown store (formerly Simpson's) still has a venerable feel.

**Marks & Spencer**. Holt Renfrew Center, 50 Bloor St. W. ☎ **416/967-6674.** Subway: Bloor/ Yonge.

This is a branch of the famous British store that's known for quality goods and clothes at reasonable prices.

## DISCOUNT

**Honest Ed's**. 581 Bloor St. W. ☎ **416/537-2111.** Subway: Bathurst.

The original store that launched Ed Mirvish to fame and fortune has perhaps the biggest, most frenetic electric sign in Toronto. Check it out—as Ed says, it can't be beat, as long as you know what you're looking for. A Toronto experience. Fun and strictly for the uninhibited.

**Marilyn's**. 130 Spadina Ave. ☎ **416/504-6777.** Subway: St. Andrew, then streetcar west.

In the heart of the garment center, Marilyn has been in business for more than 20 years, specializing in good-value discounted Canadian fashions. Each rack here carries 200 garments organized by color. The staff is trained to sift through the vast stock and create whole looks for women, dressing them from head to toe, including accessories. In this warehouse atmosphere you'll find discounts of 20% to 80%.

## FASHIONS
### MEN'S & WOMEN'S

**Asylum**. 42 Kensington Ave. ☎ **416/595-7199.** Subway: St. Patrick, then streetcar west.

Scour the racks for new and vintage clothing at this Kensington Market outlet. Dresses, reworked vintage jeans with patchwork and tattoos, men's Hawaiian shirts, belts, shoes, and skull-and-crossbone-design items—they're all here.

✪ **Club Monaco**. 403 Queen St. W. ☎ **416/979-5633.** Subway: Osgoode, then streetcar west.

If you're looking for casual wear and sportswear, this is a very pleasant shopping experience. There are other locations at the **Eaton Centre, Hazelton Lanes, 1950 Queen St. E.** in the Beaches, and the **Yorkdale Shopping Centre.**

**George Bouridis**. 193 Church St., between Dundas and Shuter sts. ☎ **416/363-4868.** Subway: Dundas.

For 30-plus years this gentleman has been fashioning custom-made shirts and blouses as well as dressing gowns. He has 400 to 500 fabrics on hand from which to choose, from Switzerland, England, France, and Germany. Women's silk blouses cost C$250 (U.S.$179) and up; men's 100%-cotton shirts, from C$125 (U.S.$89). They'd retail for much more.

✪ **Holt Renfrew.** 50 Bloor St. W. ☎ **416/922-2333.** Subway: Bloor/Yonge.

This beautiful, well-laid-out store has several boutiques, including Giorgio Armani, Donna Karan, Anne Klein, Yves St. Laurent, and more. Of course, you'll find top-quality fashions and accessories.

✪ **Irish Shop.** 150 Bloor St. W. (in Renaissance Plaza). ☎ **416/922-9400.** Subway: Bay.

This is a lovely store, well stocked with Irish fashions, lace, shawls, and accessories, as well as books and music. For men there are great sports jackets, Donegal tweeds, plus shirts, caps, and hats.

**Roots.** Hazelton Lanes, 55 Avenue Rd. ☎ **416/961-8479.** Subway: Bay.

This Canadian store proves that Canada has style. The quality of the casual clothes is good. People appreciate the hooded sweats, the Robbie Robertson jackets, and the many leather accessories including the sturdy Tuff boots. There is great children's clothing too.

    Also at Eaton Centre and other locations.

**Stollery's.** 1 Bloor St. W. ☎ **416/922-6173.** Subway: Bloor/Yonge.

This venerable store has been at this corner since 1901; it was originally a men's store, especially well known for its vast selection of shirts (with different sleeve lengths). Today it also stocks women's wear, with such English fashion names as Burberry, Aquascutum, DAKS, and Austin Reed.

## MEN'S

**Alan Cherry.** 55 Avenue Rd. ☎ **416/923-9558.** Subway: Bay.

Alan Cherry carries designer wear as well as his own private-label clothes made in Italy. At the clearance center in the back of the store the old inventory winds up at discount—it's worth a look. There's also a **women's store** at 33 Avenue Rd. in Hazelton Lanes (☎ **416/967-1115**).

**Bulloch Tailors.** 65 Front St. E., at Church St. ☎ **416/367-1084.** Subway: Union.

A Toronto institution for more than 50 years, Bulloch has a reputation for outfitting the city's doctors, professionals, military men, and politicos. The emphasis is still on custom tailoring, with suits beginning at C$900 (U.S.$643), but there's also a selection of ready-to-wear, most of which is made by Bulloch.

**Harry Rosen.** 82 Bloor St. W. ☎ **416/972-0556.** Subway: Bay.

Torontonians have been coming to this handsome, traditional English-style store for years. On three floors it features the best from Armani, Brioni, Kiton, Canali, Versace Classics, Hugo Boss, Loro Piana, and many other big names. The latest showstopper is the new Ermenegildo Zegna shop. Good shoe selection, too. Don't miss the "Great Wall of Shirts."

**Rotman Hat Shop.** 345 Spadina Ave. ☎ **416/977-2806.** Subway: Spadina, then LRT south.

This store has been in business here for over 40 years, and it retains the flavor of yesterday, when the area was more Jewish than it is today. Here you'll find the finest, light-as-a-feather Panama hats, as well as other fun headgear, like grouser hats.

**Thomas K.T. Chui.** 754 Broadview Ave. ☎ **416/465-8538.** Subway: Danforth.

For more than 25 years Mr. Chui has been dressing the wealthy and the famous. The custom suits cost from $900; there are custom-made shirts, also.

## WOMEN'S

**Benetton.** 102 Bloor St. W. ☎ **416/968-1611.** Subway: Bay.

Stylish, colorful, well-fashioned clothes at bearable prices are available for everyone. There's another outlet in the Eaton Centre.

**Chanel.** 131 Bloor St. W. ☎ **416/925-2577.** Subway: Bay.

The name says it all—classic all the way. This boutique, one of three in Canada, carries the designer's full line, including ready-to-wear and accessories—shoes, handbags, belts, and more.

**Chez Catherine.** 55 Avenue Rd. in Hazelton Lanes ☎ **416/967-5666.** Subway: Bay.

A long-established doyenne of the Canadian fashion scene, this store consists of two designer boutiques—Gianfranco Ferré and Krizia—plus a showcase of other European designers (Christian Dior, Cibertini, Lagerfeld, and more). It's known for its personalized service. There's a full line of accessories, including shoes.

**F/X.** 391 Queen St. W. ☎ **416/585-9568.** Subway: Osgoode, then streetcar west.

This ultrahip store features the latest from outrageous designer Vivienne Westwood and also Betsey Johnson, among others. They sell 150 shades of nail polish, plus other accessories to go with the garb. Also in Yorkville on Cumberland Avenue.

**Jaeger.** 50 Bloor St. W. (at Holt Renfrew). ☎ **416/966-3544.** Subway: Bloor/Yonge.

The classic British name for fashions, Jaeger requires no explanation. If you like the look, it's here.

**Krizia Boutique.** 55 Avenue Rd. (at Chez Catherine in Hazelton Lanes). ☎ **416/929-0222.** Subway: Bay.

Upbeat and creative as ever, this boutique stocks the full line from Milan—jackets, pants, sweaters, and dresses, as well as belts and jewelry.

**Lola Leman's.** Hazelton Lanes, 55 Avenue Rd. ☎ **416/921-6228.** Subway: Bay.

For truly individual hand-knits and crocheted garments fashioned from marvelous imported yarns, you can't beat this boutique. In fact, so enticing are they that some customers claim they're addicted to Lola's designs.

**Marilyn Brooks.** 132 Cumberland St. ☎ **416/961-5050.** Subway: Bay.

This is the place to come to check out Canadian designers' women's fashions. Marilyn herself has been a designer for more than 30 years, but she still supports young, up-and-coming designers.

**Suitables.** Queen's Quay, 207 Queen's Quay W. ☎ **416/203-0655.** Subway: Union, then take the LRT.

The emphasis here is on silk—silk blouses, skirts, and suits fashioned from a full range of different quality silks with prices starting as low as C$50 (U.S.$36). Needless to say, some folks come from far and wide every year to pick up a supply. The store also stocks some great Canadian cotton vests plus knits, accessories, and other unique items.

# FOOD

**Arlequin Restaurant.** 134 Avenue Rd. ☎ **416/928-9521.** Subway: Bay.

The display up front is mouthwatering—salads, pâtés, melt-in-the-mouth croissants, pastries, and more.

**Daniel et Daniel.** 248 Carlton St. ☎ **416/968-9275.** Subway: College, then walk east.

You'll find a wide selection of gourmet foods and items to take out—breakfast pastries, hot luncheon entrees, salads, soups, sandwiches, quiches, minipizzas, and desserts.

**Dinah's Cupboard.** 50 Cumberland St. ☎ **416/921-8112.** Subway: Bay.

This small, cluttered store has a fine selection of gourmet items to go, as well as frozen dishes to take home and microwave. Great salads, pâtés, vegetarian pasta, and croissants, as well as teas, coffees, vinegars, oils, and herbs.

✪ **Dufflet Pastries.** 787 Queen St. W., near Bathurst St. ☎ **416/504-2870.** Subway: Osgoode, then streetcar west.

This specialty baker supplies many restaurants with their pastries and desserts. The special Dufflet cakes include a white-and-dark-chocolate mousse, toasted almond meringue, and many other singular creations. Fine coffees and teas and light lunches are served, too.

**Global Cheese Shoppe.** 76 Kensington Ave. ☎ **416/593-9251.** Subway: St. Patrick, then streetcar west.

More than 150 varieties of cheese are discounted here. It's worth the trip to Kensington Market.

**Sweet Temptations.** 207 Queen's Quay Terminal. ☎ **416/203-0512.** Subway: Union, then take the LRT.

This store is famous for offering every kind of candy available—chocolate-covered almonds and peanuts, gummy bears, and a broad selection of Canadian and imported chocolates, including handmade Belgian chocolates that sell for C$1.50 to C$1.75 (U.S.$1.05 to U.S.$1.25) a piece. Frozen yogurt and ice cream are also available.

✪ **Ten Ren Tea.** 454 Dundas St. W., at Huron St. ☎ **416/598-7872.** Subway: St. Patrick, then streetcar west.

At this fascinating Chinatown store, you can pick up some fine Chinese tea, which is stored in large canisters at the back of the store. The tiny ceramic teapots also make nice gifts for C$30 to C$40 (U.S.$21 to U.S.$29). Many people are beginning to collect them. And while you're here the saleswomen will likely offer you a tiny cup of tea to taste.

**Teuscher of Switzerland.** 55 Avenue Rd. (in Hazelton Lanes). ☎ **416/961-1303.** Subway: Bay.

Some consider this Swiss chocolatier among the finest in the world. Teuscher produces 100-plus confections including about 20-plus kinds of truffles. The best natural ingredients—fruits, nuts, marzipan, and nougat—are used and blended together using no chemicals or additives. All are handmade in Zurich and flown in once a week.

Look for another location in **William Ashley China,** 55 Bloor St. W. (☎ **416/964-8200**).

## FURS

Fur sales take place twice a year—in summer when business is slow (the best time to negotiate a deal) and every January right after Christmas when the dealers are anxious to get rid of their inventory.

The wholesale fur warehouse is the **Balfour Building,** at 119 Spadina Ave. (subway: St. Andrew, then streetcar west); it's worth starting here and shopping all the showrooms you can find in the building.

**AlaMode Regency Furs.** 286 Bathurst St. ☎ **416/539-9999.** Subway: Bathurst.

This name includes several long-time local fur wholesalers—Sable Bay Furs, Leader Furs (established 1873), Stanley Walker, S. Kuretzky (an original), and Norcan Furs. On the premises you'll find 13,000 square feet of space divided into several showrooms. Mink is the number-one item, followed by beaver, raccoon, fox, sable, and lynx. The prices are wholesale, but in summer, when business is slow, they're even better.

**Imperial Fur Company.** 80 Bldg. D, Nashdene Rd., Unit 90–91, Scarborough. ☎ **416/292-1179.** Subway: Kennedy, then Scarborough LRT to Scarborough Center then Middlefield bus to Nashdene Rd.

Check out the factory showroom for mink, fox, raccoon, and coyote. If you don't find a design you like, they'll custom-make a coat for you. Always call ahead.

**Norman Rogul Fur Company.** 480 Adelaide St. W. ☎ **416/504-7577.** Subway: Osgoode.

This is the reputable furrier to Her Majesty the Queen and other royals and celebrities. An appointment is required.

# GIFTS & MORE

**E.K.R. Zephyr.** 292 Queen St. W. ☎ **416/593-0795.** Subway: Osgoode.

Wind chimes, jewelry, and wooden toys and rocking animals are the stock-in-trade of this appealing cooperative for Canadian crafts.

**The Gallery Shop.** In the Art Gallery of Toronto, 317 Dundas St. W. ☎ **416/979-6610.** Subway: St. Patrick.

Books, gifts, jewelry, reproductions, and rental art are all offered in this large gallery off the museum's lobby.

✪ **General Store.** 55 Avenue Rd. (in Hazelton Lanes). ☎ **416/323-1527.** Subway: Bay.

An amazing collection of gifts for the person who has everything—from ultradesigned calculators and Newtonian puzzles to Filofaxes and the best carrot peeler on the market. There's a large collection of Swatch watches, too.

✪ **Geomania.** 1 First Canadian Place. ☎ **416/364-1500.** Subway: St. Andrew or King.

Geomania is filled with highly polished, brilliantly colored pieces of minerals and stones, some fashioned into elegant jewelry, others crafted into vases, bookends, and other decorative pieces.

**J & S Arts & Crafts.** 430 Dundas St. W. ☎ **416/977-2562.** Subway: St. Patrick.

In the heart of Chinatown, this store has a variety of good, reasonably priced gifts and souvenirs—kimonos and happy coats, kung-fu suits, cushion covers, address books and diaries with handsome silk-embroidered covers, and all-cotton Chinatown T-shirts for only C$7 (U.S.$5).

**Legends of the Game.** 322A King St. W. ☎ **416/971-8848.** Subway: St. Andrew.

Anyone looking for a gift for a sports lover ought to find something at this temple to sports, complete with a Wall of Fame and baseball-handled entrance doors. Memorabilia of all sports are on sale, including autographed photos, old and new baseball and hockey cards, old and new comics, and jerseys that have been worn by players.

**Oh Yes, Toronto.** 101 Yorkville Ave. ☎ **416/924-7198.** Subway: Bay.

This is the ultimate souvenir store—everything in it features the Toronto name. Sweats, T-shirts, oven mitts, bags, buttons, and mugs range in price from C$3 to C$35 (U.S.$2.15 to U.S.$25).

There are also branches at **Queen's Quay West** (☎ 416/203-0607), **Eaton Centre** (☎ 416/593-6749), and, at the airport, **Terminal 2** (☎ 905/612-0175) and **Terminal 3** (☎ 905/672-8594).

✪ **Science City.** 50 Bloor St. W., in the Holt Renfrew Centre. ☎ **416/968-2627.** Subway: Bloor/Yonge.

A favorite of kids and adults alike, this store has an assortment of games, models, kits, and books relating to science—physics, chemistry, and biology—as well as very expensive telescopes and optics, hologram watches, trilobites, and other fossil specimens. All kinds of fun, mind-expanding stuff.

**Touch the Sky.** 207 Queen's Quay W. ☎ **416/203-0578.** Subway: Union, then take the LRT.

Kites and windsocks are the specialty here, plus wind chimes, mobiles, Frisbees, and flying toys—great inexpensive gifts.

## HOUSEWARES & KITCHENWARE

✪ **Souleiado En Provence.** 20 Hazelton Ave. ☎ **416/975-9400.** Subway: Bay.

This store has a beautiful selection of French decorative items for the home—Limoges porcelain, table settings, lamps, custom-made wrought-iron and wood furniture, and on the second floor, luxurious fabrics, pillows, and bedding by Souleiado. This is French-country style at its best.

**Fortune Housewares.** 388 Spadina Ave. ☎ **416/593-6999.** Subway: Spadina, then LRT south.

This well-stocked store has a great selection of utensils and other household/kitchen items—chopping boards, aprons, Copco pots, and other brand-name items—at 20% or more off the regular prices around town.

**Plaiter Place.** 384 Spadina Ave. ☎ **416/593-9734.** Subway: Spadina, then LRT south.

This must be the city's premier wicker emporium, bar none. Every conceivable use is made of wicker: You'll find all kinds of objects made from wicker and bamboo here—birdcages, blinds, steamers, hats, and baskets galore in all shapes, sizes, and styles.

**Tap Phong Trading Co.** 360 Spadina Ave. ☎ **416/977-6364.** Subway: Spadina, then LRT south.

All kinds of utensils, woks, bamboo steamers, ceramic and stainless-steel cookware, mortars and pestles, and terrific baskets are jammed into this small space. It's fun shopping.

## JEWELRY

**Birks Jewelers.** 220 Yonge St., in the Eaton Centre. ☎ **416/979-9311.** Subway: Bloor/Yonge.

A well-known Canadian retailer with stores in towns across Canada, Birks stocks fine silver and jewelry at fair prices. Also at the **Manulife Centre** (☎ **416/922-2266**), **First Canadian Place** (☎ 416/363-5663), and at other in-town and suburban locations.

✪ **18 Karat.** 71 McCaul St. ☎ **416/593-1648.** Subway: St. Patrick.

The owners of this store will craft jewelry on the premises according to your design. They will also do repairs and redesigns of antique settings. Show them what you have in mind and they will execute it.

**First Toronto Jewellery Exchange.** 215 Yonge St., south of Shuter St. ☎ **416/340-0008.** Subway: Queen.

Thirty stores are under one roof across the street from Eaton Centre. As you can imagine, there's a huge variety of diamonds, pearls, gold and silver rings, chains, and earrings on display.

**Peter Cullman.** Cumberland Court, 99 Yorkville Ave. ☎ **416/964-2196.** Subway: Bay.

You can watch Peter Cullman crafting his beautiful pieces that are inspired by natural and organic forms. He apprenticed in Germany and South Africa before establishing his own design studio here in 1980. All of his pieces—rings, bracelets, and necklaces—are beautifully and meticulously handcrafted.

**Silverbridge.** 162 Cumberland St. ☎ **416/923-2591.** Subway: Bay.

The sterling-silver jewelry here is designed and handcrafted by Costin Lazar and manufactured in Toronto. It's modern and reflects the talents of Mr. Lazar, who is also a sculptor. Necklaces, bracelets, rings, and earrings, as well as cuff links, money clips, and key holders are priced from C$60 to C$1,400 (U.S.$43 to U.S.$1,000).

**Yonge Dundas Jewellery Exchange.** 295 Yonge St. ☎ **416/340-0008.** Subway: Dundas.

This complex contains more than 20 stores.

## MAGAZINES & INTERNATIONAL NEWSPAPERS

**Great Canadian News Company.** BCE Place. ☎ **416/363-2242.** Subway: Union.

More than 2,000 magazines and 60 newspapers all displayed under one roof— a print-media buff's dream.

**Lichtman's News & Books.** 144 Yonge St. at Richmond. ☎ **416/368-7390.** Subway: Queen.

Local and international newspapers and magazines, as well as hard- and softcover books, are sold here and also at the Atrium on Bay, at Yonge and Bloor streets, at Yonge and Eglinton, at Yonge and St. Clair, and at Queen's Quay.

**Maison de la Presse Internationale.** 124 Yorkville Ave. ☎ **416/928-2328.** Subway: Bay.

This large store has foreign magazines and newspapers galore. It's a convenient place to pick up the *New York Times*, *Wall Street Journal*, *Financial Times*, and the like.

## MALLS & SHOPPING CENTERS

**Atrium on Bay.** Bay and Dundas sts. ☎ **416/980-2801.** Subway: Dundas.

Sixty stores on two floors sell fashions, shoes, jewelry, and more.

**College Park Shops.** 444 Yonge St. ☎ **416/597-1221.** Subway: College.

More than 100 stores spread out on two floors, this is a more intimate and less harried version of the Eaton Centre.

✪ **Eaton Centre.** 220 Yonge St. ☎ **416/598-2322** or 416/595-1691. Subway: Dundas.

This glass-domed galleria has more than 300 shops and restaurants on four levels, with plenty of places to rest and eat lunch, too. This is where the real people shop.

✪ **Hazelton Lanes.** 55 Avenue Rd. ☎ **416/968-0853.** Subway: Bay.

An elegant shopping complex featuring all the great designer fashion names along with specialty shops. About 85 stores in all on two levels. It has some pleasant dining stops, too. The stores are arranged around a lovely courtyard/skating rink, making for a unique shopping experience.

**Holt Renfrew Centre.** Bloor St. W. No phone. Subway: Bloor/Yonge.

Not to be confused with the store of the same name, which is far more upscale, the center is much more down to earth. You wouldn't find Teas 'n' Tarts in Holt Renfrew. My favorite store is Science City, on the downstairs level.

✪ **Queen's Quay Terminal.** 207 Queen's Quay. ☎ **416/203-0510.** Subway: Union, then take the LRT.

Located on the city's waterfront, this landmark warehouse now houses more than 100 shops and restaurants, including several craft galleries and fashion and gift boutiques. Open daily from 10am to 9pm.

**Royal Bank Plaza.** Bay and Front sts. ☎ **416/974-2880.** Subway: Union.

More than 60 shops are directly accessible from Union Station and the subway. Don't miss the building above.

**Village by the Grange.** 122 St. Patrick St., between Queen and Dundas sts. ☎ **416/ 598-1414.** Subway: St. Patrick.

More than 40 shops are complemented by several major restaurants. The International Food Market is good for budget dining.

## MARKETS

✪ **Kensington Market.** Along Baldwin, Kensington, and Augusta aves. No phone. Subway: St. Patrick, then streetcar west.

Originally a Jewish market, then a Portuguese market area, today it offers all kinds of ethnic foods from Middle Eastern to West Indian, with most stores open Monday to Saturday. It's a Toronto experience. See page 119 for a full description.

✪ **St. Lawrence Market.** 92 Front St. E. ☎ **416/392-7219.** Subway: Union.

This historic market is still favored by Torontonians for its fresh produce—from figs to fish. The best day is Saturday when the farmers come into town and the market opens at 5am. Hours are Tuesday to Thursday from 9am to 7pm, Friday from 8am to 8pm, and Saturday from 5am to 5pm. See page 119 for a full description.

## MUSIC

**Classical Record Shop.** 55 Avenue Rd. (in Hazelton Lanes). ☎ **416/961-8999.** Subway: Bay.

Listen to the melodies emanating from this store. It stocks a large, superb selection of CDs, audio tapes, and videos for the classical-music lover.

**HMV.** 333 Yonge St. ☎ **416/596-0333.** Subway: Dundas.

One of the city's largest music emporiums, HMV also offers an added bonus: the opportunity to listen before you buy. There are 14 other locations in the Metro area.

**L'Atelier Grigorian.** 70 Yorkville Ave. ☎ **416/922-6477.** Subway: Bay.

This store has a fantastic selection of CDs—jazz and classical only, with a really large selection of European imports.

**Record Peddler.** 619 Queen St. W. ☎ **416/504-3828.** Subway: Osgoode, then streetcar west.

This specialty store stocks British imports, LPs, and CDs in rock, blues, jazz, and reggae—no classical or country.

**Sam the Record Man.** 347 Yonge St. ☎ **416/977-4650.** Subway: Dundas.

This flagship of the famous Toronto record chain is vast and very popular. It's reputed to have the largest laser-disc selection in the city. The interactive department on the mezzanine features software and video games.

## TOBACCO

**Winston & Holmes.** 138 Cumberland St. ☎ **416/968-1290.** Subway: Bay.

Although it's not old, this store has all the appearance of tradition and age. A large selection of well-made pipes is on display behind glass; there's a broad selection of Cuban and other cigars, and all the other smoking requisites. Fine fountain pens are stocked, too, along with men's shaving accouterments, toiletries, and fine leather goods. Mail order is available. Also at **Queen's Quay** (☎ **416/203-0344**) and **2 First Canadian Place** (☎ **416/363-7575**).

## TOYS

**Carriage Trade Dolls.** 2958 Bloor St. W. ☎ **416/231-2238.** Subway: Royal York.

At this real specialty doll store, there's a good selection of antique collectibles as well as some serious modern collector pieces such as Anne of Green Gables. Although the emphasis is on collectible dolls, Carriage Trade also stocks modern vinyl and porcelain dolls, including some that are anatomically correct, dolls that you can wash, and so on.

**Kidding Awound.** 91 Cumberland St. ☎ **416/926-8996.** Subway: Bay.

Windup toys—music boxes and clockwork toys—antique toys, and other amusing items dating from the 1950s to the 1990s are found here. It's great therapy for adults.

**Kidstuff.** 738 Bathurst St., 1 block south of Bloor St. ☎ **416/535-2212.** Subway: Bathurst.

This store does not stock video and computer games, but concentrates instead on cooperative games, Lego, Playmobil, puppets, art supplies, and other imported and educational toys.

**Little Dollhouse Company.** 617 Mount Pleasant Rd. ☎ **416/489-7180.** Subway: St. Clair, then Mount Pleasant bus, or Davisville, then bus to Mount Pleasant.

This charming store makes all-wood handcrafted dollhouse kits in about 12 different styles, many Victorian, complete with shingles, siding, doors, and windows. They also sell dollhouse furniture, lighting, wallpaper, and building supplies—wood, metal, and plastic—and display 100 room settings. Dollhouse kits range from C$50 to C$500 (U.S.$36 to U.S.$357), while finished dollhouses are about twice the price.

**Science City Jr.** 50 Bloor St. W. ☎ **416/968-2627.** Subway: Bloor/Yonge.

This is a great store, full of games, puzzles, models, and books about science, and serious stuff like telescopes, trilobites, and hologram watches.

**Top Banana.** 639 Mount Pleasant Rd. ☎ **416/440-0111.** Subway: St. Clair, then Mount Pleasant bus, or Davisville, then bus to Mount Pleasant.

A traditional toy store stocking educational toys, games, and puzzles, plus books from such companies as Brio, Ravensburger, Eduframe, Playmobil, Lego, Playskool, and Little Tikes.

**The Toy Shop.** 62 Cumberland St., at Bay St. ☎ **416/961-4870.** Subway: Bay.

The two floors of creative toys, books, and games here include videos from around the world.

## WINES

You'll have to shop the LCBO outlets. Look them up in the Yellow Pages under "Liquor Control Board of Ontario," or call the info line at ☎ **416/365-5900.** The most convenient downtown locations are **20 Bloor St. E.** (☎ 416/925-1434); **87 Front St. E.** (☎ 416/368-0521); **Manulife Centre,** 55 Bloor St. W. (☎ 416/925-5266); the **Eaton Centre** (☎ 416/979-9978); and **Union Station** (☎ 416/368-9644).

True wine lovers will want to check out **Vintages** stores (also operated by the LCBO), which carry a more extensive and more specialized selection of wines. The most convenient downtown locations are in the lower-level concourse of **Hazelton Lanes** (☎ **416/924-9463**) and at **Queen's Quay** (☎ **416/864-6777**).

<hr>

## SHOPPING TOUR
### Browsing Queen Street West

<hr>

**Start:** On the north side of Queen, just west of Simcoe.

**Finish:** At one of Queen Street West's watering holes.

**Time:** 2 to 4 hours, depending on how long it takes you to shop and browse the many stores.

**Best Times:** Weekdays or Saturdays, when all the stores are open.

**Worst Times:** Early in the mornings or after 6pm, when the stores are closed.

This is one of the city's great alternative shopping and nightlife venues. The tour below includes a few stores you're most likely to enjoy browsing, but feel free to deviate from our suggestions and linger in the stores that catch your eye.

On the north side of the street, just west of St. Patrick St. at no. 200, is:

**1. Dragon Lady Comics,** for collectors of old and new comic books.

On the south side, between University and Duncan, you'll find:

**2. The Village Bookstore,** with a good selection of secondhand volumes, including some decent art books; **Cards & Presents,** which offers cool cards, paper products, and fiesta ware; and **Anji,** which has wonderful Afro-fashions created by Anji herself, as well as jewelry and crafts from local designers.

Cross Duncan and you'll come to:

**3. Noise,** which sells the latest in sneakers (Etnies and Airwalk), Arnet sunglasses, and cool colored cords, hats, and other fashion items for the Gen Xer. At the end of the block, at the corner of John and Queen, is:

**4. Citytv,** the voice and sound of the city. Here, if you have a gripe about something, you can go into the video recording box right at Speaker's Corner and complain to your heart's content. The best video clips are aired later. It's a fun, alternative TV station that also operates a music station similar to MTV and an arts channel, too.

Back on the north side of Queen is:

**5. The Queen Street Market.** Go in and you'll discover counters selling falafel, barbecue, baked goods, and fresh fruit and vegetables. Also in this block are a couple of modish shoe stores—**John Fluevog** for the brightest, most colorful, and statement-making shoes, and **Scrubbies** for Doc Martens, police- and combat boots, and other motorcycle gear at reasonable prices. Cross John Street, and at no. 256 you'll find:

**6. Pages,** a large, well-stocked bookstore selling hardcovers and paperbacks and a very wide selection of magazines.

Still on the same side of the street, cross Beverley and you'll find:

**7.** **Angi Venni,** a young Canadian designer, at no. 274. **Robin Kay's** store emphasizes environmental concerns, stocking natural-fabric fashions, duvets, and bed linens, recycled paper products, and beeswax candles. **Du Verre** (no. 280) has a wide variety of glass vases, pitchers, and plates and proudly displays a sticker identifying it as an "alternative bridal registry." It also stocks bed linens and bed-and-bath furnishings. Next door, at no. 282, the **Bakka Science Fiction Book Shoppe** amasses a vast selection in the genre. **Zephyr,** at no. 292, appeals to the natural world for inspiration, proffering polished rocks and minerals, pyramids, crystals, butterflies, and other natural collectibles. Soho Street cuts in here on the north.

On the south side, between John and Peter, are several fashion stores and some popular bistros and bars, such as:

**8.** **Black Market,** at no. 323A, which features vintage clothing and **Pegabo,** which displays the latest shoes with attitude.

☕ **TAKE A BREAK**   On both sides of the street, there are several favorite hangouts for the artsy crowd. **Le Select,** no. 328, offers a sheltered sidewalk patio and well-priced French bistro fare, whereas **Rivoli,** no. 332, is more avant garde. On the south side, **Peter Pan,** no. 373, is an art deco venue with an imaginative menu; and **The Bishop & the Belcher,** at no. 361, will answer any craving for typical bar/pub fare.

Back on the north side of the street, between Beverley and Spadina, you'll encounter some of the most venerable Queen Street clubs, such as:

**9.** **Bamboo,** which pioneered reggae and Caribbean sounds in the city, and **Rivoli,** where Holly Cole and others made their names. **David Mason** is upstairs at no. 342 and features a well-cataloged stock of antique, out-of-print, and secondhand books. **Grafix** has well-priced art supplies. **La Cache,** at no. 346, is the Canadian trade name of Canadian designer April Cornell. Stop in for her wonderful tableware, apparel, and other designs for the home. At no. 356 there's a branch of that quintessentially Canadian store, **Roots.**

Back on the south side, between Peter and Spadina, are several browsable stores. Among them are:

**10.** **Urban Mode,** at no. 387, for the latest Italian housewares; **Aldo,** for the latest foot fashions from Stone Ridge, Doc Martens, and others; **B-2,** for astonishingly high platforms and other wild shoes; and funky fashion stores like outrageous **Fashion Crimes,** at no. 395, for the most current funky and retro-style fashions or **F/X,** selling wildly flamboyant colorful clothes, feather boas, and other costume party outfits. At no. 403, **Club Monaco** offers more tailored sports fashions; and at no. 415, you'll find **Steve's Music Store,** which features a vast array of musical instruments.

Continue on to Spadina Avenue and cross it. On the south side, you'll find:

**11.** **Hype** (no. 459), offering the latest hip fashions, many of them fashioned from shimmering materials; as well as one of the street's old-time stores, **Buttons & Trims,** which is overflowing with fringes, buttons, and braids. **Siren,** at no. 463, has the latest PVC boots, leopard-pattern shirts, poet shirts fashioned from velvet, crop tops, and Danskin ankle pants for that hot club date. **Matmata** displays glorious ceramics from North Africa along with leather items, drums, and jewelry from the same region.

At no. 471, **The House of Ill Repute** features chain-mail jewelry and some appropriate lacy and velvet bodices to go with it, as well as PVC skirts, pants,

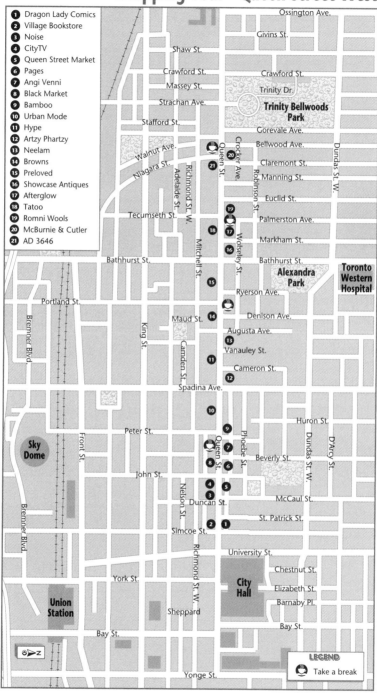

1. Dragon Lady Comics
2. Village Bookstore
3. Noise
4. CityTV
5. Queen Street Market
6. Pages
7. Angi Venni
8. Black Market
9. Bamboo
10. Urban Mode
11. Hype
12. Artzy Phartzy
13. Neelam
14. Browns
15. Preloved
16. Showcase Antiques
17. Afterglow
18. Tatoo
19. Romni Wools
20. McBurnie & Cutler
21. AD 3646

Ossington Ave.
Givins St.
Shaw St.
Crawford St.
Crawford St.
Massey St.
Trinity Dr.
Strachan Ave.
Trinity Bellwoods Park
Stafford St.
Gorevale Ave.
Walnut Ave.
Bellwood Ave.
Niagara St.
Claremont St.
Manning St.
Adelaide St.
Euclid St.
Richmond St. W.
Palmerston Ave.
Tecumseth St.
Markham St.
Mitchell St.
Bathurst St.
Bathurst St.
Alexandra Park
Toronto Western Hospital
Portland St.
Ryerson Ave.
Bremner Blvd.
Denison Ave.
Maud St.
Augusta Ave.
King St.
Vanauley St.
Camden St.
Cameron St.
Spadina Ave.
Sky Dome
Huron St.
Peter St.
Beverly St.
Dundas St. W.
D'Arcy St.
Front St.
Queen St.
Phoebe St.
John St.
Nelson St.
Duncan St.
McCaul St.
St. Patrick St.
Simcoe St.
University St.
York St.
Chestnut St.
Elizabeth St.
Richmond St. W.
City Hall
Barnaby Pl.
Union Station
Sheppard
Bay St.
Bay St.
Crocker Ave.
Robinson St.
Wolseley St.
Dundas St. W.
Yonge St.

LEGEND
Take a break

and more. The street is then taken over by a number of old-fashioned fabric and textile stores. Book lovers will want to climb up to **Robert Wright** (☎ 416/504-2065), which specializes in literature and illustrated, film, and mystery books, and **James Fraser's** store (☎ 416/504-2391), with a large collection of sci-fi, mystery, pulp, and horror titles. Farther along the street, **Steven Temple** (☎ 416/703-9908) offers fine literary first editions.

At no. 507 is the designer **Peach Berserk,** who makes her zany designs in the back room. Many of the garments carry written slogans. **Abelard** (no. 519) is one of my favorite antiquarian bookstores. Spacious and with a broad selection of fine-quality stock, it offers comforts, too—lounge chairs and sofas that invite quiet, honest-to-goodness browsing.

**Art on Beads** (no. 523) provides the beads to create whatever anyone could imagine, along with buttons, jewelry, and some great buckles. **Niknak** has some cool stuff—sunglasses, fashion-conscious fun watches imported from New York, hair accessories, jewelry, and more.

On the north side between Spadina Avenue and Vanauley Street, you'll find:

**12.** **Artzy Phartzy** (no. 394), stocking an eclectic selection of 20th-century collectibles and jewelry; an assortment of fabrics, notions, and hardware.

Cross Vanauley and you'll come to:

**13.** **Neelam Boutique,** selling Indian fashions, sarongs, sandals, incense burners, and jewelry, along with batik fashions. **Gebo Art Worx,** at no. 446, is a large collective featuring a variety of craft items and artworks by local artists—talismans, ceramics, candles, jewelry, tie-dyed T-shirts, and more. **Kimina** is great for tailored shirts and suits for women. **Maggies** (no. 450) specializes in dried flower arrangements, wreaths, and table decorations as well as fresh flowers. The **Day Before Yesterday** offers fine vintage clothing.

On the south side of this section of Queen, the highlights are:

**14.** **Browns',** at no. 545, selling Hugo Boss and other designer fashions for men 5 foot 8 and under; **Striders** for shoes; **Arka** for all kinds of Ukrainian newspapers, crafts, and books; and **Motuba** for every conceivable type of ribbon and trim. Cross Portland Street to:

**15.** **Preloved** (no. 611), a store that was opened by three models who now update secondhand clothing into hip, current fashions. You'll find great retro here in spades. At **Nikolaou,** cooks will find some bargains on restaurant equipment and cooking utensils. The **Queens Trade Centre** at no. 635 is crammed with all kinds of junk. It's known for a great selection of musical instruments from banjos and mandolins, guitars to trumpets, trombones, and accordions. **King's Outdoor Store** sells all kinds of outdoor camping gear, including terrific rain gear, ranger vests, backpacks, and great boots by Sorel that are guaranteed to keep your feet warm in minus degree temperatures. **Metro,** no. 715, sells assorted stuff from the 1950s along with art deco pieces, including a lot of kitschy souvenir items. You will now be at Bathurst.

For those who still have some energy left, cross Bathurst and continue. Here, tucked in between some of the more seedy stores, are a few gems, notably on the north side of the street:

**16.** **Showcase Antiques** at no. 610, between Bathurst and Markham, with 200 dealers on three floors selling furniture, jewelry, and decorative items from all periods and places.

Between Markham and Palmerston are:

**17.** **Afterglow,** a good hunting place for art deco stuff, and **One Tree Hill,** which sells clothing accessories, handcrafts, and skirts and blouses mainly from Turkey.

On the south side of the street, between Bathurst and Tecumseth, is:

**18.** Tatoo, a tattoo parlor, where you can pick a way-cool design and get it cut in right away. At no. 699, **Jalan** sells Indonesian and other furniture and crafts from Asia, including marble bowls from India, betel boxes from Burma, painted wood plates, and carved wooden friezes. If you're looking for some unique and bizarre decorative items to add some sparkle to your interiors, stop in at **Lynn Robinson** for one of the planters with feet or an obelisk clock. Everything is handcrafted—ceramics, glass, and jewelry. Cross to the north side at Tecumseth Street. Among the stores:

**19.** Romni Wools (no. 658) has a full range of yarns, plus sheepskin fashions and some fun sweaters; the **Tibet Shoppe** sells such sacred items as singing bowls, as well as fashions and jewelry; **The Algonquians Sweet Grass Gallery** has fine quality art deco furnishings, while **Cabaret** has some of the finest quality period clothing in the city. This is the place to purchase your retro fashions—velvet and sequined evening gowns, shoes, and that perfect smoking jacket.

Cross Euclid Avenue, and you'll encounter:

**20.** McBurnie & Cutler at no. 698, another secondhand bookstore with a good selection of Canadian first editions, as well as books on travel, philosophy, and much more.

Our last stop is on the south side, where you may wish to stop by:

**21.** AD 3646, to view its au courant furnishings, from chairs upholstered in cow skin to elaborate candleholders. At no. 795, **Rangatan** offers great Indonesian batik shirts, as well as pants, sarongs, and jackets from the region, wooden animals, bags, and more. **World Art and Decor,** at no. 803, has arts and crafts from Africa, including great batik fabrics, cushions, music, wood sculpture, drums, sandals, and T-shirts.

🍵 **WINDING DOWN**  There are plenty of places to stop for refreshment along these blocks. On the north side, between Augusta and Ryerson, is the **Epicure Cafe** at no. 512; or you can stop at the **Prague Deli,** no. 638, between Markham Street and Palmerston, and purchase take-out hot and cold sandwiches, danishes, or strudels. On the south side are several funky, fun cafes, most notably **Gypsy Coop,** east of Niagara at no. 815, with its candy in jars, assortment of teas, mismatched chairs and tables, couches, and pool table in back. There are great "skor" brownies. And at no. 787, there's **Dufflet,** for great ice-cream floats, apricot squares, and luscious cakes and tortes.

# 9

# Toronto After Dark

Toronto's performing-arts scene is terrific. On the music and dance end of things, the city's must-see companies are the National Ballet of Canada, the Canadian Opera Company, the Toronto Symphony, the Toronto Dance Theatre, Tafelmusik, and the Mendelssohn Choir. For comedy, it's hard to beat Second City, still the cradle for so many of North America's great comedy artists.

Toronto's reputation for theater is second only to New York's. Visitors can enjoy major Broadway shows at landmark theaters or explore the repertory of smaller resident companies. For additional entertainment, there are enough bars (cigar, martini, and pool bars currently being the trendiest), clubs, and cabarets to keep anyone spinning virtually all night long.

For local performances and events, check out *Where Toronto* and *Toronto Life*, as well as the *Globe & Mail*, the *Toronto Star*, and the *Toronto Sun*. For the hipper scene, get hold of a copy of the weeklies *Eye* or *Now*, both free and available in newspaper boxes, and at bars, cafes, and bookstores.

**DISCOUNT TICKETS**   For day-of-performance half-price tickets, go to the T O Tix booth at Yonge and Dundas streets outside the Eaton Centre on the southwest corner. Cash and credit cards are taken. It's open Tuesday to Saturday from noon to 7:30pm and Sunday from 11am to 3pm. For information, call ☎ **416/596-8211.**

## 1 The Performing Arts

Toronto's major performing-arts venues include **Massey Hall,** 178 Victoria St. (☎ **416/593-4822**), a Canadian musical landmark, which hosts a variety of musical programming from classical to rock; **The Hummingbird Centre,** 1 Front St. E. (☎ **416/872-2262**), home to the Canadian Opera Company and the National Ballet of Canada, which also presents headline entertainers like Celine Dion and international performing-arts companies; and the **St. Lawrence Centre for the Arts,** 27 Front St. E. (☎ **416/366-7723**), which is home to the Canadian Stage Company in the Bluma Appel Theatre, and to a variety of other ensembles and acts in the Jane Mallet Theatre including the delightful Toronto Operetta Theatre company.

**Roy Thomson Hall,** 60 Simcoe St. (☎ **416/593-4822**), is Toronto's premier concert hall and home to the Mendelssohn Choir and the Toronto Symphony Orchestra, which performs here from

## Impressions

*Toronto is known as Toronto the Good, because of its alleged piety. My guess is that there's more polygamy in Toronto than Baghdad, only it's not called that in Toronto.*
—Austin F. Cross, *Cross Roads* (1936)

*Toronto makes a Sunday in a Scotch [sic] village seem like a hashish dream!*
—Aleister Crowley, *The English Review* (1913)

September to June. It also features an array of international musical artists. The hall was designed to give the audience a feeling of extraordinary intimacy with every performer—none of the 2,812 seats is more than 107 feet from the stage. The exterior of the building itself is spectacular—dove-colored, petal-shaped, and enveloped in a huge glass canopy that's reflective by day and transparent by night. The **Glenn Gould Studio,** 250 Front St. W. (☎ **416/205-5555**), is a small 340-seat radio concert hall for chamber, jazz, and spoken word performances, and named to celebrate the great, eccentric, reclusive Toronto pianist whose life was cut short by a stroke in 1982. **The Ford Centre for the Performing Arts,** 5040 Yonge St. (☎ **416/872-2222**), is home to the North York Symphony and the Amadeus Choir and also hosts a variety of musical events and recitals in its George Weston Recital Hall, as well as such major musicals as *Sunset Boulevard* and *Ragtime* in the Apotex Theatre. The **Premiere Dance Theatre,** Queen's Quay Terminal, 207 Queen's Quay W. (☎ **416/973-4000**), was specifically designed for dance, and Toronto's leading contemporary dance companies—Toronto Dance Theatre, Dancemakers, and the Danny Grossman Dance Company—perform their seasons here.

## OPERA & CLASSICAL MUSIC

In addition to the many major musical venues mentioned above, visitors should also check to see what's on at such churches as **Trinity-St. Paul's,** 427 Bloor St. W. (☎ 416/964-6337), the home of the Toronto Consort, performers of early music; **St. Patrick's,** Dundas and McCaul streets (☎ **416/483-0559**); plus **St. James' Cathedral,** King St. E. and Jarvis St., where the Orpheus Choir sings. The **University of Toronto** also offers a full range of instrumental and choral concerts and recitals in Walter Hall and the Macmillan Theatre. For information call the **box office** at ☎ **416/978-3744.** It's also worth checking out who's performing at the **Royal Conservatory of Music,** 273 Bloor St. W. (☎ 416/408-2825).

If you're a fan of new music, look out for the **Sonic Boom concert series,** which produces concerts of new opera and other contemporary music. It's currently working on putting together a festival similar in range to the Next Wave Festival staged annually at New York's Brooklyn Academy of Music. For information, call ☎ **416/944-3100.**

**Canadian Opera Company.** 227 Front St. E. ☎ **416/872-2262.** Tickets C$30–$125 (U.S.$21–$89).

The Canadian Opera Company began its life in 1950 with 10 performances of three operas. It is Canada's largest opera company and the sixth largest in North America. It now stages six different operas at the Hummingbird Centre, spread between September and April. In 2000, the company will take a great leap forward when it opens a planned 2,100-seat downtown opera house.

**Tafelmusik Baroque Orchestra.** 427 Bloor St. W. ☎ **416/964-6337.** Tickets C$20–$40 (U.S.$14–$29).

# Downtown After Dark

TORONTO

Downtown
Toronto

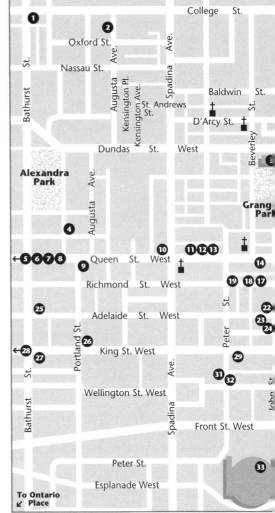

## Arts & Entertainment:

Buddies in Bad Times Theatre **34**
Canadian Stage Company/
   Berkeley Theatre **71**
Cinematheque Ontario **3**
Elgin & Winter Garden Theatre **51**
Factory Theatre **25**
Glenn Gould Studio **65**
Hummingbird Centre/
   St. Lawrence Centre **75**
Laugh Resort **53**
La Cage Dinner Theatre **49**
Maple Leaf Gardens **41**
Massey Hall **48**
Pantages Theatre **50**
Premiere Dance Theatre **78**
Princess of Wales Theatre **62**
Roy Thomson Hall **64**
Royal Alexandra Theatre **63**
Second City **31**
SkyDome **33**
St. James's Cathedral **69**
St. Patrick's Church **46**
Theatre Centre West **5**
Theatre Passe Muraille **4**
Young People's Theatre **72**

## Music, Bars & Clubs:

Al Frisco's **20**
Alice Fazooli's **23**
Atlas/Satellite Bar & Grill **19**
Bamboo **13**
The Barn/The Stables **35**
Ben Wick's **44**
The Big Easy **55**
The Bishop Belcher **14**
Bovine Sex Club **6**
Byzantium **36**
Cameron Public House **10**
C'Est What? **73**
Cha Cha Cha **61**
Chartroom **77**
The Chelsea Bun **43**
Club Lucky Cafe & Bar **21**
Churchill's Cigar & Wine Bar **60**
Consort Bar **68**
Crocodile Rock **57**
The Duke of Westminster **67**

El Mocambo **2**
Fluid Lounge **55**
Fusion **16**
The Good Queen Bess **52**
Guvernment **76**
Hard Rock Cafe **33**
The Hooch **7**
Horizons **66**
Horseshoe Tavern **11**
Industry **28**
The Joker **18**
Left Bank **9**
Limelight **56**

Lion Club **12**
Loose Moose **59**
Mambo Lounge **24**
Milano **29**
Montana **15**
Montréal Bistro Jazz Club **70**
Phoenix Concert Theatre **42**
Pints **37**
Power **58**
Queen's Head **45**
The Real Jerk **8**
The Rivoli **12**
Rockit **54**

Rotterdam **26**
Sailor **38**
Sneaky Dee's **1**
Tallulah's Cabaret **39**
Top O' the Senator **47**
Up & Down **22**
Vines **74**
Vineyards Wine Bar
   & Bistro **30**
Wayne Gretzky's/Oasis
Whisky Saigon **17**
Woody's **40**
Wheatsheaf Tavern **27**

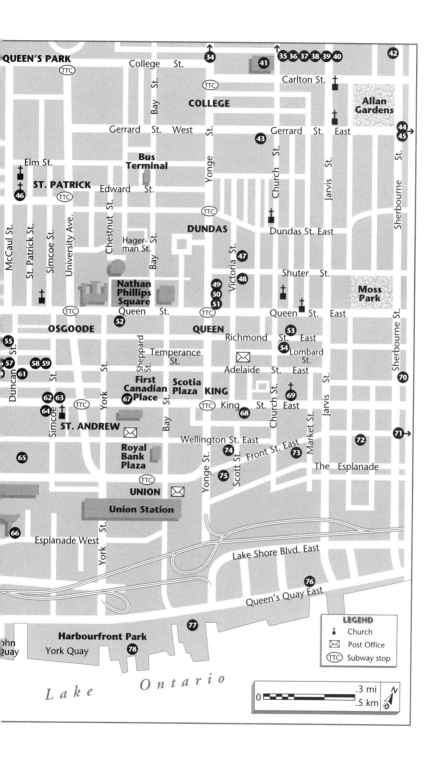

QUEEN'S PARK

College     St.

(TTC)

**COLLEGE**

Carlton St.

Gerrard    St.   West

Gerrard    St.   East

Elm St.

**Bus Terminal**

**ST. PATRICK**

(TTC)

Edward    St.

**Allan Gardens**

**DUNDAS**

Dundas St. East

Hager-man St.

**Nathan Phillips Square**

Shuter    St.

**Moss Park**

Queen    St.

(TTC)

Queen    St. East

**OSGOODE**

**QUEEN**

Richmond    St.   East

Temperance St.

Lombard St.

Adelaide    St.   East

**First Canadian Place**

**Scotia Plaza**

**KING**

King    St. East

**ST. ANDREW**

Wellington St. East

**Royal Bank Plaza**

Front St. East

The    Esplanade

(TTC)

**UNION**

**Union Station**

Esplanade West

Lake Shore Blvd. East

Queen's Quay East

**Harbourfront Park**

York Quay

ohn Quay

*L a k e*     *O n t a r i o*

**LEGEND**
✝ Church
✉ Post Office
(TTC) Subway stop

0   .3 mi
    .5 km

173

This group, which has been heralded in England as "the world's finest period band," plays baroque music on authentic period instruments, giving a series of concerts at **Trinity/St. Paul's United Church,** 47 Bloor St. W. Other performances are given in Massey Hall.

**Toronto Mendelssohn Choir.** 60 Simcoe St. ☎ **416/598-0422.** Tickets C$22–$49 (U.S.$16–$35).

A world-renowned choir, this group first performed in Massey Hall in 1895. Its repertoire ranges from Verdi's *Requiem,* Bach's *St. Matthew Passion,* and Handel's *Messiah* to the soundtrack of *Schindler's List.*

**Toronto Symphony Orchestra.** 60 Simcoe St. ☎ **416/593-4828.** Tickets C$15–$65 (U.S.$11–$46).

The symphony performs at Roy Thomson Hall from September to June. The repertoire ranges from classics to pop and new Canadian works. In June and July, concerts are given at outdoor venues throughout the city.

# DANCE

**Dance Makers.** 927 Dupont St. ☎ **416/535-8880.** Tickets C$20–$35 (U.S.$14–$25).

Artistic director Serge Bennathan's company has secured international recognition for its provocative mix of stylized physical movement and theater. Among its repertoire, the most recent and most exciting work is the Sable/Sand trilogy performed to music by Toronto composer Ahmed Hassan, which *Dance* magazine described as evoking images "at once earthy, smoldering, vulnerable, and proud."

**Danny Grossman Dance Company.** 511 Bloor St. W. ☎ **416/408-4543** or 416/531-5268. Tickets C$20–$32 (U.S.$14–$23).

A local dance favorite whose choreography is noted for its athleticism, theatricality, humor, and passionate social vision. The company performs both new works and revivals of modern-dance classics. Refreshing, fun, and exuberant.

✪ **National Ballet of Canada.** 157 King St. E. ☎ **416/366-4846.** Tickets C$15–$75.

Perhaps the most beloved and famous of all Toronto's cultural icons is the National Ballet of Canada. It was launched at Eaton Auditorium in Toronto on November 12, 1951, by English ballerina Celia Franca, who served initially as director, principal dancer, choreographer, and teacher. Over the years, the company and such stars as Karen Kain have achieved great renown. Among the highlights of its history have been its 1973 New York debut (which featured Nureyev's full-length *Sleeping Beauty*), Baryshnikov's appearance with the company soon after his defection in 1974, and the emergence of such stars as Karen Kain and Kimberly Glasco.

Besides its tours of Canada, the United States, and overseas, the company performs its regular seasons in Toronto at the Hummingbird Centre in the fall, winter, and spring and makes summer appearances before enormous crowds at the open theater at Ontario Place. Their repertoire includes the classics, as well as works by Glen Tetley (*Alice*), Sir Frederick Ashton, and Jerome Robbins. James Kudelka, who has created *The Miraculous Mandarin, The Actress,* and *Spring Awakening,* was appointed artist-in-residence in 1991.

**Toronto Dance Theatre.** 80 Winchester St. ☎ **416/973-4000** (the Premiere Dance Theatre). Tickets C$21–$35 (U.S.$15–$25).

The leading contemporary dance company in Toronto burst onto the scene 28 years ago, bringing an inventive spirit and original Canadian dance to the stage. Today, Christopher House directs the company; he joined it in 1979 and has contributed more than 35 new works to the repertoire. Exhilarating, powerful, and energetic—don't miss their *Handel Variations, Four Towers, Sacra Conversazione,* or *Pingo Slink.* The company performs two seasonal programs per year at the Premiere Dance Theatre.

## THEATER

With theaters and theater companies galore, Toronto has a very active theater scene, with a reputation in North America second only to Broadway. Many small theater groups are producing exciting offbeat drama—a burgeoning Toronto equivalent of Off Broadway. The best time to capture the flavor of Toronto's theater life is during the **Fringe Festival,** usually held for 10 days during the last week in June and the first week in July. (For more information, call ☎ **416/534-5919** or e-mail the festival at fringeto@interlog.com.) Many of the city's smaller companies have no permanent performance space and perform only erratically, wherever they can secure temporary space.

What follows is a list of those companies that have served the test of time, but for any visitor the true thrills will come in doing your own talent scouting. Always check the local newspapers and avant-garde magazines for listings of theater performances.

In addition, don't forget that two major theater festivals—the **Shaw Festival** in Niagara-on-the-Lake and the **Stratford Festival** in Stratford—are only a day trip away. See chapter 10 for details.

### LANDMARK THEATERS

In addition to the **Hummingbird Centre** and the **St. Lawrence Centre for the Arts** (see "The Performing Arts," above), the city's other big theaters include:

**The Elgin and Winter Garden Theatres.** 189–191 Yonge St. ☎ **416/872-5555** for tickets, 416/314-2871 for tour info. Tickets C$15–$85 (U.S.$11–$61). Subway: Dundas.

These two national historic landmarks vie with the royal Alex and the Princess of Wales theater for major shows and attention. Both theaters, which opened their doors in 1913 have been restored to their original gilded glory at a cost of C$29 million and are the only double-decker theaters operating today. The downstairs Elgin is larger, seating 1,500 and featuring a lavish domed ceiling and gilded decoration on the boxes and proscenium. The smaller Winter Garden possesses a striking interior with hand-painted scenic frescoes. It seats 1,000 and has a wonderful bosky atmosphere. Suspended from its ceiling and lit with lanterns are more than 5,000 branches of beech leaves, which were harvested, preserved, painted, and fireproofed. Both theaters offer everything from Broadway musicals and dramas to concerts and opera performances.

Guided tours are given twice weekly for C$4 (U.S.$2.85). Call ☎ **416/314-2871.**

**Ford Centre for the Performing Arts.** 5040 Yonge St. ☎ **416/872-2222.** Tickets C$52–$93 (U.S.$37–$66). Subway: North York Center.

This large complex contains three theaters: the 1815 Apotex for blockbuster Broadway musicals, the 250-seat Studio Theatre, and the 1000-seat George Weston Recital Hall for musical concerts ranging from classical to jazz and pop. Among the resident groups is the Amadeus Choir of Greater Toronto. Guided tours are given for C$4 (U.S.$2.85). Call for schedules.

**Pantages Theatre.** 244 Victoria St. ☎ **416/872-2222.** Tickets C$60–$100 (U.S.$43–$71); discount seats available 2 hours before the performance. Subway: Dundas.

This magnificent old theater, which opened in 1920, has been restored to the tune of C$18 million. It hosts splashy Broadway shows like *The Phantom of the Opera*, the

## Canada—The Funny Country

When Americans think about Canada—and this is rare enough—the last thing they think of is humor. But how many of those same Americans know that much of what they laugh at on TV, in the movies, and on stage is either written or performed by Canadians? Without them, there would have been no *Saturday Night Live,* no *SCTV,* no *Austin Powers;* and Ed Sullivan and David Letterman would have had to look elsewhere for their sidekicks.

For many years, Canada has exported a great number of acting talents—from Mary Pickford, the sweetheart of the silent screen, to Hollywood's most highly paid comedic actor, Jim Carrey. Famous Canadians on TV have included Lorne Greene, of *Bonanza* fame, *Star Trek's* William Shatner, and Jason Priestley of *Beverly Hills 90210.* Even Superman was invented by a Canadian, Joe Shuster.

The Canadian comedy invasion really began with Lorne Michaels, the creator of *Saturday Night Live.* Before that career-catapulting move, he honed his comedic talents by writing for Woody Allen and *Laugh In,* and helped to bring fellow Canadian humorists, like Earl Pomerantz, who wrote for *Mary Tyler Moore* and *The Cosby Show* before creating *Major Dad,* south as well. After the creation of *SNL,* Michaels continued to encourage more Canadians to pursue comedy careers in the States, most notably Dan Aykroyd, whom he asked to join the cast of *Saturday Night Live.* And, most recently, it was Michaels who brought *Kids in the Hall* to American TV, launching the career of Dave Foley, now starring on *NewsRadio.*

The early pioneers who influenced many of these comics were two stalwarts on the *Ed Sullivan Show,* Johnny Wayne and Frank Shuster, but it was Second City that became the great breeding ground for comedy actors. It launched the careers of Dan Aykroyd, Bill Murray, Mike Myers, Andrea Martin, and Eugene Levy. It was such a successful breeding ground that Second City's producer started his own TV show, *SCTV,* mainly to protect his acting talent from being stolen. In so doing, he launched another generation of comedians—John Candy, Martin Short, Rick Moranis, and Catherine O'Hara—who went on to Hollywood film careers. Second City also helped spawn a sketch comedy industry that produced *Kids in the*

---

show that reopened this theater. It was originally a silent film house and vaudeville theater. Tours are given Saturday and Sunday for C$4 (U.S.$2.85).

**Princess of Wales Theatre.** 300 King St. W. ☎ **416/872-1212.** Tickets C$40–$95 (U.S.$29–$68). Subway: St. Andrew.

This spectacular state-of-the-art theater was built for the production of *Miss Saigon* and has a stage that was large enough to accommodate the landing of the helicopter in that production. The exterior and interior walls have been spectacularly decorated by Frank Stella, who painted 10,000 square feet of colorful murals.

**Royal Alexandra Theatre.** 260 King St. W. ☎ **416/872-1212.** Tickets C$40–$95 (U.S.$29–$68). Subway: St. Andrew.

Shows from Broadway migrate north to the Royal Alex. Tickets are often snapped up by subscription buyers, so your best bet is to write ahead to the theater (260 King St. W., Toronto, ON, M5V 1H9).

The theater itself is quite a spectacle. Constructed in 1907, it owes its current lease on life to owner Ed Mirvish, who refurbished it (as well as the surrounding area) in

*Hall* and *Royal Canadian Air Farce,* among other TV shows. Many of these great comedic talents—Jim Carrey, Howie Mandel, and Harland Williams, for example—cut their teeth in Toronto's comedy clubs, such as Yuk Yuk's, which continues to groom young Canadian comics today.

Here are some of my favorite places to see comedy in Toronto:

✪ **Second City.** 56 Blue Jays Way. ☎ **416/343-0011.**

This legendary place nurtured the likes of the late John Candy, Dan Aykroyd, Bill Murray, Martin Short, Mike Myers, Andrea Martin, and Eugene Levy and continues to turn out talented young actors. The scenes are always funny and topical. Dinner and a show begins at C$33 (U.S.$24); the show only costs C$11 (U.S.$8). Reservations are required. To get there, take the subway to St. Andrew, then walk west on King.

• **Yuk-Yuk's Superclub.** 2335 Yonge St. ☎ **416/967-6425.**

Situated uptown near the Eglinton subway stop, Yuk-Yuk's is Canada's original home of stand-up comedy. Comic Mark Breslin founded the place in 1976, inspired by New York's Catch a Rising Star and Los Angeles's The Comedy Store. Some of its more famous alumni include Jim Carrey, Harland Williams, Howie Mandel, and Norm MacDonald. Other guests have included Jerry Seinfeld, Robin Williams, and Sandra Bernhard. Dinner and a show begins at C$22 (U.S.$16) and pizza and a show begins at C$15 (U.S.$11). From Sunday to Thursday, the show only costs C$5 to C$8 (U.S.$3.55 to U.S.$6), on Friday it costs C$10 (U.S.$7), and on Saturday it costs C$15 (U.S.$11).

• **The Laugh Resort.** 26 Lombard St. ☎ **416/364-5233.**

If you want to share some laughter with the likes of Gilbert Gottfried, Paula Poundstone, Ray Romano, George Wallace, and up-and-coming comics, this is the place. It's popular with those who prefer intelligent to denigrating humor. Dinner and a show costs C$23 to C$33 (U.S.$16 to U.S.$24), show only is C$5 to C$15 (U.S.$3.55 to U.S.$11). Lombard Street begins a block east of Yonge and is between Queen and King streets.

the 1960s. Inside it's a riot of plush reds, gold brocade, and baroque ornamentation, with a seating capacity of 1,493. If you can, you're wise to avoid the second balcony and also the seats under the circle.

## THEATER COMPANIES & SMALLER THEATERS

**Buddies in Bad Times.** 12 Alexander St. ☎ **416/975-8555.** Tickets C$12–$25 (U.S.$9–$18). Subway: Wellesley.

This gay, or queer (as the company prefers to be called), theater company produces radical new Canadian works that celebrate difference and blur as well as reinvent the boundaries between gay and straight, gay and lesbian, male and female. Its cutting-edge reputation has been built by American Sky Gilbert. In addition to plays that probe social boundaries, the theater also operates a popular bar and cabaret called Tallulah's Cabaret (see page 190 for a review).

**Canadian Stage Company.** 26 Berkeley St. ☎ **416/368-3110.** Tickets C$30–$60 (U.S.$21–$43); discount tickets for seniors and students sometimes available 30 min. before the performance. Subway: *St. Lawrence Centre:* Union; *Berkeley Theater:* King, then streetcar east.

The Canadian Stage Company performs an eclectic variety of Canadian and international plays in the **St. Lawrence Centre,** 27 Front St. E., and in the **Berkeley Theatre,** 26 Berkeley St. They also present free summer Shakespeare in High Park. Recent productions included the premiere of Pulitzer-winner Carol Shield's *Thirteen Hands,* Tony Kushner's *Angels in America,* and Tom Stoppard's *Arcadia.* The St. Lawrence Centre seats 500 to 600; the Berkeley Theatre is a more avant-garde, intimate place. Look for the North American premiere of an adapted *Trainspotting* in 1998.

**Factory Theatre.** 125 Bathurst St. ☎ **416/504-9971.** Tickets C$10–$23 (U.S.$7–$16). Subway: St. Andrew, then streetcar west.

Since 1970, the Factory Theatre has been a home to Canadian playwriting showcasing the best new authors as well as established playwrights. George F. Walker started his career at the factory, and the clown duo Mump and Smoot makes return appearances, too.

**Native Earth Performing Arts Theatre.** 720 Bathurst St. ☎ **416/531-1402.** Tickets C$10–$20 (U.S.$7–$14). Subway: Bathurst.

This small company is dedicated to performing works that express and dramatize the Native Canadian experience.

**Tarragon Theatre.** 30 Bridgman Ave. ☎ **416/531-1827** or 416/536-5018 for administration. Tickets C$15–$25 (U.S.$11–$18); on Sun, pay what you can afford. Subway: Bathurst.

The Tarragon Theatre, near Dupont and Bathurst, opened in 1971 and continues to produce original works by such famous Canadian literary figures as Michel Tremblay, Michael Ondaatje, and Judith Thompson, for example—and an occasional classic or Off-Broadway play. It's a small, intimate theater.

**Theatre Centre West.** 1032 Queen St. W. ☎ **416/538-0988.** Subway: Osgoode, then streetcar west.

The Theatre Centre operates this venue and also a performance development program. This is the place to see some real grassroots Toronto performances. Tickets are usually C$5 (U.S.$3.55).

**Theatre Passe Muraille.** 16 Ryerson Ave. ☎ **416/504-7529.** Tickets C$14–$28 (U.S. $10–$20).

This theater started in the late 1960s when a pool of actors began experimenting and improvising original Canadian material and has continued to produce innovative and provocative theater by such contemporary Canadian playwrights as John Mighton, Daniel David Moses, and Wajdi Mouawad. There are two stages, the Mainspace seating 220 and the more intimate Backspace seating 70.

**Toronto Truck Theatre.** 94 Belmont St. ☎ **416/922-0084.** Tickets C$23 (U.S.$16). Subway: Rosedale.

The Toronto Truck Theatre is the home of Agatha Christie's *The Mousetrap,* now in its 21st year. It's Canada's longest-running show.

✪ **Young People's Theatre.** 165 Front St. E. ☎ **416/862-2222.** Tickets C$12–$25 (U.S.$9–$18). Subway: Union.

In Toronto, you'll have no problem finding kids' entertainment, for the city takes its children's theater very seriously, as evidenced by the Young People's Theatre. Here, in a theater seating 468, such whimsical, fun productions *as Jacob Two-Two's First Spy Case,* a musical by Mordecai Richler, as well as such classics as *Anne,* from the novel *Anne of Green Gables,* are mounted. There might be one problem: Kids have been known to weep when the show ends.

## DINNER THEATER

**Famous Players Dinner Theatre.** 110 Sudbury St. ☎ **416/532-1137.** Dinner/show C$39 (U.S.$28) adults, C$36 (U.S.$26) seniors and youth, C$28 (U.S.$20) for children 12 and under. Subway: Osgoode, then streetcar west.

A unique show that can only be likened to a theatrical version of Disney's *Fantasia* plus a four-course dinner and backstage tour.

**La Cage Dinner Theatre.** 278 Yonge St. ☎ **416/364-5200.** Dinner/show C$39–$44 (U.S.$28–$31), show only C$24–$28 (U.S.$17–$20). Subway: Dundas.

This is one place to see the art of campy impersonation in a concert given by the shades of Buddy Holly, Roy Orbison, and Elvis, among others.

# 2  The Club & Music Scene

## COUNTRY, FOLK, ROCK & REGGAE

✪ **Bamboo.** 312 Queen St. W. ☎ **416/593-5771.** Call 10am–5pm. Cover C$5–$10 (U.S.$3.55–$7). Subway: Osgoode.

Bamboo is a Queen Street institution that introduced reggae to the city many years ago. Still decked out in Caribbean style and colors, it offers an exciting assortment of cutting-edge reggae, calypso, salsa, hip-hop, soul, and R&B. The club has a small dance floor and a larger area where folks dine on reasonably priced dishes inspired by Caribbean, Indonesian, and Thai flavors. The music usually starts at 10pm. There's a great summer patio, too.

**Birchmount Tavern.** 462 Birchmount. ☎ **416/698-4115.** Cover Fri–Sat C$5 (U.S.$3.55). Subway: Kennedy Rd.

This is the city's longtime country-music venue, attracting a broad range of Canadian and American artists, including Lynn Anderson, Johnny Paycheck, and many more. Wednesday to Sunday from 9pm to 1am.

**El Mocambo.** 464 Spadina Ave. ☎ **416/968-2001.** Cover varies. Subway: Spadina, then LRT south.

Still a rock-and-roll landmark, El Mocambo is the famous bar where the Stones chose to take their gig in the 1970s. Today it hosts the likes of Liz Phair upstairs. Monday's the night to see new local bands perform.

**Free Times Cafe.** 320 College St. between Major and Robert sts. ☎ **416/967-1078.** Cover C$4–$6 (U.S.$2.85–$4.30). Subway: Queen's Park, then streetcar west.

The back room is one of the city's regular folk and acoustic music venues starting around 9pm nightly. Monday night is open house. The restaurant up front offers a health-oriented menu (see page [tk] for a review).

**The Horseshoe Tavern.** 370 Queen St. W. ☎ **416/598-4753.** No cover–C$10 (U.S.$7), C$12–$25 (U.S.$9–$18) for special concerts. Subway: Osgoode.

An old, traditional Toronto venue that has showcased the sounds of the decade: blues in the '60s, punk in the '70s, New Wave in the '80s, and everything from ska, rockabilly, celtic, and alternative rock in the '90s. It's the place that launched Blue Rodeo, The Tragically Hip, The Band, and Prairie Oyster, and hosted the Toronto debuts of The Police and Hootie & the Blowfish. It attracts a cross section of 20- to 40-year-olds.

**Lee's Palace.** 529 Bloor St. W. ☎ **416/532-1598.** Cover varies. Subway: Bathurst.

Definitely grungy, Lee's Palace is a home to local alternative bands, but it also served as the venue that introduced Oasis, Sloan, and Nirvana to Toronto. The downstairs room rocks every night. There's a DJ dance bar upstairs that spins alternative rock 7 nights a week.

✪ **The Rivoli.** 332 Queen St. W. ☎ **416/597-0794.** No cover–C$10 (U.S.$7). Subway: Osgoode.

Currently this is the club for an eclectic mix of performances, including grunge, blues, rock, jazz, comedy, and poetry reading. Holly Cole launched her career here, Tori Amos made her Toronto debut in the back room, too, and The Kids in the Hall, who got started here, still consider it home. Shows begin at 8pm and continue to 2am. People dance if so inspired. Upstairs, there's a billiards room and espresso bar.

## JAZZ, RHYTHM & BLUES

Toronto is a big jazz town—especially on Saturday afternoon, when many a hotel lounge or restaurant lays on an afternoon of rip-roaring rhythm. The best time to be in the city for jazz is during the 11-day **Du Maurier Downtown Jazz Festival** in late June, when legendary international artists perform traditional and fusion jazz, blues, and gospel at 50 different venues around town. For information, call ☎ **416/ 363-8717.** For **tickets,** call ☎ **416/973-3000.**

In addition to the clubs listed below, **Bamboo,** listed under "Country, Folk, Rock & Reggae," above, also offered some of the hottest jazz in town when I last visited.

**Ben Wick's.** 424 Parliament St. at Gerrard. ☎ **416/961-9425.** No cover. Subway: College, then streetcar east.

There's jazz, usually on Saturday night only, at this comfortable English-style pub named after local cartoonist Ben Wick. The music begins at 8:30pm.

**The Black Swan.** 154 Danforth Ave. ☎ **416/469-0537.** Cover varies. Subway: Broadview.

A friendly laid-back locale for both local and visiting blues performers is casual and reasonably priced. There's pool, too.

**The Chelsea Bun.** At the Chelsea Inn, 33 Gerrard St. ☎ **416/595-1975.** No cover. Subway: College or Dundas.

The Chelsea Bun is another of my favorite Saturday-afternoon jazz spots, where the crowd gathers at 3pm and listens until 7pm. Six days a week there's also a piano player and a live band playing Top-40 tunes from 9pm to 1am.

✪ **Montréal Bistro Jazz Club.** 65 Sherbourne St. ☎ **416/363-0179.** Cover varies. Subway: King, then streetcar east.

One of the city's hottest jazz clubs. It offers a cool atmosphere for an array of local and international jazz artists—George Shearing, Oscar Peterson, Marian McPartland, and Velvet Glove. It's great, too, because the bistro is next door.

✪ **Top O' the Senator.** 249 Victoria St. ☎ **416/364-7517.** Cover C$8–$16 (U.S.$6–$11). Subway: Dundas.

Toronto's most atmospheric jazz club is a long, narrow room with a bar down one side and a distinct 1930s look. It's a great place to hear fine international jazz. Leatherette banquettes, couches alongside the performance area, and portraits of band leaders and artists on the walls create a comfortable atmosphere. Plush couches, Oriental rugs, and a humidor fully stocked with premium Cuban cigars are the attractions of the third-floor lounge.

## DANCE CLUBS

Dance clubs come and go with tremendous frequency—the hottest spot can either close or turn into one of the most decidedly unhip places almost overnight—so bear with me if some of those listed below have disappeared or changed by the time you visit. Meanwhile, here are some of the currently crowded spots on the Toronto scene.

First, let me remind you about **Horizons,** in the CN Tower, which changes from a cocktail bar into a dance club at 9 or 10pm. See "The Bar Scene," later in this chapter.

**Berlin.** 2335 Yonge St. ☎ **416/489-7777.** Cover C$8–$10 (U.S.$6–$7). Subway: Eglinton.

This is one of the more sophisticated clubs, attracting a well-heeled crowd ranging in age from 25 to 55. It plays everything from salsa to retro and even sponsors an Arabian night on Wednesdays. Latin and Greek to house music is on hand, too. Tuesday to Saturday 9pm to 3:30am.

**Easy & the Fifth.** 225 Richmond St. W. ☎ **416/979-3000.** Cover C$8–$10 (U.S.$6–$7). Subway: Osgoode.

This is the place to come if you're looking for an older crowd, as the name would suggest. The music is less frenzied, and you might even manage a conversation. The dance area is a loft-like space. In the back, there's the proverbial cigar bar furnished with Oriental rugs and comfortable armchairs, plus two pool tables.

**Cha Cha Cha.** 11 Duncan St. ☎ **416/598-3538.** Subway: Osgoode.

Above the Filet of Sole and Whistling Oyster, this supper club attracts an older crowd with its Latin rhythms (salsa and merengue), deco accents, and fireplace.

**Chick 'n' Deli.** 744 Mount Pleasant Rd. ☎ **416/489-3363.** No cover. Subway: Eglinton.

At Chick 'n' Deli, south of Eglinton Avenue, Tiffany-style lamps and oak set the background for Top-40 or R&B tunes every night. The dance floor is always packed.

Chicken wings and barbecue are the specialties, along with nachos, salads, and a selection of sandwiches. On Saturday afternoon the sounds are Dixieland. Entertainment begins at 9pm Monday to Friday (from 5pm on Sunday and from 3:45pm on Saturday with the sounds of Dixieland).

**Churchill's Cigar and Wine Bar.** 257 Adelaide St. W. ☎ **416/351-1601.** Subway: St. Andrew.

A jazz lounge with soul and Latin sounds. The couches are leatherette; the armchairs deep, soft, and comfortable; the atmosphere swank. The place attracts an older crowd. Downstairs there's an oyster bar decked out in brass and polished wood; Houston's, the dining room, features Cal-Ital specialties.

**Crocodile Rock.** 240 Adelaide St. W. ☎ **416/599-9751.** Subway: St. Andrew.

Casual and laid back, without any trace of attitude, this place spins '70s and '80s dance sounds for the 25- to 40-year-old crowd, which includes a good many suits from Bay Street. Eclectic sounds and scene. There's pool, too.

**Cutty's Hideaway.** 538 Danforth Ave. ☎ **416/463-5380.** Cover C$10–$15 (U.S.$7–$11). Subway: Chester or Pape.

This has been a Caribbean hot spot on the Danforth for a decade. Calypso and reggae bands entertain on weekends, easily luring the many island regulars out onto the dance floor. It's popular with young and old alike.

**Deluge at Atlantis.** Ontario Place. ☎ **416/260-8000.** Cover C$6–$10 (U.S.$4.30–$7). Transit: Take the Bathurst streetcar south to Exhibition Place.

House dancers get the crowd going at this waterfront venue where well-dressed yuppies come to party and check each other out. The dance floor revolves; in summer there's also rooftop lounging. Open Thursday to Saturday year-round.

**The Docks.** 11 Polson St. at Jarvis St. ☎ **416/461-DOCKS.** Subway: Union, then walk along Front St. to Jarvis and turn right, or take a cab.

Another vast waterfront party in a complex that hosts live entertainers like James Brown, Blue Rodeo, and the Pointer Sisters. The dance club boasts more than a dozen bars, the latest in lighting, and other party effects. Thursday night is foam fun. There's a restaurant and full raft of sports facilities, too. Open Tuesday to Sunday.

**Fluid Lounge.** 217 Richmond St. W. ☎ **416/593-6116.** Cover C$5–$10 (U.S.$3.55–$7). Subway: Osgoode.

Only the dressed-to-kill gain entry to this haven for the beautiful and hip, with moody lighting and a simulated underwater decor. Sport and music celebrities sometimes drop by to groove to the neo-funk, industrial, and mainstream dance sounds. No running shoes or sportswear permitted.

**Fusion.** 240 Richmond St. W. ☎ **416/977-4116.** Cover C$5–$10 (U.S.$3.55–$7) Subway: Osgoode.

The absolute latest scene. A harbinger of future design.

**Government.** 132 Queen's Quay E. ☎ **416/869-1462.** Cover C$10–$12 (U.S.$7–$9). Subway: Union, then cab. Also keep your eyes out for a shuttle bus on Front St. outside of Union, but don't count on it.

This vast space down on the waterfront features disco on Wednesday, commercial dance on Thursday and Friday, and an assortment on Saturday that usually draws a predominantly gay crowd.

**Hangar.** 100 St. George St. ☎ **416/978-4701.** Cover depends on event, generally C$2–$3 (U.S.$1.40–$2.15). Subway: St. George.

This student venue is operated by the Students Administrative Council. Live bands, pool tables, pub grub, and plenty of beer.

**Hard Rock Cafe.** 1 Blue Jays Way (enter by SkyDome's Gate 1). ☎ **416/341-2388.** No cover. Subway: Union, then walk west.

This is the only Hard Rock Cafe located in a sports stadium boasting a close-up view of the field and of other events held in the stadium. It offers a typical HRC menu and the familiar rock and roll memorabilia decor.

**Industry.** 901 King St. W. ☎ **416/260-2660.** Cover C$12 (U.S.$9). Subway: St. Andrew, then streetcar west.

Another shrine to the strobe light. Pulsating indeed. Saturday is the night to go, when the place is filled with everyone from ravers and queens to the seemingly "normal," all jumping to the sounds of house. Friday night is R&B and hip-hop with a dress code (no jeans, running shoes, or hats).

**The Joker.** 318 Richmond St. W. ☎ **416/598-1313.** Cover C$5–$10 (U.S.$3.55–$7). Subway: Osgoode.

The Joker is a huge Euro-style multilevel entertainment palace. The first floor features pool tables and Internet-surfing hardware. The second and third floors are where the dance action heats up (anything from R&B to house and retro), especially on the top floor where ravers take over.

**Limelight.** 250 Adelaide St. W. ☎ **416/593-6126.** Cover C$5–$7 (U.S.$3.55–$5). Subway: St. Andrew.

Occupying three floors, the Limelight's first floor is for dancing, the second for pool, and the third for lounging in the so-called "Greek Room." Wednesday is progressive and draws a rave crowd. A young crowd comes Thursday when prices are reduced for students. Alternative and retro sounds play on weekends. Predominantly for 20-to 30-year-olds.

**Lion Club.** 332 Queen St. W. ☎ **416/596-1908.** Subway: Osgoode.

No glitz, no decor, but a surrealistic scene and some trip-hop performers and hip DJs. The coolest scene right now.

**Loose Moose.** 220 Adelaide St. W. (between Simcoe and Duncan sts.). ☎ **416/971-5252.** No cover. Subway: St. Andrew.

This is a crowd-pleaser for the younger set, who like the multilevel dance floors, DJ, billiard tables, booze, and schmooze. Check out the moose art. Pizza, chicken, and ribs are the dinner favorites, washed down with more than 60 different brews. Starts every night at 9pm.

**Misty's.** At the Toronto Airport Hilton International, 5875 Airport Rd. ☎ **416/677-9900.** No cover–C$5 (U.S.$3.55). Open Wed–Sun.

A successful club for more than 20 plus years, Misty's is still popular thanks to its music, theme nights, pool tables, big-screen TVs, and a cool martini bar.

**Orchid.** 117 Peter St. ☎ **416/598-4990.** Cover C$5–$10 (U.S.$3.55–$7). Subway: Osgoode.

With its up-to-the minute design, this glam club attracts a  25-to-30 crowd that dances to disco sounds on Wednesday and alternative music on Thursday and weekends.

**Phoenix Concert Theatre.** 410 Sherbourne St. ☎ **416/323-1251.** Cover varies; Fri–Sat C$5–$8 (U.S.$3.55–$6). Subway: College, then streetcar east.

This rock venue showcases such artists as Screaming Headless Torsos, Patti Smith, and the Smashing Pumpkins and gets the crowds dancing on weekends to a mixture of sounds—retro, Latin, alternative, and funk. The milieu might make you think you've returned to ancient Egypt or Greece. Thursday is gay night. Open Thursday to Monday.

**Power.** 230 Adelaide St. W. ☎ **416/977-1731.** No cover–$10 (U.S.$7). Subway: St. Andrew.

This 20-something powerhouse rocks to R&B. The fashion-conscious crowd is attracted by the additional amusements staged on the multiple TVs and at the pool tables. No jeans on Saturday.

**Rockit.** 120 Church St. (south of Richmond). ☎ **416/947-9555.** No cover Fri–Sat before 11pm, C$10 (U.S.$7) afterwards. Subway: Queen.

In this pizzeria, bar, and dance club, different nights feature different sounds and attract different crowds. On Friday and Saturday, a DJ spins acid jazz, funk, soul, R&B, hip-hop, and some Latin sounds. Open weekends only.

**Satellite Lounge.** 129 Peter St. ☎ **416/977-7544.** Cover men C$10 (U.S.$7), women free. Subway: Osgoode.

Less of a lounge and more of a dance hall where the sounds are disco and retro. A real throwback.

**Sneaky Dees.** 431 College St. ☎ **416/603-3090.** No cover. Subway: Queen's Park, then streetcar west.

The pool tables and Mexican food complement the alternative rock spun by the DJ in the club upstairs until 1:30am. Downstairs, the bar is open weekdays until 3am, 5am on weekends.

**Whiskey Saigon.** 250 Richmond St. W. ☎ **416/593-4646.** Cover varies. Subway: Osgoode.

Crowds frolic to their heart's content in Euro-disco style to a variety of sounds on multiple floors—alternative, house, and retro. Thursday is cheap night. Open Thursday to Sunday.

## 3 The Bar Scene

The current night scene has spawned a flock of attractive bistros with billiard tables. You can enjoy cocktails, a reasonably priced bistro meal, and a game of billiards in a comfortable, aesthetically pleasing decor. The latest fad is the cigar bar. It seems that most clubs now have to have a cigar bar of some sort where would-be tycoons—male or female—can indulge in the latest power statement.

*Note*: Bars and pubs that serve drinks only are open Monday to Saturday from 11am to 2am. Establishments that also serve food are open Sunday, too. The drinking age in Ontario is 19.

### PUBS & BARS

First, let me list some of my favorite hotel bars. For a comfortable bar where you can really settle into some conversation, go to the rooftop bar atop the ✪ **Park Plaza** at 4 Avenue Rd. (☎ **416/924-5471**). An old literary haunt, it's comfortable and the view and outdoor terrace are splendid. Another favorite in Yorkville is **La Serre** at the Four Seasons, 21 Avenue Rd. (☎ **416/964-0411**), which offers a full range of single-malts and martinis, and welcomes cigar aficionados. It was actually named by *Newsweek* as one of the world's best bars. The fairly formal **Chartroom,** at the Westin Harbour Castle, 1 Harbour Sq. (☎ **416/869-1600**), has a good view of the lake and the island ferry. The **Consort Bar** at the King Edward Hotel, 37 King St. E. (☎ **416/863-9700**), is also comfortable. The Library Bar at the Royal York is renowned for the quality of its martinis while the **Chelsea Bun,** at the Chelsea Inn, 33 Gerrard St. W. (☎ **416/595-1975**), has a fine selection of single-malt whiskeys and good musical entertainment. If you prefer a pubby atmosphere, there's the **Good Queen Bess,** in the Sheraton Centre, 123 Queen St. W. (☎ **416/361-1000**).

Some restaurants also have adjacent wine bars with a fantastic range of selections by the glass. Among my favorites are: **Enoteca** at 150 Bloor St. W. in Yorkville; the mezzanine bar at **N. 44,** 2537 Yonge St.; and the downstairs bar at **Centro,** 2472 Yonge St.

And now for the independents.

**Al Frisco's.** 133 John St. ☎ **416/595-8201.** Subway: Osgoode.

Upstairs, people crowd around the pool tables or jam the dance floor, moving to retro sounds. Downstairs, cozy fireplaces enhance the atmosphere of this gathering spot featuring Mediterranean fare—pizzas, pastas, and such entrees as chicken breast stuffed with sundried tomatoes, prosciutto, and asiago cheese, or poached salmon wheel with spinach and red peppers in a leek-cream sauce. The extra-large outdoor patio is jammed in summer with a mix of tourists, suits, and casual professionals in their late 20s and beyond.

**Alice Fazooli's.** 294 Adelaide St. W. ☎ **416/979-1910.** Subway: Osgoode.

Baseball art and memorabilia, including a full-scale model of an outfielder making a wall catch, fill this large bar and dining room. It's always jam-packed with an older business crowd either quaffing in the bar or feasting in the back on crabs cooked in many different styles, pizza, pasta, and raw-bar specialties. The garden patio with a fountain is great in the summer. There are more than 50 wines by the glass.

**Allen's.** 143 Danforth Ave. ☎ **416/463-3086.** Subway: Broadview.

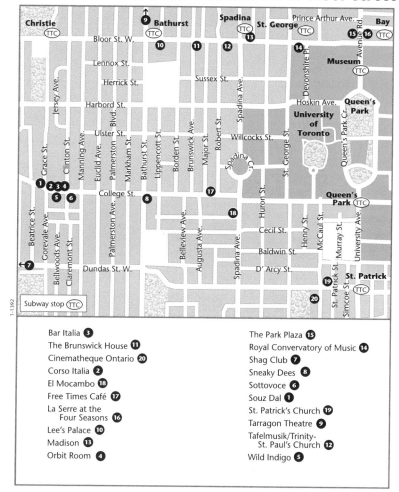

Bar Italia **3**
The Brunswick House **11**
Cinematheque Ontario **20**
Corso Italia **2**
El Mocambo **18**
Free Times Café **17**
La Serre at the
  Four Seasons **16**
Lee's Palace **10**
Madison **13**
Orbit Room **4**

The Park Plaza **15**
Royal Convervatory of Music **14**
Shag Club **7**
Sneaky Dees **8**
Sottovoce **6**
Souz Dal **1**
St. Patrick's Church **19**
Tarragon Theatre **9**
Tafelmusik/Trinity-
  St. Paul's Church **12**
Wild Indigo **5**

Allen's sports a great bar for more than 80 beer selections and 80-plus single-malts. Guinness is the drink of choice on Tuesday and Saturday night when folks reel and jig in fine abandon to the Celtic-Irish entertainment. Readers have written in to recommend the steaks here.

**Atlas.** 129 Peter St. ☎ **416/977-7544.** Subway: Osgoode.

Fashion-conscious singles in their 30s gather here, filling the sidewalk patio, jamming themselves into the downstairs bar area, or hanging out upstairs, where there's a small area for dancing to DJ sounds of funk and rock. Also upstairs, tucked away in the corner, is a dining room that offers Cal-Italian cuisine.

**Bar Italia & Billiards.** 582 College St. ☎ **416/535-3621.** Subway: Queen's Park, then streetcar west.

Downstairs, a young, trendy, and good-looking crowd quaffs drinks or coffee and snacks on Italian sandwiches. Upstairs, guys (mostly) gather around six pool tables. If you're seeking quiet, go early in the evening before the scene changes to a veritable fiesta.

**The Bishop Belcher.** 361 Queen St. W. ☎ **416/591-2352.** Subway: Osgoode.

This British-style pub offers 14 drafts on tap and a decent selection of single-malts. Their classic pub fare includes bangers and mash, shepherd's pie, and a ploughman's lunch.

**Bovine Sex Club.** 542 Queen St. W. ☎ **416/504-4239.** Subway: Osgoode, then streetcar west.

This alternative rock venue is not for the faint of heart. Intimidating metal sculptures and other shock-value art contribute to the funky atmosphere. Strictly for the nose-ring and body-pierced set. You'll recognize it by the tangle of bizarre metal that marks its exterior facade.

**The Brunswick House.** 481 Bloor St. W. ☎ **416/964-2242.** Subway: Spadina or Bathurst.

For a truly unique experience, go to the Brunswick House, a cross between a German beer hall and an English north-country workingmen's club. Waiters move between the Formica tables in this cavernous room, carrying high trays of frothy suds to a largely student clientele. Impromptu dancing to background music and pool- and shuffleboard playing drowns out the sound of at least two of the large-screen TVs, if not the other 18. This is an inexpensive place to down some beer. Upstairs, there's live-broadcast thoroughbred and harness racing from international tracks, including Hong Kong.

**Cameron Public House.** 408 Queen St. W. ☎ **416/703-0811.** Subway: Osgoode.

Old and new hippies still hang here in the front room, with its festooned bar. Local bands try out in the back room.

**Centro.** 2472 Yonge St. ☎ **416/483-2211.**

Downstairs at the restaurant, this comfortable, well-patronized bar is a relaxing place to listen to the pianist and get to know the sophisticated mid-30s-and-up crowd. Closed Sunday.

**C'Est What?** 67 Front St. E. ☎ **416/867-9499.** Subway: Union.

Located downstairs in a historic warehouse building, C'Est What? sports rough-hewn walls and a cozy, intimate atmosphere. It's casual and comfortable, attracting a diverse crowd of young and old, drawn by the ethnically varied cuisine, a choice of 28 draught beers, and the broad selection of single-malts. Live folk-acoustic music nightly. There's a cover charge of C$2 to C$10 (U.S.$1.45 to U.S.$7), depending on the group.

**Club Lucky Cafe & Bar.** 117 John St. ☎ **416/977-8890.** Subway: Osgoode.

This sophisticated cigar/piano bar opens only on weekends and draws an older crowd.

**Corso Italia.** 584 College St. ☎ **416/532-3635.** Subway: Queen's Park, then streetcar west.

This place positively glows. Up front you can sink into the couches and enjoy some good, thick coffee. The orange and yellow walls brighten the day. Four pool tables await in the back. The mural depicting a bunch of guys clinging precariously to a girder is too cool for words.

**The Duke of Westminster.** First Canadian Place. ☎ **416/368-1555.** Subway: King.

Designed in England and shipped and assembled here, this pub offers 16 beers and ales on tap, usually about C$4 (U.S.$2.85) per half pint and C$6 (U.S.$4.30) per pint for imported premium beers. The Duke of Westminster offers a classy English atmosphere that seems to attract those very English types for a good, frothy English pint and a game of darts or pool. Closed weekends.

**The Gem.** 1159 Davenport Rd. ☎ **416/654-1182.** Subway: Ossington, then bus north to Davenport.

A small, down-to-earth, retro-style spot, The Gem attracts an artist/musician crowd. The music is 1950s and 1960s, and the decor nostalgic kitsch—black, red, and vinyl in a tacky-trendy style.

**Hemingway's.** 142 Cumberland St. ☎ **416/968-2828.** Subway: Bay.

This Yorkville watering hole with a fun, large, heated rooftop patio features piano or other entertainment Thursday to Saturday in winter. A pint of beer is C$5 (U.S.$3.55).

**The Hooch.** 817 Queen St. W. ☎ **416/703-5069.** Subway: Osgoode, then streetcar west.

The Scottish word is a suitable name for this laid-back art deco–style lounge, which has live musical entertainment. It's upstairs at the **Gypsy Coop,** which serves a selection of therapeutic organic herbal infusions to cure everything from stress to colds and flu, plus teas and coffees and reasonably priced cuisine.

**Jack Russell Pub.** 27 Wellesley St. E. ☎ **416/967-9442.** Subway: Wellesley.

This comfortable local pub attracts a mixed crowd—families, professionals, and students—and is located in an old heritage house. The main pub, complete with dart board, is warmed in winter by a fire and offers a patio in summer. Upstairs on the third floor, there's a large tavern with a game room. In between, there's the Henley room, decked out with rowing regalia. A friendly place to go and chat, the Jack Russell Pub sells 14 types of draft.

**Left Bank.** 567 Queen St. W. ☎ **416/504-1626.** Subway: Osgoode, then streetcar west.

An over-25 crowd gathers in the lower-level bar at this restaurant. It's especially inviting in winter when the fire is going and folks are playing billiards or lolling on the comfortable banquettes.

**Madison.** 14 Madison Ave. ☎ **416/927-1722.** Subway: Spadina.

Madison has to be one of the city's most popular gathering places, with people (many students) jamming every floor and terrace of this town house. The newest development is the billiard room with 10 tables. Everyone seems to know everyone else.

**Mambo Lounge.** 106 John St. ☎ **416/593-4407.** Subway: St. Andrew.

Upstairs at Xango, this is a sophisticated Cuban-style piano bar and smoking lounge attracting an older crowd. It has live entertainment and dancing to a DJ. Leather couches and wrought-iron and glass coffee tables set the tone.

**Milano.** 325 King St. W. ☎ **416/599-9909.** Subway: St. Andrew.

Up front there's a bar, and beyond it lie several billiard tables. The dining area is off to the side. In summer, French doors open to the street, making for a pleasant Parisian atmosphere. The bistro-style food consists of pizza, pasta, sandwiches, and such items as salmon with an oven-roasted beet sauce.

**Montana.** 145 John St. ☎ **416/595-5949.** Subway: St. Andrew.

This is a kicky Western saloon with an upstairs log-cabin-style nook with a fireplace and a bison trophy. Live bands playing mostly nostalgic music entertain. There's billiards, too. The relaxed, casual crowd hangs out inside as well as on the sidewalk patio outside.

**Orbit Room.** 580A College St. ☎ **416/535-0613.** Subway: Queen's Park, then streetcar west.

With the sleekest decor on College, Orbit attracts a sophisticated, older crowd. Up front, there's a chrome bar with semicircular banquettes and glitzy etched glass. House bands play R&B and soul in the back.

**Queen's Head (at Pimblett's).** 263 Gerrard St. E. ☎ **416/929-9525.** Subway: College, then streetcar east.

Located downstairs in an old Victorian, this friendly pub is the kind of place where you're likely to strike up a conversation with your neighbor at the bar. Outdoor patio in summer, too.

**✪ The Real Jerk.** 709 Queen St. E. ☎ **416/463-6055.** Subway: Queen, then streetcar east.

The original Real Jerk was out east and small. It became so popular, it moved to this larger space. Here, as before, the hip crowd digs the moderately priced, super-spiced Caribbean food—jerk chicken, curries, shrimp Creole, rotis, and patties—the lively ambiance, and the hot background music. Reservations aren't accepted. Open Monday to Friday from 11:30am to midnight, Saturday 2pm to 1am, Sunday 3 to 11pm.

**✪ Rotterdam.** 600 King St. W. (at Portland St.). ☎ **416/504-6882.** Subway: St. Andrew, then streetcar west.

This brew pub is a beer-drinker's heaven, serving more than 200 different labels as well as 30 different types on draft. It's not an after-work crowd that gathers here, but by 8pm the tables in the back are filled, and the long bar is jammed. In summer the patio is fun, too.

**Sassafraz/The Catwalk.** 100 Cumberland St. ☎ **416/964-2222.** Subway: Bay.

In Yorkville, this classy gathering spot features the Bar/Bistro during the day and early evening, and later on, the Catwalk, which has two bars, a double-sided gas fireplace, and a dance floor.

**Shag Club.** 923 Dundas St. W. ☎ **416/603-2702.** Subway: St. Patrick, then streetcar west.

This is Aladdin's cave for the young, hip set, where they can trip on the projected images of the given moment without taking any acid. It's intimate and comfy-casual.

**Sotto Voce.** 537 College St. ☎ **416/536-4564.** Subway: Queen's Park, then streetcar west.

It's an appropriate name for this Euro-style wine bar-cafe where you can linger over coffee or a glass of wine and read or chat softly. Good light meals, too.

**Souz Dal.** 636 College St. ☎ **416/537-1883.** Subway: Queen's Park, then streetcar west.

This is my favorite boâte on College Street. It's dark and intimate, painted in deep-purple and mustard shades, and decorated in an exotic Moroccan fashion. Kilims adorn the walls; the bar is fashioned out of copper. The small patio protected by a trellis is lit by candles. Great selection of martinis and margaritas as well as tropical drinks, like the Havana made with rum, guava juice, and lime. Open from 8pm. Acid jazz on Thursday night.

**Up & Down.** 270 Adelaide St. W. ☎ **416/977-4038.** Subway: St. Andrew.

Velvet, leather, and other plush textures create the sultry atmosphere. Relax, play some chess, or just listen to the eclectic music.

**Vineyards Wine Bar & Bistro.** 55 John St. at King. ☎ **416/397-7148.** Subway: St. Andrew.

The decor, except for the empty wine bottles, is rather bland at this large establishment adjacent to Metro Hall, but Vineyards does have a mighty wine list. More than

100 wines are available by the glass, and there's also a selection of ports, whiskies, and cognacs, plus a decent selection of beers.

**Vines.** 38 Wellington St. E. ☎ **416/955-9833.** Subway: King.

Vines provides a pleasant atmosphere in which to sample a glass of champagne or any one of 30 wines, priced from C$4 to C$10 (U.S.$2.85 to U.S.$7) for a 4-ounce glass. Salads, cheeses, and light meals, served with fresh French sticks, are available.

**Wayne Gretzky's.** 99 Blue Jays Way. ☎ **416/979-7825.** Subway: Union.

Hockey fans will want to visit this shrine to the blond-haired hockey genius from nearby Brantford. It's filled with memorabilia—photos, uniforms, and equipment are displayed in several cases—charting Gretzky's rise from the junior leagues in Sault Ste. Marie through his professional debut with the Indiana Raptors to his career with the Edmonton Oilers. Forget the food, unless you simply have to say that you dined at *his* place. Better to have a drink at the long bar or head upstairs to the rooftop **Oasis.** There, you can sit at the cabana-style bar, which is scented with hibiscus and affords a fine view of the CN Tower.

**Wheatsheaf Tavern.** 667 King St. W. ☎ **416/504-9912.** Subway: St. Andrew, then streetcar west.

Designated a historic landmark, this is the city's oldest tavern, having been in operation since 1849. For sports mavens, it's home, with eight screens showing great moments in sports. The jukebox features 1,200 choices, and there are two pool tables and an outdoor patio.

**Wild Indigo.** 607 College St. ☎ **416/536-8797.** Subway: Queen's Park, then streetcar west.

Another small, intimate bar in Little Italy, complete with a small, atmospheric patio in the back. It attracts a youngish, intellectual, mixed crowd and features a DJ on weekends. Open daily 6pm to 2am.

## COCKTAILS WITH A VIEW

**Horizons.** 301 Front St. W. ☎ **416/360-8500.** C$12 (U.S.$8.60) charge for the elevator. Subway: Union.

From Horizons, perched on the CN Tower, gaze down on the city's lights below. It's open from 10am to 10pm Sunday to Thursday and from 10am to 1am Friday and Saturday. No jeans are allowed on Friday or Saturday nights. At 9 or 10pm, it converts from a cocktail bar to a dance club.

**Panorama.** In the Manulife Centre, 55 Bloor St. W. ☎ **416/967-0000.** Subway: Bloor/Yonge.

From this 51st-floor perch above Bloor and Bay, visitors can see north and south for 150 miles (at least on a clear day). Go for the lit skyline and the Latin ambiance (Rio carnival mural) and music. The seating is comfortable; more than a dozen types of cigars are available. Go early if you want a window seat.

## 4 The Gay & Lesbian Scene

Toronto's large, active gay and lesbian community has created a great, varied nightlife scene.

**The Barn/The Stables.** 418 Church St. ☎ **416/977-4702.** Subway: Wellesley.

This is one of the city's oldest gay bars. The second floor dance floor is jammed; the third floor is for "back room" liaisons. There are afternoon underwear parties on Sundays, and sex videos, too. Don't expect to talk.

**Byzantium.** 499 Church St. ☎ **416/922-3859.** Subway: Wellesley.

This is an attractive bar-restaurant. A good crowd gathers here for cocktails followed by dinner in the adjacent dining room.

**Pints.** 518 Church St. ☎ **416/921-8142.** Subway: Wellesley.

This pub is a friendly gathering place for a predominantly gay crowd. In summer the patio is jam-packed.

**The Rose Cafe.** 547 Parliament St. at Winchester ☎ **416/928-1495.** Subway: Wellesley, then streetcar east.

This is the city's most popular lesbian bar, with a pool table and game room downstairs that's furnished with old, cozy couches, and a restaurant and dance area upstairs. In summer, the fenced-in patio is the place to cool off.

**Sailor.** 465 Church St. ☎ **416/972-0887.** Subway: Wellesley.

This bar-restaurant is attached at the hip to Woody's. There are two bars with video screens and a good crowd, especially on weekends for brunch from 11am to 4pm.

**Tallulah's Cabaret.** 12 Alexander St. ☎ **416/975-8555.** Subway: Wellesley.

This is the place to let it all hang out. Alternative music, flamboyant dancing, and reasonably priced drinks make certain everyone has a good time. Friday is ostensibly women's night, but don't count on it.

**Woody's.** 467 Church St. (south of Wellesley). ☎ **416/972-0887.** Subway: Wellesley.

A friendly and very popular local bar, Woody's is frequented mainly by men, but welcomes women. It's considered a good meeting place.

# 5  Cinemas & Movie Houses

There are plenty of movie theaters in this city. Convenient downtown multiplexes can be found at Eaton Center, St. Lawrence Market Square, and theaters with a couple of screens at the Sheraton Centre, Bloor and Yonge, and at Yonge and St. Clair and Yonge and Eglinton. Check the newspaper for listings.

**Carlton Cinemas.** 20 Carlton St. ☎ **416/964-2463.** Tickets C$8.50 (U.S.$6) adults, C$5 (U.S.$3.55) seniors and children, discounts on Tues. Subway: College.

At the Carlton, you're apt to find that subtitled Russian film that didn't quite make it to Topeka, along with a mix of fresh independent North American films. Buy tickets early on weekends.

**Cinematheque Ontario.** Offices: 2 Carlton St. ☎ **416/967-7371** or 416/923-3456 (box office). Tickets C$8 (U.S.$6) adults, C$4 (U.S.$2.85) seniors.

This organization shows the best in contemporary cinema. The programs include directors' retrospectives, plus new films not available for commercial release from France, Germany, Japan, Bulgaria, and other countries. The films are shown at the **Art Gallery of Ontario,** 317 Dundas St. W., between McCaul and Beverley streets.

# Side Trips from Toronto

**W**ithin 2 hours of Toronto by car, there are several places that make an enjoyable day trip. My favorites—Niagara-on-the-Lake, Niagara Falls, and Stratford—are described in this chapter.

For visitor information about the area surrounding Toronto, visit the province's **Travel Centre** in the Eaton Centre at the corner of Dundas and College or call ☎ **800/ONTARIO** or 416/314-0944 from 9am to 8pm.

## 1 Niagara-on-the-Lake

Only 1¹/₂ hours from Toronto, Niagara-on-the-Lake is one of the best-preserved and prettiest 19th-century villages in North America, with its lakeside location and tree-lined streets bordered by handsome clapboard and brick period houses. Such is the setting for one of Canada's most famous events, the Shaw Festival.

### ESSENTIALS

**VISITOR INFORMATION**   The **Niagara-on-the-Lake Chamber of Commerce,** 153 King St. (P.O. Box 1043), Niagara-on-the-Lake, ON, L0S 1J0 (☎ **905/468-4263**), will provide information and help you find accommodations at one of the 120 local bed-and-breakfasts. It's open Monday to Friday from 9am to 5pm, and Saturday and Sunday from 10am to 5pm.

**GETTING THERE**   Niagara-on-the-Lake is best seen by car. Driving from Toronto, take the QEW Niagara via Hamilton and St. Catharines and exit at Highway 55.

**Amtrak** and **VIA** operate trains between Toronto (☎ **416/ 366-8411**) and New York that stop in St. Catharines and Niagara Falls. Call ☎ **800/361-1235** in Canada or **800/USA-RAIL** in the United States. From either destination, you'll need to rent a car and exit at Highway 55. Rental locations in St. Catharines include **National Tilden,** 162 Church St. (☎ **905/682-8611**), and **Hertz,** 404 Ontario St. (☎ **905/682-8695**). In Niagara Falls, there's another **National Tilden** at 4523 Drummond Rd. (☎ **905/ 374-6700**).

### THE SHAW FESTIVAL

Devoted to the works of George Bernard Shaw and his contemporaries, the festival, which opens in April and runs to November, performs 10 or 11 plays in three theaters: the historic Court House, the exquisite Festival Theatre, and the Royal George Theatre.

Some recent performances have included Shaw's *The Devil's Disciple, Pygmalion, Mrs. Warren's Profession, The Doctor's Dilemma,* and *An Ideal Husband* by Oscar Wilde.

Added attractions are the free chamber concerts Sunday at 11am, the Friday chats that introduce performances on Friday evenings in July and August, and the Tuesday evening question-and-answer sessions that follow performances.

The Shaw announces its festival program in mid-January. Unless a show bombs, tickets are difficult to get on short notice; book in advance. Prices range from C$15 (U.S.$11) for lunchtime performances to C$65 (U.S.$45) on weekends. For more information, contact the **Shaw Festival,** P.O. Box 774, Niagara-on-the-Lake, ON, L0S 1J0 (☎ **800/511-7429** or 905/468-2172).

# EXPLORING THE TOWN

**Niagara Historical Society Museum.** 43 Castlereagh St. at Davy. ☎ **905/468-3912.** Admission C$3 (U.S.$2.15) adults, C$1.50 (U.S.$1) seniors and youths 12–18, C50¢ (U.S.35¢) children under 12. Jan–Feb weekends 1–5pm; Mar, Apr, Nov, Dec daily 1–5pm; May–Oct daily 10am–5pm.

The Niagara Historical Museum houses more than 20,000 artifacts pertaining to local history, including many possessions of United Empire Loyalists who first settled the area at the end of the American Revolution.

**✪ Fort George National Historic Park.** Niagara Pkwy. ☎ **905/468-6614.** Admission C$6 (U.S.$4.30) adults, C$5 (U.S.$3.55) seniors, C$4 (U.S.$2.85) ages 6–16; free for children 5 and under; family rate, C$20 (U.S.$14). Apr 1–Oct 31 daily 10am–5pm (until 8pm on Saturdays in July and Aug.

South along the Niagara Parkway at the Fort George National Historic Park, it's easy to imagine taking shelter behind the stockade fence and watching for the enemy from across the river, even though today there are only condominiums on the opposite riverbank.

The fort played a key role in the War of 1812 until the Americans invaded and destroyed it in May 1813. Although rebuilt by 1815, it was abandoned in 1828 and not reconstructed until the 1930s. View the guard room with its hard plank beds, the officers' quarters, the enlisted men's quarters, and the sentry posts. The self-guided tour includes interpretive films and, occasionally, performances by the Fort George Fife and Drum Corps.

## A NOSTALGIC SHOPPING STROLL

A stroll along Queen Street will take you by some entertaining shops. At the 1866 **Niagara Apothecary Shop,** 5 Queen St.(☎ 905/468-3845), with its original black-walnut counters and the contents of the drawers marked in gold-leaf script, the original glass and ceramic apothecary ware is on display. **Maple Leaf Fudge,** 14 Queen St. (☎ 905/468-2211), offers more than 20 varieties that you can watch being made on marble slabs. At no. 35, **Greaves Jam** is run by fourth-generation jam makers. **Loyalist Village,** at no. 12 (☎ 905/468-7331), has distinctively Canadian clothes and crafts, including Inuit art, Native Canadian decoys, and sheepskins. The **Shaw Shop,** next to the Royal George, has GBS memorabilia and more. There's also a Dansk outlet and several galleries selling contemporary Canadian and other ethnic crafts, and a charming toy store, the **Owl and the Pussycat,** at 16 Queen St. (☎ 905/468-3081).

# Side Trips from Toronto

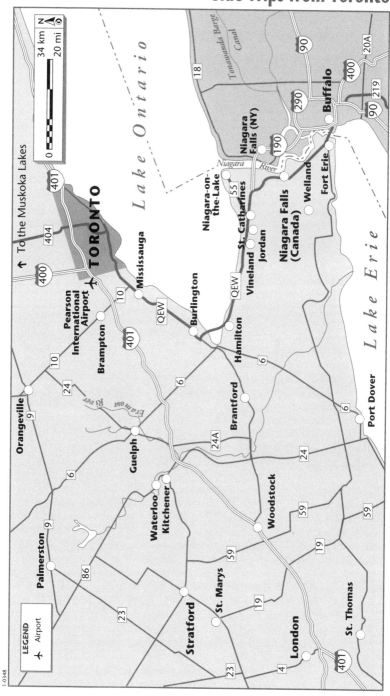

## From Vinegar to Vintage—Ontario Wines Come of Age

Not so long ago (in the early 1980s, in fact), Canadians were embarrassed about their local wines, and restaurateurs were loath to feature them on their menus, even though the government and the tax structure encouraged them to do so. Only a decade and a half later, Ontario wines are turning up all over and are prominently and proudly featured on the wine lists of top-class Canadian restaurants. In short, they have come of age, thanks very largely to the establishment of the VQA appellation in 1988.

There are three designated Ontario viticultural areas—**Niagara Peninsula, Pelee Island,** and **Lake Erie North Shore.** In order to carry each designation, wines must contain 85% grapes from the viticultural area, and must be made 85% from the variety named on the label—in order to carry a varietal name. The Ontario wine area is parallel to Provence and Languedoc-Rousillon in France, Chianti in Italy, the Rioja region in Spain, and the Mendocino Valley in California. All three Ontario regions benefit from the climatic effects of the Great Lakes, which temper the heat and cold of the seasons, and the wind buffer that the Niagara Escarpment provides.

The Niagara wine-growing region runs along the south shore of Lake Ontario from Stoney Creek to Niagara Falls. It produces good-quality wines that are winning medals in international competitions, but the region has also won worldwide acclaim for the consistent production and quality of one wine in particular—**ice wine**—so much so that Canada is now the number-one producer of this elixir that enhances desserts of every kind, except chocolate. Ice wine is made from frozen grapes, usually Riesling or Vidal, which are then pressed, producing a juice that is intensely sweet and highly acidic. Temperature is critical to the process. The frozen grapes must not melt; if they do, the concentration of the juice is diluted. Here on the Niagara Escarpment, the climate is ideal for its production. First, the grapes are left to freeze. If they survive the birds and other predators, they are harvested under unusually bitter cold conditions, then pressed while still frozen, and left to ferment. One of the reasons ice wine is so expensive is that it takes about 5 kilos of grapes to produce enough juice to make one bottle of wine (compared to 1 kilo normally).

In addition to ice wine, the region also produces some fine chardonnays, Rieslings, gewürztraminers, cabernet sauvignons, merlots, pinot noirs, and gamays. Among the major estate wineries that were the first to produce good varietal wines are: **Inniskillin,** Niagara Parkway RR #1 at Line 3, Niagara-on-the-Lake (☎ **905/ 468-3554**); **Chateau des Charmes,** 1025 York Rd., St. David's (☎ **905/ 262-4219**); and **Hillebrand,** Hwy. 55, Niagara-on-the-Lake (☎ **905/468-7123**). In addition, there are many smaller companies, which are pushing the larger estates to produce better and better wines, such as: **Cave Spring Cellars,** 3836 Main St., Jordan (☎ **905/562-3581**); **Vineland Estates,** 3620 Moyer Rd., RR #1, Vineland (☎ **905/562-7088**); **Reif,** RR #1, 15608 Niagara Pkwy. (☎ **905/ 468-7738**); **Henry of Pelham,** 1469 Pelham Rd., St. Catharines (☎ **905/ 684-8423**); **Konzelmann,** RR #3, 1096 Lakeshore Rd., Niagara-on-the-Lake (☎ **905/935-2866**); and **Stoney Ridge,** 1468 Hwy. 8, Winona, on the outskirts of Hamilton (☎ **905/643-4508**).

If you have time for only one wine tour, try Hillebrand, which in addition to an excellent tour has a good dining room (see "Dining Along the Wine Road," page 200) and even offers bike tours.

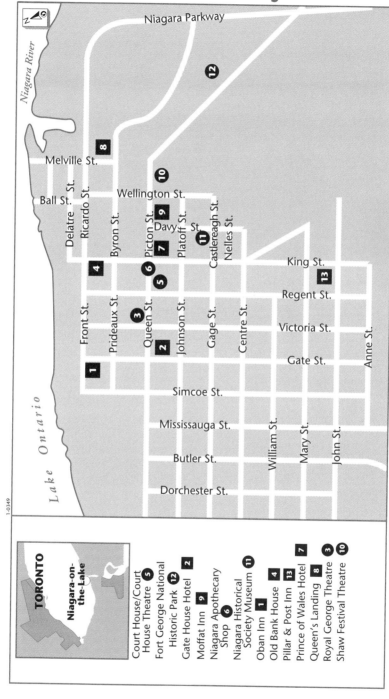

Niagara Parkway

**12**

*Niagara River*

*Niagara River*

**8**

Melville St.

**10**

Ball St.

Delatre St.

Ricardo St.

Wellington St.

Byron St.

**9**

Picton St.

Davy St.

**7**

Platoff St.

**11**

Castlereagh St.

Nelles St.

**4**

**6**

King St.

**13**

**5**

Front St.

Prideaux St.

**3**

Queen St.

**2**

Johnson St.

Gage St.

Centre St.

Regent St.

Victoria St.

Gate St.

Anne St.

**1**

Simcoe St.

Mississauga St.

William St.

Mary St.

John St.

Butler St.

Dorchester St.

*L a k e   O n t a r i o*

1-0349

TORONTO

Niagara-on-the-Lake

Court House/Court House Theatre **5**

Fort George National Historic Park **12**

Gate House Hotel **2**

Moffat Inn **9**

Niagara Apothecary Shop **6**

Niagara Historical Society Museum **11**

Oban Inn **1**

Old Bank House **4**

Pillar & Post Inn **13**

Prince of Wales Hotel **7**

Queen's Landing **8**

Royal George Theatre **3**

Shaw Festival Theatre **10**

195

## JET-BOATING THRILLS

Don a rain suit, poncho, and life jacket and climb aboard a jet boat at the dock across from 61 Melville St. at the King George III Inn. The boat will take you out onto the river for a trip along the stone-walled canyon to the whirlpool downriver closer to the falls. Trips, which operate from May to October, last an hour and cost C$48 (U.S.$34) adults, C$38 (U.S.$27) children 6 to 16. Reservations are needed. Call ☎ **905/468-4800.**

## TOURING NIAGARA-ON-THE-LAKE WINERIES

If you take Highway 55 (Niagara Stone Road) out of Niagara-on-the-Lake, you'll come to **Hillebrand Estates Winery** (☎ **905/468-7123**), just outside Virgil. It's open year-round, hosts a variety of special events, features cafe dining, and even offers bicycle tours. Winery tours are given daily from 10am to 6pm on the hour.

If you turn off Highway 55 and go down York Road, you'll reach **Château des Charmes,** west of St. Davids (☎ **905/262-5202**). One-hour tours are given daily. Open 10am to 6pm.

The **Konzelmann Winery,** Lakeshore Road (☎ **905/935-2866**), can be reached by taking Mary Street out of Niagara-on-the-Lake. Tours are given May to late September from Monday to Saturday at 2pm.

## ACCOMMODATIONS

In summer, don't despair if you're having trouble nailing down a room somewhere. Contact the chamber of commerce, which provides an accommodations-reservations service. Your best bets are bed-and-breakfast accommodations.

### IN TOWN

**Expensive**

**Gate House Hotel.** 142 Queen St. (P.O. Box 1364), Niagara-on-the-Lake, ON, L0S 1J0. ☎ **905/468-3263.** 10 rms. A/C TV TEL. C$160–$180 (U.S.$114–$129) double. AE, ER, MC, V.

Instead of being done in country-Canadian, the rooms here are decorated in cool, up-to-the-minute Milan style. Guest rooms have a turquoise marbleized look accented with ultramodern basic black lamps, block marble tables, leatherette couches, and bathrooms with sleek Italian fixtures.

**Dining: Ristorante Giardino,** one of the best places to dine in town, is located in the hotel.

✪ **Oban Inn.** 160 Front St. (at Gate St.), Niagara-on-the-Lake, ON, L0S 1J0. ☎ **905/468-2165.** 22 rms. A/C TV TEL. C$160 (U.S.$114) standard double, C$220 (U.S.$157) double with lake view. Winter midweek and weekend packages available. AE, DC, MC, V.

With a prime location overlooking the lake, the Oban Inn is the place to stay. It's located in a charming white Victorian house with a green dormer-style roof and windows, plus a large veranda. The gardens are a joy to behold and are the source of the bouquets on each table in the dining room and throughout the house.

Each of the comfortable rooms is unique. They are furnished with comfortable antique reproductions—corn-husk four-poster beds with candlewick spreads, ginger-jar lamps, and club-style sofas. Old prints might adorn the walls—it's all very homey and comfortably old-fashioned.

**Dining:** Bar snacks and light lunches and dinners are available downstairs in the pubby piano bar, with its leather Windsor-style chairs and hunting prints over the blazing fireplace. The dinner menu is priced from C$20 to C$24 (U.S.$14 to U.S.$17).

**Pillar & Post Inn.** 48 John St. (at King St.), Niagara-on-the-Lake, ON, L0S 1J0. ☎ **800/ 361-6788** or 905/468-2123. Fax 905/468-3551. 123 rms and suites. A/C MINIBAR TV TEL. C$170 (U.S.$121) double; C$185 (U.S.$132) fireplace rm; C$205–$240 (U.S.$146–$171) deluxe rm; from C$275 (U.S.$196) suites. Extra person C$20 (U.S.$14). AE, DC, ER, MC, V.

The quietly elegant Pillar & Post is located a couple of blocks from the madding crowds on Queen Street. In recent years it has been transformed into one of the most sophisticated accommodations in town, complete with a spa featuring themed treatment rooms. From the minute they set foot in the light and airy lobby furnished with fireplace, lush plantings, and comfortable seating, guests see where the emphasis is. Although all of the spacious rooms are slightly different, each room contains early Canadian-style furniture, Windsor-style chairs, a color TV tucked into a pine cabinet, and historical engravings. In the back there's a secluded pool (some rooms facing the pool on the ground level have bay windows and window boxes).

**Dining/Entertainment:** Warmed by fires on cool evenings, the two dining rooms occupy a former tomato and peach canning factory and basket manufacturing plant. The eclectic menu features everything from prime rib with Yorkshire pudding to Szechuan roast duck and bourbon-marinated beef tenderloin with a smoky bacon jus. Entrees run from C$16 to C$26 (U.S.$11 to U.S.$19). The adjoining wine bar features a curvaceous bar and a large selection of local and international wines.

**Facilities:** The spa offers a full range of body treatments and massage therapies from C$30 to C$95 (U.S.$21 to U.S.$68), plus a Japanese-style warm mineral-spring pool, complete with cascading waterfall. Other facilities include an indoor pool and an attractively landscaped outdoor pool, sauna, whirlpool, and bike rentals.

**Prince of Wales Hotel.** 6 Picton St., Niagara-on-the-Lake, ON, L0S 1J0. ☎ **800/263-2452** or 905/468-3246. Fax 905/468-1310. 101 rms. A/C TV TEL. May–Oct, C$140–$245 (U.S.$100– $175) double, from C$295 (U.S.$211) suite; Nov–Apr, C$120 (U.S.$86) double. Extra person C$20 (U.S.$14). Special packages available. AE, MC, V.

For a lively atmosphere that retains the elegance and charm of a Victorian inn, the Prince of Wales has it all: a main-street location right across from the lovely gardens of Simcoe Park; full recreational facilities; lounges, bars, and restaurants; and attractive rooms, all beautifully decorated with antiques or reproductions. Bathrooms have bidets and most rooms have minibars. The hotel's original section was built in 1864 and rooms here are slightly smaller than those in the several additions.

**Dining/Entertainment:** An impressive old oak bar from Pennsylvania dominates the quiet bar off the lobby. **Royals,** the elegant main dining room, is decorated in French style. Its menu offers a dozen classics like mustard-crusted rack of lamb or salmon with thyme beurre blanc, priced from C$18 to C$28 (U.S.$13 to U.S.$20). **Three Feathers** is a luxuriant greenhouse cafe that is perfect for breakfast, lunch, or tea. The **Queen's Royal lounge,** furnished with wingback and armchairs, is pleasant for cocktails or light evening fare.

**Facilities:** Indoor pool, whirlpool, fitness center, bike rental. Aerobics classes and massage therapy are offered.

**Queen's Landing.** P.O. Box 1180, at the corner of Byron and Melville sts., Niagara-on-the-Lake, ON, L0S 1J0. ☎ **800/361-6645** or 905/468-2195. 138 rms. A/C MINIBAR TV TEL. C$180 (U.S.$129) rm without fireplace; C$195–$205 (U.S.$139–$146) rm with fireplace; C$230–$265 (U.S.$164–$189) rm with fireplace and Jacuzzi. AE, DC, ER, MC, V.

Overlooking the river but also within walking distance of the theater, the Queen's Landing is a modern, Georgian-style mansion offering 71 rooms with fireplaces and 32 with fireplaces and Jacuzzis. The spacious rooms are comfortably furnished with half-canopy or brass beds, wingback chairs, and large desks.

**Dining/Entertainment:** The cozy **Bacchu** lounge has a fieldstone fireplace, copper-foil bar, and velvet-cushioned seating. The circular **Tiara** dining room looks out in summer over the yacht filled harbor. It's elegantly styled with a grand stained-glass ceiling—a suitable foil for the fine cuisine. At dinner, about a dozen dishes are offered. Priced from C$20 to C$29 (U.S.$14 to U.S.$21), they might include parsley-crusted sea bass slow-roasted with Estate chardonnay or roasted rack of lamb with tomato bread pudding, leaf spinach, and warm arugula oil. Breakfast, lunch, and Sunday brunch are served here, too.

**Services:** Room service from 7am to 11pm.

**Facilities:** Indoor pool, whirlpool, sauna, exercise room, lap pool, bicycle rentals.

**White Oaks Inn and Racquet Club.** Taylor Rd., Niagara-on-the-Lake, ON, L0S 1J0. ☎ **905/688-2550.** Fax 905/688-2220. 75 rms, 15 suites. A/C TV TEL. July–Aug C$145–$155 (U.S.$104–$111) double; C$165–$230 (U.S.$118–$164) suite. In off-season, rates drop slightly. AE, DC, ER, MC, V.

Not far from Niagara-on-the-Lake, the White Oaks is a sports enthusiast's paradise. Anyone can come here, spend the whole weekend, and not stir outside the resort. The rooms are as good as the facilities, each featuring oak furniture, vanity sinks, and additional niceties like a phone and hair dryer in the bathroom. Suites also have brick fireplaces, marble-top desks, Jacuzzis (some heart-shaped), and bidets. Deluxe suites have sitting rooms.

**Dining/Entertainment:** Enjoy the restaurant-wine bar, the outdoor terrace cafe, or the pleasantly furnished cafe/coffee shop.

**Facilities:** Four outdoor and eight indoor tennis courts, six squash courts, two racquetball courts, a Nautilus room, jogging trails, a sauna, suntanning beds, bike rentals, massage therapist, day-care center with a fully qualified staff.

### Moderate

**Moffat Inn.** 60 Picton St., Niagara-on-the-Lake, ON, L0S 1J0. ☎ **905/468-4116.** Fax 905/468-4747. 22 rms. A/C TV TEL. Apr 15–Oct 31 and Christmas/New Year's C$85–$135 (U.S.$61–$96) double; Nov–Apr C$65–$119 (U.S.$46–$85) double. AE, MC, V.

This is a fine and convenient choice right on Queen Street. Most rooms are furnished with either brass or cannonball beds, traditional-style contemporary furnishings, or wicker and bamboo pieces. They have built-in closets, and extra amenities include hair dryers as well as a tea kettle and supplies. Seven rooms have fireplaces. Free coffee is available in the lobby, and there's also a restaurant and bar on premises. All rooms are nonsmoking.

✪ **The Old Bank House.** 10 Front St. (P.O. Box 1708), Niagara-on-the-Lake, ON, L0S 1J0. ☎ **905/468-7136.** 6 rms (4 with private bath), 2 suites (with bath). A/C. C$90 (U.S.$64) double without bath, C$115–$125 (U.S.$82–$89) double with bath; C$145 (U.S.$104) one-bdrm suite; C$230 (U.S.$164) two-bdrm suite. All rates include breakfast. AE, MC, V.

Beautifully situated down by the river, this two-story Georgian was built in 1817 as the first branch of the Bank of Canada. All of the rooms are tastefully decorated. The most expensive suite can accommodate four in two bedrooms, a sitting room, and bathroom. Several of the accommodations have private entrances, like the charming Garden Room, which also has a private trellised deck. All but one have a refrigerator and coffee or tea supplies. The sitting room, with a fireplace, is extraordinarily comfortable and furnished with eclectic antique pieces.

## ACCOMMODATIONS ALONG THE WINE ROAD

**The Vintner's Inn.** 3845 Main St., Jordan, ON, L0R 1S0. ☎ **905/562-5336.** 9 suites. A/C TEL. C$199–$239 (U.S.$142–$171) double. AE, ER, MC, V.

Right in the village of Jordan, this modern accommodation has handsome suites, each with an elegantly furnished living room with fireplace and bathroom with whirlpool tub. Seven of the suites are duplexes—one of them, the deluxe loft, has two double beds on its second level—and three are single-level suites with high ceilings. The inn's restaurant **On the Twenty** is across the street (see "Dining Along the Wine Road," below).

# DINING
## IN TOWN

In addition to the listings below, don't forget the dining rooms at the **Pillar & Post**, **Queen's Landing,** and the **Prince of Wales,** all listed above.

Light meals and lunches can be enjoyed at the stylish **Shaw Cafe and Wine Bar,** with an outside patio, at 92 Queen St. (☎ 905/468-4772). At 84 Queen St., the **Epicurean** offers hearty soups, quiches, sandwiches, and other fine dishes in a sunny Provence-inspired dining room. Service is cafeteria-style. Half a block off Queen, the **Angel Inn,** 224 Regent St. (☎ 905/468-3411), is a delightfully authentic English pub. For an inexpensive down-home breakfast, go to the **Stagecoach Family Restaurant,** 45 Queen St. (☎ 905/468-3133). No credit cards are accepted. **Niagara Home Bakery,** 66 Queen St. (☎ 905/468-3431), is the place to stop for chocolate-date squares, cherry squares, croissants, cookies, and individual quiches.

**The Buttery.** 19 Queen St. ☎ **905/468-2564.** Reservations recommended (required for Henry VIII feast). Henry VIII feast C$47.50 (U.S.$34); tavern menu main courses C$8–$15 (U.S.$6–$11); dinner main courses C$15–$20 (U.S.$11–$14). MC, V. Summer daily 10am–11:30pm; other months daily noon–8pm except Fri and Sat when the Henry VIII feast takes place. Afternoon tea daily 2–5pm. CANADIAN/ENGLISH/CONTINENTAL.

The Buttery has been a main-street dining landmark for years, known for its weekend Henry VIII feasts, when "serving wenches" will "cosset" guests with food and wine while jongleurs and musickers entertain. You'll be served "four removes"—four courses involving broth, chicken, roast lamb, roast pig, sherry trifle, syllabub, and cheese, all washed down with a goodly amount of wine, ale, and mead.

A full tavern menu is served from 11am to 5:30pm and Monday all day, featuring spareribs; an 8-ounce New York strip; shrimp in garlic sauce; and such English pub fare as steak, kidney, and mushroom pie; and lamb curry. The dinner menu lists eight choices or so; I highly recommend the rack of lamb served with pan juices or the shrimp curry. Finish with mud pie or Grand Marnier chocolate cheesecake. Take home some of the fresh baked goods—pies, strudels, dumplings, cream puffs, or scones.

**Fans Court.** 135 Queen St. ☎ **905/468-4511.** Reservations recommended. Main courses C$10–$20 (U.S.$7–$14) AE, DC, MC, V. Daily noon–10pm. CHINESE.

Some of the best food in town can be found in this comfortable Chinese spot, decorated with fans, cushioned bamboo chairs, and round tables spread with golden tablecloths. In summer, the courtyard also has tables for outdoor dining. The cuisine is primarily Cantonese and Szechuan. Singapore beef, moo shu pork, Szechuan scallops, and lemon chicken are just a few of the dishes available. If you wish, you can order Peking duck 24 hours in advance.

**Ristorante Giardino.** 142 Queen St. in the Gatehouse Hotel. ☎ **905/468-3263.** Main courses C$22–$27 (U.S.$16–$19). AE, ER, MC, V. Summer, daily noon–2:30pm and 5–10pm. Winter, daily 5:30–9pm. ITALIAN.

On the ground floor of the Gate House Hotel is this sleek, ultramodern Italian restaurant with gleaming marble-top bar and brass accents throughout. The food is

Northern Italian with fresh American accents. Main courses might include baked salmon seasoned with olive paste and tomato concasse, veal tenderloin marinated with garlic and rosemary, and braised pheasant in a juniper berry and vegetable sauce. There are several pasta dishes too, plus such appealing appetizers as medallions of langostine garnished with orange and fennel salad. Desserts include a delicious warm gratin of wild berries and orange sbaglione.

## DINING IN NEARBY VIRGIL, ST. CATHARINES & WELLAND

**Hennepin's.** 1486 Niagara Stone Rd. (Hwy. 55) at Creek Rd., Virgil. ☎ **905/468-1555.** Tapas C$4–$8 (U.S.$2.85–$6). Main courses C$13–$24 (U.S.$9–$17). AE, ER, MC, V. Sun–Wed 11:30am–9pm, Fri–Sat 11:30am–11pm. CONTEMPORARY.

The region's first tapas bar, Hennepin's offers excitingly different cuisine. The dining rooms are fresh and light and display the works of local artists. Tapas are served all day—coconut shrimp, olive-stuffed meatballs, chicken satay, samosas—in a round-the-world medley. At dinner, there are always such temptations as escargots in pernod, or pan-seared game pâté with blueberry kirsch sauce to start. Of the main courses, game and serious meats dominate—venison bordelaise, liver in a chausseur sauce, steak, and pork tenderloin with a portabello calvados sauce. The desserts are seriously rich: As evidence, we present the death by chocolate cake. The wine list is extensive; 28 wines are available by the glass.

**Iseya.** 22 James St. (between St. Paul and King sts.), St. Catharines. ☎ **905/688-1141.** Reservations recommended for dinner. Main courses C$10–$27 (U.S.$7–$19). AE, MC, V. Mon–Fri 11:30am–2:30pm; Mon–Sat 5–10:30pm. JAPANESE.

Iseya is one of the region's few traditional Japanese restaurants, serving fresh sushi/sashimi as well as teriyaki, tempura, and sukiyaki dishes.

**Rinderlin's.** 24 Burgar St., Welland. ☎ **905/735-4411.** Reservations recommended. Main courses C$17–$30 (U.S.$12–$21). AE, DC, ER, MC, V. Tues–Fri 11:30am–2pm; Tues–Sat 6–9pm. FRENCH.

An intimate town-house restaurant, Rinderlin's has a very good local reputation for traditional French cuisine. On the dinner menu, you might find house-smoked trout with horseradish sauce, roast pork tenderloin with a honey-mustard bacon sauce, or rack of lamb with a minted onion garlic sauce, and local venison with wild mushrooms and game sauce. Desserts are seasonal—my favorite is the white chocolate torte flavored with brandy and served with a raspberry sauce.

**Wellington Court Restaurant.** 11 Wellington St., St. Catharines. ☎ **905/682-5518.** Reservations recommended. Main courses C$12–$23 (U.S.$9–$16). ER, MC, V. Mon–Sat 11:30am–2:30pm; Tues–Sat 5:30–9:30pm. CONTINENTAL.

Located in an Edwardian town house with a flower trellis, the dining rooms here feature contemporary decor with modern lithographs and photographs. The menu features daily specials—the fish and pasta of the day, for example—along with such items as a beef tenderloin in a shallot- and red-wine reduction, roasted breast of chicken served on gingered plum preserves, and grilled sea bass with cranberry vinaigrette.

## DINING ALONG THE WINE ROAD

**Hillebrand's Vineyard Cafe.** Hwy. 55 near Niagara-on-the-Lake. ☎ **905/468-2444.** Main courses C$19–$29 (U.S.$14–$21). In summer, daily 11am–11pm, in spring and fall, daily noon–3pm and 5–9pm; in winter, Wed–Sun noon–3pm and 5–9pm.

This dining room is part of the winery complex (see "From Vinegar to Vintage—Ontario Wines Come of Age," page 194). The room is light and airy and floor-to-ceiling windows offer views over the vineyards to the distant escarpment or over the barrel aging cellars. The food is superb. The menu changes seasonally but might feature such dishes as garlic-roasted Bay of Fundy salmon in a Harvest cabernet jus, or a rich and delicious sesame and molasses-glazed Ontario lamb rack on a leek, potato, and Ermite blue-cheese galette with roasted shallots. For a luxurious opener, try the baby potatoes steamed with Harvest chardonnay on blinis with smoked salmon and osetra caviar, or the thinly sliced peppercorn-seared Ontario venison strip loin with shavings of Parmesan and raspberry vinaigrette.

**On the Twenty Restaurant & Wine Bar.** 3836 Main St., Jordan. ☎ **905/562-7313.** Main courses C$20–$30 (U.S.$14–$21). AE, DC, MC, V. Daily 11:30am–3pm and 5–10pm. Closed Mon in winter. CANADIAN.

Foodies head for this gardenlike haven overlooking Twenty Mile Creek, where chef Michael Olson has finally brought some truly fine cuisine to the Niagara Falls area. The appealing dining rooms are located in an old winery. The cuisine features many local ingredients—for example, sauté of Beamsville chicken and forest mushrooms in Mennonite cream with basil buttermilk biscuit; Fundy salmon grilled over herbs with potato pancakes and sweet-pepper sauces; or smoked Ontario pork tenderloin with crisp fried shallots and quince-oxtail jus on sweet-potato celery-root gratin. To start, select the Prince Edward Island mussels steamed in lager with caramelized garlic, bacon, and scallions. Naturally, there's an extensive selection of Ontario wines, including some wonderful ice wines to accompany such desserts as lemon tart and fruit cobbler. On the Twenty is associated with the Vintner's Inn across the street (see "Accommodations along the Wine Road," above).

**Vineland Estates.** 3620 Moyer Rd., Vineland. ☎ **905/562-7088.** Reservations recommended. Main courses C$19–$28 (U.S.$14–$20). AE, DC, MC, V. Daily 11am–3pm and 5–8:45pm.

The Vineland Estates dining room is reminiscent of many a California vineyard restaurant sitting as it does overlooking the vines. On warm days you can dine on a deck under a spreading tree, or you can stay in the airy dining room furnished with white cloth–covered tables. The chef uses local ingredients wherever possible. Among the appetizers, you might find local smoked eel or house-smoked splake (a hybrid between lake trout and salmon) as well as more familiar dishes like the roasted sweet bell-pepper bisque with tomato-chive crème fraîche and Pelee Island treasures (whitefish caviar).

These can be followed by a pasta dish or one of the fresh main courses like the Wellington County lamb with roasted garlic thyme jus or chickpea-crusted halibut with a French lentil ragout. Cheese lovers will appreciate the tasting plate of Canadian farm cheeses including the wonderful Abbey St. Benoit blue Ermite. Patrons usually gasp at the delectable desserts—blueberry-cherry trifle, or the Valrhona chocolate Victoria, for example.

## 2 Niagara Falls

Niagara Falls, with its gimmicks, amusement parks, casino, wax museums, daredevil feats, and million motels (each with a honeymoon suite complete with a heart-shaped bed), may seem rather tacky and commercial, but somehow the falls still steal the show; and on the Canadian side, along the Niagara Parkway with its parks and gardens, nature manages to survive in all its glory.

## ESSENTIALS

**VISITOR INFORMATION** Contact the **Niagara Falls Canada Visitor and Convention Bureau,** 5433 Victoria Ave., Niagara Falls, ON, L2G 3L1 ( ☎ **905/**

**356-6061**), or the **Niagara Parks Commission,** Box 150, 7400 Portage Rd. S., Niagara Falls, ON, L2E 6T2 (☎ **905/356-2241**).

Summer information centers are open at Table Rock House, Maid of the Mist Plaza, Rapids View parking lot, and Niagara-on-the-Lake.

**GETTING THERE**    If you're driving from Toronto, take the QEW Niagara.

Amtrak and VIA Rail operate trains between Toronto (☎ **416/366-8411**) and New York, stopping in St. Catharines and Niagara Falls. Call ☎ **800/361-1235** in Canada or 800/USA-RAIL in the United States.

**GETTING AROUND**    The best way to get around is aboard the **People Movers** (☎ **905/357-9340**). Park at Rapid View, several kilometers from the falls. The parking's free, and from here you can take the People Mover for C$4.25 per person. Or park in Preferred Parking (overlooking the falls) for C$8 (U.S.$6) with no in/out privileges. The People Mover is an attraction in itself. It travels in a loop, making nine stops from Rapid View to the Spanish Aero Car. Shuttles to the falls also operate from downtown and Lundy's Lane; an all-day pass costs C$4.25 (U.S.$3) for adults, C$2.25 (U.S.$1.60) for children 6 to 12.

**A MONEY-SAVING PASS**    To save money, buy an Explorer's Passport, which secures admission to Journey Behind the Falls, Great Gorge Adventure, and the Niagara Spanish Aero Car, plus all-day transportation aboard the People Movers. It costs C$17.75 (U.S.$13) for adults, and C$9 (U.S.$6) for children 6 to 12.

## SEEING THE FALLS

Obviously, the first thing to do is to see the Falls, the seventh natural wonder of the world. The most exciting way to do that is from the decks of the ✪ **Maid of the Mist,** 5920 River Rd. (☎ **905/358-5781**). This sturdy boat takes you right in— through the turbulent waters around the American Falls, past the Rock of Ages, and to the foot of the Horseshoe Falls, where in a minute 34.5 million Imperial gallons of water tumble over the 176-foot-high cataract. You'll get wet, and your glasses will mist, but that won't detract from the thrill.

Boats leave from the dock on the parkway just down from the Rainbow Bridge. Trips operate daily from mid-May to mid October. Fares are C$10 (U.S.$7) for adults and C$6.25 (U.S.$4.45) for children 6 to 12; it's free for children 5 and under.

Go down under the falls via the elevator at Table Rock House, which drops you 150 feet through solid rock to the **Journey Behind the Falls** (☎ **905/354-1551**). You'll appreciate the yellow biodegradable mackintosh that you're given. The tunnels and viewing portals are open all year. Admission is C$5.75 (U.S.$4) for adults and C$2.90 (U.S.$2) for children 6 to 12; children under 6 free.

To view the falls from a spectacular angle, take a 9-minute spin (C$160/U.S.$114 for two) in a chopper over the whole Niagara area. Helicopters leave from the heliport, adjacent to the whirlpool at the junction of Victoria Avenue and Niagara Parkway, daily from 9am to dusk, weather permitting. Contact **Niagara Helicopters,** 3731 Victoria Ave. (☎ **905/357-5672**).

Or you can ride up in the external glass-fronted elevators 520 feet to the top of the **Skylon Tower Observation Deck** at 5200 Robinson St. (☎ **905/356-2651**). The observation deck is open daily from 8am to midnight from June to Labour Day (call in other seasons). Adults pay C$6.95 (U.S.$4.95), seniors C$6 (U.S.$4.25), and children 6 to 12 and under, C$4 (U.S.$2.85).

A similar perspective can be gained from the observation floors atop the 325-foot **Minolta Tower Centre,** 6732 Oakes Dr. (☎ **905/356-1501**). On-site attractions include a Volcano Mine Ride, Galaxian Space Adventure, Cybermind Virtual

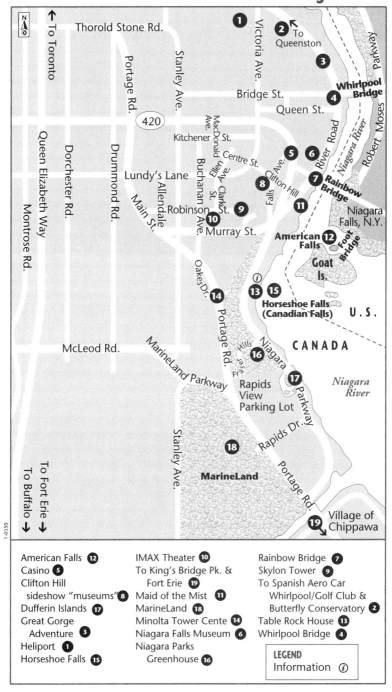

N
To Toronto
Thorold Stone Rd.
Portage Rd.
Stanley Ave.
420
Kitchener St.
MacDonald Ave.
Centre St.
Bridge St.
Queen St.
Victoria Ave.
To Queenston
Whirlpool Bridge
River Road
Robert Moses Parkway
Niagara River
Lundy's Lane
Buchanan Ave.
Ellen Ave.
Clark St.
Clifton Hill
Falls Ave.
Rainbow Bridge
Niagara Falls, N.Y.
Queen Elizabeth Way
Dorchester Rd.
Drummond Rd.
Main St.
Allendale Ave.
Robinson St.
Murray St.
Montrose Rd.
Oakes Dr.
American Falls
Goat Is.
Foot Bridge
Horseshoe Falls (Canadian Falls)
U.S.
McLeod Rd.
MarineLand Parkway
Portage Rd.
Fraser Hills
Niagara Parkway
Rapids View Parking Lot
CANADA
Niagara River
Stanley Ave.
Rapids Dr.
Portage Rd.
MarineLand
To Fort Erie
To Buffalo
Village of Chippawa

1-0-50-1

| | | |
|---|---|---|
| American Falls **12** | IMAX Theater **10** | Rainbow Bridge **7** |
| Casino **5** | To King's Bridge Pk. & Fort Erie **19** | Skylon Tower **9** |
| Clifton Hill sideshow "museums" **8** | Maid of the Mist **11** | To Spanish Aero Car Whirlpool/Golf Club & Butterfly Conservatory **2** |
| Dufferin Islands **17** | MarineLand **18** | |
| Great Gorge Adventure **3** | Minolta Tower Cente **14** | Table Rock House **13** |
| | Niagara Falls Museum **6** | Whirlpool Bridge **4** |
| Heliport **1** | Niagara Parks Greenhouse **16** | |
| Horseshoe Falls **15** | | **LEGEND** Information *(i)* |

# The Power & Pace of Niagara Falls

Seeing the falls for the first time is always a thrill. But did you know that if you were to revisit the Falls 10 years from now, you would find that they had shifted from their current location?

In fact, about 12,000 years ago Niagara Falls was 7 miles downstream from its present position. Why and how is this, you ask? Because of erosion. The tumbling waters cut away the shale and sandstone layers that are underneath the dolomite on top. Until the 1950s, the falls eroded at an average rate of 3 feet per year. Today, the rate has slowed to 1 foot every 10 years.

The approximately 35-mile-long river that tumbles over the falls is one of the world's greatest sources of hydroelectric power. It flows from Lake Erie to Lake Ontario, dropping in its short course about 326 feet between the two lakes. At the Horseshoe Falls, the drop is about 170 feet; and at the American Falls, it's anywhere from 70 to 110 feet. More than 6 million cubic feet of water go over the crest line of the falls every minute at peak daytime hours. This churning river provides the driving force for almost 2 million kilowatts of electricity from a number of power plants on the Canadian side, while another 2.4 million kilowatts—enough to light 24 million 100-watt bulbs—are generated by the Robert Moses and Lewiston plants on the American side. It's a remarkable feat, considering that the first electricity was generated in 1893 by a tiny 2,200-kilowatt plant built just above the Horseshoe Falls, in order to power an electric railway between Queenston and Chippawa. Now the river supplies power to entire cities and regions.

No tours are offered of plants on the Canadian side, but the Robert Moses Niagara Power Plant on the American side has a visitor center and tours. Call ☎ **716/285-3211** for information.

Reality, and the free *Waltzing Waters* (a computerized music, light, and water show given nightly every 30 minutes from 9pm to midnight from May to October). The tower is open daily 9am to 9pm (until 1am June to September, until 10pm March to April and October to December). Admission is C$6 (U.S.$4.25) for adults, C$5 (U.S.$3.55) for students and seniors, and free for children under 10. A day pass for the observation deck and unlimited entry to the games costs C$19 (U.S.$14), adults only. An unlimited play pass for the games only is C$14 (U.S.$10).

For a thrilling introduction to Niagara Falls, stop by the **IMAX Theater** and view the raging, swirling waters in *Niagara: Miracles, Myths, and Magic,* shown on a six-story-high screen. It's at 6170 Buchanan Ave. (☎ **905/358-3611**). Admission is C$7.50 (U.S.$5) adults, C$6.75 (U.S.$4.80) seniors and children 12 to 18, C$5.50 (U.S.$4) children 5 to 11, and free for children under 5.

In winter, the falls are also thrilling to see, for the ice bridge and other formations are quite remarkable (you'll know how remarkable if you've ever seen a building in winter after the fire department has put out the fire).

**THE FALLS BY NIGHT**    Don't miss seeing the falls lit by 22 xenon gas spotlights (each producing 250 million candlepower of light), in shades of rose pink, red magenta, amber, blue, and green. Call ☎ **800/563-2557** in the U.S., or 905/356-6061 for schedules. The show starts around 5pm in winter, 8:30pm in spring and fall, and 9pm in summer.

In addition, from July to early September, free fireworks are set off every Friday at 11pm to illuminate the falls.

# ✪ ALONG THE NIAGARA PARKWAY

The Niagara Parkway makes the Canadian side of the falls much more appealing than the American side and doubtless points up differences in cultural values. This 35-mile parkway with bike path is a refreshing respite from the honky-tonk.

You can drive all the way from Niagara Falls to Niagara-on-the-Lake on the Parkway, taking in attractions en route. The first attraction you'll come to is the **Great Gorge Adventure,** 4330 River Rd. (☎ **905/374-1221**). Stroll along the scenic boardwalk beside the raging white waters of the Great Gorge Rapids and wonder how it must have felt to challenge this mighty torrent, where the river rushes through the narrow channel at an average speed of 22 m.p.h. Admission is C$4.75 (U.S.$3.40) for adults, C$2.40 (U.S.$1.70) for children 6 to 12, and free for kids under 6.

Half a mile farther north you'll arrive at the **Niagara Spanish Aero Car (☎ 905/ 354-5711)**, a red-and-yellow cable-car contraption that will whisk you on a 3,600-foot jaunt between two points in Canada, high above the whirlpool, providing excellent views of the surrounding landscape. Admission is C$5 (U.S.$3.55) for adults, C$2.50 (U.S.$1.80) for children 6 to 12, and free for kids under 6. Open daily May 1 to the third Sunday in October; from 9am to 6pm in May, until 8pm in June, until 9pm in July and August, from 10am to 7:30pm in September, and 9am to 5pm in October.

At **Ride Niagara**, 5755 River Rd. (☎ **905/374-7433**), you can experience what it must be like going over the falls without risking your life. Before going over the falls in this computerized motion simulator, you'll see a short video showing some of the weirder contraptions folks have devised for the same journey. Then you take an elevator down to the shuttle, which takes you over the falls. Admission is C$8 (U.S.$6) adults, C$4.25 (U.S.$3.05) children 5 to 12. Open daily year-round (from 9:15am to 10:30pm in summer).

After passing the **Whirlpool Golf Club,** stop at the **School of Horticulture** for a free view of the vast gardens there, plus a look at the Floral Clock, which contains 25,000 plants in its 40-foot-diameter face. The new **Butterfly Conservatory** is also in the gardens (☎ **905/356-8119**). In this lush tropical setting, more than 2,000 butterflies (50 different international species) float and flutter among such nectar-producing flowers as lantanas and pentas. The large bright blue luminescent Morpho butterflies from Central and South America are particularly gorgeous. Interpretive and other programs are given in the auditorium and two smaller theaters. There's also a native butterfly garden outside, attracting the more familiar swallowtails, fritillaries, and painted ladies. Open daily May–June 9am–8pm; July–Aug 9am–9pm; Sept–Oct and Mar–Apr 9am–6pm; Nov–Feb 9am–5pm; closed December 25. Admission is C$6 (U.S.$4.30) adults, C$3 (U.S.$2.15) children 6 to 12.

From here you can drive to **Queenston Heights Park,** site of a famous battle during the War of 1812. You can take a walking tour of the battlefield. Picnic or play tennis for C$6 (U.S.$4.30) per hour in this shaded arbor before moving to the **Laura Secord Homestead,** Partition Street in Queenston (☎ **905/262-4851**). The home of this redoubtable woman, who threaded enemy lines to alert British authorities to a surprise attack by American soldiers, contains a fine collection of Upper Canada furniture from the 1812 period, plus artifacts recovered from an archaeological dig. Stop at the candy shop and ice-cream parlor. Tours are given every half hour. Admission is C$1.07 (U.S.75¢). Open from late May to Labour Day, daily 10am to 6pm.

Also worth viewing just off the parkway in Queenston is the **Samuel Weir Collection and Library of Art,** RR #1, Niagara-on-the-Lake (☎ **905/262-4510**), a small personal collection displayed as it was originally when Samuel Weir occupied the house. Mr. Weir (1898–1981), a lawyer from London, Ontario, was an enthusiastic collector of Canadian, American, and European art as well as rare books. Open from Victoria Day to Canadian Thanksgiving Wednesday to Saturday from 11am to 5pm, and Sunday from 1 to 5pm. Admission is free.

From here the parkway continues into Niagara-on-the-Lake, lined with fruit farms like **Kurtz Orchards** (☎ 905/468-2937), and wineries, notably the **Inniskillin Winery,** Line 3, Service Road 66 (☎ **905/468-3554** or 905/468-2187), and **Reif Winery** (☎ **905/468-7738**). Inniskillin is open daily from 10am to 6pm June to October and Monday to Saturday from 10am to 5pm November to May. The self-guided free tour has 20 stops explaining the process of wine making. A guided tour is also given daily in summer at 2:30pm and Saturday only in winter. At Reif Winery, tours costing C$2 (U.S.$1.40) are given daily from May 1 to September 30 at 1:30pm. The tasting room is open year-round.

Next stop between Niagara Falls and Niagara-on-the-Lake is the Georgian-style **McFarland House,** 15927 Niagara River Pkwy. (☎ **905/468-3322**), built in 1800 and home to John McFarland, "His Majesty's [George III] Boat Builder." It's open daily late May to June 30 from noon to 5pm, July to Labour Day from 11am to 6pm. Admission is C$1.75 (U.S.$1.25) adults and C$1 (U.S.70¢) children. The last tour is 30 minutes before closing.

A trip south along the parkway will take you by the Table Rock complex to the **Park Greenhouse,** a year-round free attraction (open daily from 9:30am to 7pm during July and August, until 4:15pm in other months).

Farther along, you can visit the **Dufferin Islands,** where the children can swim, rent a paddle boat, and explore the surrounding woodland areas, while you play a round of golf on the illuminated nine-hole par-three course. Open from the second Sunday in April to the last Sunday in October.

A little farther on, stop for a picnic in **King's Bridge Park** and stroll along the beaches before driving on to **Fort Erie,** 350 Lakeshore Rd., Fort Erie (☎ **905/871-0540**), a reconstruction of the fort that was seized by the Americans in July 1814, besieged later by the British, and finally blown up as the Americans retreated across the river to Buffalo. Guards in period costume stand sentry duty, fire the cannons, and demonstrate drill and musket practice. Open daily from the first Saturday in May to mid-September and weekends only to Canadian Thanksgiving (U.S. Columbus Day) from 10am to 6pm daily. Admission is C$5 (U.S.$ 3.55) for adults, C$3 (U.S.$2.15) for children 6 to 16, free for kids under 6.

Also in Fort Erie, the **Mildred M. Mahoney Dolls House Gallery**, 657 Niagara River Pkwy. (☎ 905/871-5833), displays more than 120 fully furnished dollhouses representing a variety of styles of architecture from Colonial to contemporary. Admission is C$3 (U.S.$2.15) adults, C$2.50 (U.S.$1.80) seniors, C$2 (U.S.$1.45) children 6 to 17. Open daily May to December 31 10am to 4pm.

Another Fort Erie attraction is the scenic historic **Fort Erie horse-racing track,** 320 Catherine St. (☎ **905/871-3200**) that's open in summer. Take the Bertie Street exit from the QEW to get to the track.

## MORE NIAGARA FALLS ATTRACTIONS

The newest Niagara attraction is **Casino Niagara**, 5705 Falls Ave. (☎ **905/374-3598**), featuring 123 tables that offer blackjack, roulette, baccarat, several different pokers, plus 3,000 slot and video poker machines. The casino contains five restaurants, including the Hard Rock Cafe. It's open 24 hours a day, 365 days a year.

Founded in 1827, the **Niagara Falls Museum,** 5651 River Rd. (☎ **905/356-2151**), has exhibits ranging from Egyptian mummies to an odd mixture of

Indian and Asian artifacts, shells, fossils, and minerals, plus the Freaks of Nature display. Open in summer daily from 8:30am to 11pm; in winter 10am to 5pm. Admission is C$6.75 (U.S.$4.80) for adults, C$6.25 (U.S.$4.45) for seniors, C$5 (U.S.$3.55) for students 11 to 18, C$4 (U.S.$2.85) for children 5 to 10; under 5, free.

Everyone loves **White Water,** 7430 Lundy's Lane (☎ 905/357-3380), where you don your bathing suit and swoop around the corkscrew turns of the five slides into the heated pools at the bottom or frolic in the wave pool. If you prefer to wallow in the hot tub, you can do that, too. The little 'uns can ride three small slides designed specially for them. Take a picnic and spend the greater part of the day (there's also a snack bar). Admission is C$15 (U.S.$11) for adults and C$10 (U.S.$7) for children 12 and under. Open daily 9am to 6pm in July and August, 10am to 4pm in spring and fall. Closed mid-October to late April.

Families won't want to miss **Marineland,** 7657 Portage Rd. (☎ **905-356-9565**), on their trip to the falls. At the aquarium-theater, King Waldorf, Marineland's mascot, presides over performances given by killer whales, talented dolphins, and sea lions. In 1998, Friendship Cove will open, a 4¹/₂-million-gallon breeding and observation tank for killer whales. Another aquarium features displays of freshwater fish. At the small wildlife display, kids enjoy petting and feeding the deer and also seeing bears and Canadian elk.

Marineland also has theme-park rides, including a roller coaster, Tivoli wheel, Dragon Boat rides, and a fully equipped children's playground. The big thriller is Dragon Mountain, a roller coaster that loops, double-loops, and spirals its way through 1,000 feet of tunnels. There are three restaurants, but you can picnic at one of several tables provided.

In summer, admission is C$23 (U.S.$16) adults, C$20 (U.S.$14) children 5 to 9 and seniors, free for children under 4. It's lower in other seasons. Open July to August daily from 9am to 6pm; mid-April to mid-May and September to mid-October from 10am to 4pm; mid-May to June from 10am to 5pm. The park is closed from November to April. Rides open in late May and close the first Monday in October. In town, drive south on Stanley Street and follow the signs; from the QEW take McCleod Rd. exit.

## ACCOMMODATIONS

Every other sign in Niagara Falls advertises a motel. In summer, rates go up and down according to the traffic, and some proprietors will not even quote rates ahead of time. So be warned. You can secure a reasonably priced room if you're lucky enough to arrive on a "down night," but with the casino in town that's becoming a rare occurrence. Still, always request a lower rate and see what happens.

### EXPENSIVE

**Renaissance Fallsview Hotel.** 6455 Buchanan Ave., Niagara Falls, ON, L2G 3V9. ☎ **800/363-3255** or 905/357-5200. Fax 905/357-3422. 262 rms. A/C MINIBAR TV TEL. C$109–$309 (U.S.$78–$221) double; C$189–$220 (U.S.$135–$157) whirlpool rms. AE, DC, DISC, ER, MC, V. Free parking.

The Renaissance features tastefully furnished rooms with oak furniture and TVs tucked away in cabinets. Bathrooms have double sinks and all the modern accouterments. Renaissance Club rooms have three telephones and a Jacuzzi tub.

**Dining:** There's a restaurant and a rooftop cafe on the 18th floor.

**Facilities:** Indoor pool, whirlpool, health club with saunas, squash and racquetball courts, fitness and weight room.

**Skyline Brock.** 5685 Falls Ave., Niagara Falls, ON, L2E 6W7. ☎ **800/263-7135** or 905/374-4444. 233 rms. A/C TV TEL. Mid-June to Sept, C$129–$219 (U.S.$92–$156) double; Oct–Dec and Apr to mid-June, C$99–$145 (U.S.$71–$104) double; winter, C$80–$115 (U.S.$57–$82) double. Children under 18 stay free in parents' rm. Extra person C$10 (U.S.$7). Special packages available. AE, DC, DISC, ER, MC, V. Parking C$7 (U.S.$5).

For an unmarred view of the falls, try the Skyline Brock or the Skyline Foxhead. The Brock has been hosting honeymooners and falls visitors since 1929. It still has a certain air of splendor, with a huge chandelier and marble walls in the lobby. About 150 of the rooms face the falls. City-view rooms are slightly smaller and less expensive.

**Dining/Entertainment:** The 10th-floor **Rainbow Room,** with a lovely view, serves a popular continental menu that includes half a roast chicken with cranberry sauce, salmon hollandaise, and prime rib, priced from C$16 to C$25 (U.S.$11 to U.S.$18). **Isaac's Bar** is available for drinks, and there's also the **Lobby Cafe.**

**Skyline Foxhead.** 5875 Falls Ave., Niagara Falls, ON, L2E 6W7. ☎ **800/263-7135** or 905/374-4444. 399 rms. A/C TV TEL. Mid-June to Sept C$169–$279 (U.S.$121–$199) double; Oct–Dec and Apr to mid-June C$125–$175 (U.S.$89–$125) double; winter, C$90–$120 (U.S.$64–$86) double. Extra person C$10 (U.S.$7). Children under 18 stay free in parents' rm. Special packages available. AE, DC, DISC, ER, MC, V. Valet parking C$10 (U.S.$7).

The Foxhead has 399 rooms (about half with balconies) spread over 14 floors. In the last few years, the rooms have been renovated in a tasteful manner. Each room has a private bath or shower, a color TV with in-room movies, and climate control.

**Dining:** The 14th-floor penthouse dining room takes fair advantage of the view with its large glass windows and serves a daily buffet for breakfast, lunch, and dinner, with nightly dancing to a live band (in season). Or there's the **Steak and Burger** for reasonably priced fare.

**Facilities:** An outdoor rooftop pool.

## MODERATE

**The Americana.** 8444 Lundy's Lane, Niagara Falls, ON, L2H 1H4. ☎ **905/356-8444.** Fax 905/356-8576. 120 rms and suites. A/C TV TEL. Late June to late Aug, C$130–$170 (U.S.$93–$121) double; Sept–June, C$80–$120 (U.S.$57–$86) double. Extra person C$10 (U.S.$7). AE, DISC, ER, MC, V. Free parking.

The Americana is one of the nicer moderately priced motels on this strip, set in 25 acres of grounds with a pleasant shady picnic area, one tennis court, indoor and outdoor swimming pools, a whirlpool, sauna, and squash court. The large rooms are fully equipped with telephones, color TVs, vanity sinks, and full bathrooms. Some suites have whirlpool tubs and fireplaces. A dining room, lounge, and coffee shop are on the premises.

**Holiday Inn by the Falls.** 5339 Murray St. (at Buchanan), Niagara Falls, ON, L2G 2J3. ☎ **905/356-1333.** 122 rms. A/C TV TEL. Late-June to Labour Day, C$105–$195 (U.S.$75–$139) double; late Apr to late June, C$65–$155 (U.S.$46–$111) double; Labour Day to mid-Oct, C$85–$165 (U.S.$61–$118) double; mid-Oct to late Apr, C$65–$135 (U.S.$46–$96). Extra person C$10 (U.S.$7); rollaway bed C$10 (U.S.$7); crib C$5 (U.S.$3.55). AE, DC, DISC, ER, MC, V.

The Holiday Inn by the Falls has a prime location right behind the Skylon Tower, only minutes from the falls. It's not part of the international hotel chain (the owner had the name first and still refuses to sell it). Each room is large, with ample closet space, an additional vanity sink, color-coordinated modern furnishings, a telephone, and a color TV. Most of the rooms have balconies. Lounge and dining room, a gift shop, indoor and outdoor heated pools, and a patio are available.

**Michael's Inn.** 5599 River Rd., Niagara Falls, ON, L2E 3H3. ☎ **800/263-9390** or 905/354-2727. Fax 905/374-7706. 130 rms. A/C TV TEL. June 16–Sept 15 C$98–$208 (U.S.

$70–$149) double. Sept 16–May C$59–$178 (U.S.$42–$127) double. AE, CB, DC, ER, MC, V. Free parking.

At this four-story white building overlooking the Niagara River gorge, the large rooms are nicely decorated with modern conveniences. Many are whirlpool-theme rooms like the Garden of Paradise or Scarlett O'Hara rooms. There's a solarium pool out back. The Ember's Open Hearth Dining Room is just that: The charcoal pit is enclosed behind glass so you can see all the cooking action. There's a lounge, too.

### INEXPENSIVE

**Nelson Motel.** 10655 Niagara River Pkwy., Niagara Falls, ON, L2E 6S6. ☎ **905/295-4754.** 25 rms. A/C TV. June 16–Sept 12, C$55–$90 (U.S.$39–$64) double; Sept 13 to mid-Nov and mid-Mar to June 15, C$40–$55 (U.S.$29–$39) double. Closed mid-Nov to mid-Mar. Rollaways and cribs extra. MC, V. Free parking.

For budget accommodations, try the Nelson Motel, run by John and Dawn Pavlakovich, who live in the large house adjacent to the motel units. The units have character, especially the family units with a double bedroom adjoined by a twin-bedded room for the kids. Regular units have modern furniture. None has a telephone, and singles have a shower only. All units face the fenced-in pool and neatly trimmed lawn with umbrellaed tables and shrubs. The Nelson Motel is located a short drive from the falls overlooking the Niagara River, away from the hustle and bustle of Niagara itself.

**The Village Inn.** 5685 Falls Ave., Niagara Falls, ON, L2E 6W7. ☎ **800/263-7135** or 905/374-4444. 205 rms. A/C TV TEL. Mid-June to Oct from C$90 (U.S.$64) double; Apr to mid-June C$70 (U.S.$50) double. Special packages available. AE, DC, DISC, MC, V. Closed Jan–Mar. Parking C$4 (U.S.$2.85).

Located right by Casino Niagara, behind the two Skylines, the Village Inn is ideal for families—all its rooms are large. Some family suites measure 700 square feet and include a bedroom with two double beds and a living room.

### A PLACE TO STAY IN NEARBY QUEENSTON

✪ **South Landing Inn.** At the corner of Kent and Front sts. (P.O. Box 269), Queenston, ON, L0S 1L0. ☎ **905/262-4634.** 23 rms. A/C TV. Mid-Apr to end of Oct, C$90–$110 (U.S.$64–$79) double; Nov to mid-Apr, C$60–$70 (U.S.$43–$50) double. AE, MC, V. Free parking.

The original section of Queenston's South Landing Inn was built in the 1800s and today has five attractive rooms furnished with early Canadian furnishings, including four-poster beds. Other rooms are across the street in the modern annex. There's a distant view of the river from the inn's balcony. In the original inn you'll also find a cozy dining room with red-gingham-covered tables, where breakfast is served for C$4 (U.S.$2.85).

## DINING

If you really want to dine well, I recommend making the effort to secure a table at one of the dining rooms in the wine-country towns of Jordan, Virgil, or Vineland or else at one of the selections listed in Niagara-on-the-Lake. Our reviews for these begin on page 199.

Alternatives in Niagara Falls include the **Pinnacle,** 6732 Oakes Dr. (☎ **905/356-1501**), which offers a Canadian and continental menu and a remarkable view, since it's located atop the Minolta Tower. There's also a vista from atop the 520-foot tower at the **Skylon Tower Restaurants,** 5200 Robinson St. (☎ **905/356-2651,** ext. 259), where you can enjoy reasonably priced breakfast, lunch, or dinner buffets in the Summit Suite dining room, or pricier continental fare for lunch and dinner in the Revolving Restaurant.

## EXPENSIVE

**Casa d'Oro.** 5875 Victoria Ave. ☎ **905/356-5646.** Reservations recommended. Main courses C$15–$24 (U.S.$11–$17). AE, DC, DISC, ER, MC, V. Mon–Fri noon–3pm and 4–11pm, Sat 4pm–1am, Sun 4–10pm. ITALIAN.

For fine Italian dining amid gilt busts of Caesar, Venetian-style lamps, statues of Roman gladiators, and murals of Roman and Venetian scenes, go to Casa d'Oro. Start with clams casino, or the *brodetto Antonio* (a giant crouton topped with poached eggs, floating on a savory broth garnished with parsley, and accompanied by grated cheese). Follow with specialties like saltimbocca alla romana, or sole basilica (flavored with lime juice, paprika, and basil). Finish with a selection from the dessert wagon or really spoil yourself with cherries jubilee or bananas flambé.

**Happy Wanderer.** 6405 Stanley Ave. ☎ **905/354-9825.** Reservations not accepted. Main courses C$10–$26 (U.S.$7–$19). AE, MC, V. Daily 9am–11pm. GERMAN.

Warm hospitality reigns at the chalet-style Happy Wanderer, which offers a full selection of schnitzels, wursts, and other German specialties. Transport yourself back to the Black Forest among the beer steins and the game trophies on the walls. The several rooms include the Black Forest Room, with a huge, intricately carved sideboard and cuckoo clock, and the Jage Stube, with solid wood benches and woven tablecloths. At lunch there are omelets, cold platters, sandwiches, and burgers. Dinner might start with goulash soup and proceed with bratwurst, knockwurst, rauchwurst (served with sauerkraut and potato salad), or a schnitzel-wiener, Holstein, or jaeger. All entrees include potatoes, salad, and rye bread. Desserts include, naturally, Black Forest cake and apple strudel, both under C$5 (U.S.$3.55).

## MODERATE

**Betty's Restaurant & Tavern.** 8921 Sodom Rd. ☎ **905/295-4436.** Main courses C$8–$16 (U.S.$6–$11). AE, MC, V. Mon–Sat 7am–10pm, Sun 9am–9pm. CANADIAN.

Betty's is a local favorite for honest food at fair prices. It's a family dining room where art and generosity surface in the food—massive platters of fish-and-chips, roast beef, and seafood, all including soup or juice, vegetable, and potato. There are burgers and sandwiches, too. If you can, save room for the enormous portions of home-baked pies. Breakfast and lunch also offer good low-budget eating.

## NIAGARA PARKWAY COMMISSION RESTAURANTS

The Niagara Parkway Commission has commandeered the most spectacular scenic spots, where it operates some reasonably priced dining outlets. **Table Rock Restaurant** (☎ 905/354-3631) and **Victoria Park Restaurant** (☎ 905/356-2217) are both on the Parkway right by the falls and are pleasant, if crowded. **Diner on the Green** (☎ 905/356-7221) is also on the Parkway, but at the Whirlpool Golf Course near Queenston. It's very plain. The listing below offers the best dining experience.

**Queenston Heights.** 14276 Niagara Pkwy. ☎ **905/262-4274.** Reservations recommended. Main courses C$19–$26 (U.S.$14–$19). AE, MC, V. Daily 11:30am–3pm; Sun–Fri 5–9pm, Sat 5–10pm. Closed Jan to mid-Mar. CANADIAN.

The star of the Niagara Parkway Commission's eateries stands dramatically atop Queenston Heights. Set in the park among fir, cypress, silver birch, and maple, the open-air balcony affords a magnificent view of the lower Niagara River and the rich fruit-growing land through which it flows. Or you can sit under the cathedral ceiling with its heavy crossbeams where the flue of the stone fireplace reaches to the roof. At dinner, among the selections might be fillet of Atlantic salmon with a Riesling-chive hollandaise, prime rib, or grilled pork with apples and cider-dijon mustard sauce. Afternoon tea is served from 3 to 5pm in the summer season. If nothing else, go for a drink on the deck and the terrific view.

# 3  Stratford

Home of the world-famous Stratford Festival, this city manages to capture the prime elements of the Bard's birthplace, from the swans on the Avon River to the grass banks that sweep down to it. Picnic under a weeping willow before attending a Shakespeare play.

## ESSENTIALS

**VISITOR INFORMATION**    For first-rate visitor information, go to the **Information Centre** (☎ **519/273-3352**) by the river on York Street at Erie. From May to early November it's open daily from 9am to 5pm (until 8pm Thursday to Saturday). At other times, contact **Tourism Stratford,** 88 Wellington St., P.O. Box 818, Stratford, ON, N5A 6W1 (☎ **800/561-SWAN** or 519/271-5140).

**GETTING THERE**    Driving from Toronto, take Highway 401 west to Interchange 278 at Kitchener. Follow Highway 8 west onto Highway 7/8 to Stratford.

   **Amtrak** and **VIA Rail** operate several trains daily along the Toronto–Kitchener–Stratford route.

## ✪ THE STRATFORD FESTIVAL

Since its modest beginnings on July 13, 1953, when *Richard III,* starring Sir Alec Guinness, was staged in a huge tent, Stratford's artistic directors have all built on the radical, but faithfully classic base originally provided by Tyrone Guthrie to create a repertory theater with a glowing international reputation.

   Stratford has three theaters: the **Festival Theatre,** 55 Queen St. in Queen's Park, with its dynamic thrust stage; the **Avon Theatre,** 99 Downie St., with a classic proscenium; and the **Tom Patterson Theatre,** an intimate 500-seat theater on Lakeside Drive.

   World famous for its Shakespearean productions, the festival also offers both classic and modern theatrical masterpieces. Recent productions have included *Camelot, The Taming of the Shrew, Oedipus Rex, Death of a Salesman,* and *Little Women.* Among the company's famous alumnae are Dame Maggie Smith, Sir Alec Guinness, Sir Peter Ustinov, Alan Bates, Christopher Plummer, Irene Worth, and Julie Harris. Present company members include Brian Bedford, Al Waxman, Cynthia Dole, Martha Henry, and Barbara Byrne.

   In addition to attending plays, visitors may enjoy "Meet the Festival," a series of informal discussions with members of the acting company, production, or administrative staff; "Post Performance Discussions" that follow Thursday evening performances; and backstage or warehouse tours, offered every Wednesday, Saturday, and Sunday morning from early June to mid-October. The tours cost C$5 (U.S.$3.55) for adults and C$3 (U.S.$2.15) for seniors and students; they should be reserved when you purchase tickets.

   The season usually begins early in May and continues until mid-November, with performances Tuesday to Sunday and matinees on Wednesday, Saturday, and Sunday. Ticket prices range from C$48 to C$64 (U.S.$34 to U.S.$46). For tickets, call ☎ **800/567-1600** or 519/273-1600**;** or write to the Stratford Festival, P.O. Box 520, Stratford, ON, N5A 6V2. Tickets are also available in the United States and Canada at Ticketmaster outlets. The box office opens for mail and fax orders only in late January; telephone and in-person sales begin late February.

## EXPLORING THE TOWN

Summer pleasures in Stratford besides theater? Within sight of the Festival Theatre, **Queen's Park** has picnic spots beneath tall shade trees or down by the Avon River. There are also some superb dining and good shopping prospects.

Past the Orr Dam and the 90-year-old stone bridge, through a rustic gate, lies a very special park, the **Shakespearean Garden.** Here in this formal English garden, where a sundial measures out the hours, you can relax and contemplate the herb and flower beds and the tranquil river lagoon, and muse on a bust of Shakespeare by Toronto sculptor Cleeve Horne.

If you turn right onto Romeo Street North from highways 7 and 8 as you come into Stratford, you'll find the **Gallery/Stratford,** 54 Romeo St. (☎ **519/271-5271**), located in an historic building on the fringes of Confederation Park. Since it opened in 1967, it has mounted fine, Canadian focused shows, often oriented to the theater arts. If you're an art lover, do stop in, for you're sure to find an unusual, personally satisfying show in one of the four galleries. Open daily in summer 9am to 6pm; Tuesday to Sunday off season. Admission is C$4 (U.S.$2.85) for adults, C$3 (U.S.$2.15) for seniors and students 12 and up.

Stratford is a historic town, and 1-hour **guided tours of early Stratford** are given Monday to Saturday July to Labour Day, leaving at 9:30am from the visitors booth by the river. There are also many fine shops worth browsing along Ontario and Downie streets and tucked down along York Street. Antique lovers will want to visit the nearby town of Shakespeare (7 miles out of town on Highway 7/8), which has several stores.

Paddleboat and canoe rentals are available at **the Boathouse,** located behind and below the information booth. It's open daily from 9am until dark in summer. Contact Avon Boat Rentals, 40 York St. (☎ **519/271-7739**).

## A COUPLE OF EXCURSIONS FROM STRATFORD

Only half an hour or so away, the twin cities of **Kitchener** and **Waterloo** have two drawing cards: the **Farmer's Market** and the famous 9-day **Oktoberfest** (for Oktoberfest information, write K-W Oktoberfest, P.O. Box 1053, 17 Benton St., Kitchener, ON, N2G 4G1 (☎ **519/570-4267**). The population of these cities is 60% German, many of whom are Mennonites. Starting at 6am you can sample shoofly pie, apple butter, kochcase, and other Mennonite specialties at the Saturday market in the Market Square complex at Duke and Frederick streets in Kitchener. For additional information, contact the **Kitchener-Waterloo Area Visitors and Convention Bureau,** 2848 King St. E., Kitchener, ON, N2A 1A5 (☎ **519/748-0800**), open 9am to 5pm weekdays only in winter, daily in summer.

Five miles north of Kitchener, people enjoy visiting the town of **St. Jacobs,** drawn there by close to 100 shops located in venues such as a converted mill, silo, and other factory buildings. For those interested in learning more about the Amish-Mennonite way of life, **the Meetingplace,** 33 King St. (☎ **519/664-3518**), shows a short film about it (daily in summer, weekends only in winter).

## ACCOMMODATIONS

When you book your theater tickets, you can also, at no extra charge, book your accommodations. The festival can book you into the type of accommodation and price category you prefer, from guest homes for as little as C$40 (U.S.$29) to first-class hotels charging more than C$125 (U.S.$89). Call or write the **Festival Theatre Box Office,** P.O. Box 520, Stratford, ON, N5A 6V2 (☎ **800/567-1600** or 519/273-1600).

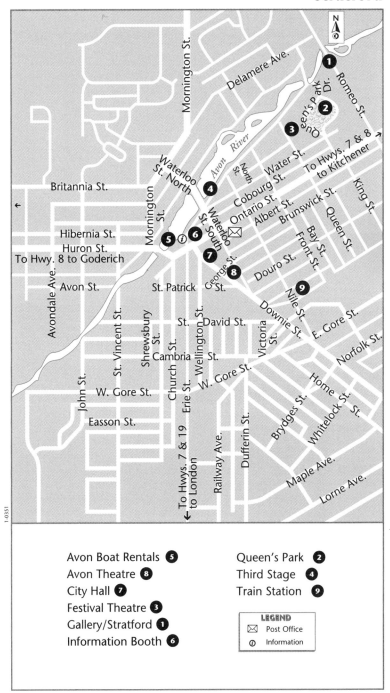

Avon Boat Rentals **5**

Avon Theatre **8**

City Hall **7**

Festival Theatre **3**

Gallery/Stratford **1**

Information Booth **6**

Queen's Park **2**

Third Stage **4**

Train Station **9**

LEGEND

⊠ Post Office

ⓘ Information

## HOTELS/MOTELS

**Bentleys.** 107 Ontario St., Stratford, ON, N5A 3H1. ☎ **519/271-1121.** 13 suites. A/C TV TEL. Apr–Nov C$145 (U.S.$104) double; Nov–June C$90 (U.S.$64). Extra person C$20 (U.S.$14). AE, DC, ER, MC, V.

The soundproof rooms here are in fact luxurious duplex suites, each with a bathroom, telephone, air-conditioning, a color TV, and an efficiency kitchen. Period English furnishings and attractive drawings, paintings, and costume designs on the walls make for a pleasant ambiance. Five of the suites have skylights.

**Festival Motor Inn.** 1144 Ontario St. (P.O. Box 811), Stratford, ON, N5A 6W1. ☎ **519/273-1150.** Fax 519/273-2111. 183 rms. A/C TV TEL. C$84–$130 (U.S.$60–$93). Extra person C$10 (U.S.$7). Winter rates about 30% lower. AE, DC, MC, V.

With its black-and-white motel-style units, the Festival Motor Inn is set back off highways 7 and 8, in 10 acres of nicely kept, landscaped grounds. The place has an old-English air with its stucco walls, Tudor-style beams, and high-back red settees in the lobby. The Tudor style is maintained throughout the large modern rooms, all with wall-to-wall carpeting, matching bedspreads and floor-to-ceiling drapes, reproductions of old masters on the walls, and full bathrooms. Some of the bedrooms have charming bay windows with sheer curtains, and all rooms in the main building, north wing, and annex have refrigerators. Other facilities include a dining room, coffee shop, and an indoor pool with outdoor patio.

**The Queen's Inn.** 161 Ontario St., Stratford, ON, N5A 3H3. ☎ **519/271-1400.** Fax 519/271-7373. 31 rms. A/C TV TEL. May–Nov 15 C$105–$130 (U.S.$75–$93) double, C$165–$190 (U.S.$118–$136) suite. Nov 1–May 1 C$65 (U.S.$46) double, from C$85 (U.S.$61) suite. AE, MC, V.

Conveniently located in the town center, The Queen's Inn has recently been restored. The rooms, all with private bath, have been pleasantly decorated in pastels and pine. Facilities include the Boar's Head Pub and a restaurant specializing in Southwestern cuisine.

**23 Albert Place.** 23 Albert St., Stratford, ON, N5A 3K2. ☎ **519/273-5800.** Fax 519/273-5008. 34 rms. A/C TV TEL. C$81–$100 (U.S.$58–$71) double; C$110 (U.S.$79) minisuite; from C$130–$140 (U.S.$93–$61) suite. MC, V.

Right around the corner from the Avon Theatre, the Albert Place sports large rooms with high ceilings. Furnishings are simple and modern. Some rooms have separate sitting rooms. Complimentary coffee, tea, and donuts are available in the lobby for guests in the early morning.

## A PICK OF THE BED & BREAKFASTS

For more information on the Stratford bed-and-breakfast scene, write to **Tourism Stratford,** P.O. Box 818, 88 Wellington St., Stratford, ON, N5A 6W1 (☎ **519/271-5140**). It's open 9am to 5pm Monday to Friday.

**Acrylic Dreams.** 66 Bay St., Stratford, ON, N5A 4K6 ☎ **519/271-7874.** 3 rms (all with bath). A/C. C$90–$100 (U.S.$64–$71) double; C$115–$135 (U.S.$82–$96) suite. Rates include breakfast. 2-night minimum on weekends. No credit cards.

Acrylic Dreams has a fun, modern artsy atmosphere as its name would suggest, thanks to its artist owners. The house is furnished with cottage-style antiques, except for the living room, which is furnished in a New Wave style with transparent acrylic furniture. Upstairs, there's a suite decorated in Provençal colors with a private bath and sitting room with TV and refrigerator. The bedroom contains a white iron bed. On the ground floor, there are two doubles with bath. The largest is decorated with angel-patterned wallpaper and contains an antique white iron and brass bed. The smaller room is decorated in a buttery yellow with cherubs and has an antique double bed. Both share a guest fridge. The full breakfast varies from day to day, but might include peaches and peach yogurt, scrambled eggs, and homemade scones and preserves using ingredients from the garden (there's never any meat because the owners are vegetarian). There's a phone for guests' use. Yoga ($10 per class) and reflexology can also be part of the experience.

**Ambercroft.** 129 Brunswick St., Stratford, ON, N5A 3L9 ☎ **519/271-5644.** 4 rms (all with bath). A/C. C$100 (U.S.$71) double. All rates include continental breakfast. MC, V

This inviting 1878 home in a quiet downtown area is convenient to the theaters and restaurants. There's a comfy front parlor, a small TV room, and a front and rear porch. Guests have the use of a refrigerator. An extended continental breakfast is served—seasonal fruits, cereals, homemade baked goods, and more. No smoking.

**Avonview Manor.** 63 Avon St., Stratford, ON, N5A 5N5. ☎ **519/273-4603.** 4 rms (2 with bath). C$80–90 (U.S.$57–$64) double. All rates include breakfast. No credit cards.

Located on a quiet street in an Edwardian house, Avonview Manor has four rooms with fans, all attractively and individually furnished. Three have queen-size beds, while the suite contains four singles and also has a sitting room and private bath.

A full breakfast is served in a bright dining room overlooking the garden, and a kitchen equipped with an ironing board is available on the first floor. The living room is very comfortable, particularly in winter, when guests can cozy up in front of the stone fireplace. Smoking is allowed only on the porch. There's also an in-ground pool and hot tub.

**Brunswick House.** 109 Brunswick St., Stratford, ON, N5A 3L9. ☎ **519/271-4546.** 6 rms (none with bath). C$65 (U.S.$46) and up. All rates include breakfast. No credit cards.

If you stay here you'll enjoy the very literate surroundings created by owners Geoff Hancock and Gay Allison—portraits of Canadian authors and poetry on the walls, books everywhere, and the chance to run into a literary personality. There are six rooms sharing two baths, all nicely decorated, and with ceiling fans. One is a family room with a double and two single beds. Each room has a personal decorative touch—a Mennonite quilt, posters by an artist friend, or a parasol atop a wardrobe. A full breakfast is served. Smoking is restricted to the veranda. It's very conveniently located within walking distance of the center of town and theaters.

✪ **Deacon House.** 101 Brunswick St., Stratford, ON, N5A 3L9. ☎ **519/273-2052.** 6 rms. A/C. C$95–$120 (U.S.$68–$86) double. Extra person C$20 (U.S.$15). All rates include breakfast. Off-season packages available. V.

Deacon House, a shingle-style structure built in 1907, has been restored by Dianna Hrysko and Mary Allen. They have six rooms, all with baths, that are decorated in a country style, with iron-and-brass beds, quilts, pine hutches, oak rockers, and rope-style rugs. My favorites are the quirky rooms on the top floor. The living room, with a fireplace, TV, wingback chairs, and a sofa, is comfortable. The guest kitchen is a welcome convenience; so too is the second-floor sitting/reading room. This is a great location, within walking distance of everything.

**Flint's Inn.** 220 Mornington St., Stratford, ON, N5A 5G5. ☎ **519/271-9579.** 2 rms (with shared bath), 1 suite (with bath). A/C. C$65 (U.S.$46.45) double; C$70 (U.S.$50) double or twin, C$90 (U.S.$64) suite. All rates include breakfast. No credit cards.

This steep-mansard-roofed house, built in 1862, has three air-conditioned units. One is a large suite with a sun porch, a balcony, a private bath, and a refrigerator. The iron-and-brass bed sports an old quilt, and among the decorative features are an old butter churn and a bottle collection. The other two rooms share a bathroom with bidet. The double has an attractive window seat and the twin has chintz wallpaper, a brass and iron bed, dresser, and trunk. The living room, with its marble fireplace and pine furnishings, is inviting. At breakfast, homemade muffins, juice, and coffee are accompanied by eggs Benedict or something similar. The garden is well kept and filled with the wonderful scent of lilac in season.

**Woods Villa.** 62 John St. N., Stratford, ON, N5A 6K7. ☎ **519/271-4576.** Fax 519/271-7173. 6 rms (all with bath). A/C TV TEL. C$120–$175 (U.S.$86–$125) double. All rates include breakfast. DISC, MC, V.

This handsome 1870 house set on 1-acre grounds is home to Ken Vinen, who collects and restores the Wurlitzers, Victrolas, and player pianos found throughout the house. In the large drawing room there are six—and they all work. Ken will happily demonstrate, drawing upon his vast library of early paper rolls and records. The six rooms, all with private bath (five with fireplaces), include a handsome suite with canopy bed. Rooms are large and offer excellent value. In the morning, coffee is delivered to your room, followed by a full breakfast prepared to order and served in the dining room. Guests are welcome to use the attractively landscaped outdoor pool and terrace.

## A NEARBY PLACE TO STAY & DINE

✪ **Langdon Hall.** RR #3, Cambridge, ON, N3H 4R8. ☎ **800/268-1898** or 519/740-2100. Fax 519/740-8161. 41 rms, 2 suites. A/C TV TEL. C$209–$379 (U.S.$149–$271) double. All rates include continental breakfast. AE, DC, ER, MC, V.

The elegant house that stands at the head of the curving, tree-lined drive was completed in 1902 by Eugene Langdon Wilks, youngest son of Matthew and Eliza Astor Langdon, a granddaughter of John Jacob Astor. It remained in the family until 1987, when its transformation into a small country-house hotel was begun. Today its 200 acres of lawns, gardens, and woodlands make for an ideal retreat. The main house, of red brick with classical pediment and Palladian-style windows, has a beautiful symmetry. Inside, a similar harmony is achieved. Throughout, the emphasis is on comfort rather than grandiosity, whether in the conservatory, the veranda where tea is served, or Wilks' Bar, with its comfortable club chairs.

The majority of the rooms are set around the cloister garden. Each room is individually decorated; most have fireplaces. The furnishings consist of handsome antique reproductions, mahogany wardrobes, ginger-jar porcelain lamps, and armchairs upholstered with luxurious fabrics, fine Oriental rugs, pictures, and such nice touches as live plants and terry bathrobes. The light and airy dining room overlooking the lily pond offers fine regional cuisine with main courses priced from C$23 to C$30 (U.S.$16 to U.S.$21). Beyond the cloister, down a trellis arcade and through a latch gate, lies the herb and vegetable garden and beyond that the swimming pool (with an attractive poolhouse), tennis court, and croquet lawn. Other facilities include a whirlpool, sauna, exercise room, billiard room, the spa, and cross-country ski trails.

## DINING
### EXPENSIVE

✪ **The Church.** At the corner of Brunswick and Waterloo sts. ☎ **519/273-3424.** Reservations required. Summer fixed-price dinner C$49–$53 (U.S.$35–$38) or main courses C$21.50–$32 (U.S.$15–$23). AE, DC, MC, V. Tues–Sat 11:30am–1am; Sun 11:30am–10pm. May be open Mon if there's a musical performance or some other special event at the theaters. CONTINENTAL.

The decor at The Church is just stunning. The organ pipes and the altar are still intact, along with the vaulted roof, carved woodwork, and stained-glass windows, and you can sit in the nave or the side aisles and dine to the appropriate sounds of, usually, Bach. Fresh flowers, elegant table settings, and a huge table in the center graced with two silver samovars further enhance the experience.

In summer, there's a special four-course fixed-price and an a la carte dinner menu, a luncheon on matinee days, and an after-theater menu. Appetizers might include asparagus served hot with black morels in their juices, white wine, and cream; or sauté of duck foie gras with leeks citron and mango and ginger sauce. Among the selection of eight or so entrees you might find Canadian caribou with port and blackberry sauce, cabbage braised in cream red-wine shallots and glazed chestnuts, or lobster salad with green beans, new potatoes, and truffles scented with caraway. Desserts are equally exciting, like the charlotte of white chocolate mousse with summer fruit and dark chocolate sauce or the nougat glace with kiwi sauce.

If you want to dine here during the festival, make reservations in March or April when you buy your tickets; otherwise you'll be disappointed. The upstairs Belfry Bar is a popular pre- and post-theater gathering place.

✪ **The Old Prune.** 151 Albert St. ☎ **519/271-5052.** Reservations required. 3-course fixed-price dinner C$51.50 (U.S.$37). AE, MC, V. Wed–Sun 11:30am–1:30pm; Tues–Sat 5–9pm, Sun 5–7pm. After-theater menu also available Fri–Sat from 9pm. Call ahead for winter hours. CONTINENTAL.

Another of my Stratford favorites, delivering a perfect and magical dinner to patrons, is run by two charming, whimsical women—Marion Isherwood and Eleanor Kane. Set in a lovely Edwardian home, it has three dining rooms and an enclosed garden patio. Former Montrealers, the proprietors have brought with them some of that Québec flair, which is reflected in both decor and menu. Artist Marion created the subdued, dreamy palette of the walls, which are graced with her own inspired paintings.

Chef Bryan Steele selects the freshest local ingredients, many from the dedicated community of organic farmers in the region, and prepares them simply to reveal their abundant flavor. Among the main courses you might find Perth County pork loin grilled with a tamari and honey glaze and served with shiitake mushrooms, pickled cucumbers, and sunflower sprouts; or steamed bass in Napa cabbage with curry broth and lime leaves; or rack of Ontario lamb with a smoky tomatillo-chipotle pepper sauce. Among the appetizers there might be an outstanding house-smoked salmon with lobster potato salad topped with Sevruga caviar or a refreshing tomato consommé with saffron and sea scallops. Desserts, too, are always inspired, like rhubarb strawberry Napoleon with vanilla mousse. The Old Prune is also lovely for lunch or a late supper when such light specialties as sautéed quail with grilled polenta with Italian greens, mushrooms, roasted tomatoes, and balsamic jus and smoked trout terrine are offered for C$7 to C$14 (U.S.$5 to U.S.$10).

✪ **Rundles.** 9 Cobourg St. ☎ **519/271-6442.** Reservations required. 3-course fixed-price dinner C$52 (U.S.$37). Gastronomic menus C$56–$62 (U.S.$40–$45). AE, ER, MC, V. Wed and Sat–Sun 11:30am–1:30pm; Tues 5–7pm, Wed–Sat 5–8:30pm, Sun 5–7pm. Closed during the winter; it functions occasionally as a cooking school until theater season comes again. INTERNATIONAL.

Rundles provides a premier dining experience in a serene dining room overlooking the river. Proprietor Jim Morris eats, sleeps, thinks, and dreams food; and chef Neil Baxter delivers the exciting, exquisite cuisine to the table. The three-course fixed-price dinner will always offer a full selection of palate-pleasing flavor combinations. Among the five main dishes there might be poached Atlantic salmon garnished with a mixture of Jerusalem artichokes, wilted arugula and yellow peppers in a light carrot sauce, or fatless pink roast rib eye of lamb with ratatouille and rosemary aïoli. Every appetizer will appeal, from the shaved fennel, arugula, artichoke, and Parmesan salad to the warm seared Québec foie grass with caramelized endive, garlic-flavored fried potatoes, and tomato and basil oil. My dessert choice would be the glazed lemon tart and an orange sorbet, but the hot mango tart with pineapple sorbet is also a dream. Tables are covered with fine white cloths, chairs are swathed in gray fabric, and the room features some whimsical contemporary art by Victor Tinkl.

## MODERATE

**Keystone Alley Cafe.** 34 Brunswick St. ☎ **519/271-5645.** Reservations recommended. Main courses C$14–$19 (U.S.$10–$14). AE, DC, MC, V. Mon 11am–3pm, Tues–Sat 11am–4pm and 5–9pm. CONTINENTAL.

Theater actors often stop in for lunch—perhaps soup, sandwiches (muffeleta with Creole mayonnaise), salads (Jamaican chicken salad with mango and pineapple salsa), or an entree like fish-and-chips or crab and jicama ceviche. At night a full dinner menu features eight or so main courses, such as roast sea bass with a potato crust accompanied by jalapeño tartare sauce, roast rack of lamb with a mango sweet-pepper barbecue sauce, or a vegetarian dish and pasta of the day.

**York Street Kitchen.** 41 York St. ☎ **519/273-7041.** No reservations. Main courses C$8–$10 (U.S.$6–$7). AE, V. Daily 8am–8pm.

This small, narrow restaurant is a fun, funky dining spot loved for reasonably priced but high-quality fare. You can come here for breakfast burritos and other breakfast fare and for luncheon sandwiches, which you can build yourself by choosing from a list of fillings. In the evenings, expect to find comfort foods like meat loaf and mashed potatoes or barbecued chicken and ribs.

## INEXPENSIVE

**Bentley's.** 107 Ontario St. ☎ **519/271-1121.** Reservations not accepted. Main courses C$5–$13 (U.S.$3.55–$9). AE, DC, ER, MC, V. Daily 11:30am–1am. CANADIAN/ENGLISH.

For budget dining and fun to boot, go to Bentley's, the local watering hole and favorite theater company gathering spot where you can shoot a game of darts, watch the big game on TV, or relax in one of the wingbacks. In summer you can sit on the garden terrace and enjoy light fare—grilled shrimp, burgers, gourmet pizzas, fish-and-chips, shepherd's pie, and pasta dishes. More substantial dishes—including lamb curry, sirloin steak, and salmon baked in white wine with peppercorn-dill butter—are offered at dinner. Beer drinkers appreciate the 16 different drafts on tap.

**Let Them Eat Cake.** 82 Wellington St. ☎ **519/273-4774.** Reservations not accepted. Lunch items under C$6 (U.S.$4.30); desserts C$1–$4 (U.S.72¢–$2.85). V. Mon 7:30am–4pm, Tues–Fri 7:30am–8pm, Sat 8:30am–6pm, Sun 9am–4pm. Winter open until 4pm only. LIGHT FARE.

Let Them Eat Cake is great for breakfast (bagels and scones) and lunch (soups, salads, sandwiches, quiche, and chicken potpie), but best of all for dessert. There are about 15 to 20 to choose from—pecan pie, orange Bavarian cream, lemon bars, carrot cake, Black Forest cake, and chocolate cheesecake among them.

## PICNICKING IN STRATFORD

Stratford is really a picnicking place. Take a hamper down to the banks of the river or into the parks; plenty of places cater to this business. **Rundles** will make you a super-sophisticated hamper; **Café Mediterranean,** 10 Downie St. in the Festival Square building, has salads, quiches, crepes, and flaky meat pies and pastries. Or go to **Picnics Gourmet Food Shop,** 40 Wellington St. ( ☎ **519/273-6000**), which offers all kinds of salads—pasta, grains, and vegetables—and pâtés; fish, chicken, and meat dishes; soups; and breads and pastries. Open in summer Tuesday to Friday from 10am to 6pm, Saturday 10am to 4pm (closed 2 weeks in January).

# Index

See also separate Accommodations and Restaurant indexes, below.

**GENERAL INDEX**
Accommodations, 37–60.
    *See also* Accommodations
    Index
    best bets, 38–39
Airlines, 21, 22, 23
Airports, 23–24. *See also*
    Pearson International
    Airport
Air tours, 124, 202
Algonquin Island, 105
Allan Gardens, 36, 120
American Express, 17
American Falls (Niagara
    Falls), 202, 204
Amsterdam Bridge, 129
Amtrak, 24, 191, 202
Amusement parks, 105,
    111–12, 121, 207
Annex, The, 30, 99
Antiques, 104, 129, 146,
    148–49, 168, 212
Aquarium, 207
*Archer, The* (Moore), 106,
    116, 136
Architectural highlights,
    116–17
Area code, 33
Argonauts, 126–27
Art Collection, McMichael
    Canadian (Kleinburg), 4,
    111
Art galleries, 104, 129,
    141, 142, 149–51
Art Gallery of North York,
    112
Art Gallery of Ontario,
    4–5, 106–7, 122, 141,
    190
Artists. *See* Group of
    Seven; Moore, Henry
Art museums, 4–5, 106–7,
    110, 111, 112, 122, 141,
    205–6
ATMs, 15–16

Atrium on Bay, 162
Auto racing, 18, 126
Avon River, 212

Bakeries, 159
Balfour Building, 160
Ballet, 170, 174
Bamboo, 179, 180
Bank of Commerce, 134
Bank of Montréal, 138
Bars, 184–89
    gay, 189–90
Baseball, 4, 126
Basketball, 5, 126
Bata Shoe Museum, 112
Bat Cave Gallery, 107,
    212
Bathurst Pier, 104
Bay, The, 135, 146, 156
BCE Place, 138
Beaches, on Lake Ontario,
    126
Beaches, the, 4, 30, 114
Beardmore Building, 139
Bed & breakfasts, 38
Bell Canadian Open, 19,
    127
Bicycling, 33, 124, 205
Black Creek Pioneer
    Village, 112–13, 122
Blue Jays, 4, 106, 126
Blues music, 180
Boating, 104, 125, 212
    jet, on Niagara River,
    196
Boat tours. *See* Cruises
Bookstores, 140, 151–54,
    165, 168
Brown, George, House,
    142
Buses, 31
    to/from airports,
    23–24
    to Toronto, 24
    tours, 123

Business hours, 34, 146
Butterfly Conservatory
    (Niagara Parkway), 205

Cabbagetown, 11, 30, 124
Cable car, 205
Cabs, 31
Cafes, 98–99
Calendar of events, 17–19
Cambridge, 216
Campbell House, 118,
    136
Canada Life Assurance
    Building, 136
Canada Permanent Trust
    Building, 135
Canada Sports Hall of
    Fame, 113
Canada's Wonderland,
    Paramount (Vaughan),
    111–12, 121
Canadian Broadcasting
    Centre, 122–23
Canadian Imperial Bank
    of Commerce, 134
Canadian National
    Exhibition, 18–19
Canadian Opera
    Company, 170, 171
Canadian Stage Company,
    177–78
Canoeing, 125, 212
Caribana, 18
Caribbean Corner, 144
Car racing, 18, 126
Car rentals, 33
Car travel, 33
    to Toronto, 24–25
Casa Loma, 116, 122
Casino Niagara, 206
Cavalcade of Lights, 19
CBC Museum, 123
Cemeteries, 120–21
Centre Island, 105, 121,
    124

Centreville (Centre Island), 105, 121
Ceramic Art, Gardiner Museum of, 107, 110
Chateau des Charmes (Niagara-on-the-Lake), 194, 196
Children
  accommodations, 53
  bookstores, 140, 152
  restaurants, 94
  shopping, 164
  sights and activities, 121–22
  theater, 121, 178
Children's Festival, Milk International, 18, 121
Children's Film Festival, 121
Children's Village, 101, 121
China, 154
Chinatown, 4, 5, 28, 114
  guided walking tour, 124
  restaurants, 65, 77
  walking tour, 141–45
Chudleigh's (Milton), 122
ChumCity, 123, 165
Churches, 117, 132, 140, 171, 174
Cinemas, 190
Cinesphere, 101
City Hall, 19, 116, 135–36
CityTV, 123, 165
Classical music, 171, 174
Climate, 17
Clothing, shopping for, 156–58, 162–63, 166, 168
CN Tower, 105–6, 121, 130
  bar atop, 4, 181, 189
  revolving restaurant atop, 62, 68
Colborne Lodge, 118
Coles The World's Biggest Bookstore, 153
Comedy, 176–77
Concerts, 171, 174, 179–80, 183

Consulates, 34
Country music, 179
Crafts, 141, 142, 144, 155–56, 169
Craft Studio, 104, 129
Cross-country skiing, 125
Cruises, 5, 123–24
  Niagara Falls, 202
Cullen Gardens & Miniature Village (Whitby), 122
Currency and exchange, 15–16, 34
Customs regulations, 15
Cycling, 33, 124, 205

Dance, 170, 174–75
Dance clubs, 180–84
  gay, 189–90
Danforth, the, 4, 6, 30, 114
Danforth Avenue, restaurants, 93–95
Dentists, 34
Department stores, 156
Design Exchange, 113
Desserts, 98
Dining. *See* Restaurants
Dinner theatre, 179
Dinosaur Gallery, 107, 121
Disabled travelers, 20
Discount stores, 156
Doctors, 34
Dolls House Gallery (Fort Erie), 206
Doll stores, 164
Don Mills, 12, 59, 110
Downtown, 27
  accommodations, 37, 39–49
  restaurants, 61
  sightseeing, 105–7
Downtown East
  restaurants, 81–85
  walking tour, 136–40
Downtown West, restaurants, 65–81
Dragon City, 114, 144
Drugstores, 35
Dufferin Islands, 206

Du Maurier Downtown Jazz Festival, 18, 180
Du Maurier Ltd. Open, 19, 127
Dundas Street, 141–42

East End, 30, 114. *See also* Danforth, the, restaurants, 93–95
Eaton Centre, 35, 116–17, 162
  accommodations, 46
  shopping, 153, 154
Eaton's, 146, 156
Edwards Garden, 120
Elgin Theatre, 175
El Mocambo, 145, 179
Embassies, 34
Emergencies, 34
Entry requirements, 15
Erie, Lake, 194
Etobicoke, 57, 58, 127
Exhibition Place, 19, 113

Farmer's markets, 119–20, 139, 144–45, 163, 165, 212
Farms, 122, 206
Fashions, 156–58, 162–63, 166, 168
Ferries, 33, 105
Festivals, 5, 17–19
Film Festival, Toronto International, 19
Financial District, 27
  walking tour, 130–36
First Canadian Place, 132, 134, 154, 161
First Night Toronto, 19
Fitness centers, 125
Flatiron Building, 139
Folk music, 179–80
Foodstuffs, 158–59
Football, 126–27
Ford Centre for the Performing Arts, 171, 175
Forest Hill, 30
Fort Erie, 206
Fort Erie Race Track, 127
Fort George National Historic Park, 192

Fort York, 7, 8, 118, 121
Fringe of Toronto Festival, 18, 175
Front Street, 138–39
Fruit farms, 206
Furs, 159–60

Gallery/Stratford, 212
Gardens, 120, 212
Gardiner Museum of Ceramic Art, 107, 110
Gay & Lesbian Pride Celebration, 18
Gay men and lesbians
    bookstore, 153
    information sources, 21
    nightlife, 177, 189–90
    special events, 18
George R. Gardiner Museum of Ceramic Art, 107, 110
Glass, 154
Glen Abbey Golf Club (Oakville), 19, 125, 127
Glenn Gould Studio, 171
Golf, 125, 205
    tournaments, 19, 127
Gooderham Building, 139
Gourmet foods, 158–59
Grange, The, 106–7
Great Gorge Adventure (Niagara Parkway), 205
Great Gorge Rapids, 205
Great Library, 136
Grenadier Pond, 120
Gretzky, Wayne, 122, 189
Group of Seven, 4, 11, 106, 111, 151
Guided tours. See Tours

Haida, 101
Halls of fame, 113, 122, 138
Hamilton, 194
Handcrafts. See Crafts
Harbourfront Antiques Market, 104, 129, 146, 148
Harbourfront Centre, 4, 27, 104
    bicycle rentals, 33, 124
    for children, 121

development of, 13
    ice-skating, 126
    special events, 18, 19, 104, 121
    visitor information, 14, 26, 35
    walking tour, 128–29
Harbourfront Reading Festival, 104
Harbourside Boating Centre, 104, 125
Hard Rock Cafe, 182, 206
Hazelton Lanes, 5, 115
    shopping, 148, 162
Health centers, 125
Helicopter tours, 124, 202
High Park, 120, 125
Hillebrand Estate Wineries (Niagara-on-the-Lake), 194, 196, 200–201
History, 6–13
Hockey, 4, 127
Hockey bar (Wayne Gretzky's), 189
Hockey Hall of Fame, 113, 122, 138
Holidays, 17
Holt Renfrew Centre, 163
Honest Ed's, 115, 132, 156
Horizons, 181, 189
Horse racing, 127, 206
Horseshoe Falls (Niagara Falls), 202, 204
Horse Show, Royal, 19
Hospitals, 34
Hostels, 49
Housewares, 161, 166
Hudson's Bay Company, 135, 146, 156
Hummingbird Centre, 139, 170, 175

Ice cream, 99
Ice hockey. See Hockey
Ice-skating, 126
Ice wine, 194
IMAX theaters, 101, 105, 122, 204
Immigration, 5, 8–12, 141
Industrial tours, 122–23
Information sources, 14–15, 26

In-line skating, 126
Inniskillin Winery (Niagara-on-the-Lake), 206
Insurance, 20
Inuits, 106, 111, 134, 150, 155, 192
Island, Toronto. See Toronto Islands
Itineraries, suggested, 100–101

Jazz, 18, 180
Jet boating, Niagara River, 196
Jewelry stores, 161–62
Jogging, 126
John Quay, 104, 129
Jordan, 194, 198–99, 201

Kensington Market, 119, 141, 144–45, 146, 163
Kids in the Hall, 176–77
King's Bridge Park, 206
King Street, 139–40
King Street West Theater District, 27–28
Kitchener, 19, 212
Kitchenwares, 161
Kleinburg, 4, 111
Konzelmann Winery (Niagara-on-the-Lake), 194, 196

Lake Erie North Shore, 194
Lakefront, 13, 27, 114. See also Harbourfront Centre
    accommodations, 46
    attractions, 101, 104–5
Large Two Forms (Moore), 141
Laugh Resort, 177
Laundry, 34
Legends of the Game, 131, 160
Legislature, Ontario, 117
Lesbians. See Gay men and lesbians
Libraries, 115, 117, 136, 145
Liquor law

Liquor stores, 35, 165
"Little Greece," 93–95, 114
Little Italy, 4, 6, 30, 114
  cafes, 99
Live music, 179–80, 183
Lost property, 35
Lower Don Valley bike trail, 124

McCaul Street, 141
McFarland House (Niagara Parkway), 206
Mackenzie, William Lyon, 9
  House, 118
McMichael Canadian Art Collection (Kleinburg), 4, 111
Magazines, 35, 162
Mahoney Dolls House Gallery (Fort Erie), 206
*Maid of the Mist* (Niagara Falls), 202
Malls, shopping, 162–63
Maple Leaf Gardens, 4, 12, 127
Maple Leaf Quay, 129
Maple Leafs, 4, 127
Maps, 35
Marineland (Niagara Falls), 207
Marine Museum, 113
Maritime museums, 113
Markets, 119–20, 139, 144–45, 163
Markham Village, 59, 146
Marks & Spencer, 156
Martin Goodman Trail, 124, 126
Massey Hall, 170
Metro Hall, 132
Metropolitan Toronto Reference Library, 115, 117
Metropolitan Zoo, 110–11, 121
Midtown, 27
  accommodations, 37, 49–55
  restaurants, 61
  sightseeing, 107, 110

Midtown East, restaurants, 93–95
Midtown West, restaurants, 85–93
Milton, 122
Minolta Tower Centre (Niagara Falls), 202, 204
Mirvish, Ed, 114–15, 131–32, 132, 156, 176–77
Mirvish Village, 114–15
Mississauga, 56, 58, 122
Molson Amphitheatre, 101, 104
Molson Indy, 18, 126
Molson Place, 104
Money, 15–17
Moore, Henry, 116, 136, 141
  Sculpture Centre, 4–5, 106
Moss Park, 36
Mount Pleasant Cemetery, 120
Movie theaters, 190
Museum for Textiles, 113–14
Music, 179–80
  blues, 180
  classical, 171, 174
  jazz, 18, 180
  opera, 170, 171
  shopping for, 163–64, 166

Nathan Phillips Square, 19, 106, 116, 126
National Ballet of Canada, 170, 174
National Club Building, 135
Native Canadians, 6, 178
  arts and crafts, 149, 150, 155
  exhibits, 106, 111, 134
  Toronto International Pow Wow, 19
Necropolis, 120–21
*Ned Hanlan,* 113
Neighborhoods, 27–30, 114–15. *See also specific neighborhoods*

New City Hall, 116, 135–36
Newspapers, 35, 162, 170
Newstands, 162
New Year's Eve, 19
*Niagara: Miracles, Myths, and Magic,* 204
Niagara Falls, 201–4, 205
  accommodations, 207–9
  attractions, 202, 204, 206–7
  facts about, 204
  money-saving pass, 202
  at night, 204
  restaurants, 209–11
  seeing the falls, 202, 204
  traveling to, 202
  visitor information, 201–2
Niagara Falls Museum, 206–7
Niagara Historical Society Museum (Niagara-on-the-Lake), 192
Niagara-on-the-Lake, 191–92, 194, 196–201, 206
Niagara Parkway, 201, 205
  restaurants, 210–11
Niagara Peninsula, 194
Niagara Spanish Aero Car (Niagara Parkway), 205
Nightlife, 170–90. *See also* Ballet; Bars; Comedy; Dance; Dance clubs; Movie theaters; Music; Performing arts; Theaters
  current schedule, 170
  tickets, 170
North York, 30

Oktoberfest (Kitchener), 19, 212
Old City Hall, 116, 135
Omnimax Theatre, 110
Ontario, Lake, 6, 126
  beaches, 126
  islands. *See* Toronto Islands
Ontario Legislature, 117

Ontario Place, 18, 101, 104, 121
Ontario Science Centre, 4, 110, 121
Opera, 170, 171
Organized tours. *See* Tours
Orr Dam, 212
Osgoode Hall, 118–19, 136

Panama hats, 144
Pantages Theatre, 175–76
Paramount Canada's Wonderland (Vaughan), 111–12, 121
Parking, 33
Parks, 120, 125, 212
Partridge, David, 135–36
Pearson International Airport, 23, 26, 35
   accommodations, 37, 56–57
Pelee Island, 194
People Movers (Niagara Falls), 202
Performing arts, 170–79. *See also* Ballet; Dance; Music; Theater
   current schedule, 170
   tickets, 170
Perkins Building, 139
Pharmacies, 35
Phillips, Nathan, 12
   Square, 19, 106, 116, 126
Phoenix Concert Theatre, 183
Pioneer Village, Black Creek, 112–13, 122
Playdium (Mississauga), 122
Police, 35
Politics, 5, 6
Post office, 35
Power Plant Contemporary Art Gallery, 104, 129
Premiere Dance Theatre, 171
Princess of Wales Theatre, 131, 176
Pubs, 184–89

Queen's Park, 30
Queen's Park (Stratford), 212
Queen's Quay Terminal, 104, 128–29
   shopping, 146, 163
Queenston, 205–6, 209
Queenston Heights Park, 205
Queen Street East, 114
Queen Street Market, 165
Queen Street West, 4, 13, 29, 115
   cafes, 99
   restaurants, 65
   shopping tour, 165–69
   streetcar, 4, 31

Radio, 35
Raptors, 5, 126
Recreational activities, 124–26
Reggae music, 179
Reif Winery (Niagara-on-the-Lake), 194, 206
Restaurants, 61–98. *See also* Restaurant Index
   best bets, 62–63
   by cuisine, 63–65
   dinner theatre, 179
Rexdale, 56, 57–58
Ride Niagara (Niagara Parkway), 205
Riverdale Farm, 122
Robert Moses Niagara Power Plant (Niagara Falls), 204
Rock music, 179–80, 183
Rolling Stones, 145, 179
Rosedale, 30
Ross Lord Park, 125
Royal Alexandra Theatre, 132, 176–77
Royal Bank Plaza, 117, 138, 163
Royal Horse Show, 19
Royal Ontario Museum (ROM), 107, 121
Royal Trust, 134
Royal York Hotel, 138
Roy Thomson Hall, 132, 170–71, 174

Safety, 36
Sailing, 125
St. Andrew's Presbyterian Church, 132
St. Catharines, 200
St. Jacobs, 212
St. James Cathedral, 140, 171
St. Lawrence, walking tour, 136–40
St. Lawrence Centre for the Arts, 139, 170, 175
St. Lawrence Hall, 139–40
St. Lawrence Market, 4, 27, 119–20, 139, 146, 163
St. Patrick's Day Parade, 18
Samuel Weir Collection and Library of Art (Queenston), 205–6
*Saturday Night Live,* 176
Scadding House, 117
Scarborough, 59–60, 110–11
Science Centre, Ontario, 4, 110, 121
Science City, 161
Scotia Tower, 134
Sculptor's Society Gallery, 132
Second City, 177
Secord, Laura, Homestead (Queenston), 205
Senior citizen travelers, 20
Shakespearean Garden (Stratford), 212
Shaw, George Bernard Festival (Niagara-on-the-Lake), 5, 175, 191–92
   Shop (Niagara-on-the-Lake), 192
Sheraton Centre, 45, 53, 136, 184, 190
Shoe Museum, Bata, 112
Shopping, 146–69
Sightseeing, 100–122
Silver, 154
Skating, 126
SkyDome, 4, 5, 13, 19, 106, 126

Skylon Tower Observation Deck (Niagara Falls), 202

Spadina, 119

Speakers Corner, 123, 165

Special events, 17–19

Sporting goods, 168

Sports, 124–26
spectator, 126–27

Sports Hall of Fame, Canada, 113

Sports memorabilia, 131, 160

Standard Life, 134

Stella, Frank, 131, 176

Stock Exchange Building, 113, 123, 132

Stratford, 211–18
accommodations, 212, 214–16
restaurants, 216–18
sightseeing, 212
traveling to, 211
visitor information, 211

Stratford Festival, 5, 175, 211

Streetcars, 4, 31

Student travelers, 20–21

Subway, 31

Sun Life Centre, 132

Sunnybrook Park, 125

Swimming, 126. *See also* Water parks

Symphonies, 171, 174

Table Rock House (Niagara Falls), 202

Tafelmusik Baroque Orchestra, 171, 174

Taxes, 36, 61

Taxis, 31

Telephone, 36

Television, 123

Temperatures, average monthly, 17

Tennis, 126
tournaments, 19, 127

Ten Ren Tea, 142, 159

Textiles, Museum for, 113–14

Theater, 175–79
for children, 121
Fringe of Toronto Festival, 18, 175
Shaw Festival (Niagara-on-the-Lake), 5, 175, 191–92
Stratford Festival, 5, 175, 211

Thomson Hall, 132, 170–71, 174

Tickets, 180
discount, 170

Tommy Thompson Trail, 126

Toronto Argonauts, 126–27

Toronto Blue Jays, 4, 106, 126

Toronto Dance Theatre, 174–75

Toronto Dominion Centre, 134

Toronto Dominion Gallery of Inuit Art, 134

Toronto Exchange Tower, 123, 132

Toronto Harbour, 113
cruises, 123–24

Toronto Island Airport, 23

Toronto Islands, 1, 4, 27, 105, 121
beaches, 126
bicycling, 124
cruises, 123–24
ferries, 33, 105

Toronto Maple Leafs, 4, 127

Toronto Mendelssohn Choir, 174

Toronto Raptors, 5, 126

Toronto Sculpture Garden, 140

*Toronto Star,* 35, 170

Toronto Stock Exchange, 123, 132

*Toronto Sun,* 35, 170

Toronto Symphony Orchestra, 170–71, 174

Toronto Transit Commission (TTC), 30–31

Tourist information, 14–15, 26

Tours, 122–24
by boat, 123–24
by bus, 123
guided walking, 124
by helicopter, 124, 202
industrial, 122–23

Toy stores, 164

Train travel, 24, 191, 202, 211

Transit information, 36

Transportation, 30–33
to/from airports, 23–24

Traveling to Toronto, 21–25

Travel insurance, 20

Trinity Church, 117

Twenty Mile Creek, 201

Underground Toronto, 27

Union Station, 138

University of Toronto, 30, 145, 171

University of Toronto Athletic Centre, 126

University of Toronto at Scarborough, 59

Uptown, 27
accommodations, 37, 55
restaurants, 61, 95–98

Vaughan, 111–12

VIA Rail, 202, 211

Village by the Grange, 141, 163

Vineland, 201

Vineland Estates, 194, 201

Vineyards. *See* Wine and vineyards

Vintage clothing, 156, 166

Virgil, 200

Visitor information, 14–15, 26

Walking tours. *See also walking tours chapter (chapter 7),* 128–145
organized, 124

Ward's Island, 105

War of 1812, 7, 192, 205

Waterfront. *See* Lakefront

Waterloo, 212

Water parks, 112, 122, 207

Weather, 17
  updates, 36

Web sites, 22

Weir Collection and Library of Art (Queenston), 205–6

Welland, 200

Whitby, 122

White Water (Niagara Falls), 207

Wildwater Kingdom, 122

Wine and vineyards, 194, 196, 206
  shopping for, 165

Winter Garden Theatre, 175

Women travelers, 21

Wonderland, Paramount Canada's (Vaughan), 111–12, 121

Woodbine Beach, 126

Woodbine Racetrack (Etobicoke), 127

World War I, 11

World War II, 12

YMCA, 125, 126

Yonge Street, 7, 26, 29

York Quay Centre, 104, 129

Yorkville, 9, 12–13, 30, 115

Yuk-Yuk's Superclub, 177

Zoo, 110–11, 121

## ACCOMMODATIONS

Acrylic Dreams (Stratford), 214–15

Ambercroft (Stratford), 215

Americana, The (Niagara Falls), 208

Avonview Manor (Stratford), 215

Bentleys (Stratford), 214

Best Western Primrose Hotel, 46–47

Best Western Roehampton Hotel, 55

Best Western Toronto Airport, 57

Bond Place Hotel, 47

Brunswick House (Stratford), 215

Cambridge Suites Hotel, 39, 42

Clarion Essex Park Hotel, 47

Comfort Inn–Airport, 57–58

Crowne Plaza Toronto Centre, 39, 42–43

Days Inn Carlton Inn, 47

Days Inn–Toronto Airport, 58

Deacon House (Stratford), 215

Delta Chelsea Inn, 39, 47–48, 53

Delta Meadowvale Resort & Conference Centre, 58

Festival Motor Inn (Stratford), 214

Flint's Inn (Stratford), 215–16

Four Points Hotel, 58

Four Seasons Hotel, 38, 39, 49, 52, 53

Gate House Hotel (Niagara-on-the-Lake), 196

Guild Inn (Scarborough), 59–60

Hilton International, 43

Holiday Inn by the Falls (Niagara Falls), 208

Holiday Inn on King, 39, 48

Hotel Selby, 55

Hotel Victoria, 48–49

Inter-Continental, 52–53

King Edward Hotel, 38, 42

Langdon Hall, 38–39

Langdon Hall (Cambridge), 216

Metropolitan Hotel, 43

Michael's Inn (Niagara Falls), 208–9

Moffat Inn (Niagara-on-the-Lake), 198

Neil Wycik College Hotel, 49

Nelson Motel (Niagara Falls), 209

Novotel, The, 44

Oban Inn (Niagara-on-the-Lake), 196

Old Bank House (Niagara-on-the-Lake), 198

Park Plaza, 53–54

Pillar & Post Inn (Niagara-on-the-Lake), 197

Prince of Wales Hotel (Niagara-on-the-Lake), 197

Quality Hotel, 49, 54–55

Queen's Inn (Stratford), 214

Queen's Landing (Niagara-on-the-Lake), 197–98

Radisson Plaza Hotel, 54

Radisson Plaza Hotel Admiral, 38, 39, 44

Regal Constellation Hotel, 57

Renaissance Fallsview Hotel (Niagara Falls), 207

Royal York, 39, 44–45

Sheraton Centre, 45, 53

Sheraton Gateway at Terminal Three, 56

SkyDome Hotel, 39, 45–46

Skyline Brock (Niagara Falls), 208

Skyline Foxhead (Niagara Falls), 208

South Landing Inn (Queenston), 209

Strathcona, The, 49

Sutton Place Hotel, 54

Toronto Airport Hilton International, 56

Toronto International Hostel, 49

Toronto Marriott Eaton Centre, 46

23 Albert Place (Stratford), 214

University of Toronto at Scarborough, Student Village, 59

Venture Inn, Yorkville, 39, 55

Venture Inn at the Airport, 58

Victoria University, 39, 55

Village Inn (Niagara Falls), 209

Vintner's Inn (Jordan), 198–99

Westin Harbour Castle, 39, 46

Westin Prince Hotel, 59

White Oaks Inn and Racquet Club (Niagara-on-the-Lake), 198

Woods Villa (Stratford), 216

Wyndham Bristol Place, 56–57

## RESTAURANTS

Acqua, 68–69

Aïda's Falafel, 91

Al Frisco's, 82

Alice Fazooli's, 82

Annapurna Vegetarian Restaurant, 91–92

Arlequin, 89–90

Astoria, 93

Avalon, 69

Babur, 72

Bagel, The, 78

Bamboo, 82

Barberian's, 69

Bentley's (Stratford), 218

Betty's Restaurant & Tavern (Niagara Falls), 210

Biagio, 81, 82

Bistro 990, 85, 88

Black & Blue Smoke Bar, 89

Bloor Street Diner, 92

Boba, 88

Borgo Antico, 90

Boulevard Café, 92

Brownes Bistro, 97

Buttery, The (Niagara-on-the-Lake), 199

Byzas, 93–94

Cafe Diplomatico, 82

Canoe, 69–70

Casa d'Oro (Niagara Falls), 210

Centro, 62, 95

Chiado, 63, 70

Chiaro's, 68

Church, The (Stratford), 216–17

Cities, 72

Coppi, 96

Dufflet Pastries, 63

Eating Counter, The, 78

Fans Court (Niagara-on-the-Lake), 199

Far Niente Napa Grill, 68

Filet of Sole, 72

Four Seasons, 63

Fred's Not Here Smokehouse and Grill, 72–73

Free Times Café, 78

Galileo, 81

Grano, 97

Grappa, 73–74

Happy Wanderer (Niagara Falls), 210

Hemingways, 82

Hennepin's (Virgil), 200

Herbs, 62, 96

Hillebrand's Vineyard Cafe (near Niagara-on-the-Lake), 200–201

Il Fornello, 78–79

Il Posto, 88

Indian Rice Factory, 92

Iseya (St. Catharines), 200

Jacques Bistro du Parc, 90

Jerusalem, 94, 98

Joso's, 63, 90

Jump Cafe and Bar, 62, 70

Kalendar, 79

Kensington Kitchen, 92–93, 94

Keystone Alley Cafe (Stratford), 218

KitKat Bar & Grill, 74

La Bodega, 74

La Fenice, 70–71

Lai Wah Heen, 71

La Maquette, 81–83

Langolino Wine Bar & Grill, 74

Lee Garden, 79

Left Bank, 75

Le Papillon, 84

Le Paradis, 98

Le Select, 74–75

Let Them Eat Cake (Stratford), 218

Lolita's Lust, 82, 94

Masa, 75

Mercer Street Grill, 71

Messis, 90–91

Mildred Pierce, 63, 75–76

Montana, 82

Montréal Bistro and Jazz Club, 83–84

Mori, 93

Movenpick Bistretto, 91, 94

Movenpick Marché, 79

Myth, 93

N 44, 62, 95

Nami Japanese Seafood, 83

N'Awlins, 76

Old Prune, The (Stratford), 217

Omonia, 94

Opus, 88

Ouzeri, 63, 94–95

Palavrion, 62, 76

Pangaea, 88–89

Pan on the Danforth, 62, 93

Peter Pan, 76–77

Pink Pearl, 77

Prego della Piazza, 63, 89
Pronto, 96–97
Queen Mother Cafe, 79
Queenston Heights (Niagara Parkway), 210–11
Red Tomato, 79–80
Revolving Restaurant, 62, 68
Rinderlin's (Welland), 200
Ristorante Giardino (Niagara-on-the-Lake), 199–200
Rivoli, 80
Rodney's Oyster House, 84
Rundles (Stratford), 217–18
St. Tropez, 77, 82

Sassafraz, 82
Scaramouche, 62, 63, 95–96
Senator, The, 83
Shopsy's, 84
Sicilian Ice Cream Company, 63
Southern Accent, 91
Souz Dal, 82
Spiaggia, 84
Splendido Bar and Grill, 89
Studio Cafe, 63
Taro Grill, 77
Thai Magic, 98
Tiger Lily's, 80
Toby's Goodeats, 80, 94
Trapper's, 97
Trattoria Giancarlo, 77–78

Truffles, 85
On the Twenty Restaurant & Wine Bar (near Niagara-on-the-Lake), 201
Vanipha, 80–81
Vineland Estates, 201
Wah Sing, 81
Wellington Court Restaurant (St. Catharines), 200
Whistling Oyster Seafood Cafe, 78
Wild Indigo, 82
Xango, 62, 63, 71–72
York Street Kitchen (Stratford), 218
Young Thailand, 85
ZooM Caffe & Bar, 83

## FROMMER'S® COMPLETE TRAVEL GUIDES

*(Comprehensive guides to destinations around the world, with
selections in all price ranges—from deluxe to budget)*

Acapulco, Ixtapa &
   Zihuatenejo
Alaska
Amsterdam
Arizona
Atlanta
Australia
Austria
Bahamas
Barcelona, Madrid &
   Seville
Belgium, Holland &
   Luxembourg
Bermuda
Boston
Budapest & the Best of
   Hungary
California
Canada
Cancún, Cozumel & the
   Yucatán
Cape Cod, Nantucket &
   Martha's Vineyard
Caribbean
Caribbean Cruises & Ports
   of Call
Caribbean Ports of Call
Carolinas & Georgia
Chicago
China
Colorado
Costa Rica
Denver, Boulder &
   Colorado Springs
England

Europe
Florida
France
Germany
Greece
Hawaii
Hong Kong
Honolulu, Waikiki & Oahu
Ireland
Israel
Italy
Jamaica & Barbados
Japan
Las Vegas
London
Los Angeles
Maryland & Delaware
Maui
Mexico
Miami & the Keys
Montana & Wyoming
Montréal & Québec City
Munich & the Bavarian Alps
Nashville & Memphis
Nepal
New England
New Mexico
New Orleans
New York City
Northern New England
Nova Scotia, New
   Brunswick
   & Prince Edward Island
Oregon
Paris

Philadelphia & the Amish
   Country
Portugal
Prague & the Best of the
   Czech Republic
Provence & the Riviera
Puerto Rico
Rome
San Antonio & Austin
San Diego
San Francisco
Santa Fe, Taos &
   Albuquerque
Scandinavia
Scotland
Seattle & Portland
Singapore & Malaysia
South Pacific
Spain
Switzerland
Thailand
Tokyo
Toronto
Tuscany & Umbria
USA
Utah
Vancouver & Victoria
Vienna & the Danube
   Valley
Virgin Islands
Virginia
Walt Disney World &
   Orlando
Washington, D.C.
Washington State

## FROMMER'S® DOLLAR-A-DAY GUIDES

*(The ultimate guides to comfortable low-cost travel)*

Australia from $50 a Day
California from $60 a Day
Caribbean from $60 a Day
Costa Rica & Belize
   from $35 a Day
England from $60 a Day
Europe from $50 a Day
Florida from $50 a Day
Greece from $50 a Day
Hawaii from $60 a Day
India from $40 a Day

Ireland from $50 a Day
Israel from $45 a Day
Italy from $50 a Day
London from $60 a Day
Mexico from $35 a Day
New York from $75 a Day
New Zealand from $50 a Day
Paris from $70 a Day
San Francisco from $60 a Day
Washington, D.C., from
   $60 a Day

## FROMMER'S® PORTABLE GUIDES

*(Pocket-size guides for travelers who want everything in a nutshell)*

Bahamas
California Wine Country
Charleston & Savannah
Chicago

Dublin
Las Vegas
London
Maine Coast
New Orleans

Puerto Vallarta, Manzanillo
& Guadalajara
San Francisco
Venice
Washington, D.C.

## FROMMER'S® NATIONAL PARK GUIDES

*(Everything you need for the perfect park vacation)*

Grand Canyon
National Parks of the American West
Yellowstone & Grand Teton

Yosemite & Sequoia/
Kings Canyon
Zion & Bryce Canyon

## FROMMER'S® IRREVERENT GUIDES

*(Wickedly honest guides for sophisticated travelers)*

Amsterdam
Chicago
London

Manhattan
New Orleans
Paris

San Francisco
Santa Fe

Walt Disney World
Washington, D.C.

## FROMMER'S® BY NIGHT GUIDES

*(The series for those who know that life begins after dark)*

Amsterdam
Chicago
Las Vegas
London

Los Angeles
Madrid
& Barcelona
Manhattan

Miami
New Orleans
Paris

Prague
San Francisco
Washington, D.C.

## THE COMPLETE IDIOT'S TRAVEL GUIDES

*(The ultimate user-friendly trip planners)*

Cruise Vacations
Las Vegas
New Orleans

New York City
Planning Your Trip
to Europe

San Francisco
Walt Disney World

## SPECIAL-INTEREST TITLES

Arthur Fommer's New World of Travel
The Civil War Trust's Official Guide to
the Civil War Discovery Trail
Frommer's Caribbean Hideaways
Frommer's Complete Hostel Vacation
Guide to England, Scotland & Wales
Frommer's Europe's Greatest
Driving Tours
Frommer's Food Lover's Companion
to France
Frommer's Food Lover's Companion to
Italy
Israel Past & Present
New York City with Kids
New York Times Weekends

Outside Magazine's Adventure Guide
to New England
Outside Magazine's Adventure Guide
to Northern California
Outside Magazine's Adventure Guide
to the Pacific Northwest
Outside Magazine's Adventure Guide
to Southern California & Baja
Outside Magazine's Guide to Family Vacations
Places Rated Almanac
Retirement Places Rated
Washington, D.C., with Kids
Wonderful Weekends from New York City
Wonderful Weekends from San Francisco
Wonderful Weekends from Los Angeles

# WHEREVER YOU TRAVEL, *H*ELP IS NEVER FAR AWAY.

From planning your trip to providing travel assistance along the way, American Express® Travel Service Offices are always there to help you do more.

---

### *Toronto*

---

American Express Travel Service
Holt Renfrew Building
50 Bloor St. West
Toronto
416-967-7113

American Express Travel Service
Royal York Hotel, #133-134
100 Front Street West
Toronto
416-363-3883

do more **AMERICAN EXPRESS**
**Travel**

http://www.americanexpress.com/travel
**American Express Travel Service Offices
are found in central locations
throughout Canada.**